CHESS

This book is intended both for those who know nothing of Chess but wish to learn and for those who are experienced in the game and can benefit from a scientific analysis of its many aspects. It is accordingly carefully graduated: Part I introduces the chess pieces, describes their powers and values, and explains the elementary endgame; Part II deals with the middle game, and tactics and strategy; and Part III discusses the openings and some refinements in the endgame, and includes a selection of illustrative games. It aims to teach the reader to think like a chess player, to see moves for himself rather than rely on his memory.

TEACH YOURSELF BOOKS

A thorough study of this work should indeed give the student an adequate grounding in the art of chess.

The Guardian

A comprehensive and well-illustrated guide.

The Times Literary Supplement

CHESS

Gerald Abrahams

TEACH YOURSELF BOOKS
Hodder and Stoughton

First printed 1948
New edition 1953
Ninth impression 1982

ISBN 0 340 26417 9

Printed in Great Britain for
Hodder and Stoughton Educational, a
division of Hodder and Stoughton Ltd,
Mill Road, Dunton Green, Sevenoaks, Kent
by Richard Clay (The Chaucer Press) Ltd,
Bungay, Suffolk

PREFACE TO FIRST EDITION

The philosopher Mendelssohn gave up Chess because he found it too serious to be a game and not serious enough to be an occupation. If, in disregard of that great example, the reader desires to immerse his mind in this scientific Lido, then the author undertakes in these pages to prevent him from drowning, and so to exercise him that his general mentality will be strengthened rather than weakened by his new pursuit. And in these pages swimming lessons are also available to those who have long disported themselves in the water.

In other words, the author has endeavoured, in this book, to produce something that shall be useful to many classes of persons interested in Chess, ranging from those who know nothing at all about it but wish to learn, to those who are experienced in the game and can benefit (as who cannot?) from a scientific analysis of its many aspects.

The book sets out from the belief that there are many readers completely ignorant of Chess but possessed of a fair intelligence and a desire to learn. It is believed that the number of people desirous of learning Chess is increasing. It is important that these shall learn the moves, but not stop at that; and this book is written on the assumption that such readers not only want to know the moves, but wish for an education in the game that shall bring them to a stage at which they are participating in an undertaking of skill and not a mere game of chance.

The book is accordingly graduated; graduated according to the expectation that, at any point after the earliest pages, the reader will have improved as a Chess player through having mastered what has gone before. He is expected to absorb and understand—and practise—what he reads; not to learn it by heart. If he understands what he reads, then, as he works his way through the second chapter, he will find himself acquiring a certain capacity to think for himself about moves. After the second chapter he may even be thinking like a Chess player. From that stage on, the book should be of some interest even to players of considerable experience. In this respect, *inter alia*, it is claimed that this book differs in its method and purpose from other books available to beginners.

Naturally, such an undertaking—the undertaking to educate in Chess, rather than to equip with minimal knowledge —has been incompatible with the simultaneous or continuous presentation of all aspects of the game at the same level. But, in the author's view, the Chess mind does not require such a preliminary presentation of knowledge before it can

PREFACE

be educated. Also it fortunately happens that Chess is sufficiently organic a science for the reader who is struggling with the rudiments of the game to be made aware of processes that he will have to study at a later stage.

In his ordering of the book in the light of these purposes the author has used a method that is original without being heretical. For many reasons the book does not commence with the openings, though indications of the nature of the openings present themselves on early pages. In the author's view, the learning of opening variations immediately after the learning of the moves is a quite false approach to the game. Most of the present masters were good players before they learned any opening variations. A move in an opening, like a move at any other stage, is a good, bad, or indifferent move. There are very few moves recommended in the openings which are not independently recognisable as reasonably good moves. Now the important thing about Chess is the need for seeing good moves at every moment of time when it happens to be the player's turn to move. There is no stage of the game at which this capacity is not the factor of highest importance. If a student sets out with the idea that he will be materially assisted by learning a series of moves by heart, then he is the victim of at least one fallacy. He is doing precisely what a traveller would do if he tried to make a phrase-book act as a substitute for the knowledge of a language. Phrases are important to those who already have a grasp of a language. In the same way Chess learning is only useful to those who can already play. That is why the proper place for a study of the openings is at the end of a Chess book, not at the beginning.

Again, since the author is convinced that intelligence and imagination, rather than memory, are the qualities of mind to be developed in Chess, he has abstained from the presentation of large numbers of opening variations. What he has undertaken is to give to the reader some conception of the strategic purposes that are expressed in the various openings. If the reader becomes able to see a move, and gains some notion of what is important strategically, then he will not go seriously wrong either in the openings or at any other stage of the game.

And there is a final thought that is worth elaborating. The book is subordinate to the game. The game dwarfs all the advice that is given about it. A book, therefore, should not recommend moves, only say: thus and thus try to find the best move. Moreover, few games are lost through

PREFACE

the failure at any particular moment to find the very best move. Often the very best move does not exist. Besides, there is such an elasticity in Chess that advantages are easily reduced, and resources are usually available. At all stages the player is advised to look for the best that he can see, and not regard himself as controlled by any convention. To achieve that state of mind he must play—play hard and think much—rather than read. When he reads, let his reading be subordinate to what he is discovering in play. Whatever learning (whether from books or from other players) a student of Chess acquires is only valuable in the degree that it makes his mind receptive to the possibilities of the board, to the ideas and the notions that pervade the board, and in so far as it widens and deepens his awareness of a rich and enjoyable field of experience.

The author wishes to express his appreciation of the invaluable help given to him at proof stage by Mr. J. H. Williams, the tireless librarian of the Manchester Chess Club.

PREFACE TO 1962 EDITION

Much Chess has been played since there was delivered to me at a London Tournament in 1948, amid cries of "too late", the advance copy of *Teach Yourself Chess*.

But Chess is timeless. In the 13 and more years that have elapsed since the book was written, new figures have ascended the high places of the Chess world—and some have descended again—but the game is still fought along the same lines: if I may say so, along the lines of thought that I described in the first edition.

There have been changes of fashion in opening play, and these continue to occur, as do fashions in lady's hats; but "time writes no wrinkles" on Caïssa's brow. I think her smile that favoured Botwinnik in 1961 is the same that favoured him in 1948; and is, indeed, the same that was seen by all the earlier generations of great players.

To the student of Chess, then, there is no need for any restatement of any truths that are basic in the game. Nor would later instances and examples improve on earlier ones, whether as sources of instruction or as sources of pleasure.

Apart, then, from a few alterations of phrase, in order to excise possible ambiguities, I have found nothing to alter in this book. All I had to take away was the dated word "recent." All I could have added—had there been space—was quantity.

GERALD ABRAHAMS

CONTENTS

PART I

THE ELEMENTS

CHAPTER I

PRELIMINARY

INTRODUCING THE CHESS MEN: THEIR FUNCTIONS AND VALUES: THE SCIENCE OF CHESS

In the diagram on this page the reader will see a Chess Board with the Pieces, or Men, set up in the position they occupy at the beginning of an ordinary game of Chess.

The Board and Men at the commencement of a game.

The Board has been compared to a battle field, and the two sets of Pieces (White and Black) to contending armies. That comparison is a useful one to bear in mind because, in learning Chess, the average reader will find himself in contact with players and writers who think in terms of attack and defence, threats, manœuvres for position, captures, ambushes (traps as they are sometimes called), and many other terms suggesting combat. Eventually he will himself absorb, and act upon, notions which are of the first importance in war and other modes of activity, as well as in Chess : for example, the notion of strategy, and the related notion of tactics. From elementary ideas such as capturing and recapturing, advance and retreat, he will proceed to think in terms of strong-points, blockade, tempo and general development. In the light of these accumulating notions he will be able to assess the real forces underlying threats and parades of strength. While doing this he will gradually be acquiring a control over affairs, and learning that the real opposition consists in nothing other than the limits of the material and his own limitations —his lack of confidence or of capacity ; and at the end of his development he will discover, as every good General does, that he has mastered not only an opponent, but a Science.

Perhaps the best standpoint that the reader can adopt if he wishes to justify to himself the expenditure of time on Chess, is that he is studying a Science ; not a Science as exact as Pure Mathematics, but a relatively unpredictable system of Dynamics analogous to the Dynamics of War. With the material available one has to set about achieving an ultimate object—the capture of the King. That involves scientific planning, and calls for the capacity to appreciate future developments. Moreover, Chess is scientific in that those who understand it find their operations determined, not by their own tastes, but by the limits and the possibilities of the material in which they are working. Chess has its beauties, but its essence is mental discipline such as only a Science can give. And Chess has the further advantage that its rules are universal—a fact which distinguishes it from the many games with which it is sometimes classified.

HISTORY

Chess, moreover, being well established in time, enjoys a considerable history and literature. Its earliest history is of antiquarian interest. Having originated in some part of Asia as a war game—claims have been made for India, China and Persia*—it seems to have become crystallized in its present form at the time when books were first written about the subject ; that is to say, in Spain during the period of the mediaeval Arab culture. Since the invention of printing

---

*There is evidence of an early Indian game (3rd century C.E.) called Chaturanga (four corners). The accepted theory (based on the scanty contemporary literature) is that this is the original game of Chess ; and that Chinese and Persian forms of the game are later derivatives from it.

there has been no important change—save that the popularity of the game has moved northward from Iberia to modern Siberia. After the decline of the Moors, the game continued to flourish in Spain—the prolific Ruy Lopez having contributed to Chess as well as to literature—and became popular also in Italy and France.

In England, Chess was well known in Shakespeare's day. It may be inferred (from *The Tempest*) that the game was popular in Court circles. But before that time, Chaucer knew Chess well—and there is a Ballad of some Chess interest.

Caxton, one of the first English printers, has provided us with an excellent book descriptive of Chess in its modern form. But it was not till the nineteenth century that England, and the northern nations, Germany and Russia, took over the initiative in the development of Chess. In these countries, and cognate America, the leadership of Chess has now rested for a century. Meanwhile in Asia the development of the game —more or less standardized by the Arabs—has lagged a little behind the European development ; but the modern Indian game (there is an old form, Desi) differs in so little from the European game (the Pawn's first move, and a limitation on promotion) that in this century a native Indian found himself able to win the British Championship. To all intents and purposes it may therefore be said that Chess has the advantages of age and universality over most other games; and the rules set out herein are applicable wherever it is played. Finally, being describable in notation, Chess is completely communicable, and a player in any part of the world can follow developments in any other part of the world.

THE BOARD AND MEN

The Board on which Chess is played is a chequered Board— i.e., divided into 64 squares of alternating colour—and is the same board as that required for the modern form of Draughts.*

*Although the two games have a scientific character in common, they are of different origin. Chess is Asiatic ; Draughts appears to have originated in the Mediterranean lands. Perhaps that explains its less dynastic appearance. The chequered board seems to have been known all over the world. For English readers it may be interesting to observe that this Board is the ultimate origin of the title " Exchequer." It may also be interesting to notice that the name Bishop for one of the Pieces is indigenous to England—which suggests the conjecture that this name was given at a time when Ecclesiastics controlled the Exchequer. On the continent, the Piece we call Bishop is described as " le fou," or " laüfer." These words, which suggest " Court Jester," or " Courier," are probably corruptions of the Arabic Alfil (Elephant), the Moorish name for the Piece, adopted in Spanish. (cf. Italian Alfieri.) The Russian name is Slon (Elephant).

On this Board all the moves are from square to square and only one Piece is allowed to remain on any one square at any given time.

The Board is set out with a Black corner square at each player's left hand side. The Chess Men of each colour—two complete sets of 16 White and 16 Black Men respectively being involved—are arrayed along the two back " ranks " nearest the player who is handling that particular colour. Referring to the first diagram, and reading from left to right, they are : White's back row ; Rook, Knight, Bishop, Queen, King, Bishop, Knight, Rook. (Those which the Queen separates from the King are called Queen's Rook, Queen's Knight, Queen's Bishop, to distinguish them from King's Rook, King's Knight, King's Bishop : this nomenclature is for the purpose of notation and does not correspond to any difference of powers.) Along the front rank (second row) stand the Pawns. The corresponding Black Men are directly opposite ; King (fourth from Black's left) facing King, Queen facing Queen, etc., etc.

Thus it will be seen that each player has, at the outset, two Rooks, which stand on the corner squares, and are, of course, equal to each other in value, two similarly equivalent Knights, which stand on the squares next to the Rooks, two Bishops, again equivalent to each other, but with the difference that one is confined to the Black squares and the other to the White squares ; these flank the King and Queen respectively. Also one Queen, which always starts the game on a square of its own colour (White Queen on White square, Black Queen, opposite, on Black square) ; one King, the only Piece on the Board which dare not be lost, and which stands next to the Queen, i.e., always on a square of its opposite colour; finally, eight Pawns, which stand along the second rank.

The Chess Men, or Pieces, of opposite colour move alternately, i.e., White, Black, White, Black, White having the not negligible privilege of the first move ; and each player must move at his turn to move. The Pieces proceed from their original positions, according to their powers and when they are not obstructed, along the " files " (vertical lines), " ranks " (horizontal lines), and diagonals ; and, with the exception of the promoted Pawn, they retain their original and normal powers of movement throughout the game.

They can all capture hostile Pieces (not more than one per move). This they do, not, as Draughtsmen, by jumping over the victim, but by occupying (except in one very special case) the square of the hostile occupant. The latter is automatically removed from the Board for the duration of the game, unless and until the promotion of a Pawn, in an appropriate case, recalls it. Conversely, subject to one restriction, the Pieces can all be captured.

The restriction on capturability is that the capture of the King is the end of the game. Whoever loses his King, or finds himself so placed that his King must be lost before his opponent's, loses the game. This is another way of saying that *the object of a game of Chess is the capture of one's opponent's King*.

The tactical and strategic consequences that follow from the special character of the King—the divinity which hedges it—will be considered after we have dealt with the geometric moves of the Pieces. Here, suffice it to mention two terms which are of the first importance. (1) When the King is attacked—in the sense that an opponent threatens to capture it next move by bringing a Piece to occupy its square —there is in being a situation which is called *Check*. It is usually said that the King is in Check.* (2) When the King is in Check, and there is no way of terminating the Check, the King is *Check-Mate* or *Mate*. (Check is a corruption of Shah : Mate is a Semitic word, meaning dead.)

These cannot be illustrated conveniently until the reader has learnt the moves (which follow). It is also important for the reader to learn the notation, which enables Chess players to read Chess as musicians read music. Incidentally, it will be necessary to know the notation in order to read this, or any other, Chess book. The notation is given at the end of the Chapter.

THE MOVES

The powers of the Pieces, as distinct from their tactical and strategical importances and their relative values, are quite easily described and grasped.

On the battle field which is the Chess Board there are three obvious directions—as it were, three sets of ready-made roads—along which Pieces can operate, viz. the ranks, the files, and the diagonals. The powers of five, out of the six, functionally different units—that is to say the powers of Rook, Bishop, Queen, King and Pawn—can be simply

*It is customary, but not obligatory, to announce Check orally. This is, however, unrequired, albeit not discourteous, when one's opponent is a good player. On the other hand there is no custom of announcing an attack on the Queen or any other Piece. Such an announcement is "not done."

described as specific movements in these various directions. Rooks move on ranks and files, Bishops on diagonals, Pawns on files (with capturing power on the diagonals), King and Queen along ranks, files and diagonals. The sixth mode of movement, that of the Knight, which, being the Cavalry of the game, seems to make its own special path across the Board, can also be grasped without much difficulty in terms of the same geometry.

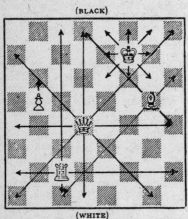

(BLACK)

(WHITE)

Paths of 5 pieces.

THE ROOK (French, Tour; German, Turm; Russian, Ladj; English notation R).*

The Rook has a relatively simple linear move along any rank or any file. That is to say, it can move as few or as many squares as are desired and are available along any rank or file on which it happens to find itself at the moment of moving. Along a file it can move backwards or forwards, i.e., towards or away from its own side of the Board From any square on an empty Board the Rook has a range of 14 possible moves, and can, in one move, " cover " any other square of the 64.

*The term Rook, if it were derived, as some think, from the Italian Rocca, or the French Roche, would—like the archaic name Castle—do no credit to this Piece's mobility. Its function suggests the Tank rather than the Fortress. But the real origin of the word Rook, the Persian Rukh, meaning a wind or a spirit, does express the notion of mobility. In the Persian game the Rook was, indeed, the most mobile and powerful of the Pieces. That was before the powers of what is now the Queen were increased to their modern magnitude.

THE BISHOP (French, Fou ; German, Laüfer ; Russian, Slon ; English Notation, B).

The Bishop moves as few or as many squares as are desired and available, backwards or forwards, along any diagonal on which it finds itself at the moment of moving. Since that square will be either a Black square or a White square and since each set of diagonals is monochrome, it follows that the Bishop starting on a White square stays on White squares, so long as it is on the Board. If it were not such a militant Piece, one might say that each Bishop is confined to its own diocese. From a centre square the scope of either Bishop is 13 possible moves.

THE QUEEN (French, Dame ; German, Dame ; Russian, Firze ; English Notation, Q)*.

The Queen, which is the most powerful, though, as we have seen, not the most important, Piece on the Board, combines the powers of the Rook and the Bishop ; more accurately, the Powers of the Rook and either Bishop, because by virtue of her linear movement, she can find herself on either diagonal —so is not confined to one. Briefly then, the Queen can move as many or as few squares as are desired and available along any rank or along any file or along any diagonal ; and, in the case of movement along the files or diagonals she can move backwards or forwards. From a centre square, the Queen has a range of 27 squares out of the 64†.

*Nobody knows exactly when, or why, the most powerful piece on the Board became called the Queen. The name was probably adopted earlier than the period of the great Catherines and Elizabeths—but the famous Isabella may be the responsible influence. A Hebrew poem, attributed to Ibn Ezra (12th century), but probably later (because it refers to the modern Pawn move), describes the Queen or Consort as a Piece having a range of three squares in any direction. Certainly, in the original Indo-Chinese game, no Piece had such great power as the modern Queen, and in those days the King is believed to have been at least as powerful as its neighbour. The earliest Moorish records describe a Piece somewhat less powerful than the modern Queen as the Vizier. Vizier has, since the invention of printing crystallized the rules of Chess, become generally known in Europe as the Queen or Lady. An interesting relic of the Mediaeval name is that in Russia the Queen is called Firze, which is derivative from Vizier. Students of English literature may be reminded of the old Romance of the Rose : "When he took my Fers away, then I could no longer play." In the days of Elizabeth I the Queen had developed her present powers—"checking the world."

†AVAILABLE SQUARES AND CAPTURES. At this point, having dealt with the long range Pieces, it may be convenient to point out to any reader who has not already inferred it, that, in Chess, Pieces only travel over empty squares. With three exceptions, which are either apparent only, or else specially explicable, the Chess Pieces do not jump. The exceptions are : the Knight's move (which is only apparently exceptional

THE KNIGHT (French, Chevalier ; German, Springer ; Russian, Konj ; English Notation, Kt ; sometimes S, or N, in order to avoid possible confusion with K).

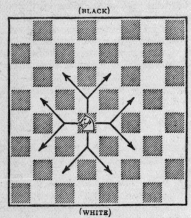

(BLACK)

(WHITE)

THE KNIGHT

Geometrically, the Knight's move may be described as the shortest possible move in which a Piece can change both its rank (or file) and its diagonal. An easier description is to say that the Knight moves from corner to corner of any rectangle three squares by two, of which its own square is a corner square. More easily, for the purpose of visualizing, one can because the Knight does not " sweep " any complete square that it passes), Castling, and the Pawn's Capture En Passant. These remain to be described.

For the benefit of the reader who approaches Chess from Draughts, it should be repeated that the Chess Pieces do not capture by jumping. With one exception (the Pawn capturing En Passant), they capture by moving on to the square of a hostile occupant and remaining there, the captured Piece being removed from the Board. To this general rule about capturing, the Knight's move is not an exception, because the Knight does not affect any Pieces that it appears to pass. It can only take a Piece on a square which is its destination.

Needless to say, with the apparent exception of the Knight, no Chess Piece can pass one of its own coloured Pieces on its direct line of motion; and no Chess Piece can capture any Piece of its own colour.

For the further benefit of the Draughts player approaching Chess, it should be noted that all the Pieces, except the Pawns, can move either forwards or backwards.

Finally, capturing is optional. There is no huffing at Chess. A capture is only compulsory when it is the only move available to terminate a state of Check, or the only move that does not expose the King to Check.

say the Knight moves one square along the rank, or along the file (backwards or forwards), and then one square along the diagonal away from its point of origin. Alternatively, one square along any diagonal, followed by one square along the rank or file away from the point of origin.

In this path the Knight ignores any Pieces of its own or hostile colour on the squares it appears to pass, and is only concerned with any Piece that may occupy the square of its destination. In other words, the Knight appears to jump, or to

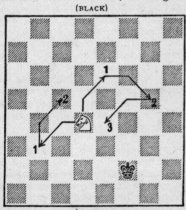

The Knight takes 3 moves to arrive at the square adjacent to it on the rank or file, 2 moves to reach an adjacent diagonal square, and 3 moves to check a King 2 diagonal squares away.

Knight cannot move. If, instead, the Pawns were on adjoining squares (all 8 of them), they would not affect the Kt's move.

cross, occupied squares. Pedantically that is not quite correct, because the Knight's path does not sweep out any complete square ; rather it is across the edges of squares. It is as if, on the battlefield which is the Chess Board, the Knight does not move along any special road, but always alights at places which happen to be on the recognised roads.

From any rank or file except the two sets of double ranks and files bordering the Board, the Knight has a field of 8 possible squares ; 8 squares around the edges of a field of 25 squares ; and each move of the Knight creates a new area for it. It is thus an important " middle range " Piece. It has great difficulty in reaching squares adjacent to its point of origin on the rank and file (these require three moves to reach). It takes two moves to reach an adjacent square on the diagonal, four moves to reach the next but one on the diagonal, i.e., 3 moves to Check a King there. Also it takes several moves to cross the Board. On the other hand, as we shall see when we come to compare it with the heavier Pieces, there are many ways in which its powers give the Knight a value as great as that of the Bishop.

THE PAWN (French, Pion ; German, Bauer ; Russian, Peshka : English Notation, P).

The Pawn differs from the other Pieces* in several respects. All the other Pieces can move either forwards or backwards at will. Only the Pawn, the Infantry of the game, is condemned to a perpetual advance. The range of other Pieces is not confined in both extent and direction ; the Pawn resembles the Infantryman in that the extent of its range as well as its direction is limited. The Pawn's normal move is one square forward on the file, with the alternative of a two move advance for each Pawn's first move only. (This right, incidentally, cannot be reserved. If a Pawn moves one square at its first move, it cannot move 2 on its second). Further, other Pieces capture opponents that purport to block their path. The Pawn cannot do so. Anything standing the square ahead of it on the file stops its normal advance. One the other hand, the Pawn captures in a direction which is not that of its normal move, viz., one square ahead

---

*So far, the word Pieces has been used to include, in its denotation, Pawns. There will be contexts, however, in which the word Piece or Pieces is used in contrast to the word Pawns, e.g., as where a Piece is said to be lost for a Pawn.

This ambiguity is inevitable in Chess literature (not only Anglo-American Chess literature). It is hoped that in every case the context will make the meaning clear.

on either diagonal. Thus a Pawn can change its file, but only with the aid of the hostile Pieces that it captures. Finally, the Pawn has this compensation, that it can be translated to a higher realm. The values of other Pieces become translated according to the position. Only the Pawn changes its nature. This is called *promotion*. When a Pawn reaches the eighth rank it must cease to exist; and there is substituted for it, at the player's will, either a Queen, Rook,

(BLACK)

THE PAWN.

(WHITE)

Bishop or Knight. Something must take its place. The player can choose which Piece he pleases. The normal choice, of course, is the Queen, but, as we shall show, there are instances where a sub-promotion (to Rook, Bishop or Knight) is preferable.

It follows that a player can possess, at some stage of a game, more than one Queen, and/or more than two Rooks, Bishops or Knights. There has, indeed, been a famous win, King and three Knights against King and one Knight. The tactical and strategic value of the Pawn will be considered later. Here suffice it to say that promotability obviously raises it above the ordinary Infantry standard. Because of this it can be said that the Pawns are the only Infantry that the General regards as more than cannon fodder.

THE PAWN'S FIRST MOVE AND THE CAPTURE EN PASSANT

The right of the Pawn to move, at the player's option, two squares forward instead of only one, on the first move, is a modern invention. It does not exist in the Indian game even now*. The option of a double move does not affect the advancing Pawn's power of capture. Thus a Pawn on the second rank cannot capture on the adjoining file on the fourth rank, but only on the third. The option of two squares instead of one applies to an ordinary advance, not to a capture.

On the other hand, the Pawn's double first move has been

(BLACK)

(WHITE)

EN PASSANT.
If the Black pawn advances 2 squares in one move, then, on the next move only, the white pawn can behave as if the Black pawn had moved one square.

offset by the award to opposing Pawns of a special kind of capture. Thus, if a Pawn is standing on its fifth rank, and a hostile Pawn on an adjoining file has not yet moved, then obviously, if that hostile Pawn moves to its third rank (our Pawn's sixth), there can be a capture. If, however, the hostile Pawn moves two squares, apparently there can be no capture. This is where the En Passant rule comes into force. If in those circumstances (where a Pawn stands on the fifth rank) a Pawn on an adjoining file makes a double move (i.e., its first move), then, *on the next move, and the next move only,* the Pawn on its own fifth rank of the adjoining file (the advancing Pawn's fourth rank) can capture the Pawn that has made the double move—exactly as if it had made a single move. Thus, in terms of the notation ; a White Pawn is standing on KB5 A Black Pawn from its KKt2

*Also, the Indian game differs in respect of promotions. There, the Pawn is promoted to a Piece equivalent to that on whose file it gets promoted. On a Rook's file, it becomes a Rook, on a Bishop's file a Bishop, on a Knight's file a Knight ; on the Queen's file or King's file it becomes a Queen.

moves two squares to Kt4   The Pawn on KB5 can capture
that Pawn immediately as if it had moved to KKt3. The
captured Pawn is removed from KKt4 and the capturing
Pawn stands, not on that square (its own Kt5), but on Kt6.
This is the only case in Chess of a capture in which the
capturing Piece does not occupy the square of the Piece
captured.

(BLACK)

(WHITE)

PAWN CAPTURES.
P, on KR file cannot
move.
If P on Kt file
advances, Black P
on R file can capture
it or be captured by
it.
P on KB file can
either capture P on
K file, or advance
one square without
capturing.
P on K file can cap-
ture or be captured.
P on Q file if it
advances one square
can be captured by
either flanking pawn.
P on Q file if it
advances 2 squares in
one move, can, on
the next move, be
captured by either flanking pawn as if it had moved one square only.

To make the matter clear beyond doubt, let it be repeated
that any Capture En Passant must either be done immediately,
or else not at all. It is a right that cannot be reserved beyond
the immediate occasion of its creation. If the Pawn is not
captured En Passant on the opponent's immediately following
move, then it cannot be captured En Passant at all.

THE KING (French, Roi ; German, König ; Russian, Korolj ;
English Notation K).
 Last, by reason of its greatest importance, and in some
senses least, of the Pieces, lacking the Knight's distance and
the Pawn's promotability, the King yet has a quite considerable power. The King's move is the Queen's move in
miniature, one square in any direction ; that is to say, one
square either way along the rank, or one square backwards or
forwards along the file or diagonal. Thus it has a range,
from any square not on the edge of the Board, of eight

possible moves. This we shall see to be a not negligible power at any stage of the game. The King is most potent in the Endgame, among Pawns, and it can reach squares closed to either of the Bishops as the case may be*.

Many restrictions hedge in the King, since, as we have seen, in this war game (which continues dynastic, even while the King's power has constitutionally diminished), the King remains the *sine qua non* of the game. If the King is lost, everything is lost.

CASTLING (French, Rochade ; German, Rochade ; Notation, 0–0 ; 0–0–0).

To compensate for the diminution in the King's power in the modern game, there has developed the privilege in which

(BLACK)

(WHITE)

After Castling K side.

the unmoved King participates together with an unmoved Rook. It is, incidentally, a quick method of bringing the Rook nearer to the centre of the Board.

For Castling to take place, the King, and the Rook with which it is proposed to Castle, must stand on their original squares—not having moved—and there must be no Piece in between. Then the King can move two squares to its right or

*There is reason to believe that before the rise of the Vizier (now Queen) the power of the King was greater than now (no one knows how great). Yet the name has not been changed. Even in Republican countries this Piece is still called the King, and nobody has yet suggested G.H.Q., or War Office, or any other name that signifies a military function at once highly important and not too dynamic.

left as the case may be; and the Rook towards which it moves jumps over it, and lands on the square between the original King's square and the square to which the King has moved. Thus, in Castling King's side, the King moves to the King's Knight's square and the King's Rook moves to the King's Bishop's square. In Castling Queen's side, the King moves to the Queen's Bishop's square and the Queen's Rook moves to the Queen's square*

(BLACK)

After Castling Q side

(WHITE)

A number of conditions govern Castling, which, incidentally, is the only instance in Chess of two Pieces of the same colour simultaneously altering their positions. For Castling to take place :

1. Obviously the King and Rook concerned must be on their original squares with no Pieces intervening.
2. Neither the King nor the Rook concerned may have made a previous move. If the King has moved there can be no Castling at all for the player whose King it is. (It follows that one cannot Castle twice.) If only the Rook has moved there can be no Castling with that particular Rook, though there can still be Castling with the other Rook if that has not yet moved. Obviously

*It is normal, in Castling to move the King first because that particular King's move necessarily implies that you are Castling, whereas if you move the Rook first your opponent may think that you have made a complete move. As the rule in serious Chess is that a Piece touched must be moved, the policy of moving the King first in Castling avoids technical objections of a pedantic nature.

there can be no Castling with a " promoted Pawn "
Rook.

3.   The King must not be in Check. It is not true to say,
as many bad players think, that once the King has been
in Check there can be no Castling. That is just incorrect ;
but at the moment of Check the King cannot get out of
Check by Castling. That is very important.

4.   The square to which the King must move, and the square
which the King must pass in order to Castle, must not be
under attack by a hostile Piece. Thus, in Castling King's
side, not only must you not be in Check, but your King's
Bishop's square and your King's Knight's square must
not be immediately reachable by a hostile Piece. On
the other hand the fact that the Rook is attacked does
not matter at all. In Castling Queen's side, the Queen's
square and the Queen's Bishop's square must not be
immediately reachable by a hostile Piece. The Queen's
Knight's square and the Queen's Rook's square do not
matter.

(BLACK)

(WHITE)

CASTLING.
White cannot Castle
either side, and if the
Kt be placed one
square right or left,
White cannot Castle
for a different reason
(i.e., being in Check).

Since Castling can be quite an advantage—it usually
is—an opponent will prevent Castling if he can. The
ways of doing this follow from the rules given above. To
cause the King to move, or to cause to move that Rook
with which the King is likely to Castle, or to cause both
Rooks to move, is a good method but not an easy one.
A more usual method, and very effective if the situation can

be maintained, is to have Pieces stationed so as to control the squares that the King has to pass or arrive at in order to Castle. To achieve this without loss is usually to achieve superiority.

On the other hand, it must be pointed out that Castling is not always good. Sometimes the King is best placed in the middle of the Board (e.g., when the Endgame is approaching.) It is also true that Castling can, on occasion, incur a quick loss because the opponent's attack may be, in the circumstances, more easily directed to the wing than to the centre. Typical is what is sometimes called the " Greek Gift Sacrifice." It is a warning that in Chess there is no room for automatism. (See next Chapter.)

CONSEQUENCES OF THE SPECIAL IMPORTANCE OF THE KING

The treatment of the King was purposely left until after the other Pieces had been considered, because, whereas other Pieces are only limited by their geometric scope, the King, whose geometric move is tactically and strategically important, is also limited by the fact that it alone of all the Pieces dare not be lost. Other values can be transvalued, but not the importance of the King.

(BLACK)

(WHITE)

CHECK.

White King in Check. This Check can be terminated.

(a) by K move.
(b) by capture of B.
(c) by interposition of KT.

The reader has already been introduced to the ideas of Check and Mate. It is now proposed to consider them in detail. *Check* differs qualitatively from all other attacks, because it is obligatory upon the player checked to terminate the Check. Other Pieces can be allowed to be lost—can be left, or placed, En Prise.* Obviously, since the purpose of the game is the capture of the King, it may come about that you can allow your opponent to capture any of your Pieces, because the loss will leave you in a position, immediately or ultimately, to effect the downfall of your opponent's King. Then the Piece concerned is said to have been sacrificed. A sacrifice is one instance of what has been called above " transvaluation," where the formal values of the Pieces are subordinated to the functions of all the Pieces operating in the game. By virtue of that reasoning, the King can never be allowed to sacrifice itself.

Again, other Pieces may be lost unsacrificially, but their loss, whether in exchange for something or not, does not necessarily put an end to the game. But the King, be it repeated, must not be lost if the game is to be continued.

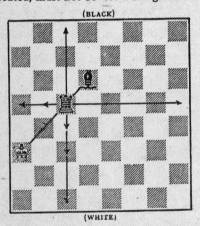

(BLACK)

(WHITE)

DISCOVERED CHECK.
DOUBLE CHECK.
If the R moves away, White is in Check (Discovered Check). If the R moves 2 squares to the White side of the Board or 2 squares to White's left the Check is Double Check.

It follows that a state of Check must be terminated. A simple Check (by one Piece) can be terminated either by the capture of the checking Piece, or by the interposition of a Piece between the King and the attacking Piece (evidently this cannot be done when the attacking Piece is a Knight or a Pawn, or a Piece on an adjacent square to the King); thirdly, by moving the King. This can coincide with the

*En Prise is a useful term to express the capturability of a Piece—especially capturability for insufficient exchange. The term is never abbreviated to e.p., which is the shorthand for en passant.

first method when the checking Piece is adjacent to the King and unguarded (i.e., its square is not covered by another Piece of the same colour).

These three methods apply also when the Check is a discovered Check. A discovered Check arises when a Piece, which does not itself give Check, moves out of the path of a long-range Piece opening a battery on the King. A diagram illustrates this. The distinction between discovered Check and simple Check is only psychologically important; discovered Check gives alarm to weak players.

(BLACK)

(WHITE)

CROSS-CHECK.

If the Black Rook moves, say, one square, White can Cross-check by moving the King or interposing the Kt. If the Black Rook gives Double-check, a King move gives a Cross-check. In the case of a Cross-check by interposed piece, the fact that the checking piece is pinned is immaterial. (The first King to fall loses.)

More difficult to deal with is double Check. That is a discovered Check with the addition that the Piece unmasking the battery itself gives Check. Then there are two Pieces checking the King; a Rook or a Queen on the rank or file, and a Knight, Bishop or Pawn also checking; alternatively, a Queen or Bishop checking from long range on the diagonal and a Knight or Rook checking independently. Double Check is an extremely useful weapon because it forces the King to move. Sometimes it can be followed up with very great advantage.*

To complete the account of Check, a player can extricate himself from Check, in the same move giving Check, e.g., he can interpose a Piece in answer to a simple Check, which Piece, moving to the square required, either itself gives Check, or discovers Check; alternatively, the King, by moving, can open a battery on the opponent's King. On the other

*It stands to reason that there cannot be a treble Check.

hand, the King's move can never give double Check, because the King itself cannot give Check. On similar reasoning, the reply to a Check cannot be the capture of the opponent's King, because that would imply that the opponent, in giving Check, has either exposed his own King to Check—which he must not do—or has failed to terminate the condition of Check in which his own King stood at the moment of moving.

It remains only to be added that the value of Check varies with the position. Check can be a bad move, if the position after the Check has been replied to is more favourable to the player who has been checked than it was before. The only Check which is bound to be good is Mate. On the other hand, the player who said, " Never miss a Check, it might be Mate," was contributing to the humour of the game, not to its serious study.

MATE AND LOSS

If, unhappily, a player is in Check, and has at his disposal no move that can terminate the Check, then he is Check Mate, or, as it is more usually called, Mate. Mate is the state of

(BLACK)

This is Mate.

(WHITE)

the game when your opponent's next move will be the capture of your King, whatever move you make in the meantime. Since the object of the game is the capture of the King, it follows that to be mated is to lose.

Mate can happen after few moves or after many moves— but it is always the end of the game.

Conversely, the game is not lost, strictly speaking, until Mate. But in most games it happens that the player who realises that Mate of his King later has become inevitable, in the light of the position, and on the assumption of his opponent's capacity to bring it about, anticipates the Mate by resigning. So for practical purposes, it may be said that the game is lost —and resignation justified—when Mate is either immediately

(BLACK)

(WHITE)

This is Mate.

(BLACK)

(WHITE)

This is also Mate. It arises from the following play :

1. P to K4 ; P to K4
2. Kt to KB3 ; Kt to QB3
3. B to Kt5 ; P to QR3 (Ruy Lopez)
4. B to R4 ; Kt to B3
5. O—O ; Kt × P
6. P to Q4 ; P × P
7. R to K1 ; P to Q4 (Riga Defence)
8. Kt × P ; B to Q3
9. Kt × Kt ; B × Pch
10. K to R1 ; Q to R5
11. R × Ktch ; P × R
12. Q to Q8ch ; Q × Q
13. Kt × Qch ; K × Kt8
14. K × B, P to KB4 ?
15. B to KKt5 Mate.

impending, or certain though not immediate. Mate, or the reasonable certainty of Mate, is, then, the condition of loss. The reasonable certainty of Mate may exist in an infinite variety of circumstances, but the main characteristic of most positions that are resigned is a decisive preponderance

(BLACK)

(WHITE)

LOSS.
This is a typical instance of loss. White will soon be a Queen to the good and will force Mate.

of force. This may vary from a Queen, or more than a Queen, to the good, down to the preponderance of a single Pawn in a position where sooner or later it can be promoted. Those are instances of material advantage, which, other things being equal, give one side the conditions of victory. But let the reader notice that the expression used above was preponderance of force. That is not the same thing as excess of material. Excess of material only wins, other things being equal. Now Chess is one mode of activity where other things are very rarely equal. In Chess it can quite often be said that the many have been delivered into the hands of the few. A player may sacrifice much of his material in order to bring about a Mating attack, and may finally achieve Mate when materially he is several Pieces to the bad. Or it may be the case that a player is material to the bad, but his Pieces are so well placed that he controls the Board and can win his opponent's material at his leisure. Then what he has is a preponderance of force. But where neither player is in a position to control the Board or to force a decisive series of moves, then, and then only, material counts; because in those circumstances material can be turned into effective force, and a sufficient excess of material will guarantee victory.

Thus it may be said that there are two main types of victory in Chess—victory by Mate, or victory, of a more sedate kind, by the accumulation of an overpowering advantage in the form of force, which may be positional dominance, or excess of material not offset by positional disadvantage. Most games of Chess are struggles to achieve this kind of accumulation—the mediate victory rather than the immediate Mate. But it must be borne in mind that at all stages of the game Mate is a factor. The threat of immediate Mate may be part of a forcing process by which you compel your opponent to yield ground and/or material. Thus it may happen that an attack against an opponent's King results, not in Mate, but in a considerable gain in material; it may also happen that, in the struggle for material, the player that succeeds in gaining or saving material finds himself the victim of a Mating attack. It follows that in a well contested game there is always a dovetailing and an integration of purposes; and the game must always be looked at as a whole.

It remains only to be added that, although the loss of the King is the loss of the game, in practice the game never ends that way. If a player exposes his own King to attack, or fails to terminate a state of Check, he must correct the move. That is the only move which, in ordinary Chess, is allowed to be retracted. Games are lost, either by Mate, or by resignation in anticipation of immediate or eventual Mate.

Stalemate and Other Types of Draw

There is one special situation, which is so important that it affects the whole nature of Chess, where a preponderance of force—and that of a striking character—produces not a win, but a draw. That is when one of the players is not in Check but is in such a position that he cannot make any move at all without exposing his King to immediate capture. This position is called *Stalemate*. It must not be confused with what we describe in the Continental term Zugzwang, where the player whose turn it is to move incurs disadvantage through having to move. In Stalemate the important fact is that any move allows the capture of the King on the move, though the King as it stands at the moment of moving is not attacked. Roughly, it is Mate without a Check. This position can come about when there are quite a number of both coloured Pieces on the boards. That, however, is rare. More usually it comes about in an Endgame where the forces are small. Then the player with the passive—usually, but not necessarily, the lesser—material can find himself with his Pawns, for example, blocked, other Piece or Pieces pinned (i.e., in such a position that they stand between the King and an attacking Piece and cannot move without allowing Check), and the King itself without an available square. One of the most important situations, however, is where one player has an excess of force just

STALEMATE.
If it is Black's turn to move.

STALEMATE.
If White has to move.

insufficient to bring about Checkmate. Thus, as we shall see, a King and Bishop alone, or a King and Knight alone, cannot bring about the Mate of a lone King; but they can bring about Stalemate. A King and two Knights can Mate a lone King, but they cannot force Mate. The most that they can force is Stalemate. Again, a King and Pawn can defeat a King if the Pawn can be brought to promotion; but if the defending King is properly placed relatively to the other, and no mistakes are made, again all that can happen is Stalemate. The foregoing are the circumstances where Stalemate is most frequent; and it is from these circumstances that it derives its importance. For the consequence of the Stalemate rule is that there is a margin of excess of force which is not adequate for victory. There is a margin of Draw, so to speak, on either side of equality. That fact makes Chess a harder game to win even than might be expected. Needless to add, it is almost invariably easy to lose !*

Another type of Draw—theoretically the normal—is where both sides have absolute equality of material and force and neither side has any available process of seeking victory. The extreme case, of course, is King against King. But a draw can be agreed—and usually is agreed among good players—where it is clear that neither side has any preponderance, or any likelihood of achieving preponderance.

*Very rare is the draw that results from the fact that the player whose turn it is to move *physically* cannot move.

(BLACK)

(WHITE)

DRAW.

A ridiculous, but not impossible position. White to move, cannot move

This kind of situation can develop even when the Board is crowded with Pieces. It happens when the skirmishing is over and the strategic lines of the game are so set that neither side can attempt any attack without incurring the risk of loss.

(BLACK)

(WHITE)

AGREED DRAW.

This is a typical situation, fairly early in the game, where a draw can easily be agreed.

In addition there are rules of the game which increase what has been called above the margin of Draw. One of these rules is that *perpetual Check* is a Draw. This can happen early in the game, but it usually happens towards the Endgame, when the side with inferior chances has available a powerful Piece like the Queen, or a couple of Pieces, which can so move as to keep the opposing King in Check move after move without being stopped. In some instances the geometry of the Board is the factor that prevents the Checks from being stopped. In other cases, the Check could only be stopped by heavy loss of material. Both of these types are illustrated later. The rule, shortly stated, is that an unending series of Checks bringing about no change in the position, amounts to a Draw.

Perpetual Check is a draw by way of terminating the interminable. A harder rule relates to the occurrence, 3 times or more, of an identical position in the same game. Then, a claim to a draw may be made, *instead of a move,* (a) by the player whose move can cause the recurrence : (b) by his opponent, when the recurrence has taken place.

Another rule is that if 50 moves have been played without any change in the material, and with no Pawn having been moved, the game is also a Draw. (See note at end of chapter).

The last rule is relatively rare in its direct operation. But the rule about repetition can operate at any stage where both players refuse to commit themselves to any change of plan.

(BLACK)

(WHITE)

DRAW.
White, at a material disadvantage and in great danger, draws by repeating the Checking moves . . . Q to Kt5 and B6.

In conclusion, let it be said—and this may already have occurred to the reader—that by reason of the margins that exist in Chess, the normal result of a well-contested game should be a Draw. But that does not mean that a winning advantage has got to be a perceptibly big advantage. A winning advantage can be slight and subtle. That slight and subtle advantage will be the thin edge of a wedge. What requires to be pointed out is that all advantages are not winning advantages. There is usually counter-play ; and in the hands of a good opponent the counter-play will usually be dangerous and will suffice at least to prevent the eventual difference that crystallizes from being sufficient for your victory.

NOTATION

The rules governing the English (or Descriptive) notation are as follows :

1. Each file is named after the Piece whose original square is at the base of that file. Thus we have Queen's Rook's (QR) file, QKt file, QB file, Q file, K file, KB file, KKt file, KR file. (Where there is no ambiguity the K or Q in QR, KKt, etc., etc., can be dropped.)

2. Pieces are referred to by their initials ; e.g., K, Q,

QB, KR, etc. (Where there is no ambiguity, the extra letter can be dropped as in the case of the names of the files.) Each Pawn is named, not after its original file, but according to the particular file on which it happens to be at the moment of the move being registered. A Pawn can be QR P, QKt P, etc., etc. (Where there is no ambiguity, one or both of the extra letters can be dropped, leaving, e.g., BP or P.)

3. The destination of any Piece or Pawn is described by the specific square to which it moves on any particular file.

4. To this end the squares along each file are numbered 1 to 8. Thus a move is registered as P to K4, B to Kt5, R to K1, etc., etc.

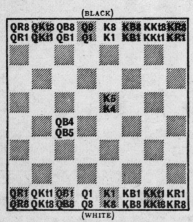

(BLACK)

THE NOTATION.
The Black description of each square is below the White description.

(WHITE)

5. Each player numbers the Board, for the purpose of describing his own moves, from his own back rank, counting that as 1, his second rank as 2, and so on to 8. His opponent describes his (the opponent's) move, and he describes his opponent's moves, from his opponent's end. Thus the Board falls into two completely overlapping frames of reference ; one for White moves, the other for Black moves.

Thus, White, moving his King's Pawn two squares on the first move, writes P to K4. If Black replies with a similar move, that is registered in Black's column (by both players) as P to K4. Now suppose Black did not make that move, but some other, e.g., P to K3, and White, on his next move, advanced his Pawn one square further, that is registered in the White column as P to K5.

Once it is remembered that the system of description is double—one frame of reference for White's moves, and one frame of reference for Black's moves—there is no difficulty. The method has been described as clumsy, but there is something natural about it.

6. Certain symbols are useful; viz., × means Captures, e.g., P×P. 0–0 (or 0–0–0) signifies Castles (K side or Q side). Ch. signifies Check. The plus sign is sometimes used for Check, but as this sign also means "with advantage," the former use is relatively rare.

ALGEBRAIC NOTATION

So far the English notation. The continental, or Algebraic, notation will be found described in the next diagram. It only requires to be explained that the files are a, b, c, d, e, f, g, h, *from White's left to White's right, and the numbering of the squares on the files is always from White's side of the Board, whether Black is moving or White is moving, i.e., there*

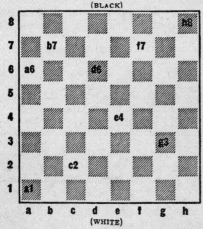

(BLACK)

ALGEBRAIC NOTATION·

(WHITE)

is only one frame of reference. Further, in the continental notation, Pawns, the object of militaristic disregard, are never described by initials; P to K4 is e2 to e4. Further, "Captures" is described by a semi-colon, and the Piece captured is not mentioned—only the square on which the capture takes place, e.g., B g 8; Finally, an obelus signifies Check†. A double obelus, Mate‡.

FORSYTH NOTATION

This is a neat and ingenious method of recording the position without the labour of making a diagram.

Looking at the Board from White's side, one reads off from the top left-hand corner—as in ordinary reading—the number of vacant squares and the names of Pieces present on the back rank, the next rank and so downwards from rank to rank.

White Pieces are described by a Capital initial ; Black Pieces by a small initial. Thus, suppose Black's King is on his King's square and the White King is facing it on the next rank but one (i.e., White's K6), and there is a White Queen on the right of the White King (i.e., White's KB6).

This position, which, incidentally, is a good example of Stalemate, would be described in the Forsyth notation as follows : 4k3 ; 8 ; 4KQ2 ; 40.

Any position can be quite quickly written down by this method, however crowded the Board.

Note on the 50-move rule.

There are some (very few) endgame positions in which the win that is demonstrable occupies more than 50 moves unpunctuated by captures or by Pawn moves.

Instances are : some cases of King and 2 Knights against King and Pawn ; some cases of King, Rook and Bishop against King and Rook, and at least one case of King, Rook and Pawn against King, Bishop and Pawn.

Because of these demonstrations it has become the practice of organizers of Chess events to declare their acknowledgement of certain exceptions to the 50-move rule, and to declare the number of moves, in excess of 50, that they allow in the various exceptional classes of position. (This practice is pursuant to amendments to the Laws of Chess made by F.I.D.E. during the 1950's. The new form of the rule about the Draw by repetition of position (p. 34) derives from the same source.)

CHAPTER II

THE FUNCTIONS AND RELATIVE VALUES
OF THE PIECES :
THE ELEMENTARY ENDGAME.

IN the language of the Persian poet the purpose of the Chess
player is to " mate and slay." He judges the value of his
Pieces in terms of their capacity to capture other Pieces and to
mate the King. At all stages of the game these capacities
vary. But this varying is more likely to occur on a crowded
Board than on a relatively empty Board. It is on the relatively empty Board that it is easiest to compare the strength
of the Pieces. Particularly, their power to co-operate in
Mate is a good index to their value ; and the reader would
be well advised to master as soon as he can some of the
operations of mating that can take place on an open Board.
It may appear to him that in doing this he is starting at the
end, not at the beginning. In making this criticism he will
have grasped an important truth about Chess—that the study
of it starts at the end. The final purpose is what matters
from the beginning. As we have seen, the game is won by
preponderances of force sufficient to carry out an eventual
mating operation. A very simple strategic process (too
simple to be the whole of strategy, but always an aspect of it)
is to aim at acquiring more material than your opponent
possesses ; then, by repeated exchange of Pieces, to leave
yourself with some striking force in addition to your own
King against your opponent's lone King. Now there is no
purpose in carrying this out unless, having achieved that final
superiority, you can turn it into eventual Mate. Nor indeed
will you be able to force the simplification unless you can Mate.
Therefore, one must begin the study of the game by learning
how to finish the game. In studying this one learns to see
the game as a whole ; also one acquires some degree of
intimacy with the functions of the Pieces.

MATING BY THE QUEEN

A surprising number of games liquidate themselves eventually into King and Queen against King. King and Queen
against King is the logical finish of any closely contested game
where the final difference in force is a Pawn that can be

promoted. If, then, resignation does not take place, that Pawn gets promoted into a Queen, rapidly disposes of anything that requires to be disposed of, and the King and Queen are left working together to bring about Mate.

Now the Queen, though extremely powerful, cannot mate unaided, because, as will already be evident to the reader, the 27 squares that she controls cannot include the same squares as the 9 that constitute the hostile King's field (the square on which the King stands and the 8 squares to which it has the choice of moving). This follows from the fact that the Queen cannot occupy the King's square at the moment of the King's occupancy.

(BLACK)

The Queen about to give Mate.

(at e2 or c1)

(WHITE)

Moreover, even if the King's scope be reduced to 5 squares (at the edge of the Board), or to 3 squares (at the corner of the Board), the Queen unaided cannot Mate. To do so she would have to include in her capacity the power of making a Knight's move, which, of course, she does not possess. (That, incidentally, may be a reply to those would-be reformers who wish to add to the Queen's power the power of moving like a Knight).

At the side of the Board (a fortiori at the corner of the Board) the Queen and the King combined can bring about Mate. They cannot Mate in the middle of the Board. But they can so co-operate as always to drive the hostile King to the side of the Board. Then Mate is easy, though the player must always be careful to avoid the risk of Stalemate.

The first diagram shows a position just before the end. From this position, in order to Mate, the Queen must arrive either at a square immediately in front of the hostile King on the file and guarded by her own King ; or else must be able to check on the rank when her own King is so placed as to prevent the checked King from escaping from the back rank. If one gives the Board a quarter turn, the same effect can be

(BLACK)

(WHITE)

K and Q *v.* K.

Most favourable position for Black.

White wins as follows.

1. Q to Kt4 ; K to B4
2. K to B2 ; K to K4
3. K to B3 ; K to Q4
4. K to K3 ; K to K4
5. Q to Kt5 Check.

and the process is repeated until the Black K is on the back rank.

(BLACK)

(WHITE)

STALEMATE

seen on the file edge of the Board. It may be observed that the King is a particularly useful co-operator with the Queen. Together they can give a bigger range of Mates than could the Queen and Bishop together or the Queen and Knight together.

The diagram on page 40 shows the mating process being completed. But the reader must learn how to bring this final stage about. The next diagram shows the Pieces separated from each other, with the hostile King in the centre.

The series of moves beside the second diagram shows the method of bringing about the kind of position that we saw in the first diagram. The third diagram shows a possible mishap. In approximating with the Queen and King, White has contrived to give not Mate but Stalemate. His last move should have been not K (from K2) to B1, but Q to Kt4—a more patient move.

(BLACK)

(WHITE)

A possible Mate.

The Queen's power as a mating Piece will be better realised when mating processes by other Pieces have been considered. Meanwhile, in case there is any misunderstanding, let it be made clear that the Queen can appear at her maximum strength on a full Board as well as on an empty Board. On a full Board, for example, it can happen that the Queen delivers Mate single-handed. That is when the hostile King is hemmed in by its own Pieces. Here are two examples. One early Mate (in which the Queen's full powers are not seen, but which the reader should learn) consists in the so-called

Fool's Mate. This is the quickest Mate in Chess—on the second move. It can only be done by Black—and that when White plays extremely badly.

White plays P to KKt4, a weak move which does very little development and puts a Pawn on a square where it is not useful yet. Black replies P to K4, a reasonable move developing some Pieces and occupying a good square. White then plays a perfectly horrible move P to KB3 and Black replies Q to R5 ; and, if you look at that, you will see that the Queen is delivering a Check to which there is no answer

The diagram on p. 42 (also illustrative of the Queen's power) shows a position that can come about more rationally. Black has Castled Queen's side. White's Bishop has taken a Pawn on his QR6, Black has recaptured with a Pawn from Black's Kt2, and White's Queen, moving down the diagonal from KB3, arrives at QR8 and Black is mated, because the King is hemmed in in all directions that the Queen's range does not cover.

More usually the Queen mates in co-operation with at least one other Piece. Here, e.g., is the Scholar's Mate—in four moves—

White	Black
1. P to K4.	P to K4.
2. B to B4.	B to B4.
3. Q to R5. Not really a good move, because there is a good answer to it ; but it threatens two things, including the capture of the Pawn on White's K5.	P to Q3. Guarding the Pawn on his K4, but overlooking another threat. Necessary was Q to B3 or K2. Less good than that would be P to KKt3, allowing Q × KP Check, followed by capture of the Rook.
4. Q × BP Mate.	

The above are occurrences that do not often take place. Nobody invites the Fool's Mate ; and nobody tries to do the Scholar's Mate, because Q to R5 is not a good move if Black makes the correct reply. As will be seen later, it is not wise to parade the Queen round the Board except for very good reason.

The following few moves constitute one instance of a vigorous Queen move early in the game. This same example shows the importance of Mate as a tactical threat. The Mate is not achieved but material is won.

White	Black
1. P to K4.	P to K4.
2. Kt to KB3 apparently attacking a Pawn.	Kt to QB3 defending the Pawn.
3. B to B4	B to K2. Not bad, but not vigorous. Better is B to B4.

White	*Black*
4. P to Q4. A vigorous developing move.	P × P. Not a good capture: Kt × P is not so bad, but P to Q3 is better.
5. P to QB3. The sacrifice of a Pawn: if, e.g., 5 . . . P × P 6. Kt × P. White will have lost 2 Pawns for one. The capture, however, is a pitfall.	P × P. A mistake. P to Q3 (or Kt to B3) is necessary.
6. Q to Q5. And now Mate on KB7 is threatened. Black is now forced to play . . .	Kt to KR3. Losing a Piece but stopping the Mate. He could not play P to Q3 because of 7. Q × BP Ch. K to Q2 8. B to K6. Mate.

White will now capture this Knight with his Queen's Bishop; Black will not have time to recapture, but will be obliged to Castle (in order to stop the Mate) and the Bishop will return home, having won a Piece for the Gambit Pawn. Incidentally, White's task will still not be easy; because his own development is now imperfect—as often after a successful skirmish.

As well as a good mating Piece, the Queen is also, and obviously, a good capturing Piece. On a Board where the Pieces are in any degree spreadeagled, the Queen's power to attack in several directions simultaneously can be devastating. The next diagram shows a simple instance of this.

(BLACK)

(WHITE)

The Queen attacking three unguarded Pieces.

And even earlier in the game, on a crowded Board, a Queen's move can force the win of material quite soon in the game. Typical is the following variation :—

White	Black

White

1. P to K4.
2. Kt to KB3.
3. B to B4.
4. P to Q4.
5. P to QB3. A sacrifice similar to that in the previous example.

Black

P to K4.
P to Q3. Defending the Pawn.
B to K2.
P × P.
B to Kt5. With the idea of preventing the King's Knight from moving. This is called "Pinning" the Knight. At this early stage it is a mistake. P × P would also be dangerous, because of 6 Q to Q5 B to K3. 7 Q × KtP. The best answer is 5 . . . Kt to KB3.

6. Q to Kt3. With a double threat. The Queen is attacking the Knight's Pawn ; and the Bishop, supported by the Queen, is attacking the King's Bishop's Pawn.

It is impossible for Black to parry both threats.

This type of manœuvre is very frequent ; but it should be added, as a warning, that if both sides are equally well-developed (as they are not in the example given), the capture of the Queen's Knight's Pawn can be dangerous to the capturer because it loses a lot of time, and may involve the Queen in remaining badly mobilized ; and that consideration may be well worth a Pawn to the opposition. (An example of this is given in the Chapter on Strategy.)

LIMITS OF THE QUEEN'S POWER

On a crowded Board the Queen can be far from omnipotent. Indeed a Master, expert in the use of all the Pieces, can give the odds of a Queen to players of mediocre skill and can win.

On a crowded Board, the Pieces are usually not loose or spreadeagled unless they are being very badly handled. Most of the Pieces will be guarded ; that is to say, if they are captured, another Piece (Pawns are particularly useful here) will be standing ready to recapture. In that kind of situation —which is the normal one—the Queen's power is limited by her own value ; and that value can only be ignored if a process is in operation which justifies some loss of value for its fulfilment. Failing this, a wandering Queen can amount to a helpless target, prevented by her value from engaging in combat and exchanges with lesser Pieces.

Here are some examples to illustrate the vulnerability of the Queen and her liability to capture by a combination of weaker Pieces. Two at least of these examples, incidentally, should be useful to the reader as illustrations of the aggressive power of the Knight.

The first is a short game played about 1923 by the author :—

White (The Author)

1. P to K4.

2. P × P.
3. Kt to QB3. Attacking Queen and gaining a move. The minor Piece comes out without the opponent being able to develop a corresponding minor Piece immediately.
4. P to Q4. Opening the game up and controlling the centre.

5. B to Q2. Creating a masked battery against the Queen. The danger is not immediate however.

6. B to QKt5. Pinning the Knight. One threat is P to Q5. The other will be seen next move. Actually P to Q5 is not a threat unless the other is a threat as well. But in practical Chess it is very easy to see some possibilities without seeing the full implications.
7. Kt to Q5. Winning the Queen. Thus, if Q × KB, Kt × P Check, forking the King and Queen—a good example of the Knight's " fork." If, instead, B to QKt5, intervening between the Queen and the Bishop that is attacking it, then simply B × B, and the situation is unaltered because the Knight is pinned—a good example of the effect of a pin.

Black (W. R. Thomas)

P to Q4. The Centre Counter Opening, now a little out of favour, but quite playable. It solves some problems of development quite early, but loses a tempo.
Q × P.
Q to R4.

Kt to QB3. An experimental move invented by Mieses. The idea is to lure White into too quick an attack with P to Q5. Better than the text, and usual, is P to QB3, guarding the centre and affording the Queen a retreat.

Kt to KB3. A plausible move, but not the best. Had Black realised what White's Pieces could do in the next two moves, he would have played B to Q2 with the idea of Castling on the following move. It should be added, however, that White's threat, though short, was hard to see among the many possible lines of play that Black had to consider.

P to K3. A move with some positional merits, but revealing that Black has not seen what is going on. At this stage his only safe moves are awkward ones, like K to Q1 or Q to Kt5, the latter with the idea of replying to P to Q5 with P to QR3, etc., driving the Bishop away or bringing about exchanges.
Resigns. For the reasons given opposite. The best Black can do is to play Q × QB Check followed by the capture of the Knight at Q5. Then he will have given a Queen for two minor Pieces—which, at this early stage, is insufficient, especially in view of the fact that White's development is very good.

There have, in fact, been games when one player has given a Queen for two minor Pieces, and by that sacrifice has been enabled to win. An historic position from the Match between McDonnell (a North Irish Master of the 1840's) and La Bourdonnais (one of the last known really great French Chess Masters) is shown in the accompanying diagram.

(BLACK)

From the 50th game between La Bourdonnais and McDonnell. Black plays Kt × Kt!

(WHITE)

McDonnell played

White	Black
13. . . .	Kt × Kt.
14. B × Q.	Kt to K6 Ch.
15. K to K1.	K × B.

And Black has an overwhelming attack unless White resacrifices. La Bourdonnais was too opinionated to do so.

The above two examples took place on the full Board. Here,* now, is a composition by Adamson (an English Composer who specializes in the construction of elegant Endgame positions) in which the Queen is rendered helpless on the relatively open Board. With a very big range, she is so situated in relation to the King that she cannot escape capture.
1. B to B6. And now the Queen is in difficulties, e.g. she cannot go to KKt8 because of the immediate Kt to B3 Ch. — This " fork," as it is called, is impossible, however, to avoid: e.g. 1. . . . Q to R4. 2. BK4! (threatening Kt to B3 Ch. and Kt to B6 Ch. to follow) and the threat cannot be avoided. If, again, 1. . . . Q to R2. 2. Kt to B3 Ch. K to Q6. 3. B to K4 Ch.—and the Queen is lost next move. The advanced student can easily work out other variations.

*Diagram on next page.

This example, together with the others, should be sufficient to show the reader that the values of Chess Pieces are not constants, but variables in the context which is the

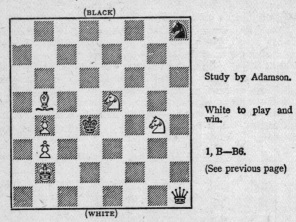

(BLACK)

(WHITE)

Study by Adamson.

White to play and win.

1, B—B6.

(See previous page)

position—i.e. the possibilities of the combined forces at the stage of the game that is being considered.

OTHER RELATIVE VALUES

The last example will have shown the difficulty of assessing the value of the Queen against a combination of two other Pieces. When processes are in operation, involving the possible promotion of Pawns, attacks on King, etc., etc., the valuation must entirely depend on the position. But geometrically, on an empty Board, it may be said that the Queen is definitely better than any two minor Pieces. Her range is evidently greater than the combined range of two Knights, or the combined range of two Bishops (even at their maximum range which they rarely enjoy) ; and it is greater than the range of Rook and Bishop, for these can never control a total of 27 squares unless they are mutually unguarded ; and, in addition, the Queen will always be able to find diagonal moves that the Bishop in question cannot find.

Nevertheless, it does not follow that King and Queen against King and two minor Pieces, or King, Rook and one minor Piece can win. That, too, will depend on the position. Provided the lesser Pieces are well placed and the play is careful, a draw should be the result. In the case of Queen against two Knights, which is the weakest of these oppositions, the processes of winning and drawing respectively have taxed Chess Masters beyond their powers.

Two Rooks

Two Rooks are demonstrably superior to the Queen on an empty Board, given that they are mutually defending, and are not forced to abandon mutual defence in order to stop a Mating threat; but the difference in value is slight, and normally insufficient to win because of the Queen's enormous checking power and pinning power.

But the slight superiority that they have is evident from this consideration : that two Rooks can force Mate without the aid of their own King; the Queen, as we have seen, cannot do so.

Mate by 2 Rooks.

The diagram shows a Mate by two Rooks. And this is quite easily brought about. The King is checked down the Board by alternating Rooks. Thus, for example, a Rook checks on the fourth rank or file driving the King to the third or fifth. The Rook that has checked stays where it is, and the other Rook checks on the rank or file, as the case may be, to which the King has gone. Thus the King is driven further towards the edge of the Board. Again the Rook that has last checked stays where it is and the other Rook checks the King; and so on until the edge of the Board is reached—when the Check that is given will be Mate.

If the King, while this is going on, approximates to one of the Rooks, or to a square that a Rook requires to go to, that only delays the process, but does not alter it. The Rook in question simply moves to the other end of the rank or file as the case may be, and the process continues.

Another aspect of the strength of two Rooks as compared with the Queen can be seen when there are Pawns to be attacked or defended. A Queen is insufficient to defend an attacked Pawn (or any attacked Piece, or attacked square) against two Rooks—or indeed against any two Pieces—for the simple reason that the Queen is only one Piece.

It follows that two Rooks and a Pawn represent winning chances against Queen and Pawn, because, assuming that one of the Pawns is defended by Queen and King, the two Rooks can give themselves up for the Pawn and Queen, leaving King and Pawn against King. Everything will then depend on the relative position of the Kings and the remaining Pawn. And, of course, while this situation is developing, much will depend on the Queen's checking power—i.e. the relative position of the King and the various Pieces involved.

(BLACK)

(WHITE)

Q *v.* 2 ROOKS
The Queen, to move, wins.

The accompanying diagrams show the resources of a Queen against two Rooks. In the first diagram a position is shown in which the Queen, by a short series of Checks, captures one of the Rooks. The moves are as follows: Q to Q7 Ch. If the King goes to the back rank, Q to Q8 Ch. wins a Rook: if the King comes its 3rd rank, Q to K6 Ch. wins a Rook.

Then the Queen is left, playing one Rook, and that is a win, though it has to be carefully handled. The process is to bring up one's own King; squeeze, as it were, the King and Rook; then, failing Mate, find a series of Checks that leads to the capture of the Rook. The following line of play is illustrative—1. K to Kt6 R to K3 Ch. 2. K to B7 R to K2 Ch. 3. K to Q6 R to KB2. 4. Q to K5 Ch. K to Kt3. 5. K to K6

(BLACK)

(WHITE)

White to move, wins (K to Kt6, etc.).
Black to move, draws (R to K4).

R to KKt2. 6. Q to B4 (not 6. Q to B5 Ch. K to R3. 7. K to B6 R to B2 Ch. draw) and Mate or the capture of the Rook will follow quickly.

The reader is not advised to try and learn this kind of process by heart.

The main task of the beginner is so to grasp the possibilities of the Pieces that he can see any process when required. Chess is a matter of vision, not of memory. All that one can learn is sufficient acquaintance with the possibilities of the Board to be able to recognize them and discover new ones; i.e. exactly as a Medical man learns to diagnose.

PERPETUAL CHECK

It is when a Queen is alone against two Rooks that one is most likely to find the game ending in the special type of draw which is Perpetual Check. (Other Pieces, of course, can be the instruments of Perpetual Check, but the Queen is the most likely Piece to bring it about.)

In the next diagram the Black Rooks are safely placed,

guarding each other on QKt2 and KKt2. The King is at QKt1. Now Black is safe but cannot win, wherever the White King is, if it is White's move. The Queen can Check at her Q8 (Black's Q1); the King must go to R2. Then the Queen checks at R5, King goes back to Kt1, Queen checks at Q8 and so on for ever. That is a Draw.

QUEEN against
2 ROOKS
Perpetual Check.

Now alter the position in this diagram by putting the White King on its KR8; put the Black King on its QR1. Add a Black Knight on Black's QKt6 and let the Queen be checking on QB8. Now the King will go to R2 (if the Rook goes in, pinning the Queen, Queen captures with Check, then the King captures the remaining Rook leaving King and Knight against King—which is a Draw). At this point White makes his Perpetual Check by playing Q to QR8 Check. If the King takes it the result is Stalemate; if the King goes to Kt3 then the Queen goes to QR6 Check again, and so on indefinitely. That is the kind of trick that the Queen is capable of performing.

The Queen is, indeed, so resourceful that she has been known to force a Draw against Queen and Rook. This can happen when the Pieces are grouped in the corner. Thus place the Black King on White's QR8, the Black Queen on White's QKt8, and the Black Rook on White's QKt7 (let the White King be on King's square). Now, if the White Queen can manage to check on QR5, there is a perpetual Check in being; because whichever Piece intervenes the

Queen will have either Q5 or Q8 to check on; after that she will have QR5 or Q5 or Q8 to check on as the case may be; and so on for ever.

Finally, illustrative of the Queen's power in combination with other forces, here is a position that occurred in a game played in 1907 by the late Emanuel Lasker.*

(BLACK)

A finish by Lasker (Black).

(WHITE)

At the end of a brilliant middle game, in which Lasker, as Black, has obtained the advantage by the creation of subtle threats, White seems to be on the point of equalizing.

White	Black
35. R to QB1. Threatening (after the Bishop's move) to take the Knight's Pawn with the Queen and bring the Rook up to QB6 with an attack.	B × KtP! A sacrifice that White had not anticipated.
36. R × B.	B × Kt.
37. P × B.	R to Q8 Ch.
38. K to Kt2.	Q to Q4 Ch.
39. K to B2.	Q to R8 !
40. Q × P. One of many possible moves; but there is none to save the game.	Q to B8 Ch.
41. K to K3.	R to Q6 Ch.
42. K to K4.	Q to B6 Ch.
43. K × P.	Q to K6 Ch.
44. Q to K4.	P to B3 Ch., followed by Mate.

* Emanuel Lasker. Distinguished Mathematical Philosopher who was one of the greatest Chess players in the history of the game. Held the World Championship a generation (1894-1921), and after that, until his death in 1941, remained in the very forefront of Chess Masters.

ONE ROOK

From any of the foregoing examples it will be clear to the reader that the Queen is much more powerful than one Rook.

King and one Rook lose against a Queen. King and one Rook with something else, even a Pawn, may draw if the position is favourable, may even win in exceptional positions. But King and Rook alone can only save the game if, at the moment the position crystallizes, the Rook can capture the Queen by a pin or a fork or a thrust. (Diagram on page 51 with Black to move.) Failing that, it is only a question of time. The process was shown above.

Nevertheless, the Rook is a powerful Piece. The Rook does not exceed the Bishop or the Knight to the extent to which the Queen exceeds the Rook, because the win by Rook against Bishop or against Knight is exceptional—the win by Queen against Rook almost invariable. But the Rook has this in common with the Queen ; that the Rook and the Queen are the only Pieces which, alone save for a King, can force Mate. Also, the Rook is the only Piece, apart from the Queen, which in one move can put itself within reach of any given square on the Board. The King and the Knight can reach any square given time ; the Bishop only operates on one half of the Board (squares of a specific colour).

If a Rook is lost, or given, for a Bishop, or for a Knight, the player giving up the Rook is said to be losing, or sacrificing *The Exchange*—and, of course, the other player is winning The Exchange. Some players use the phrase Major Exchange, to signify the difference between the Queen and the Rook. The description is not very accurate, because, as we have seen, the difference is disproportionately bigger; but the expression is quite often used. Again, some players describe the gain of a Bishop in exchange for a Knight as a gain of the Minor Exchange. But this, too, can be misleading because the superiority of Bishop to Knight is entirely a function of position ; and it can happen, quite easily, that a Knight is more valuable than a Bishop. This will be discussed later in the Chapter. Suffice it here to say that for practical purposes the Bishop and Knight can be regarded as roughly equal. Vis-à-vis the Rook, they are both inferior (hence the expression " loss " of the Exchange when a Rook is lost for either), and the degree of inferiority is similar. On an empty Board the Bishop (against the Rook) is a little more likely to hold its own than the Knight. For the rest, Bishop and Knight together are definitely a stronger force than a rook ; so, in a sense, are two Knights—a fortiori two Bishops. But their joint superiority, though definite, is slight. Roughly, it may be said that a Rook and Pawn are almost equivalent to two *minor Pieces* (the term applied to Bishop and Knight); Rook and two Pawns are slightly better.

MATING BY KING AND ROOK

The main superiority of the Rook to a minor Piece consists in its capacity to Mate in conjunction with the King alone. The process is not easy, and depends on the principle of Zugzwang, i.e. at a critical stage the lone King will be short of moves and will have to move to its detriment.

(BLACK)

(WHITE)

Mate by K and R.

The above diagram shows a King and Rook having Mated. It will be observed that this reproduces one of the possible Mates available to the Queen; but the Queen has others, e.g., on Q2 in this diagram—or, with the Black K on White's K1 or QB1: at K2 or KKt1 in the one case, at QB2 or QR1 in the other.

Now how to get this position. The next diagram shows the King not directly opposite the King. A finesse is now required. The Rook wastes a move, R to B3 or 5,6,7,8, not conceding any space, but leaving the King to go back to the square opposite the King. Then it Mates.

Now by a similar method, starting from anywhere, the King can be forced down the Board. From time to time it will be necessary to use that little finesse to make the King lose ground. This is well illustrated in the following series of moves. The White King is at its K3, R on KB2. Black King at its Q4; and the moves are somewhat as follows—1. R to QB2 K to K4, 2. R to B5 Ch. K to Q3, 3. K to Q4 K to K3, 4. K to K4 K to Q3, 5. R to QB4 K to K3, 6. R to B6 Ch. and so on.

The reader will appreciate that the Zugzwang here depends on the emptiness of the Board. But it can happen that the Rook is so placed as to be able to "squeeze" a King and

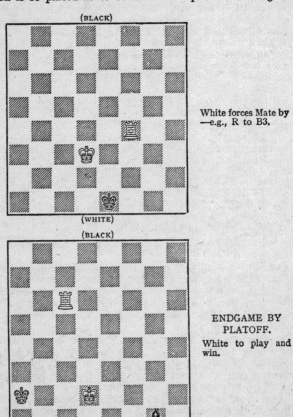

White forces Mate by —e.g., R to B3.

ENDGAME BY PLATOFF.

White to play and win.

Bishop or King and Knight. Here is an ending by Platoff.

White wins by 1. K to B3 K to Kt8. 2. K to Kt3 B to R2 (best to avoid double threats) 3. R to QR6 B to B4 (best) 4. R to R6. If now 4. . . . .B to Kt8 5. RR1 wins If 4. . . .K to B8 R to QB6 wins. If 4. . . . .B to K6 5. R to R1 Ch. B to B8 6. R moves on rank and wins. If at move 1 Black plays B to K6, 2. K to B2 wins, and there are other variations in which White can threaten mate and attack the Bishop alternately until both threats arrive together.

THE EFFECT OF THE "EXCHANGE"

The Platoff ending shows the superiority of Rook to Bishop on an empty Board. There are similar chances (also rare) of a squeeze by K and R against K and Kt. These, be it repeated, are rarities. But the Rook has other superiority. Thus, a King and Rook can usually draw against King, Rook and Pawn ; King and Bishop, or King and Knight, generally speaking, cannot do so. Among other things the Rook can cut the hostile King off from the part of the Board where King and Pawns are operating against the Bishop or the Knight.

Again, when it comes to destructive work among Pawns, the Rook is evidently superior.

(BLACK)

White, with the Exchange down, does not lose.

(WHITE)

On the other hand, a Bishop with aggressively placed Pawns can defeat a Rook with Pawns. Thus a Rook on its Rook's square, can find itself hemmed in by a Bishop at its Kt8 and a Pawn at R7, while, elsewhere on the Board, the Bishop's

King establishes a winning advantage among the remaining Pawns. Again, a well-placed Bishop or Knight with the aid of the King may prevent a Rook from penetrating among the Pawns. Exceptionally a Bishop can hold its own against Rook and Pawn—a Knight, more rarely.*

As we go back earlier into the game, we find that the more

(BLACK)

(WHITE)

Bishop draws against Rook and Pawn.
The Bishop keeps the King away.
If P to B7, of course K to Kt2.

(BLACK)

(WHITE)

Sacrifice of Rook.
If 1 ... B × R
2. Q × Kt P. R—B1
3. B—Kt5 wins.
If 1 ... K—B1.
2. B—R3 Ch. K—Kt1
3. R—Kt1 B—Kt2.
4. R—Kt3 B—R4.
5. Q × Kt P Ch. K × Q
6. R—Kt 3 Ch. K—R3
7. B—B1 Ch. K—R4
8. B—K2 Ch. K—R5
9. R—R 3 mate

*A locus classicus is the following position defended by Emanuel Lasker against Edward Lasker (New York 1924).
32: Kt K3 k2, 1p 4r1, 16: Drawn because White King can be kept away.

crowded the Board is the less likely the Exchange is to matter
A Rook is slow of development on the crowded Board. Until
it is fully mobilized it is worth less than its nominal value.
Aggressive players would as soon give odds of a Rook as of
a Minor Piece.* Nevertheless, in the absence of good
reason (defence or attack), the loss of the Exchange
should be resolutely avoided. Other things being equal, the
loss of the Exchange is at least as serious as the loss, without
compensation, of a Pawn.

The last diagram shows an instance of the total sacrifice of
the Rook at an early stage in the game. A mobilized Minor
Piece is removed from the defence, while the attack only
loses an unmobilized Rook.

It follows that the sacrifice of the Exchange can be tactically
advantageous when the Piece removed is important to the
defence.

THE MINOR PIECES

The Rook is a major Piece ; the Bishop and Knight are
minor Pieces—though not infantile.

The relative valuation of the Bishop and the Knight forms
one of the most difficult features of Chess.

At first sight it would seem that a Bishop, with a maximum
range of 13 squares, is better than a Knight with a maximum
range of 8 squares. Yet no good Chess player regards himself
at a disadvantage merely because he has given a Bishop for
a Knight. In very many openings this exchange is normal.
Everything will depend on the utility of the Knight one is
left with. If it is well placed, e.g. established (supported and
unassailable by Pawns) on a central square, such as K5, its
power can be considerable.

There is more to be said for the superiority of two Bishops
to two Knights than for the superiority of one Bishop to one
Knight. Here is an extreme case : White K on K6, Bishops
on K4, Q4 ; Black K at K1, Kt on KR5, QR5 : clearly Black
loses. Two Bishops fully mobilized control 26 squares, 10 more
than 2 mobilized Knights. Again, this may be an illusory
advantage if the Knights have plenty of work to do—e.g.
attacking Pawns, etc., while the Bishops are merely covering
empty space.

It may be conceded that on a relatively empty Board two
Bishops with a Rook, or with Pawns, are likely to win against

---

* When odds of a Rook are given the player can still Castle, making the
King's move only, unless the square of the Rook in question has been
occupied by a hostile Piece.

two Knights with a Rook, or with Pawns, as the case may be. But to value these Pieces from that point of view is to oversimplify. Nor is it advisable to dwell on the fact that two Bishops can force Mate whereas two Knights cannot force Mate. These endings are rare.

In practice, as the game comes towards its climax, Minor Pieces tend to be exchanged for an infinite variety of reasons. And if a player tries so to conduct his game as to avoid the loss of Bishop for Knight, he will find his scope restricted, and will find himself losing tempo—which, incidentally, may be much more important than any slight difference in formal value. A good example of that slight error is seen in the diagram below.

(BLACK) AUTHOR

White to move—
Best is B x P.

(WHITE) MENCHIK

Here B×P, allowing exchange of Kt for B, is better than Kt×P which after Kt exchanges and P to B4 for Black (with gain of tempo) leaves Black well placed. And there are numerous other examples.

To sum up : although, formally, the Bishop appears to be stronger than the Knight, and although, strategically, it would seem desirable to keep Bishops against one's opponent's Knights, in practice the vicissitudes of the game do not allow players to attach importance to what differences there are. Theoretically a Bishop can immobilize a Knight. If, e.g. the hostile Knight is on your Q1, your Bishop on Q4 deprives it of all its scope. If one could maintain a position like that, the advantage would be clear. But in a fairly level game the probability is that the Bishop would not be allowed to stay there, or could only be maintained by, e.g., a King which would thereby be prevented from proceeding with its work among the Pawns.

Also a Bishop can guard Pawns, and attack Pawns, from longer range than a Knight—which is an advantage. On the other hand, Pawns can be so grouped that a Bishop cannot touch them while a Knight may be able to work havoc among them. Moreover, they cannot avoid the pursuit of the Knight by changing the colour of their squares, as they would avoid the attack of a Bishop. Indeed an endgame can quite easily crystallize in which the Pawns are so placed that the player with the Knight will win against the player with the Bishop.

(BLACK)

(WHITE)

KNIGHT AMONG PAWNS.

Typical Endgame in which Knight is superior to Bishop.

Further, although a King can do more damage to Pawns guarded by a Knight than to Pawns guarded by a Bishop (especially if the Knight is in front of the Pawns), it can happen that a Knight and Pawn can win where a Bishop and Pawn cannot win ; that is, when the Pawn is a Rook's Pawn whose Queening square is of a different colour from the squares controlled by the Bishop.

To show the difficulty of assessment, it may be added that there is one position in a King and Rook's Pawn ending where a Knight is inferior to a Bishop, because of the Knight's inability to lose a move !

Finally, although a Bishop can do so much more in one

move than a Knight, in two moves or three moves the differ-ence diminishes.

For the rest, the powers of the two Pieces are so different, and their scope varies so much from position to position, that no valuation is reliable which attempts to establish the super-iority of one Minor Piece to the other. It comes down to a question of taste and style. The late J. R. Capablanca* who

B and RP v. K.

Once the King is in the corner, the Bishop is powerless to evict it.

DRAW.

The Knight can never drive the hostile King away, because it cannot approach without Check and cannot lose a move. If this Kt were at K6 or K4 with Black to move, White would win.

*J. R. Capablanca. A Cuban Chess prodigy. World Champion 1921-1927

aimed at subtle simplifications, preferred the Bishop. The late Alexander Alekhine*, a player whose style lent itself to combinations on the crowded Board, seemed to prefer the Knight. Typical of Capablanca's style is his play from the following position—play which incidentally shows how strong Bishops can be when the diagonals are available to them.

(BLACK)

(WHITE)

Capablanca *v.* N.N.

After a badly played Stone-wall Defence, Black made a try for freedom with 11. . . . P to K4. Capablanca now proceeds to take excellent advantage.

White	Black
12. P × KP.	Kt × P.
13. P × QP.	P × P. Kt × B Ch. loses a P.
14. Kt to B4 ! Pretty and forcing.	P × Kt. Slightly better was KKt to B2, but even that yields White an overwhelming attack.
15. B × P Check.	KKt to B2. Best.
16. R × B.	Q × R.
17. Kt × Kt.	B to K3. At move 14 Black (if he saw so far) had probably relied on this and the next for salvation.
18. R to Q1.	Q to K2. The only alternative was Q to Kt3, which would be met by 19 Kt to Q7 !

* Alexander Alekhine. A great Russian player, who won the world Championship from Capablanca in 1927—and held it, with a gap of two years (1935-7), until his death in 1946.

White	Black
19. R to Q7.	B × R.
20. Kt × B.	KR to QB1 (If Q × Kt .21 Q to B3).
21. Q to B3.	R × B.
22. P × R.	Resigns. The best that Black can hope for is an ending with Rook against Bishop, Knight and Pawn, and those so well placed as to give him no drawing chance.

The above is an excellent example of the power of Bishops, and carries many strategic lessons.

(BLACK)

(WHITE)

Alekhine
v. Bogoljubow
(5th game of the first Match.)

In contrast the diagram position from a game in a Match between Alekhine and Bogoljubow is an interesting example of the Knight's powers. In the moves leading up to the diagrammed position, it is probable that Bogoljubow failed to anticipate the finesse consisting in the threat of a Knight's fork after the capture of a Pawn—which threat deprived him of the tempo required for equalization.

The moves played were as follows—

White	Black
23. . . .	QR to Kt1.
24. Kt to Kt5.	Kt × Kt.
25. R × R.	R × R.
26. Kt × P.	R to Kt1
27. Kt to B5	K to K2.
28. P × Kt.	and White has gained a Pawn.

THE KNIGHT'S FORK

The Knight's fork, which is seen threatened in the last example, is different from the normal attack by any Piece on two other Pieces simultaneously, because the Knight is usually attacking two Pieces which cannot react along the line of attack, because they are not Knights. The Knight, which, incidentally, is very difficult to deprive of moves,

THE KNIGHT'S FORK.

THE KNIGHT'S FORK.

Black is threatening Kt × Q : also Kt to B6 Ch.
If (1) Q to K4 Q × Q (2) B × Q, Kt K7 Ch. wins a piece.
But White can meet the immediate danger with B to K4.

can execute a long series of changing threats; these are difficult to prevent, and, psychologically, difficult to follow. The eight squares of its range are on the edges of quite a large rectangle, and every move made brings into its range a different area. The vast number of possible courses that the Knight can trace in any two or three moves makes it the commando of the Chess Board.

PIN.
The Knight is pinned by the Bishop. The KP is pinned by the Rook. Therefore, White can play Kt × QP.

PIN.
White wins by P to B6, because if R × P, B to B7 pins and wins the Rook. Of course, if 1 ... R to QR2 2. B × P Ch.

THE PIN

A tactical device that the Bishop and the Major Pieces can carry out, though the Knight cannot do it, is the Pin. That is the holding down, on a rank or file (in the case of a Rook), on the rank, file or diagonal (in the case of a Queen), on the diagonal (in the case of a Bishop), of some Piece which cannot move without exposing to capture either the King, or some-

(BLACK)

(WHITE)

BLACK WINS.
A pretty pin 1... R to R5 enables the Black Pawn to be promoted.

(BLACK)

(WHITE)

A KNIFE-THRUST
(see p. 68)
"Accipe hoc."
B to Kt7 Ch. wins the Queen

thing else of value, which it covers by its presence. Pins can be important or unimportant. Their effect may be temporary or permanent. They may bring about the loss of an Exchange, or even of a Queen. Applied to a Rook, the Bishop's Pin is particularly effective, because it gives the player with the Bishop the option of winning the Exchange.

Some examples of the Pin are shown in the diagrams on pages 66 and 67.

Good examples of the Bishop's Pin will also be found in later chapters, e.g., in Morphy v. Isouard, and in Alekhine against Böök, in which the great Master of Knight manœuvres is seen handling Bishops to superb advantage.

OTHER TACTICAL POWERS

Different from the Pin is another power that the Knight lacks, a power, as it were, to stab in the back. One example of it (p. 67) shows the Bishop able to check the King along a diagonal where there is another opposing Piece on the other side of the King, and winning that Piece in consequence. In contrast to the Knight's fork this might be called " the Bishop's Knife." That, however, is not the technical term—nor is there a term to describe this type of thrust. (" Skewer" is used.)

(BLACK)

(WHITE)

A DELAYED THRUST.
1. White Queens ; if 1 . . . Black Queens, then Q to R8Ch. wins. But Black can draw by 1 . . . K to Kt7.*

Looking at it more generally, one sees that this power is not peculiar to the Bishop, but is possessed by any long range

* But not if the White King were one square further left (e.g., on e2). In that case white manœuvres so that the Queen arrives at c3 with check. Then follows K—Kt8 for Black; and White, with K—Q2 creates a threat of mate, forcing Black to promote Pawn to Knight (and lose).

Piece. The Rook has it on the rank or file; the Queen has it on the rank, file and diagonal.

This can be an extremely important tactical feature, especially when it takes the form of a resource at the end of a line of play; e.g., 2 Pawns (one Black, one White) are racing for promotion; one Queens: the other Queens immediately after; but the first promoted Pawn, now a Queen, may be able to give a Check along a file, rank or diagonal which will involve the loss of his opponent's newly-made Queen. The diagram opposite illustrates such a situation.

Obviously the Knight can do nothing like this, though it can come away from a sub-promotion giving a damaging fork. But the reader has already been sufficiently warned not to infer on that account that the Knight can now be written off as inferior. As we have seen, there are things that only the Knight can do. Among them is a special kind of Smothered Mate.

SMOTHERED MATE

We have seen that the King can be Mated with the aid of its own Pieces, in that their presence deprives the King of flight squares. When this happens the King may be said to be smothered in some degree. But the expression Smothered Mate is normally applied to a Mate which can only be carried out by the Knight. One of the simplest forms of this results from the position in the next Diagram.

(BLACK)

(WHITE)

PHILIDOR'S
LEGACY.

1. ... K to R1.
2. Kt to B7 Ch ; K to Kt1.
3. Kt to R6 Dble. Ch. ; K to R1.
4. Q to Kt8 Ch. ; R ×Q.
5. Kt to B7 Mate.

The moves which follow have been called Philidor's Legacy on the assumption that the method was discovered by the great French Master of the eighteenth century. But there is reason to believe that the idea is older. Here are the moves: Black, being in Check, plays K to R1. White plays Kt to B7, Check. Black can now give up the Rook for the Knight, but, not seeing the danger, or because there may be a Mate on the back rank if the Rook moves off it, finds himself unable to do so. He therefore plays K to Kt1. Then comes Kt R6 Double Check. The King is forced to R1. There follows a thunder bolt, Q to Kt8 Check, sacrificing the Queen. (A player who thinks in terms of the formal values of the Pieces would never anticipate this move, which is only possible to a player who thinks in terms of the functions of the Pieces.) Black must take this Queen with the Rook. Then White plays Kt to B7 Mate.

The above is the best known Smothered Mate; but it is not the only kind. Much less familiar is that which occurs in the position shown in the second diagram.

(BLACK)

(WHITE)

A FINISH BY
NAJDORF.

The position in the diagram was reached by Najdorf, the Polish Master, on one of his Boards in a simultaneous blindfold display. He announced Mate in four. It may be remarked that the Mate in four would not be apparent to the majority of really strong players playing with sight of the Board and not simultaneously. It is a fine example of vision in Chess.

The moves are as follows:

White	*Black*
Q to R5. This threatens Q×BP Mate.	B×QP. Stopping the Mate. Had Black played P to Kt3, then Q×RP would have been Mate. Q×R. Forced, and apparently winning the Exchange.
R×B. Removing the defender. This is a sacrifice of the Exchange.	
Q×BP Check. Sacrificing the Queen, a beautiful surprise. Its real value, to a Chess player, consists in the fact that the Master making the move saw it before he announced his Mate in four—perhaps a good deal earlier.	Q×Q. Forced; apparently winning the Queen, but in reality doing exactly what the Rook did in the previous example.
Kt–Q7 Mate. A very fine example of Smothered Mate.	

To conclude this survey of the Minor Pieces, let the reader realize that these are the Pieces to be mobilized first in any game—and they, with one or two Pawns, bear the brunt of the opening. Also they have endgame functions.

How to Mate with two Bishops and with Bishop and Knight. See diagrams.

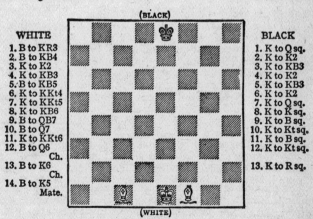

(BLACK)

WHITE

1. B to KR3
2. B to KB4
3. K to K2
4. K to KB3
5. B to KB5
6. K to KKt4
7. K to KKt5
8. K to KB6
9. B to QB7
10. B to Q7
11. K to KKt6
12. B to Q6 Ch.
13. B to K6 Ch.
14. B to K5 Mate.

BLACK

1. K to Q sq.
2. K to K2
3. K to KB3
4. K to K2
5. K to KB3
6. K to K2
7. K to Q sq.
8. K to K sq.
9. K to B sq.
10. K to Kt sq.
11. K to B sq.
12. K to Kt sq.
13. K to R sq.

(WHITE)

K, B, B *v.* K.

In order to reach the end position, the Bishops quickly limit the King's field, making an " edge " to the field of play.

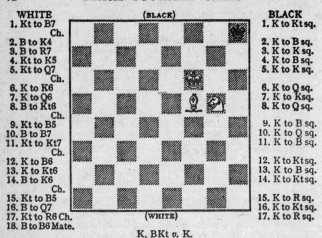

WHITE		BLACK
1. Kt to B7 Ch.		1. K to Kt sq.
2. B to K4		2. K to B sq.
3. B to R7		3. K to K sq.
4. Kt to K5		4. K to B sq.
5. Kt to Q7 Ch.		5. K to K sq.
6. K to K6		6. K to Q sq.
7. K to Q6		7. K to Ksq.
8. B to Kt6 Ch.		8. K to Q sq.
9. Kt to B5		9. K to B sq.
10. B to B7		10. K to Q sq.
11. Kt to Kt7 Ch.		11. K to B sq.
12. K to B6		12. K to Kt sq.
13. K to Kt6		13. K to B sq.
14. B to K6 Ch.		14. K to Kt sq.
15. Kt to B5		15. K to R sq.
16. B to Q7		16. K to Kt sq.
17. Kt to R6 Ch.		17. K to R sq.
18. B to B6 Mate.		

K, BKt v. K.

In order to reach this position, it is fairly easy to force the King to the side, since B, Kt and King can create a directive pressure. If, above, 4. K–Q1, 5. B–K4, with Kt–B4, prevents escape to a black corner.

THE CHANGING VALUE OF THE PAWN

We have seen, already, that a factor inhibiting the movement of those Pieces that seem to control a good deal of the Board consists in the normal undesirability of their being taken in exchange for Pieces of lesser value. Since, formally, the Pawn is the least of the Pieces (because its move is so limited), it acquires tremendous tactical importance as an inhibitor of all other Pieces. If a Pawn is guarding something, then what it is guarding is well guarded—particularly against attack by anything larger than the Piece attacked. Pawns guarding Pawns can, consequently, form a barrier that can only be broken either by Pawns or else by the sacrifice of value. Moreover, the Pawn as an instrument of attack is a force not to be under-estimated. In a crowded centre of the Board a feature of the play is always likely to be the power of a Pawn to fork two Pieces such as a Bishop and Knight, or else to advance, dislocating a minor or major Piece from a good square, and, to that extent, disrupting the defence of, e.g., the castled King. From this point of view, the centre Pawns tend to be more important than the Pawns on the wings. The nearer they are to the centre, the more likely they are to be participating in the attack, given that the game is reasonably open. We shall see that, in the ordinary way, Pawns are stronger when they are not doubled and when they are not isolated. In the centre their isolation, or their doubling, can be a source of strength as well as an element of weakness.

Because of the fact that the tactical value of the Pawn is functional rather than formal, depending entirely on what the Pawn is doing or likely to be doing in the immediate future, it comes about that, during tactical operations, players are apt to treat the loss or gain of a Pawn as relatively unimportant—as a difference which is transitory, as a cheap sacrifice. This is particularly true of the attitude adopted to idle Pawns on the wings, or Pawns that are being used to cause the vacation of important squares. But, as the strategic lines of the game become set, the Pawn is likely to gain in importance. If the strategy is along the simple lines of " saving up and exchanging down," it may well be that the extra Pawn will mean victory. No hard and fast rules can be laid down. One Pawn may be so placed as to be worth two or even three Pawns. But, other things being equal, it is safe to say that as the Endgame approaches, or in so far as one is playing with a view to the Endgame rather than the middle game attack, the importance of the Pawn increases. On a relatively empty Board a Pawn progressively acquires the status of a Piece. No transvaluation in Chess is more important than the promotion of the Pawn. Therefore, in most games, some Pawns at least will not be regarded, or disregarded, as cannon fodder. Indeed, as we have already seen, at the end of the game the possession of a Bishop or a Knight with a lone King is inadequate for victory. The possession of a Pawn, on the other hand, can bring about victory.

If, then, a Pawn is to be lost, it is only well lost if the loser of the Pawn is gaining sufficient in tempo, or mobility, or general control of the Board, etc., etc., to make him confident that his game as a whole is superior to his opponent's, and that at the worst, he will be able, sooner or later, to regain at least the material that he has lost. On the other hand, a player will think twice about deploying his forces, however temporarily, in order to win a Pawn. In a well integrated game, where everything depends on the availability of counter moves to many possibilities, any excursion away from the main scene of operations, even by one square, may be fatal. The consequences may be immediately demonstrable, or they may be more mediate—possibly strategic rather than tactical ;

in either case they are likely to be of more importance than
the Pawn concerned. In a word, then, the gain of a Pawn
can win a game ; it can also lose a game. Once again, everything depends on the position.

GAMBITS

At the very outset of the game some Pawns in their original
positions need to be moved, so as to give the major Pieces
access to the open Board. Also it is usually thought desirable
to move them in such a way that they will exert pressure on
the centre, thereby creating a maximum of manœuvring
space for the other Pieces. For those reasons it very often
happens that, as early as the second move, Pawns are moved
where they can be taken without immediate compensation.
Such moves are called Gambits. Thus, after the moves
1. P to K4, P to K4, a very popular move used to be 2.
P to KB4—the King's Gambit. This opening is less frequent
now than it was. Nevertheless, it is still formidable and
introduces play of great interest and difficulty to both sides.
On the other wing one of the most frequent openings
in Modern Chess consists in the moves P to Q4, P to Q4.
2. P to QB4. This is the Queen's Gambit, which introduces
a slower but more lasting development, less likely than
the King's Gambit to result in a too early skirmish, from
which it may be difficult to ensure the retention of a permanent advantage.

Both of these Gambits can either be accepted, by the
immediate, or slightly postponed, capture of the Gambit
Pawn: or they may be declined. The Queen's Gambit is
more frequently declined than accepted ; the King's Gambit
is more usually accepted than declined. If a Gambit is
accepted, it usually happens that the player who has won
the Pawn allows his opponent to regain a Pawn at a later
stage, when the continued holding of the Gambit Pawn involves
either the loss of tempo in development, or the undertaking
of a difficult line of play in which the player does not wish
to become involved. In this way a Gambit differs from a
sacrifice. In a Gambit the Pawn is rather lent than given.
However, there are Gambits, such as the Wing Gambit (P to
K4, P to QB4. 2. P to QKt4), in which the Gambiteer may
lose interest in the offered Pawn and go for long without
attempting to recover it.

A clear example of the difference between a Pawn sacrifice
and a Gambit may be seen in one of the normal variations
of the Queen's Gambit declined.

White	*Black*
1. P to Q4.	P to Q4.
2. P to QB4.	P to K3.
3. Kt to QB3.	Kt to KB3.
4. B to Kt5. A move made popular by the American Master, Pillsbury. It is a developing move which pins the Knight, not with any serious threat, but by way of creating a slight pressure.	QKt to Q2. A good developing move, offering the sacrifice of a Pawn. Apparently, since the King's Knight is pinned, the Queen's Pawn, twice attacked and only once guarded, can be won by White. This, however, is an illusion.
5. P × P.	P × P.
6. Kt × P, falling into a trap.	Kt × Kt. Black is not sacrificing the Pawn after all. What he is sacrificing is his Queen.
7. B × Q.	B to Kt5 Ch.
8. Q to Q2, the only move.	B × Q Ch.
9. K × B.	K × B. And Black is a Piece to the good.

Because of the existence of this pitfall, White on the fifth move usually plays P to K3 or Kt to KB3. Then the threat is on; because Black's checking resource will no longer win the White Queen. Therefore, in answer to P to K3 or Kt to KB3, Black usually plays some such move as B to K2 (unpinning the Knight) or P to QB3 (giving additional support to the Pawn at Q4).

Incidentally, the point of declining the Queen's Gambit (which will be considered more fully later on) is to prevent White from establishing a Pawn on K4, from which point it can make a dangerous thrust forward; also the Queen's Pawn can become dangerous; and, generally, the Black Pieces will find less space in which to operate than is available to White.

The acceptance of the Gambit involves a different strategy. Black allows White the occupancy of the centre, crystallizes it so as to allow squares like KB4, QB4, etc. to the Black Pieces, and later undermines the centre, or attacks it from a distance along the diagonal. These methods have become very popular in modern times, owing to the example of players like Niemzovitch, Alekhine, Tartakower, and the Modern School generally.

When, however, a player achieves (from any opening) a good development of the centre Pawns as well as of the minor Pieces, then, if his opponent is behind-hand in development, the Pawns can be instrumental in bringing about a devastating attack. (See Illustrative Games; e.g., by Bird).

Isolated, Doubled, and Passed Pawns

Pawns are at their strongest if they are on adjoining files, preferably on the same rank, but also if one is guarding the next. If a Pawn has no allied Pawn on either flank, then it is said to be an *Isolated Pawn*. Because it can only be guarded by Pieces, it is more vulnerable to attack by Pieces than if it could be guarded by a Pawn. This matters at all stages of the game. It is only unimportant when the Pawn in question is a factor in the attack. Then many things may happen. It may change its file through a capture. It may advance until a hostile Pawn is exchanged for it. It may be captured on terms that the possessor of it wins some other Pawn, or even a Piece. But if the game settles down into relative stability the isolated Pawn is usually a permanent target for the enemy. In a King and Pawn Endgame its strength or weakness will depend on the position of the Kings.

(BLACK)

(WHITE)

The White Pawns on QKt file are *doubled and isolated*.
The Black Pawns on KB file are *doubled* but not isolated.
The White RP is isolated. It is also a Passed Pawn.

When two Pawns stand on the same file they are said to be *Doubled*. *Doubled Pawns*, formally regarded, are evidently less than two Pawns on different files, because one inhibits the other. In conjunction with adjoining Pawns, doubled Pawns can be very useful, creating a special kind of Pawn chain. Doubled-Isolated Pawns are, however, very weak, unless they are playing a tactical rôle (e.g. controlling central squares in the middle game).

From the standpoint of the ending, one of the things that matters about Pawns is their ability, or inability, to proceed without interference from hostile Pawns. If a Pawn has a clear run forward with no hostile Pawns on either of the flanking files, then it is a *Passed Pawn*. Left to itself a Passed Pawn is easily promoted. Therefore it amounts to a danger. An Isolated Passed Pawn, and doubled isolated Passed Pawns,

(BLACK)

(WHITE)

POWER OF PAWNS.

White to move wins by advancing either Pawn. Obviously if both White Pawns were on the 6th it would be a win even with Black to move. As it is, Black to move, wins.

1. ...   R to K8 Ch.
2. K to Kt2, R to KKt8.
3. K to B3, R to Kt4, etc.

(BLACK)

(WHITE)

POWER OF PAWN.

White to move, draws. If the Rook were at Kt8, checking, it would still be a draw.

are, of course, relatively easy to stop.   United Passed Pawns are extremely difficult to cope with.

On the assumption that the hostile King is out of striking distance, two united Passed Pawns on the sixth rank can cope with and defeat a Rook or a Knight or a Bishop, unless the Piece in question can capture one of them immediately. Making the same assumption, it follows that two united Passed Pawns, one on the fifth, one on the sixth, can defeat a Rook, Knight or Bishop if it is the turn to move of the player who has the Pawns, and if he can advance from the fifth to the sixth without either of the Pawns being immediately capturable (see Diagram on p.77).

One advanced Pawn, accompanied by the King, can force a hostile Rook, Bishop or Knight to sacrifice itself for the Pawn, provided the hostile King is far enough away (see Diag on p.77).

Moreover, a Passed Pawn on the seventh rank of the Bishop's file or the seventh rank of the Rook's file can, if its King is correctly placed, enable a player to draw with minimal force against King and Queen.

(BLACK)

A DRAW.

Black to move, can only draw. The pawn is uncapturable. White to move, will play K to Kt8.

(WHITE)

The reason for this is the Stalemate resource available to the King when the Pawn is on one of those squares and the King is at R8.   If the Pawn is on Kt7, Q7 or K7, the draw is not available because the player with the Queen can gain a tempo every few moves so as to bring his King to join in the attack opposite.   The Process is shown beside the next diagram Also a proximate hostile King can upset the drawing plan wherever the Pawn is.

(BLACK)

(WHITE)

BLACK WINS.

1. K to Q8, K to K5
2. K to K7, Q to B2
3. K to K8, Q to K4
    Ch.
4. K to B7, Q to Q3.
5. K to K8, Q to K3
    Ch.
6. K to Q8 and the
Black King can move
again.

PAWNS FACING EACH OTHER

Equal numbers of Pawns facing each other are effective, of course, to hold each other off. An interesting exception to this rule exists in the following position. Pawns at, e.g., QR5, QKt5, and QB5, are facing Pawns at R2, Kt2, B2. White to move plays P to Kt6. If RP×P, White replies P to B6, and the Rook's Pawn (or Bishop's Pawn) will Queen. If, on the other hand, BP×P, White plays P to R6, and now the Bishop's Pawn (or Rook's Pawn) will Queen. Had the Black Pawns stood at QR3, QKt2, QB3, White to move could do nothing. This is an exception to the rule that Pawns are at their best horizontally adjacent to each other.

SUB-PROMOTION.

The next diagram affords an interesting example of the struggle that can take place when a Pawn is nearing promotion and the opposition consists of a powerful Piece which is just not in a Position to stop it. The play also illustrates the point that the promotion to a Queen is not always the best promotion. Finally, the example shows the mental act in Chess—the act of seeing further than the obvious, and then seeing further than that.

Thus in the accompanying position, which was reached in a game between two English amateurs of the last century, Fenton and Potter, the Rook cannot stop the Pawn, but the Rook's Checks involve a resource. If the King goes alongside the Pawn, the Rook pins the Pawn and next move sacrifices itself for the Pawn. If, on the other hand, the King comes quickly onto the B file, the Rook comes down to the back rank and when the Pawn Queens, wins the Queening Pawn immediately by Check (the thrust mentioned above). Therefore the King must pursue a path which brings it on to the B file low enough down the Board for the Rook's thrust not to be possible. But at that point the player with the Rook finds a neat resource. He places his Rook where, when the

(BLACK)

(WHITE)

FENTON *v.*
POTTER.

WHITE WINS.

1. K to Kt5, R to Q4 Ch.
2. K to Kt4, R to Q5 Ch.
3. K to Kt3, R to Q6 Ch.
4. K to B2, R to Q5. (Now, if White Queens, R to B5 Ch. effects Stalemate, therefore) . . .
5. P=R threatening Mate. 5 . . . R to R5.
6. K to Kt3 wins.

Pawn Queens, it can sacrifice itself giving Stalemate. Again, very clever. But the player with the Pawn double crosses him. He makes a Rook. Now it would appear that the game is level; but it so happens that owing to the position of the Kings, Black is in a mating net and loses a very pretty ending.

THE KING

Normally, the Piece that is called upon most frequently to cope with Pawns is the King. More will be said on this topic when we deal further with the end game. Here, suffice it to show one or two features of the King's power against and with Pawns.

The accompanying diagram shows what is called the Square. If you want to know whether the King can stop a Pawn, an easy way of reckoning it, according to some people, is to draw an imaginary line making a square based on the number of squares the Pawn has to travel in order to become a Queen. Now, if the King is within that square when the Pawn moves it can stop the Pawn. Allowance must be made for the Pawn's first move, so that if the Pawn is on the second rank, the square must be drawn as if it were on the third rank because of the Pawn's double first move. Some players,

(BLACK)

(WHITE)

THE SQUARE.
White to move wins, because the King cannot overtake the Pawn.
Black to move, draws.

(BLACK)

(WHITE)

Endgame, by Reti.

White to play, draws!

(Solution overleaf).

including the author, find it easier to work out the King's moves without the aid of this device.

It can happen that the King, if it has on its side another Pawn, even of apparently innocuous character, will gain moves sufficient to get itself into the square. A famous Reti ending is an exceedingly pretty example of this. The play is as follows :

1. K to Kt7.	P to R5.
2. K to B6.	P to R6.
3. K to K7	forces his own Pawn forward.

Therefore on move 2 Black must play K to Kt3. Then follows 3. K to K5 threatening K to Q6—If then 3 . . . K×P, 4. K to B4 and White catches the Pawn.

If the hostile King is otherwise engaged, a King within reach can hold off two Pawns, though, paradoxically, it is as strong against two united Pawns as against two separated Pawns. The diagram shows this. Also, there can be a position where a King holds off three united Pawns, though it may have to let them through if and when it has to move.

(BLACK)

(WHITE)

DRAW.
White can play K to B3, but cannot capture a Pawn. Black cannot capture either and must play carefully. Thus:
1. K to B3, K to B2.
2. K to Kt2, K to B3 for if 2 . . . K to Kt1, P to B6 and the Black K is squeezed.

THE OPPOSITION

The basis of all End game play is King and Pawn against King. In the diagram the player with the Pawn, having the move, can only force Stalemate. But let it be Black's move or (which is the same thing) put the Black King opposite the Pawn, with White to move, then the Pawn can be forced

Draw, if White to move.
1. P to K7 Ch., K to K1.
2. K to K6 Stalemate.
If (1) K to B5, K to K2; (2) K to K5, K to K1.
Then if —
(3) K to B6, K to B1.
If (3) KB5, KK2, etc.

THE OPPOSITION.

White to move, loses. Black to move, draws, by K to B2 or K to Q2, but *not* by K to K2, which loses (to White's K to K5).

through. The difference may be described by saying that in one case Black has the *Opposition ;* in the other case White has the *Opposition.* This, incidentally, is only one instance of a relationship which is dealt with more fully in the chapter on End Games. Here, let it be said that the Opposition is a relationship between the Kings such that when it comes to a King's move, the player who has to move out of Opposition is at a disadvantage. It is a sort of Zugzwang, and is particularly important when Kings are facing each other, each preventing the other from access to the hostile Pawns. According to the position of the Pawns, the Opposition may amount to victory, or it may fall short of that. Normally it is a great advantage. In the last diagram White to move loses, because he has to concede a square on which Black can attack and capture one of his Pawns. Black to move, however, does not lose provided that he does not make the error of K to K2, when White could play K to K5, and Black to move would lose. On his first move therefore, Black must play K to Q2 or K to B2. If then White plays K to K5, K to K2 regains the Opposition temporarily. Then White has to be careful and must play K to Q4, so as to be able, in answer to K to K3, to play K to K4.

The Opposition can sometimes be an effective drawing factor (even a winning factor) when the Pawns are not equal in number, and the side with the Opposition has fewer Pawns. Normally, however, the Opposition matters when there is equality. Then, as the diagram position has shown, it can be aggressively decisive or defensively adequate.

It follows that one of the most important factors in the end game is the position of the King. And this is true irrespectively of Opposition theory. As the middle game turns into end game, the King should be as favourably placed as possible for co-operation with its own Pawns, or for dealing with hostile Pawns, whichever is the more important. As the Board clears, the King must be mobilized. To make the King a fighting Piece is always good policy, so long as the danger of a mating attack can be controlled. In the transvaluations that take place in Chess it may be said that the King, and with it the Pawns, increase considerably in value as the end game approaches. " The King is a fighting piece." (*Steinitz*). In Master Chess, at even an early stage of the game, players are careful to have their Kings where they are most useful for the total purpose.

TRANSVALUATION AND REVALUATION.

At this stage the reader may find himself discovering that though he started with a fairly clear idea of the degrees of power of the various Pieces, he is now not at all sure which are strong and which are weak. If that is his experience let him be comforted. What has happened to him is typical of the growth of the mind in Chess, and in most other subjects to which the mind applies itself. Eventually he will arrive at valuations which are subtler because they are more fluid ; at the same time firmer because they are arrived at after criticism and not before criticism.

In other words, the reader is moving from Chess statics to Chess dynamics. He has seen the formal values of the Pieces. Then he has seen their functions, in which the formal values become blurred in the light of the general purpose. As the general purpose becomes clear, and as the reader learns to appreciate the points of any position, the fluid values will steady themselves. Just as, in learning a language, one needs very much-more than the bare meanings of words—one needs to know how to use each and every word in different contexts —so the Chess player has to learn more than the simple recognition of the Pieces. As the reader learns to use the Chess Men, the fact that their values vary from time to time will cease to puzzle or disturb him any more than he is puzzled by the easily recognised ambiguities of well known words.

To put the matter of sacrificing simply, once the reader has grasped that in Chess the Pieces co-operate together to carry out processes and to achieve purposes, there should be nothing difficult in the realisation than an individual Piece can fulfil its function in the game by giving itself up in order to make possible some move or series of moves that is decisive. The difference between sacrifice and loss is not difficult. When there is positive total advantage—and not merely the staving off of worse consequences—then the giving up of a Piece is a sacrifice. How to sacrifice or when to sacrifice cannot be taught, just as to see or to do the best move cannot be taught, and just as the neat and effective use of words cannot be taught, because these things imply the recognition by the mind's eye of the point or purpose of some given situation. But, just as through reading and listening one improves one's capacity for using the instrument of language, so the student of Chess may be assisted by having his attention drawn to some examples. Since the essence of Chess is vision, the only way of learning Chess in general is to have features of the game pointed out. By concentrating on these the student does not learn a fixed rule that he can apply universally, but, in some mysterious way, he acquires a capacity for the recognition of possibilities when they are present. Be it added that he will also, as his familiarity with the Board increases, acquire some conception of the impossibilities as well as of the possibilities. He will see, when he appreciates the point of any given sacrifice that such a sacrifice is not always on, and that he need not cramp his style through a constant fear of miracles.

Some Illustrative Sacrifices.

Sacrifices are quite impossible to classify. Any kind of position, or any purpose that you are carrying out, may contain the possibility of ignoring the value of any given Piece. To take a very elementary example. While your opponent is attacking your Queen, you threaten Mate with other Pieces. You are sacrificing your Queen. There is nothing very clever in that. What is clever is to see, some moves ahead, that as your purpose develops you need not be side-tracked by the attack on your Queen because you have a threat so strong as to make it impossible for your opponent to capture the Queen. In such a situation, any time he may have relied on gaining by the attack on the Queen may prove not to be gainable. A manoeuvre of this type is shown in the first diagram. There the play is good because Black's move is made in the knowledge that when his Queen is attacked he will be able to proceed with a threat which even at that point is not terribly obvious. The sacrifice is a good sacrifice and all the better if it has been seen a relatively long way ahead.

(WHITE)

(BLACK)

QUEEN
SACRIFICE
(Author—1929)

Black plays Q to R5 allowing P to KKt3, because this is met by Kt to Kt4.

The second diagram shows a position that developed between Euwe and Yanofsky, the young Champion of Canada, in a tournament at Groningen in 1946.

EUWE
YANOFSKY
1. B to B5.
With winning chances.

The ending is a particularly difficult ending for White to win, because when the Bishops are of opposite colour each Bishop controls squares from which the hostile Bishop cannot shut it off. Therefore, each player can make the advance of his opponent's Pawn exceedingly difficult. It follows that clever manoeuvring is necessary if, and when, there is a win to be extracted from such an endgame. Here there were chances; and Euwe's first move from the diagrammed position was B to

ENDGAME
(AFTER
TROITZKI)
White to play and win.
(Solution overleaf)

B5, putting his Bishop *en prise*. That is an instance of a sacrifice for the specific purpose of closing a path to an opponent; alternatively it gains a Pawn.

Adapted from a composed ending we have a subtle example of sacrifice in order to close a line to an opponent's Piece. 1. B to Q4. Then if P × B, K to Q3 blocks the Bishop's line of action. If B × B 2. K to Q3B to R8 3 to K to K4 has the same effect. N.B.—Not 1. K to Q3 P to K5, ch. 2. K × P K to K2 and draws.

If the reader will look back through this book he will find that already he has seen examples of sacrifices in positions of a very different type, and different from each other. For example, we have Capablanca's sacrifice of the Knight in order to open the lines for his Bishop. We have Najdorf's sacrifice of the Queen in order to bring about a smothered Mate. In the games cited in later chapters the reader will find more than one sacrifice of material in order to carry through a long and decisive attack. All these are subordinations of the formal value of the Pieces to the purposes of the game.

(BLACK)

STEINITZ
LASKER

(WHITE)

Here is another—and historic—example.

In the diagram is a position, from which Emanuel Lasker rapidly demolished his opponent's defences by the sacrifice of two of his minor Pieces. This is a fine sacrificial attack because it had to be determined so accurately that the opponent had no intervening moves to upset Lasker's plan. Lasker

played 15 . . . Kt×P. 16. K×Kt B×P Ch. 17. K to B2:
(If K×B, some Queen Checks are followed by R to K5, etc.)
17 . . . P to KB3, followed by P to KKt4 and with logical play
Lasker overwhelms his opponent.

COMBINATION

Play of the type illustrated above is sometimes called
combinative play. Strictly speaking all Chess is combinative
in that a player aims at co-operation and combination among
his Pieces so as to achieve a decisive advantage. But in
practice there is a distinction between logical processes and
imaginative undertakings, between relatively safe play,
making good developing moves, logical moves, sound strategic
moves, and, on the other hand, the play which introduces
big changes into the position through moves in apparent
disregard of the value of the Pieces. Players of Chess of
the latter type, combative, sacrificial, surprising and convincing, have come to be called combinative players ; the less
imaginative tend to be called positional players. The great
players are of course well equipped for combinative as well as
for positional play. At that level the difference is one of
degree only—a difference of style.

At an earlier period of the game (during the 19th century
in particular) the outstanding players, Morphy, Anderssen,
Zukertort and others won their best games with the aid of
fine and spectacular sacrifices. The plethora of sacrificial
combination during this, the Romantic, period of Chess is
due in part to the fact that the great Masters were playing
against players not only deficient (relatively to them) in
Chess genius, but ill-equipped in the strategy which enables
relatively weak players to-day to preserve themselves against
the greater violences. Steinitz and his successors have
equipped the ordinary player with a strategy and technique
which reduce the scope for the unexpected. Consequently
the great combinative players of the 20th century, players
like Alekhine, have only been able to produce their sacrifices
after some subtleties of strategic manœuvring. They occur
then as variations, lines of possible play in a struggle to
restore the balance of position. The modern sacrifices include
many of great beauty, and with a value enhanced by the fact
that they rest on finer differences and have to be calculated
more closely and further ahead. For the rest, spectacular
sacrifices of the traditional type imply, if not a considerable
difference in the playing strength of the players, then a considerable deficiency in the position of one of them. The difference

of level is, as it were, re-capitulated in the progress of players as they pass through a stage where they are annihilated by sacrifices, before they reach (if ever) a stage at which they can only be annihilated by the thunderbolts of outstanding genius. Such a thunderbolt can, however, still strike in this century—witness the famous endgame Capablanca—Bernstein (diagram). Forty years later, it may be added, we find Bernstein avenging his own memory with a

(BLACK)

(WHITE)

A THUNDERBOLT

Black (Capablanca) has allowed a Pawn on c3 to fall (after exchanges) and now plays Q to Kt7, winning outright.

(BLACK)

(WHITE)

BERNSTEIN— KOTOV (1946)

White wins.
1. R to R8 Ch., K to Kt3.
2. P to B5 Ch., P × P.
3. Q × RP Ch., P × Q.
4. QR—KKt8 Mate.

thunderbolt against a Russian aspirant to the Capablanca
succession.

The spectacular classical (or some would say Romantic)
attacks are wonderfully illustrative of the way in which well
co-ordinated forces can destroy larger, less well-organized,
arrays of pieces. Typical is the attack with which Morphy
disposed of that quite considerable player Paulsen. In the

PAULSEN—
MORPHY

diagram it is noticeable that Paulsen's position is not at all
integrated.

The Pawns and Pieces are spreadeagled, i.e., not well co-
ordinated. Paulsen has relied on his last move Q to R6 to
free himself. Morphy who has played, not only with greater
insight, but along lines of more reasonable development, is
now able to demolish Paulsen's position with a few powerful
moves, including a Queen sacrifice. 1. ... Q × B 2. P × Q
R to Kt3 Ch. 3. K to R1 B to R6 4. R to Q1 (forced: if R to
Kt1 4. ... B to Kt7 Ch., and 5. ... R to K8 Ch., with mate
next move) 4. ... B to Kt7 Ch. 5. K to Kt1 QB × P Dis. Ch.
6. K to B1 to Kt7 Ch. 7. K to Kt1 B to R6 Ch. 8. K to R1
B × P 9. Q to B1 (forced) 9. ... B × Q 10. R × B R to K7
11. R to R1 R to R3 12. P to Q4 B to K6 and mate follows
after a few moves.

Even more meritorious is the finish to the Evergreen Game
achieved by Anderssen against Dufresne. The whole game
deserves reproduction.

THE EVERGREEN GAME

	White ANDERSSEN		Black DUFRESNE
1.	P to K4.	1.	P to K4.
2.	Kt to KB3.	2.	Kt to QB3.
3.	B to B4.	3.	B to B4.
4.	P to QKt4. **The Evans**	4.	B × KtP.
	Gambit.		
5.	P to B3.	5.	B to R4.
6.	P to Q4.	6.	P × P.
7.	0—0.	7.	P to Q6.
8.	Q to Kt3.	8.	Q to B3.
9.	P to K5.	9.	Q to Kt3.
10.	R to K1.	10.	KKt to K2.
11.	B to R3.	11.	P to Kt4.
12.	Q × P.	12.	R to QKt sq.
13.	Q to R4.	13.	B to Kt3.
14.	QKt to Q2.	14.	B to Kt2.
15.	Kt to K4.	15.	Q to B4.
16.	B × QP.	16.	Q to R4.
17.	Kt to B6 **Ch.**	17.	P × Kt.
18.	P × P.	18.	R to Kt sq.
19.	QR to Q sq. (See diagram.)	19.	Q × Kt.
20.	R × Kt Ch.	20.	Kt × R.
21.	Q × QP Cb.	21.	K × Q.
22.	B to KB5 Double Ch.	22.	K to K1.
23.	B to Q7 Ch and Mate follows.		

(BLACK)

(WHITE)

ANDERSSEN—
DUFRESNE

Black plays 19 . . .
Q × Kt.
Then follows :
20. R × Kt Ch., Kt
× R.
21. Q × QP Ch., K
× Q.
22. B to B5 Dble.
Ch., K to K1.
23. B to Q7 Ch. and
Mate next move.

The position in the diagram, which is the consequence of strategically inferior play by Dufresne (who started a counter attack before he had dealt with his opponent's more dangerous looking offensive) is yet a very close affair. Black also has chances ; and moves like 19. . . . Kt to K4, or 19. . . .

R×KtP Ch. only just fail. Dr. Lasker has gone so far as to suggest that 19. . . . R to KKt5 would give White great difficulty; and Lasker suggests that White would have done better at move 19 to play a quiet move like B to K4 instead of the brilliant QR to Q1. Nevertheless it is generally held that Anderssen's move was sound as well as brilliant (if what is called brilliance does not imply soundness) and the whole undertaking is of the greater beauty because White had to see a large number of variations clearly; the slightest oversight would have turned his advantage into a loss. That ability to see conclusive sequences through many variations is the essence of fine Chess.

Many sacrifices occur in positions where the unbalance is so obvious, or the possibilities so clear, that no great merit attaches to them. In point is the frequent sacrifice of the Bishop at KR7, or B or Kt at KB7. Sometimes this is easy to follow mentally, sometimes hard—and the merit varies directly with the difficulty. The Diagram on page 94 shows the penalty being exacted for the cramping of Black's game. Sacrifices are the normal consequences of this kind of cramp.

But what good Chess players regard as the best sacrifices are those lines of play which, in an apparently level game, with resources available to both, determine the game in favour of one player. Examples of such sacrifices are seen in later chapters.

(BLACK)

(WHITE)

"THE GREEK GIFT."
B × RP Ch. K × B.
Kt to Kt5 Ch.
If 2. . . . K to Kt1.
   3. Q to R5.
If 2. . . . K to Kt3.
   3. Q to Kt4, et seq.

(BLACK)

(WHITE)

Sacrifice against
Cramped Position

White wins by :
B × P Ch., K × B.
Kt to K6 ! K × Kt.
Q to B4 Ch., etc.

In conclusion, the last few examples amount to excellent proof that what matters on the Chess Board is not the aggregation of material but the dynamic of efficient force. In Chess, as in War, the many can be delivered into the hands of the effective few. What was shown repeatedly in recent world history is not a novelty to the Chess player. In Chess as in War, the operator can ignore quite large arrays of force because they are not mobile. They only matter if the attack does not decisively conclude the campaign. At all stages, therefore, the player must look through and beyond the value of the Pieces—all the Pieces other than the King. In appreciating any possibility of disregarding the obvious the learner is taking an important step towards competence in a game where the obvious is always becoming doubtful and the not obvious always becoming clear.

That is not to say that the obvious must be ignored. It must be included and transcended. In an elementary position the formal values of the Pieces are a safe enough guide. But the player who is learning can never be sure—and must never let himself feel sure without reflection—that the position is elementary. Later he will appreciate the stresses and tensions that make a position promising for sacrifices. At the present stage every position has difficulties and latent problems that are likely to make it into a task. If a player is not conscious of what is going on—or what can be going on—then he is not in control, and his opponent may well produce something unexpected, something surprising, a departure, so to speak, from the conventions. He will suddenly put a Piece where it can be captured ; he will ignore your attack on one of his Pieces ; he will take a small Piece in exchange for a big Piece. In a word, he will depart from the logic that is based on a formal valuation. Then, probably, you will have the melancholy alternative of allowing him to retain the advantage that he has unconventionally acquired, or else of accepting his sacrifice and finding yourself involved in some forcing sequence which will culminate in your discomfiture.

Let it be emphasised that in most cases the sacrificer is not doing anything remarkable. The player who allows the sacrifice is playing badly. A sacrifice is just a move, necessary for the achievement of some object, which happens to allow material to be captured. A sacrifice only becomes praiseworthy when it is at once unexpected and part of a long plan. A sacrifice seen in the distance is valuable. (Capablanca's sacrifice against Bernstein was such a one). So is an immediate sacrifice whose consequences are distant or difficult (see the game, Zukertort-Blackburn in a later Chapter). But there are many other moves besides sacrifices that are meritorious—quiet moves that bring about a control of the Board, gain time subtly, etc., etc. Sacrifices are most likely to surprise the novice only because the formal values of the Pieces are dominant in his mind. At a later stage he may find quiet moves harder to see than sacrifices. But the general factor is that one has to see beyond the immediate ; beyond the apparent valuation ; and, more widely, beyond the present situation. Seeing through the values of the Pieces is one instance of seeing ahead. Seeing ahead is the essence of Chess. In every tactical situation—that is to say in every Chess position—what matters is not only what exists but what is going to happen. The reader who has learnt the moves, and some of the functions of the Pieces, has to learn to interpret situations in which these values and these functions are the elements and the total significance. So far the reader has learnt the meanings of some words, some rules of accidence, some principles of syntax. What he has to acquire, however, is the art of understanding what he reads. Eventually he will want to construct sentences, paragraphs, arguments of his own.

PART II

TACTICS AND STRATEGY.

CHAPTER III

THE MIDDLE GAME AND INTRODUCTION TO TACTICS.

PHASES OF CHESS

Chess is conventionally divided into three phases, Opening, Middle Game and End Game. The distinction is convenient because it corresponds to a difference of scope. The endgame, which is not always reached—because the game can be lost to a middle-game, or even opening, attack—comes into being when the game is reduced to relatively small forces, and (usually) Pawns, with their capacity for promotion, become rather more important individually than they were in the early stages. The endgame calls for exactitude, subtlety, and that blend of skill and experience of the general pattern which is called technique.

The Opening on the other hand, is more crowded with Pieces and possibilities. In the opening, a certain amount of book learning can be useful, though its importance must not be exaggerated. But the normal phase of Chess, and therefore, that part to which the student should quickly be introduced, is the Middle-game. Indeed, from one standpoint, Chess is all Middle-game, because if you do not know book variations in the openings, and if you do not know the standard types of position that constitute the endgame, you can still do well by using, if you have attained it, that capacity for seeing variations which is the essence of Chess, and which is the main equipment required for the Middle-game.

At the outset then, it is advisable to treat Chess as if it were all Middle-game, to imagine yourself faced at any particular moment with a critical position in which you are called upon to find the best move. To see the best move means to see a number of possible moves, the answers to those moves, the answers to the answers, working out each series separately and deciding which move is going to produce the relatively best position that you can achieve. What you have to work out, for the most part, is tactical. That is to say you are concerned with moves, which, if they are constructive, endeavour to bring something into being—something perceptible and completely advantageous Both you and your opponent are initiating processes which, if uninterfered with, will bring about a definite result. For the most part the pursuit of these processes, and the conflict of processes, is analogous to close fighting and skirmishing in warfare. In Chess the forces are generally so interlocked that clever fighting is always necessary and usually going on.

The game is largely tactical. But tactics do not exhaust the game. The student will eventually discover that there is such a thing as choosing the terrain, avoiding conflicts on occasion, preparing for one type of attack rather than another, so playing as to induce an attack, or to prevent it, according to choice, etc., etc. These are features of strategy. They are different from tactics but inseparable. At the outset, however, it is more important to be able to fight than to try and arrange the battlefield. Consequently the first lessons in Chess must be lessons in tactics. In any event tactics are the bulk of the game. A Chess player is always playing tactics as a person is always talking prose. Just as it is important to be conscious of what is going on when one is talking prose, so the student may be assisted by considering what kind of mental operation he is undertaking when he plunges into the tactical complexities of the Middle-game, i.e., whenever he plays Chess.

MENTAL APPROACH

When Edgar Allan Poe said that in Chess one calculated, he was demonstrating to Chess players his complete innocence of their mental processes. In Chess there is very little of the deductive, very little of the arithmetical; and there is hardly anything in the way of formula that can help a man of limited vision to work out—or calculate—what he should do. The reader will, indeed, eventually encounter and acquire certain abstract principles, such as the unlikelihood of attacking successfully against a superior development. These principles, though useful, are negative, regulative, disciplinary, rather

than constructively helpful to the student who wants to learn
how to approach the Chess Board.   Again, there are certain
concepts derived from experience—particularly of the endgame
—which enable a player to consider his position in the light of
the ultimate Pawn structure, etc.   These help to the formation
of one's strategic equipment.   But they, too, are not useful
unless and until the player possesses the faculty for seeing
what is going on among the Chess Pieces in any given position.
If he cannot see the specific possibilities—and impossibilities—
of any concrete situation, then he is lost in the skirmishes ;
he is incapable of tactical effort, or the control of the tactical
situation—which is any situation on the Chess Board.   From
tactical operations strategy is inseparable ; in abstraction
from them it is meaningless.

Very good examples of how the Chess mind works have been
given on occasion by the leading Masters in their explanations
of their own play.

Here is a position from the match between Lasker and
Marshall, in which Lasker has explained his reasoning.
Lasker was Black.

(BLACK)

MARSHALL
LASKER
Black plays P to KB3

(WHITE)

Black has to consider his twelfth move.   Now there are
quite a number of safe moves to consider, but what Lasker
selects is a choice of two aggressive moves.   Strategically,
Black is no longer at the disadvantage of tempo that he
normally has to struggle against in the opening.   Now it is
his   turn   to   take   the   initiative ;   he   does   not   wish   to

give his opponent a chance for further development. The two most aggressive moves available are 12. . . . P to KB4 and 12. . . . P to KB3 ; both of these moves being attempts to give effective attacking value to Black's King's Rook.

Now consider 12. . . . P to KB4. If the Pawn captures *e.p.* the Rook is already in action ; if the Pawn does not capture there is a threat of P to KB5.

Now suppose White, faced with this threat, counter-attacks :

White	*Black*
12. . . .	P to KB4.
13. P to KB3.	P to B5.
14. P × Kt.	P × B, and now there is a serious threat of Q to B7 Ch. followed by the clever P to K7. White cannot avoid this by Q to K2, nor by R × P, without heavy loss. If he plays R to KB1 he loses a Pawn at least ; and after Kt to QB3 he remains under severe pressure.

But all this is short-circuited by the consideration that in answer to 12. . . . P to KB4 White can reply with P to KB4 ; and the result is not so convincing : thus :—

White	*Black*
12. . . .	P to KB4.
13. P to KB4.	P to KKt4. Now White can defend with Q to B1, or more boldly—
14. P to KKt3.	Kt × P (the most vigorous).
15. P × Kt.	Q × P Ch.
16. K to R1.	And Black, although he has perpetual Check (since the White King dare not go to B1), has no way of bringing additional material into the attack in time to prevent White from mobilizing his Queen's Rook and Knight to the defence. Thus Black cannot play P × P while his Queen is at Kt6 because of R to Kt1 ; he cannot mobilize the Bishop along the diagonal Kt2 to KR8 because White can block that diagonal by playing B to B5. Also the Black Rook can only penetrate the game slowly via squares B2 and Kt2. Against this, White has time for QKt to Q2 and either Q to KB3 or Kt to KB1.

Black therefore considers a different line of play, to which White's only vigorous reaction must be a counter attack.

	White	*Black*
12.	. . .	P to KB3.
13.	P to KB3.	P × P.
14.	P × Kt.	P to Q5.

And Lasker judged that, at this point, if the Bishop surrendered itself Black would have a winning endgame with Bishop against Knight and better placed Pawns, and at least one open file; whereas if White plays to keep the Bishop with 15 B to Q2, Black's attack, with B to Kt5 and R to B7 would be too good to need analysing. (The threat would be a Mating attack involving the possibility of R × P Ch.)

In the result Marshall played in answer to 12. P to KB3, 13. P to KB3 (there was nothing better) and play proceeded.

	White	*Black*
12.	. . .	P × P.
14.	P × Kt.	P to Q5.
15.	P to KKt3.	Q to B3.
16.	B × P.	P × B.
17.	R to KB1.	Q × R Ch.
18.	Q × Q.	R × Q Ch.
19.	K × R.	R to Kt1.
20.	P to Kt3.	R to Kt4.
21.	P to B4. To stop eventual R to B6.	R to KR4.
22.	K to Kt1.	P to B4.
23.	Kt to Q2.	K to B2.
24.	R to KB1. Ch.	K to K2.
25.	P to QR3.	R to KR3.
26.	P to KR4.	R to QR3 with a winning endgame.

The mental processes involved in that piece of Chess are most interesting. It will be seen that Lasker mainly used direct vision of move and counter move. At one or two points that vision included the perception of surprises, unexpected moves, threats that would not readily be anticipated. This means that Lasker was using that degree of vision which is imagination. On the other hand in some phases of the game he was not endeavouring to see exhaustively, but was seeing general characters of the position, and the general scope, i.e., he was using judgment, and applying his grasp of strategy.

Another position, fairly easy to understand, is taken from the first match game between Zukertort and Steinitz, and illustrates a failure to think clearly or judge adequately.

(BLACK)

(WHITE)

ZUKERTORT—
STEINITZ

In this position, which arises after an opening in which Black has played strategically more wisely than White, there is a threat impending of a profitable sacrifice by Black on K6. This is typical of what requires to be seen. A bad player would miss it. There is hardly room to doubt that Zukertort saw it—and saw that tactically his game would be much improved if he played Kt to Kt3 giving his King a flight square. Zukertort probably thought that that would make his Queen's side attack too slow, and took a risk. He may have judged that Steinitz's attack would prove unsound, and/or sufficiently failed to analyse the sequences that would follow the sacrifice.

There followed 14. P to Kt5, KtR5. 15. P to Kt3, Kt Kt7 Ch. 16. K to B1, Kt×KP Ch. 17. P×Kt, KB×KtP. 18. K to Kt2, B to B2 and White cannot prevent a winning attack from developing. The moral of this story is that one cannot afford, in complexities, not to work out the sequences in analytic detail.

Alternatively it is possible that Zukertort got out of his own depth and relied on possibilities that later proved unfounded.

From the standpoint of practical Chess the average good

player in that position would regard the situation as relatively easy, and take it for granted that he needed to take the precaution of Kt to Kt3 in order to provide his King with a flight square.

There are many positions in Chess comparable to this: in that they can be regarded as easy if one wishes to avoid risks, and are extremely difficult if insecurity is contemplated.

THE TACTICAL COMPLEX

The Chess position is never isolated, never static. It is a phase in an argument. If one is obsessed with the difficulty of spelling out and translating the words, the argument cannot be followed. But once the elements can be interpreted, one is able to perceive the sort of argument that is going on— the consideration of possible changes in the given position, and the consequences of those changes. Each move considered is a step in an argument, and is effective, or interesting, according to the answers that are available, and the way in which the moves can be followed up. There may be many answers or few; and each answer may have many answers or few; each of these in turn has its few or many answers. What the Chess player requires to do is to follow as many possible lines as he can, each separately, and each as far as he can. His vision, therefore, must be wide and deep—and above all, clear.

The essence, let it be repeated, is clear vision. That, be it emphasized, is something that does not follow automatically from knowing the moves, or from knowing the maximum of which each Piece is capable, or from knowing particular devices. Always you have to see the reality of a changing situation, and see it as a whole.

Vision, as we have seen, varies from something like ready wit to the higher degree which is imagination; just as the capacity for argument varies with the capacity to give adequate answers varying from the obvious to the ingenious, original or profound.

For the rest, vision is not the only mental activity that goes on in Chess, as we have seen, or, indeed, in any intellectual undertaking; but it is fundamental. The important thing about vision, as distinct from items of information, and from technique, etc., is that it is the least capable of mental operations of being taught. We all enjoy it in some degree. We can all, somehow, learn to see; but nobody can be taught to see. One is reminded of Dr. Johnson's observation that he could convey reason but not understanding. In Chess a player can be shown examples of what people have apprehended. He can be presented with situations in which he himself has to find the truth of the matter. If he has some faculty of vision, he will find himself acquiring, quite mysteriously, from his studies, the capacity to apprehend different possibilities in totally different positions. And then he will be quite amazed that he could not see before what is now so obvious. The puzzle picture should not have been puzzling! That is how the mind grows. But let no one attempt to achieve this by learning examples by heart; that way staleness lies. Be it repeated, there is no direct teaching of how to apprehend, just as there is no teaching that will make the obtuse acute.

What, however, can be done—and that is the purpose of these pages—is to direct the reader's mind to essentials. A study of examples, and illustrative games, should make the reader more ready to recognize what is important, i.e. what he requires to concentrate on in most positions. The examples already given have served to show that he is no longer concerned with isolated Pieces; that he is concerned with a tactical complex made up of all the powers of all the Pieces. The second stage is the recognition that not all the powers of all the Pieces matter equally all the time. On every Chess Board something is important and something relatively unimportant; something is relevant to the argument, something is irrelevant.

RELEVANCE

Before passing to examples, this general truth may usefully be re-stated. The good Chess player, like the good arguer, concentrates on the relevant. Once the reader has passed the stage at which the Board is a polychromatic mystery, he will appreciate that, in the mass of possibilities that exist in any given Chess position, a great many possibilities are likely to be unimportant. One does not approach one's move on the assumption that the choice is between all the available moves of all the available Pieces. There will be some moves that are clearly not to be thought about Just as in any argument a great deal of one's vocabulary, and masses of knowledge, are not in point, so on the Chess Board there is always the distinction between what is in issue and what is not in issue. Having passed the stage of general confusion, the Chess player manages to focus his vision on the relevant. He must recognize it. There is no way of showing anybody how to pick out the relevant. That is an act of vision, which, as we have seen, is unteachable. But if in looking at the Chess Board the reader sees something going on, sees, for example, that a Piece is attacked, defended, can be again attacked, and again defended, then he is already isolating some relevant point ; and, in some degree, he is playing Chess. At first his field of relevance will be narrow. Concentration makes it so. As vision improves, and concentration becomes more dynamic, the field of relevance widens and/or lengthens. A Pawn that one player disregards may be very important to another player, who is planning a long series of moves and has to consider, for example, a check upon, or an escape to, a square guarded by that Pawn. Even at that advanced stage the good player will not be laboriously working out the consequences of every possible move by every possible Piece. His vision, trained, by practice, in seeing the essentials in that kind of material, is grasping a sort of pattern—a group of possibilities arranging themselves into purposes. Much of what he is considering would never occur to the weaker player ; on the other hand he will have seen his way through, and be excluding from consideration, much that obsesses the novice, and will be paying no more attention to it than the artist who chips away the material round the figure that he has seen in the marble.

How, then, to set about finding the relevant, and improving one's grasp of possibilities ? First, *concentrate*, consider one line at a time and do not let the attention be diffused on to other thoughts. Take particular care of the absence from the Board of Pieces that will have been removed. After you have concentrated, then the mind will expand to let in outside ideas that will prove relevant. Second, a good idea is suggested by the military metaphor with which this book opened. Chess has something in it of combat. A good approach, therefore, is to think in terms of a quasi-military type. Think bellicosely. Think of threats and manifestations of force. These will not exhaust the possibilities that are latent in your position. But they will give you some kind of guide through the sequence of moves. Eventually what you thought was a threat may prove not to have been a threat. What you thought forced may prove not to have been forced, and you may have failed to see what was necessary for you to do. But in so far as you have thought in terms of these necessities, you have been playing constructively. Eventually you will find yourself seeing wider plans, and you will make no move without a sufficient reason.

Threats and Forcing Moves

From the very beginning there is something going on on the Chess Board—one or other of the infinite variety of processes that are called tactics. These are the things that require to be seen, the possibilities of winning Pawns, embarrassing minor and major Pieces, threatening to Mate the King, etc., etc. Some players start their careers by evading this task of seeing. They endeavour to learn long opening sequences by heart. This is an idle undertaking. The strain on the memory is likely to be greater than the strain on the mind's eye that exists in direct vision. Also, what the learner will have learnt by heart amounts to nothing more than a number of tactical operations that good players have undertaken because they saw what to do; and they did that by looking at the position and not by reference to memory; and they would have made equally good moves in other positions, and in answer to other lines of play, which is precisely what the player who approaches Chess mnemonically will not be able to do. For the rest, the effort to learn Chess by heart pre-supposes enormous difficulties at all stages in a game of which a great many aspects and processes are really quite easy.

To show the logic of the game, and to illustrate the idea of threats and forcing moves, let us examine some elementary opening play. White plays: 1. P to K4. Already he is playing constructively. This move allows two Pieces access to the Board—the Queen and the Bishop, the latter being the more important because it is less effective on its original square than in the centre of the Board. Also P to K4 gives a certain control over the centre squares, and in some degree inhibits the opponent.

Black now replies P to K4, with the same kind of end in view, and challenging White's control of the centre.

Now White plays Kt to KB3. This move has several advantages including the fact that it makes a Piece that was very much out of the game participate actively in it. But the main feature of this move is that now Black's Pawn is attacked. If nothing else were to happen White could capture it.

This threat is, in fact, not immediately so serious as it looks. If White were to capture the Pawn, probably there would be counter-attack by Q to K2 etc. which would re-capture it. But it is generally considered advisable either to defend the King's Pawn, or else to counter-attack immediately with Kt to KB3. These are, incidentally, good moves of development. Of Defence, the most usual moves in this position are for Black 2. . . .Kt to QB3 or (slightly less popular) P to Q3, the defect of the latter being that it gives Black's KB less scope than is possessed by White's KB.

Let us, however, consider a plausible move for Black. 2. . . .P to KB3. At first sight this move looks rational, because it defends a Pawn with the aid of a Pawn, which, as has been pointed out, is a good guard since it is a cheap one. Black has, of course, taken a square away from his King's Knight, but if he is only worried about the Pawn that fact will not concern him unduly.

But let us concentrate first on the question whether the Pawn is guarded. This is the concentration on the relevant that is the first essential of Chess ; and one does not stop concentrating on a relevant line of Chess argument simply because something looks obvious. Is Black correct in supposing that P to KB3 makes Kt×P impossible for White ?

Look, then, at 3. Kt×P. What happens? The logic of P to KB3 suggests 3. . . . P×Kt. But if White has looked at this he will have seen that after P×Kt, White has 4. Q to R5 Ch. In answer to this Black has a limited choice ; and we are encountering, thus early in the game, a good specimen of forcing play ; moves that threaten, and replies that are forced. If Black plays 4. . . . K to K2, then he is in trouble. White plays 5. Q×P Ch. Black is forced to play 5. . . . K to B2 ; and there follows a most destructive attack commencing with 6. B to B4 Ch. The Black King (after the QP has desperately sacrificed itself) is driven on to a most awkward square, and White has many ways of winning Therefore, on the fourth move Black must play P to Kt3. In the ordinary Chess sense this is forced, a move being forced when it is the best available and others involve worse consequences.

After 4. . . . P to Kt3 White plays 5. Q×KP Ch., capturing the Rook on the next move. He will then have gained two Pawns and the Exchange.

At this point the reader may be quite convinced that 2. . . . P to KB3 is a bad move. And that may now seem obvious. But the good Chess player does not stop at that. He is always looking beyond the obvious. If a complete analysis is required, there is still quite a lot to think about before P to KB3 is abandoned.

First, it may occur to the player that after 5. Q×KP Ch., then, if the Black Queen intervenes at K2 and White plays 6.

Q×R, Black's 6th move Kt to KB3 will put the White Queen out of play and into danger of encirclement.

To cut a long story short, the answer is that it takes Black a number of moves to encircle the Queen. He will have to get in P to Q4, then K to B2 (which the former move enables) : then a QKt or QB move, so that there is no loose Piece on the back line ; then B to Kt2 attacking the Queen. While this is being done White can organize an excellent rescue with P to Q3, Kt to Q2, Kt to KB3 ; and at the proper moment Kt to Kt5, which, if correctly timed, may even be Mate.

Another line of thought is as to what happens if, in reply to Q×R, Black plays Q×P Ch. The answer is that very little happens that Black can be pleased about. White moves King to Q1, threatening soon to operate on the open King's file with the Rook. In the result Black is short of material and the Black Queen is badly placed.

At this stage the analyst is more than ever satisfied that P to KB3 is a bad move. But he still has one feature to look at. What if, after 3. Kt×P, Black replies not 3. . . . P×Kt, but Q to K2 ? Then 4. Q to R5 Ch. may seem good for White, but is bad, because, if Q to R5 Ch., Black plays 4. . . . P to Kt3. Now, if the Knight takes the Pawn, the Pawn cannot recapture, because the Queen will capture the Rook. So it looks good. But Black can reply to Kt×KtP with Q×KP Ch. Then, if the Queen retreats to stop the Check, there will be exchange of Queens and the Pawn will take the Knight ; if anything else, if e.g. B to K2 is played, the Queen can take the Knight. Black will then have to be careful not to lose his Queen by a Bishop pin : but if he sees that, he will be in no danger of loss. It follows, therefore, that after 3. . .. Q to K2 the White Knight must retreat and the Black Queen will recapture the Pawn with Q×P Ch. But, then, after 5. B to K2, what has happened is that two White Pieces have developed, the Black Queen is wandering loose around the Board, where it will be attacked in a moment by the developing Queen's Knight or Queen's Pawn ; and the square that should be occupied by the Black King's Knight is occupied by a Black Pawn doing nothing. At the end of all this analysis Black is justified in deciding that 2. P to KB3 is a bad move.

The above example shows not only the occurrence of necessary continuations—forcing lines and demonstrations that certain moves are impossible—at a very early stage in the game : it also shows how, at an early stage, there can be several variations, some short and some in which long range vision, verging on the speculative, may be called for. Indeed, there is no stage of the game where it is impossible to find oneself plunged into the depths of remote continuations.

This vision of lines of play is the essence and the quintessence of Chess. But in the course of playing many games most players acquire, or manifest, a certain ability to economize mental effort. The average Chess player would reject 2. . . . P to KB3, in the variation shown, by an act of judgment. Without going into the various continuations in detail he would have a general notion of the shape that the game would take ; and he would also reject the move because of its relative lack of immediate utility ; it develops nothing and it creates tension. This judgment, which operates at all stages of the game, is a great labour saver ; but when the line has to be clearly seen, then vision, not judgment, is invoked. In practice, and in the ordinary mind, these functions are not separable in the simple way that this analysis might suggest. In Chess, as in other activities, the mind uses many methods ; but vision is the moving edge of the Chess mind. That is the important fact that the player has to act upon.

To illustrate the perpetual necessity for vision and vigilance, and to show incidentally the importance of thinking about moves like P to KB3, here is a famous opening in which many masters for long assumed that P to KB3 was unplayable :—

White	Black
1. P to Q4.	P to Q4.
2. P to QB4.	P to QB3. The Slav Defence.
3. Kt to QB3.	Kt to KB3.
4. Kt to KB3.	P × P.
5. P to QR4, in order to put pressure on the Pawn that may defend the Black Pawn on White's QB4.	
5. . . .	B to B4.
6. Kt to K5.	P to K3.
7. P to KB3.	

This was long thought to be a preparation for something unsound and was avoided even in world Championship games. Nevertheless it is good, because if now

White	Black
7. . . .	B to QKt5.
8. P to K4.	B × P.
9. P × B.	Kt × P.
10. B to Q2.	Q to R5 Ch.
11. P to Kt3.	Kt × P.
12. P × Kt.	Q × R.
13. Q to Kt4 with a splendid game.	

If, instead,

	White	Black
10.	. . .	Q × QP.
11.	Kt × Kt.	Q × Kt Ch.
12.	Q to K2.	B × B Ch.
13.	K × B.	Q to Q5 Ch.
14.	K to B2.	White has more material than is compensated for by Black's attack.

Thus, again, we see speculative possibilities cropping up early in the game. Some of them require a long analysis before they are adopted or dismissed.

The important thing is to see the forcing line. That does not necessarily mean that it is to be adopted. Here is a study in a quite early forcing line which is useful because it shows that the forcing line does not necessarily achieve advantage.

	White	Black
1.	P to K4.	P to K4.
2.	Kt to KB3.	Kt to QB3.
3.	B to B4.	Kt to KB3. The Two Knights Defence.
4.	Kt to Kt5. This is a forcing move because it makes a serious threat which the defender cannot afford to ignore.	P to Q4. Forced : i.e., the only way of preventing White from winning the KBP. But Black's move, though compelled, is good on its own merits.
5.	P × P.	Kt to R4. Black starts forcing now.
6.	P to Q3.	P to KR3.
7.	Kt to KB3.	P to K5.
8.	Q to K2.	Kt × B.

And Black has a good deal of freedom in exchange for his Pawn. It is only fair to add that no less an authority than Lasker prefers White ; but that is a matter of taste. It should be noted, incidentally that on move 6, White can play B to Kt5 Ch., which can lead to highly speculative play after P to QB3, 7. P×P, P×P, 8. Q to B3, etc.

An even better refutation of a vigorous line is due to the Russian Master, Rabinovitch.

	White	Black
1.	P to K4.	P to K4.
2.	Kt to KB3.	Kt to QB3.
3.	B to Kt5.	P to QR3.
4.	B to R4.	Kt to B3.
5.	0–0.	P to QKt4. Not the best, but playable, as the continuation shows.
6.	B to Kt3.	P to Q3.

And now if White plays the apparently good 7. Kt to Kt5, forcing P to Q4, then he is a victim of Fata Morgana, because if 8. P×P, Black develops a highly interesting counter-attack with 8. . . . Kt to Q5. 9. P to QB3, Kt×B. 10. Q×Kt, Q×P, with good play for Black—and there are other, more speculative variations.

It follows that while the forcing process is an important feature of Chess, it is not to be considered good merely by virtue of its vigour. If the forcing move can be met by play which yields the opponent an advantage, then it must not be pursued.

The player who sees a possible forcing line, and a convincing answer to it, and therefore abandons it in favour of something else, is improving as a Chess player. He is playing the board —not the man—playing against all possibilities. He is now seeing battles as part of the war ; seeing the whole as an inter-play of forces, in which the various campaigns are variations to be analysed. But, be it understood, the process which forces something positive to your advantage must be adopted, because it is desirable that the player shall control the game so as to make as much as possible of it follow of necessity. This control cannot always be achieved ; and there is such a thing as losing through trying to force the pace. But if you can proceed vigorously without causing your opponent's game to become better integrated, if you can keep him cramped by threats while you develop, evidently it is good play to do so ; and given the choice between static play and dynamic play, the dynamic line should be chosen. Lasker's game against Marshall, with which this chapter opened, is an excellent demonstration of the proof that in Chess there is no room for Micawbers. If you wait for it, it won't turn up.

EXAMPLES OF FORCING PROCESS

If the reader will turn back to the Lasker position, he will see that even when Lasker had gained some advantage, he still chose forcing moves wherever he could find them. On move 19 he played R to Kt1, forcing P to Kt3 and incidentally depriving White's Knight of that square. Then he brought the Rook to Kt4, threatening R to B4 and eventual R to B6 ; so that White was forced to move the QBP, leaving his game hollower than ever.

The next diagram shows a neat and pointed forcing series. White is threatening a process of Pawn promotion on the King's wing, with the aid of a Knight's sacrifice, but it appears as if Black can hold the threatened attack with the aid of the King and the two Pieces, so that 1. Kt×RP will fail after K×Kt. 2. R to R8 Ch., K to Kt2. 3. R to R7 Ch. K to Kt1, etc.

White therefore plays 1. R to QKt8, threatening to win a
Pawn and to break up the Q side. 1. . . . P to B3 is no
defence because of R to QB8. Black therefore plays 1. . . .
B to Kt3. Now an important change has been made in the
position. White can now play 2. Kt×RP, K×Kt. 3. R to
R8 Ch., K to Kt2. 4. R to R7 Ch., K to B1 (forced because
the Bishop no longer guards the Rook). 5. P to R6 wins,
because after R×R, P×R the King cannot stop the Pawn.

(BLACK)

White to move.

(WHITE)

It is worth noticing that if on move 1 Black plays R to
Q2, aiming at counter play, the sacrifice is also on, for a similar
reason ; and if the Rook checks a couple of times, it gets
hopelessly entangled : but the sacrifice is perhaps no longer
necessary ; the game can be won without it by R×P and
R to Q5 if required. Incidentally, the reader must not suppose
that one achieves a piece of play like this by thinking in
terms of " purpose " (" the Bishop is a nuisance—let me
displace it "). These things are seen as a whole—or not
at all.

There is no need for an accumulation of examples of forcing
processes because the reader will discover, in every game he
plays, or plays through, that a certain amount of compulsion
characterises the play at some stages, whereas in other stages
there is relative freedom. What is important is to see, if possible,
the obscure possibility that makes something necessary to
the player who sees it, or makes his opponent able to achieve
something if the defender does not see it.

The diagram shows an ingenuity by Alekhine. Playing against Tartakower at San Remo, in a position which was slightly advantageous, but which looked as if it might have been tenable by the defender along logical lines, Alekhine introduced the finesse which brought about a decisive result quickly. After 32. ... Kt to K1, giving the diagram position, Black was sure that White could not get any advantage from Kt × P, B × Kt; B × B Ch., K × B; R to K3 Ch., K × P, etc. What he failed to appreciate was a change of order. 33. B × P Ch., B × B. 34. P to Kt4 Ch. and now if 34. ... K to B5. 35. Kt to K6 is Mate. Therefore Black must play 34. K to B3 leaving White to capture the Bishop with full control of the game.

(BLACK) TARTAKOWER

White to move.

(WHITE)   ALEKHINE

An interesting feature of this position is that another point of order makes White's manoeuvre harder to see. To play P to Kt4 Ch. before B × P does not give the same result as the line played, because after K to B5, B × P could be met by R × Kt, leaving an endgame of tremendous difficulty.

For the rest, do not confuse forcing moves with "loud" moves. The threat need not be of an immediate capture.

In the next diagram position the "loud" move is 1 R to Q6, hitting something, and if Q to K2 of course White is in trouble, e.g., 1. ... R to Q6. 2. Q to K2, KR to Q1. 3. 0-0, B × Kt, etc. If 3. Kt to Q4, B × Kt. 4. P × B, KR × P. 5. 0-0, R to KKt6! wins.

However, White is not obliged to play Q to K2. 2. Q to

B4 is playable—and Black cannot comfortably double Rooks, although his game is still good. If he doubles Rooks—each player wins a Bishop, and after exchanges Black has a slightly superior endgame.

But if Black plays 1. . . . R to Q3—less loud, but still threatening, White is relatively helpless. If 2. Q to K2, B to Kt4. If instead, 2. Q to B4 2. . . . B to R3 is playable, and B×Kt and KR to Q1 are threatened. If 3. Q to B5 Ch., R to K3 Ch. 4. B to K3, R×P. 5. Q×BP, R×B Ch. wins.

(BLACK)

(WHITE)

Black to move.

WHAT ARE TACTICS : SOME HINTS

By this time the reader, whom it is the aim of these pages to teach to think like a Chess player, may have noticed, or been disappointed to find, that in a Chapter relating to tactics he has not been given any rules. If he is already thinking like a Chess player, he will have the answer ; that tactics do not lend themselves to rules. Tactics consist in dealing with a situation according to the forces available and the nature of the situation. Knowledge of tactics is simply the awareness of the powers of the Pieces and the geometry of the Board, plus the ability to control (i.e. plan in the light of) those factors. There is no rule about dealing with them effectively. The materials that one is using are the functions of the Pieces described in the second chapter. When the player has mastered the functions of the Pieces to the extent of being able to use them in his plans, then he is a tactician.

Most of tactics consists in the straightforward use of the Pieces in the light of common sense. Common sense is not quite an accurate description, because the ability to think in terms of the Chess moves already places the reader beyond ordinary common sense. But it is common sense relatively to the more imaginative degrees of vision. Bringing to bear as much force as possible in attack or defence of any given point ; capturing the greater with the lesser ; making squares of escape for Pieces that are hemmed in, etc., etc., these are tactics. The tactical efficiency of a player increases in the measure to which the powers of the Pieces and their idiosyncracies have become part of his equipment.

Important factors in tactical operations include several that the reader has already been made aware of.

The pinning of Pieces and Pawns by the Pieces that can pin (Bishop, Rook and Queen) is one important feature of the tactical complex. To know this is not enough, because the pinning operation may in the total situation be unimportant. That is something that can only be assessed by the player who has learned to concentrate and to seek for answers to all his threats. Imagine for example that your opponent has moved his Queen's Pawn, so that you can, with your Queen, pin his Knight at QB3 by placing your Queen at QR4 or QKt5. That may be a very good undertaking if it is part of a general pressure and creates threats in addition to the temporary immobilization of the Knight.

For example it may be coupled with an attack on the Queen's Knight's Pawn or Queen's Rook's Pawn, which it may or may not be safe to capture. Or it may be coupled with a threat of P to Q5 and the possibility of winning the Knight. On the other hand your move may in the long run be useless as the opponent's Bishop may be able to place itself at Q2. It may be that you want to compel it to go there. On the other hand B to Q2 may embarrass you, not your opponent. He threatens to " unmask a battery " by a Knight move. If nothing else, this may cause you to lose tempo.

The unmasking of batteries is quite an important feature of tactics. The principle is that of discovered check. It can quite easily come about that even a light pinning Piece can be lost, even when it is pinning against a heavy Piece. Thus, your Queen is on K1, your Knight on QB3, your opponent's Bishop is on his QKt5, his Queen on K2, and he has castled King's side. Your move Kt to Q5 may win a Piece, because if he takes your Queen, you take his Queen with Check, and capture the Bishop next move. The efficacy of this depends

on whether the Knight can later extricate itself. Probably, if
the worst comes to the worst, it can sell itself for a Pawn.
That, too, suggests a feature of tactics. In Chess as in other
undertakings it is wise to play with the bookmaker's money.
The so far unrecaptured Piece, the " hanging Piece," so to
speak, is a tactical weapon ; it can sell itself for what it likes
and whatever return it obtains is profit.

But let the reader not endeavour to learn Chess by making
a list of notions like unmasking batteries, hanging Pieces, etc.
If the student is getting familiar with the powers of the Pieces
these manoeuvres will be perceptible by him even if he does
not know the name of each manoeuvre. Knowing the name is
an advantage only because it may heighten awareness. But
the awareness must come first.

To revert to pins, there are many ways of relieving a pin.
One of the most familiar is the relief of the pin of the Queen's
Knight by P to QR3 and P to QKt4. That is particularly
effective against a Queen : it may also upset a Bishop. In
the Noah's Ark Trap (later in this Chapter) it helps to win a
Piece. On the other hand, while this may be good counterplay
(and incidentally a method of developing the QB) it may also
create a weakness on the QB file.

On the King's wing the manoeuvre P to KR3, P to KKt4
has a similar effect but may be more dangerous to the defender,
because it often happens that the attacker can sacrifice a
Knight for the KtP, recapture with the Bishop and have a
permanent pin.

A permanent, unrelievable pin is a very good thing if it is
not purchased at too high a price. It is sometimes worth
while to sacrifice in order to hold a Rook permanently (or
even for a move or two) pinned on KB7 while forces can
be brought up to attack it. The so called Dilworth Defence
to the Ruy Lopez illustrates this principle (see chapter on
openings).

Another instance of permanent pin can happen when a
Rook checks on the back rank, and a Bishop is forced to
interpose itself, and the defender finds it impossible, or
laborious, to get his King off the back rank without at the
same time losing the Bishop. If he can move his Pawns, he
can escape, but the Pawn moves may be dangerous because
they may open new lines of attack.

Obviously your opponent's King and Queen are good pieces
to have behind the Piece you are pinning; they make the pin
more serious.

A few lines of opening play are understandable when one

considers that they turn on the fact that, if a minor Piece captures a Pawn on the King's or Queen's file, that Piece may be pinned against the King or Queen by a Rook, while a Pawn comes up to attack it. It may well be that there is tactical counterplay as in the diagram position below. Once again the total situation has to be taken into account, but the pinning possibility is always to be borne in mind. Again, the Queen is not a very good Piece to pin with unless it is clear that there is no effective counter such as a masked battery. Queens that pin at Kt5 are usually attacking at the same time a Knight's Pawn. But tactically the capture of the Knight's Pawn may be dangerous.

(BLACK)

(WHITE)

TACTICAL COMPLEX

Black to move:
1. ... Kt × P.
2. Kt × Kt, Q × Kt.
3. R to K1, Kt to K5 with counter-play.

Suppose you are attacking a Knight's Pawn and your opponent Castles on the other wing; the capture may put your Queen into difficulties. These difficulties constitute a feature of the tactical complex.

White	Black
1. P to Q4.	P to Q4.
2. Kt to KB3.	B to B4.
3. P to QB4.	P to K3.
4. Q to Kt3 taking advantage of the weakness of the QKtP.	Kt to QB3. A clever reply.
5. Q × P.	Kt to Kt5. And the Queen is in difficulties. There is a threat at least to draw by the repetition R to Kt1, R to R1, etc.

Here is another example—a position reached by the author, in which Black has played Q to Kt3 attacking a Bishop and putting pressure on the centre, but White replies Kt to QB3, threatening Kt to R4; and if Q×B, that same Kt to R4 actually wins the Queen.

(BLACK)

(WHITE)

TACTICAL POINT

White to play:
1. Kt to QB3.

In this last example the Knight's powers are well illustrated as part of a Chess situation. The reader has already seen examples of the Knight's fork—another instrument of tactical operations. The reader has also seen the Smothered Mate. It may also be mentioned that a Knight can find itself hemmed at the edge of the board. Thus, place it on QR4; give the opponent a Pawn on Q5, a B on K2, a P on QR2, and if you have a Pawn on QKt2, then your opponent's P to QKt4 may win the Knight; and examples could be multiplied.

All the Pieces have their peculiarities, some of which are harder to appreciate than others; and the harder ones are worth mentioning. Thus in the next diagram, the advantage of Black's last move P to QR4 is that now it takes White four moves to get his Pawn to QKt4. 1. P to QKt3 (not P to QR3 which is answered by P to QR5) 2. P to QR3 3. B to Kt2 (this is necessary to guard the Rook) and finally P to QKt4. Very often, therefore, a player who wishes to establish a Kt on B4 precedes this move with P to QR4.

This diagram, incidentally, shows a kind of pin in being— the Rook's prevention of 3. P to Kt4:P×P 4. P×P R×R.

This rather differs from the Rook's pin on the King's file, e.g. when a capture of a Pawn is under consideration.

The Pawn, incidentally, is quite a hard Piece to master. In the centre of the Board it has latent threats. Thus given a Bishop on QB4, your opponent may be able to play Kt × KP, and in answer to Kt × Kt, P to Q4. Or again this may be quite ineffective because either the Knight or the Bishop may be able to move away with a threat or a check, gaining a tempo to save the second piece—another instance of the hanging Piece.

(BLACK)

(WHITE)

TECHNICAL POINT

Effect of Pawn on R4.

Here is a harder example. Your opponent has a Rook on his QR4, a B on QB4, a Knight on Q5. You have a Kt on Q1, Pawns on QKt2 and QB2 ; P to Kt4 wins a Piece ; because if B × P, P to QB3 forks Kt and B.

This last example illustrates the difficulty and the inutility of attempting to make a list of tactical factors. They are too empirical, too numerous, too inconstant. The functions of the Pieces are always functions varying with the positional setting.

Some Masters have claimed to be able to teach Chess, including the art of sacrificing, on rational mathematical lines. They speak of bearing in mind the maximum moves of each Piece : or thinking of the most " restrictive " moves. That is an error due to the analysis of some combinations into mathematical statements. The Rook, e.g. which sacrificed itself in some particular position made its maximum move, finally putting itself *en prise*. On the other hand, some Rooks sacrifice themselves without going so far. Again, going too near the enemy, restrictively, may not be the best (see Diagram on page 113). If you try to think of all the powers of all the Pieces you will be considering a great many irrelevancies; you will be doing the opposite of what is required above all else in Chess, concentration on the relevant. The relevant is intuited, not worked out mathematically. If you have absorbed the functions of the Pieces your capacity for the perception of the relevant is better; that is all that can be said.

Acccording to your grasp of the Board, you will be less liable to surprise. The element of surprise is always present in Chess. Even good players can be surprised. There is

(BLACK)

(WHITE)

ALEKHINE
NIMZOWITCH

A STUDY IN
PINNING.

White wins :
16. KR to K1, B to
   K5.
17. B to R5, Kt × B.
18. R to Q8 Ch., K to
   B2.
19. Q × Kt. Resigns.
Note the achieve-
ment of a permanent
pin.

always something beyond any player's field of vision. The reader has already seen several examples of surprise ; and he will see many more ; the putting of Pieces *en prise*, in order to gain a square, to effect a pin for a critical moment, to inveigle a Major Piece into a difficult situation, etc., etc. All these require to be seen rather than deduced.

That very good players can be surprised by manœuvres not many moves deep, but yet having an element of unexpectedness in them, is illustrated by the play in the above and two following positions. These were three of a great number of triumphs that Alekhine achieved at Bled in the days of his supremacy. They were scored against Nimzowitch and Flohr, at that time two of the very greatest players in the world.

Each of these positions is describable, after play, in terms of some geometry—open lines, closed lines and the like. But good players proceed with the manoeuvres they wish to execute, even when they do not like all the geometrical features, because it is very rare to have the kind of position in which one likes all the geometrical characteristics. Besides, and more important, the existence of open lines, masked

(BLACK)

(WHITE)

**NIMZOWITCH
ALEKHINE
COMPROMISING
THE QUEEN.**

12. ... Kt to Q4 Ch.
13. B to Q2, Q to Kt3.
14. Q × R Ch. K to Q2 and White's Queen is in difficulties.

There followed :

15. O–O Kt to B2.
16. B to R5, Kt × Q.
17. B × Q, Kt × B, etc.

(BLACK)

(WHITE)

**ALEKHINE
FLOHR**

Unusual effect of a " battery."

28. P to K5. P to B4.
29. R to B8. Wins.

batteries, possibilities of pins, etc., are insufficient to constitute a decisive process. They condition the process—not bring it about. If the good player cannot see his opponent's exploitation, it may be because the opponent cannot do anything decisive. But a particularly clever opponent sometimes finds ingenuities and resources in a position that the other has missed; (equally, the best of players might fail to extract anything from an apparently more favourable setting). That is how good players fall victim to surprise. They engage in hard combat; and the enemy finds somewhere a source of strength, effects a neat hold, which, in close combat, is quite easy for the victim not to anticipate.

The student of Chess may learn from these examples that the very best players fail to deduce dangers that exist, and fail to see them. It follows that the student cannot hope to work out a Chess geometry, or a set of mechanics which will keep him safe. The only safe structure for the Chess Pieces is the box in which they are contained. On the other hand better players, relying on their vision and their judgment, enter into compromised positions which the student should avoid—at least approach cautiously. The Master, whose position is compromised, has that position because he is endeavouring to gain something or to hold something, or to defy the consequences of something which he thinks, to use a colloquialism, that he can get away with. The student, if he is experienced enough to grasp that a position is strained, or subject to stress—compromised in some way, will proceed more cautiously ; and he will avoid the kind of situation in which he has to leave in being masked batteries, dangerous pins, etc. He will not, without great thought, leave a Piece to be recaptured for any length of time. That is the kind of situation to be careful of, because the opponent may be able to use that Piece sacrificially. Your Piece that the opponent has in hand is a Desperado. (That term is also applied, for no good reason, to either player's Piece which is apparently blocking his line of attack and which can be sacrificed in order to gain a tempo.) More fundamentally, it is important not to play a line in which you will have to spend a number of moves restoring safety, restoring the equilibrium, while your opponent proceeds with his game.

To put the matter shortly, it is wise to avoid any tactical compromise, unless your opponent is worse compromised. Avoid looseness in a position ; also avoid tensions and stresses. Avoid loss of time. Some of the tactical possibilities described above are the features that constitute strain and stress.

But more important than any rules enabling one to judge whether one's position is safe or dangerous, is the general principle laid down above that the Chess player must endeavour to see the consequences of what he does. The Chess player must keep within his depth. If Chess is a cold bath for the mind (as a distinguished amateur has described it), then it also has analogies to swimming. In Chess, as in swimming, it is important to keep within one's depth; it is also hard to know what that depth is. What the reader can see from examples is the kind of whirlpool to avoid. Experience will make him conscious of the dangerous waters and the relatively safe shallows. It will also teach him to keep swimming.

(BLACK)

(WHITE)

DESPERADO PIECE.

The Knight gives itself away to clear two lines.

1. Kt to Kt5, P × Kt.
2. B × P Ch., K to R1.
3. B × KtP Ch., K × B.
4. Q to Kt6 Ch., K to R1.
5. R to R3, Q to Q2.
6. B to Kt8 Ch., Q × R.
7. P × Q wins.

Once again, let it be stated, one cannot play Chess under guarantees of security. You have to move forward. If you are swimming correctly, there is no reason to suppose that the waves will easily overwhelm you. Chess is a dangerous game, not a safe game. If your position is reasonably well developed you should not be afraid of becoming involved in a struggle. Indeed you must seek it, as Lasker did against Marshall. When Marshall's play lacked incisiveness, Lasker attacked and won. To adopt the metaphor of combat, in Chess your forces are joined with your opponent's as in a duel or wrestling bout, and you cannot escape him by doing nothing, nor can you easily disentangle yourself. In Chess as in war the maxim is " engage the enemy." If he is developing you too must develop, and at the same time limit his development. If he is not developing, move aggressively against him. When you are doing that you may be embarking on an undertaking of which you cannot see all the consequences. What is important is to see that, in the position which you can see ahead, your affairs seem to be in good order. If you cannot see that, then do not start the operation.

To recapitulate, the essence of tactics is finding effective moves, undertaking effective operations. Those things have to be seen. Awareness of the possibilities of the Pieces will make you better at seeing the possibilities with some degree of completeness. In addition some elementary arithmetic and common sense will always help your thinking. One of the great features of Chess is the need for doing as much as can be done with what force is available. Therefore, be economical of material and of time. But above all of time. Do not do in two moves what you can do in one. If you can alter the order of your moves so as to bring about a certain situation in three moves rather than four, then play it that way. It is nearly as bad in Chess to lose a tempo as to lose a Pawn. To lose two tempi against a good player is to invite destruction. In the relative developments, when forces are involving themselves with each other, the speed is a function of the total energy that is being exerted. If therefore, you can save a move, or cause your opponent to lose a move, you have, as it were, advanced a step further, thrown forward a little more weight than your opponent. If you think about it you will realize that many of the advantages that are involved in batteries, forks, etc., consist in gains of time. You are doing more than your opponent can cope with in the time at his disposal. It is reasonable to play on the assumption that if you keep pace with your opponent you will not incur disadvantage. Therefore, conserve tempo. It does not, of course, pay to gain a tempo at the cost of dislocating your position. The reader will see examples of the doubtfulness of some gains of tempo in the chapter on Openings. Again, when a position has crystallized, it may be that time matters less; the processes are clear, and extra precautions can be taken, preparations made, without detriment. The decision in such circumstances is a strategic one. But in general it is safe to say that the player who gains time gains an advantage.

How Far Chess Players See

The consideration of some practical processes brings us to a question frequently heard among beginners, rarely heard among good players; how far does a good player see? Good players know this question to be unanswerable in terms of number of moves. Everything depends on the position. Some positions are, so to speak, opaque ; the short range is hard to see. Typical of this is any situation in the openings where Pawns can capture each other and there are great varieties of recapture. Or it may be desired to advance a Pawn to K4 or Q4, and there are so many possible lines, most of them short range, that the effort of exhausting them is considerable ; and there may be one variation which has to be followed a long way. Other positions are more translucent. The possibilities are fewer or more logical, are visible further ahead and are not hard to follow. Many Chess positions have aspects of both translucence and opacity. Most of the variations are easy ; one is hard. That makes the whole position hard. Again we have seen that any position can be characterised by the possibility of a cleverness which, ex hypothesi, is hard to see.

(BLACK)

(WHITE)

White to move.
Advisable is:
1. R to QKt1.
1. P to Q7 is wrong,
    because of 1 . . .
    R × P.
(1. K to B6 is not
    bad.)

Of the phases of the game, it may be said that in the end game one sees a greater number of moves ahead than earlier in the game, because much of it is the counting of Pawn moves and King moves. On the other hand endgames may be extremely difficult, because clevernesses on an empty board are harder than on a crowded Board, if only because one expects them less. Here is a not very hard point of order. The player who has relied on forcing his opponent to give Rook for Pawn is surprised to find that he has done it at the wrong moment.

In the endgame, and in the transition to the endgame, what one is looking for may be a method rather than an immediate line of play: what Pawn structure is being aimed at ; how that Pawn structure can be exploited. The execution of the process—a break-through by Pawns—may be long delayed ; but it need not be difficult to grasp.

Also at this stage of the game one encounters short specific problems that are not hard, though they involve accuracy.

(BLACK)

White to move.

(WHITE)

For example in the diagram position your opponent's Rook is threatening to play havoc among your Pawns. If you panic and start throwing your Pawns forward your opponent will win. But you have a neat resource, you simply move your King to K1. Now if your opponent's Rook comes to Q7, you can play R to Q1 forcing exchanges, because if he takes your Pawn you can mate him. That is not hard to see. What, however, may be hard to see is this same move when you are looking at it from the beginning of a long middle-game process, in which Pieces are to be exchanged and the whole game simplified. And it often happens that a Master wins a game by a reduction of all the forces and an entry into the endgame with the power to gain an important tempo, or seize an important point, with the aid of some cleverness or other ; after which the win follows by careful exploitation of what has become a permanent advantage.

In the middle-game what the good player requires to see is not so much a number of moves as a number of stages. He

sees quite a long variation up to a position where some other
operation may be starting ; and that other operation has to
be followed ; and that operation may work itself out into a
situation where something else starts. What makes these
analyses difficult, apart from following clearly all the exchanges
and removals of pieces, is the intrusion of the unexpected—
a manoeuvre which gives a different twist to the game. A good
example is the position in the following diagram, reached between Euwe and Lasker at Zurich in 1934. Euwe had seen
quite a long way, but had failed to appreciate the effect of
Lasker's Queen sacrifice—or had taken it for granted that the
loss of the Queen could not be tolerated by his opponent.

(BLACK)

(WHITE)

EUWE—LASKER
A QUEEN
SACRIFICE

White has played
35. Kt to K4.
Black replies
35. ... Q × P.
36. Kt to B6 Ch., Q
× Kt.
37. R × Q, Kt × R
(f6).
38. R to QB1, Kt to
K5 with advan-
tage.

Typical of the short range are the following positions from
a game in an English Masters' Tournament (1947). In the
first position White has just made the mistake of playing
QR to QB1, allowing Black to play 14. ... Q to K3. Now
15. B to B3 for White failed to save a Pawn because of Kt × P
16. Kt × Kt P to Q4. Black is well co-ordinated enough to
leave a Piece in his opponent's possession for a moment, in the
certainty of winning it back with profit. Actually Black went
further than this. There followed ; 17. B to Q4 P × Kt, 18. B × B
P × B (sacrificing for the attack) 19. B × R Q to K6 Ch., 20. K
to R1 P × P Ch. 21. K × P Kt to Q6, and we have a typical
middle-game situation in which, opening complications, threat
and counter threat, enriched by one or two ideas, have given
Black an attack sufficiently good to justify him in leaving at

least one Piece "in the air." The threat of R to Q1 is sufficient to give White no time to attempt to save the Bishop. The game proceeded as follows—22. R to B4 (not R to B3 because after Kt×P Ch. R×Kt Q×R the Bishop still cannot escape by B×P because of Q to K5 Ch ; Black is already beginning the transition to an endgame with Pawns to the good). 22. . . . R×B, with ample compensation in middle-

YANOFSKY —AITKEN.

White to move.
Black is on the point of winning a Pawn.
1. B to B3, Kt × P.
2. Kt × Kt, P to Q4
(If 1. B to B4, P to Q4 is good for Black.)

YANOFSKY —AITKEN.
(contd.)

Strength of a Knight at the 6th.
If R to Q1, Kt to K8, etc.
If P × P, Kt × KP etc.

game and endgame advantages, for the Exchange. There followed 23. Q to Kt4 P to B4, 24. Q to Kt3 Q to Q7 Ch., 25. K to Kt1 R to Q1, 26. Q to B3 P to K4, giving another interesting position, which illustrates, among other things, the immense tactical advantage of a Knight established on a square like Q6 or K6. Note that White cannot free himself with R to Q1, because of the neat Kt to K8. This is the kind of cleverness that is apt to turn up in a promising position. The finding of it near to hand is Resource, or Ingenuity, as distinct from the vision which takes place when it is seen a long way ahead.

White played 27. P×P (the advance of the Pawn being too serious to contemplate) 27. . . . Kt×KP 28. Q to B4 Kt×R 29. Q×Kt Ch. Black has now won the Exchange back ; and were he to play 29. . . . K to Kt 2, should win very easily because of his considerable endgame advantage, to say nothing of his control of a great many open lines. However, the diagram shows one of the curious little features of the

(BLACK)

(WHITE)

YANOFSKY —AITKEN (concluded)
A PIT-FALL (Crosspin)
R to Q1 wins for White.

geometry of the Chess Board, which even a very good Chess player (under fatigue) is apt to miss. Black played 29. . . . Q to Q4, giving the diagram position ; and White with 30. R to Q1 wins. The point is that after Q×Q R×R Ch. gains a tempo, allowing subsequent P×Q and White is a Rook to the good. This cross-pin is highly amusing as a resource, and illustrates one of the very many difficulties that stand in the way of the player who is endeavouring to turn an advantage into a win. Not the least difficult of Chess operations is the winning of won games.

SOME VARIETIES OF ERROR

The fortunate winner of the game above described (Yanofsky, his opponent being Aitken, the Scottish Master) was the beneficiary of an equally amusing error some years earlier. In the diagram position from the Canadian Championship,

(BLACK)

(WHITE)

ALMGREN—
YANOFSKY

White to play.
1. P to QKt4, P × P e.p.
2. K × P, R to Q5 Ch., wins.

White (Almgren) can probably draw comfortably with Kt×P— and there are other moves. He played however, P to QKt4; and this is quite a good tactical idea. If P×P e.p., then the idea is to capture the QP, and when the Knight's Pawn advances to stop it with the King and the Knight. This is a quite reasonable way of breaking up dangerous Pawns. However, Black plays P×P e.p., White replies K×P, and is astonished when Black plays R to Q5 Ch. winning, because, after K×R P to Kt7 forces promotion.

From the other side of the world, here is a classic. In the next diagram position White (Rabinovitch) is clearly dominant, and can improve his position with an advance of the KRP.

Evidently Black's strategy has been defective. He plays, now, Kt to K5, in order to dislodge the White Queen. White allows himself to be dislodged into Q to R6, forcing mate. The idea, which the reader has already seen, is pretty but not difficult, and was probably entertained as a possibility by the

Russian Master before he allowed his Queen to occupy so exposed a square as Kt5.

(BLACK)

(WHITE)

RABINOVITCH —GOGLIDZE.

Black played :
1 . . . . Kt to K5,
and White replied :
Q to R6, winning.

Sometimes the oversight is actually a failure to see a quick win. One of the classics is the game Marco-Popiel. In the diagram position Marco, with Black, appears to be in great difficulties ; in fact he seems to be on the point of losing a Piece. For that reason he resigns. He had however a

(BLACK)

(WHITE)

POPIEL—MARCO.

Black to play, re-signed, but could win by 1 ... B to Kt8.

better move, viz : B to Kt8 winning. By failing to see this
Marco achieved the wrong kind of immortality.

Enough examples have now been shown to illustrate how easy
it is to overlook the unexpected over a very short range.
Over the longer range what happens is that play and counterplay produce positions which were terribly difficult to assess in
the distance. That follows from the fact that they are quite
difficult when one comes right up to them. Here is an example.
The diagram shows the kind of situation that can develop

(BLACK)

(WHITE)

White to move.

in a closely fought middle-game. Black has evidently sacrificed the Exchange in order to hold on to his strong though
isolated, centre Pawn, and in exchange for some open lines.
White has to move, and evidently has to think hard about
Black's threat of B to B3 Ch. White can play 1. B to K4 ;
but that is met by B to R5—a quite hard move to see even
at one move distance.

White cannot take the Bishop without landing into serious
trouble by Q × B Ch. followed by Q to K7. Failing that
capture, White must lose material. It follows that B to K4
cannot be played on the first move. The only other moves
to be considered are KR to K1 and QR to K1. The answer to
KR to K1 is relatively easy ; 1. . . . B to B3 Ch. 2. B to K4
B × B Ch. 3. Q × B Q × Q Ch. 4. R × Q Kt to B7 Ch. wins a Piece.
Therefore White must play 1. QR to K1, and that is met by, and
involves, some clever play thus, 1. QR to K1 B to B3 Ch.
2. B to K4 P to Q6. If now White captures the Queen, he

loses by 3. . . . P×Q 4. QR to K1 B×B Ch. 5. R×B Kt to B7 Ch. winning a Piece, because the Rook cannot leave the back rank.

If, then, on move 3 White tries, as he must, to guard the Bishop, he also has difficulty. Thus, 3. Q to B4 (an awkward move), Kt to B7 Ch. 4. K to Kt1, which looks safe because the Queen is still attacked; however, 4. . . . B×B wins, because if 4. Q×B Black wins a Piece, and if instead 4. R×Q Kt to R6 is mate.

On move 3, then, White has only one move Q to KKt2; and there follows 3. . . . B×B 4. Q×B Kt to B7 Ch. 5. R×Kt Q×R (on B7) and, remarkably, Black has an endgame win. This is quite hard to establish; but the point is that White is not going to be able to capture the dangerous QP. Thus if 6. Q to K3 Q to B7 7. R to QB1 P to Q7; and there are many other variations. Only a remarkable player, seeing, in middle-game complications, that he was likely to arrive after a few moves, at the diagram position just analysed, could be sure that White was incurring a loss.

Even without the intrusion of clever ideas a series of moves can be very hard to see through; particularly a series involving many exchanges.

Here is an example from the openings—

White	*Black*
1. P to K4.	P to K4.
2. Kt to KB3.	Kt to QB3.
3. B to B4.	P to Q3.
4. P to B3.	B to Kt5.
5. Q to Kt3.	Q to Q2.

Here White might be tempted to play for the win of material as follows :

White	*Black*
6. B×P Ch.	Q×B.
7. Q×P.	K to Q2.
8. Q×R.	B×Kt.
9. P×B.	Q×P.
10. R to B1 or Kt1.	Q×KP Ch.
11. K to Q1.	Q to B6 Ch.

And now the game has burnt itself out into a draw, because if White tries to escape the perpetual check by K to B2, Kt to Kt5 Ch. wins the Queen; and that is something that could hardly be seen by the player meditating 6. B×P Ch. at a stage long before a diagonal, that was then full, had cleared itself of obstructive material.

Celebrated is the quick win of Reti over Tartakower, in

which the former took unexpected advantage of some experimental play by his very strong opponent.

White	Black
1. P to K4.	P to QB3. The Caro-Kahn, not nearly so bad as it looks.
2. P. to Q4.	P to Q4.
3. Kt to QB3.	P × P.
4. Kt × P.	Kt to KB3. More usual is B to B4, the real object of the opening being to obtain mobility for the QB.
5. Q to Q3.	P to K4. This is very enterprising and looks good ; of course, B to B4 had become impossible because of Kt × Kt Ch.
6. P × P.	Q to R4 Ch. In order to win the Pawn back.
7. B to Q2.	Q × P. With a dangerous looking pin. White, who could have prevented this by the retreat of the Knight on move 7, has evidently seen the remarkable sequel.
8. O-O-O.	Kt × Kt. Probably assuming that White is relying on R to K1 to recapture the Knight. It is quite probable that Black has spent all his thought on the series of moves that follow R to K1. But he has completely failed to see his opponent's idea.
9. Q to Q8 Ch. A thunderbolt.	
9. . . .	K × Q.
10. B to Kt5, double Check, with mate next move—a beautiful performance.	

The richest Chess is seen when cleverness follows cleverness ; when during, or after, a fairly logical process, an ingenious idea intrudes, and is met by an ingenious idea, and so on. That means that both players are exploiting the hidden resources of the board. Here is an example of some very nice Chess. After the opening moves 1. P to K4 P to K3, 2. P to Q4 P to Q4, 3. Kt to QB3 Kt to KB3, 4. B to Kt5 P × P, 5. Kt × P B to K2, 6. B × Kt B × B, 7. Kt to KB3 Kt to Q2, 8. B to Q3 P to B4, 9. P × P Kt × P, 10. B to Kt5 Ch. K to K2, 11. Q × Q Ch. R × Q, it seems that White wins a Piece by 12. Kt × Kt. But there is an answer 12. . . . R to Q4 winning a Piece in return. Fairly straightforward. But is White now obliged to sit still and lose back his Piece ? He is playing with his opponent's material ! 13. Kt to R6.

Now follow the consequences. If Black captures the B, then Kt to B7 forks the Rooks ; if he captures the Kt, B to

B6. But the resources of Black's science are not exhausted
—13. . . . B×KtP ; and if Kt to B7, of course B×R—
But how does this bear on the problem ?   What if White
quietly plays R to Kt1 ?   There lies the concealed cleverness.

White	Black
14. R to QKt1.	R×B.
15. Kt to B7.	B to B6 Ch.

and one of the Rooks that are forked gets away giving a tempo
to the other in which to escape.

Very neat, but not conclusive ; because there is an answer
that is equally neat—

White	Black
14. R to Kt1.	R×B.
15. Kt to B7.	B to B6 Ch.
16. K to K2.	R×R.
17. R×R.	R to Kt1.
18. Kt to R6. Forces a draw by repetition of moves.	

The player who saw all that, back on move 10, was only
seeing eight moves.   But he was seeing a great deal more than
the man who, approaching an elementary Pawn ending, can
see about 20 by simple counting of Pawn and King moves in
reasonable order.

An opening that the reader has already seen (Ruy Lopez) is
rich in examples of the scope for vision and error.

White	Black
1. P to K4.	P to K4.
2. Kt to KB3.	Kt to QB3.
3. B to Kt5.	P to Q3. (The Steinitz Defence.)
4. P to Q4.	B to Q2.

At this point the variation to be seen is 5. B×Kt B×B,
6. P×P P×P,   7. Q×Q Ch. R×Q, 8, Kt×P B×P—
showing that the defensive move B to Q2 amounted to a
counter-attack on the King's Pawn.   In a small way, the
logic of taking and retaking has been departed from and an
idea introduced.   To continue :

White	Black
5. Kt to QB3.	Kt to KB3. White has defended his own King's Pawn, and Black has attacked it again. White can pin this Knight of Black's, but if Black defends with 6 . . . B to K2 then when B×KKt there will be an additional Piece defending Black's King's Pawn. White therefore develops.
6. 0–0.	B to K2.
7. R to K1.	

Here we are presented with an object lesson on the need for vision in Chess. Black wants to Castle ; and he feels safe in castling. His judgment tells him that castling is a logical developing move. But what about the attack on the Pawn ? White's King's Pawn is twice guarded. Therefore if White wins Black's King's Pawn, Black cannot immediately regain it. But Black, not being entirely without vision, may have seen something. He may have seen that after the Exchanges 8. B×Kt B×B, 9. P×P P×P, 10. Q×Q R×Q, 11. Kt×KP, Black's B can take the White KP because the White Rook is tied to the back row. That is quite a perception ; and the judgment that we have spoken of may support it, because it looks as if Black is at least as well developed as White.

However, to cut a long story short, the move 7. . . . Castles on the part of Black loses material. There follows 8. B×Kt B×B, 9. P×P P×P, 10. Q×Q QR×Q, 11. Kt×P, B×P (best, because the answer to Kt×P would be Kt×B and the possibility of the Check gains a tempo for the recapture of the Knight). And now 12. Kt×B Kt×Kt, 13. Kt to Q3 terminates Black's mating possibility ; and leaves the White Rook attacking the Knight and pinning it against the unguarded Bishop.

But there is still a stage further to go—and this illustrates the process previously described. Black plays 13. . . . P to B4. This is answered by 14. P to KB3. Black plays 14. . . . B to B4 Ch. ; there is nothing better ; and obviously it creates a problem for White, because if he plays K to B1, then after Black retreats the Bishop to Kt3, White cannot safely capture the Knight. However, White has 15. Kt×B Kt×Kt, 16. B to KKt5 ; and now White wins the Exchange thus; 16. . . . R to Q4, 17. B to K7 R to K1, 18. P to QB4. and in order to save the Knight Black has to lose the Exchange.

At the end of it all Black has lost material. He is a victim of what is called, inaccurately, the Tarrasch Trap, because the Master Marco succumbed to this play against the great Tarrasch. What Marco was really a victim of was the intrusion into the game of ideas that he had not seen.

The so-called Tarrasch Trap is one of the most difficult pieces of Chess to see through unaided ; and is one of the few variations whose existence justifies a player in learning some lines by heart. For the rest the line has other aspects of great interest. First it proves that on move 7 Black was forced to play P×P. That is a new conception of the word forced.

It was necessary, not through an immediate compulsion, but in a long perspective. In that sense the best-move (where there is a single best move) is always forced. Finally the line shows the strain that can be put on vision, even when the general principles of the game do not indicate the presence of stresses and strains.

TRAPS.

When an opponent makes a move that seems to lose a Piece, and you accept it and find yourself involved in a forcing sequence that leads to great loss, you may hear yourself said to have fallen into a trap. That is not a very accurate way of describing it. A good player rarely makes moves on the assumption that his opponent will make a mistake. He makes the objectively best move ; one variation arising from which may be unobvious because it involves a disregard of conventional values. You, who have not anticipated this, now find that your opponent had a strong move that you thought was not available, if indeed you thought about it at all. The move need not necessarily be sacrificial, but in so called traps it usually is. If, on looking at it, you find that you can refuse your opponent's sacrifice and have a very good game, then his move probably only amounted to a trap ; and he was playing bad Chess, because he was playing the man not the Board. Needless to say, if your opponent's sacrifice can be accepted to your advantage, then he has simply made an unsound sacrifice. Perhaps his position was bad and he was trying to bluff. Perhaps on the other hand. he was just playing badly.

A good example of the kind of play that is conventionally, and inaccurately, called a trap, is known to Chess players as " The Sea-Cadet " because in the operetta which bears that name these moves were executed by living Chess men.

	White	*Black*
1.	P to K4.	P to K4.
2.	Kt to KB3.	P to Q3.
3.	B to B4. More vigorous is 3. P to Q4, met by 3. . . . Kt to Q2. 4. P × P P × P in White's favour.	P to KR3. A very bad move. Moves of the Rook's Pawn for the purpose that animated this move (to prevent Kt to Kt5) are known as " provincial moves." Kt to Kt5 might, indeed, be the answer to Kt to KB3. But B to K2, followed by Kt to KB3 is good developing play.

White	*Black*
4. Kt to B3.	B to Kt5. A move which at this early stage is aimless—apart from the fact that the player of it missed the reply which this move allows. He intended to tie down White's Knight and is very surprised to discover that this very attempt enables the White Knight to move profitably.
5. Kt × P. A move made possible by Black's last, in conjunction with Black's inferior development. If the Pawn captures the Knight, White has Q × B, showing a profit of a Pawn. The capture of the Queen is bad because of what follows in the main line.	B × Q.
6. B × P Ch.	K to K2
7. Kt to Q5 Mate.	

Now a good commentary on the above play is afforded by the following lines where the same idea is available for White but is not so good—in fact the move loses.

White	*Black*
1. P to K4.	P to K4.
2. Kt to KB3.	P to Q3.
3. B to B4.	Kt to QB3. Obviously better than the provincial move.
4. 0–0. Not the most vigorous.	B to Kt5. Better than in the previous game. While not the best move, this pressure on the Knight is more useful now that White has Castled than it would be otherwise.
5. P to Q3. Quite good.	Kt to KB3.
6. Kt to QB3. Not the best. Better would be B to K3, allowing the Queen's Knight the option of Q2 in order to guard the King's Knight.	Kt to Q5. A good move, made possible by White's last, but not fatal. It creates some inconvenience for White on the King's side. White now requires to play very carefully in order to prevent a disadvantage from becoming a loss.
7. B to KKt5. Not the best. It is only reasonable on the assumption that here, and on the next move, White is expecting his opponent to play bad moves. This may be because White does not see the alternatives clearly ; or it may be that he is playing the man—setting a trap. Correct was 7. B to K3.	P to KR3. Good, but not the best—if this move were not reasonably good in itself it might be said to be setting a trap for the trapper. It is, however, a fairly good move, because, if the White Bishop retreats, Black has gained a tempo for a Pawn move which in this type of position may be useful. If White takes the

White	Black
	Knight with the Bishop the Black Queen recaptures, with a winning attack on White's King's side. (Mate, or the gain of the Queen is threatened in the next few moves.) The text gives Black the advantage.
8. Kt × KP. The Sea-Cadet out of his depth. If Black takes the Queen, there follows, of course, B × P Ch., K to K2, Kt to Q5 Mate. Very pretty, but in Chess prettiness is not enough. White has overlooked or ignored a simple answer in his preparation of this move.	Best, however, was B × Kt, followed by Q to Q2. P × Kt. With advantage. Evidently White can do nothing. If Q × B, Kt × Q, B × Q, R × B and Black is a Piece to the good. If, instead, B × Kt, B × Q, B × Q, R × B, R × B, Kt × BP and Black holds considerable positional advantage.

The above example shows at once the possibilities that exist in Chess for disregarding the obvious formal values of the Pieces, and it also shows that that in turn is insufficient. What is necessary is clear vision of all the sequences, including moves which would be unexpected to conventional players ; also moves which can be unexpected to unconventionally-minded players.

Here is a well-known opening variation with a move that may be described as a trap rather than an objectively good move.

White	Black
1. P to K4.	P to K4.
2. Kt to KB3.	Kt to QB3.
3. B to B4.	Kt to Q5. Clever, but not good. The correct answer to it is probably P to QB3 with gain of tempo. But Black has given White a scope for error.
4. Kt × P. A mistake.	Q to Kt4. Unexpected, because it ignores a threat, and illustrative of the Queen's power to make two divergent attacks.
5. Kt × BP. A desperate effort to win some material. B × P Ch. is no better because after K to Q1, White simply has another piece misplaced. Possibly 5. Kt to Kt4 allowing Black to play P to Q4 is the best of many evils. White may emerge with 2 Pawns for a Piece.	Q × KtP.
6. R to B1. Forced.	Q × KP Ch.
7. B to K2.	Kt to B6. Mate. Another interesting example of Smothered Mate.

Now, in that line of play, we saw that Kt to Q5, though clever, was not really good because P to QB3 deprives it of all point and gains time for the opponent. There is, however, one opening variation where this move Kt to Q5 is a good move.

White	*Black*
	P to K4.
1. P to K4.	Kt to QB3.
2. Kt to KB3.	B to B4.
3. B to B4.	

4. P to QKt4. The Evans Gambit, a famous opening of British invention, which allows a Pawn to be captured in exchange for gain of tempo. Many brilliancies emerged from this opening in the 19th century. It gives a hard and interesting game to both sides.

    B to QKt3. Declining the Gambit. Although there is much to be said for accepting the Gambit and fighting to retain the Pawn, the text, favoured by Dr. Lasker, is undoubtedly a safe line.

5. P to Kt5. Apparently forcing the gain of a Pawn (KP).

    Kt to Q5.

Now, if White plays Kt × KP, he falls victim to the disaster that starts with Q to Kt4.

The difference between Kt to Q5 in this variation and Kt to Q5 in the previous example is that here Kt to Q5 is an eminently reasonable move to save the Knight, and possibly to exchange Knights without loss of tempo, because White has used two tempi to get his Queen's Knight's Pawn up to Knight's fifth, where it is not very useful.

It may be mentioned, also, that whereas a player will think twice about taking the Pawn that is offered to him in the variation that we call the trap, he will find the danger harder to see when the move Kt to Q5 has some obvious other reason such as escaping from capture. Psychologically, the point of a sacrifice is hard to see when the player to whom it is offered thinks that his opponent is being compelled to give up the Pawn or Piece as the case may be. This fact does not amount to an encouragement to disguise one's traps, but as a warning to look for concealed dangers in lines that appear to be nothing more than logical. It is easy to be misled by the obvious "reason" for a move. What matters about a move is its consequence. The player who can see the unexpected consequence in the midst of logical processes may be said to have imagination.

Traps, in general, do not need learning. Most of them amount to short clear variations.

E.g. In the Lopez it requires little skill not to fall into the Noah's Ark Trap.

White	*Black*

After—

P to K4.	P to K4.
Kt to KB3.	Kt to QB3.
B to Kt5.	P to QR3.
B to R4.	P to Q3. Steinitz Deferred.
5. P to Q4 is only playable as a Gambit, because after—	
5. . . .	P to QKt4.
6. B to Kt3.	Kt × P.
7. Kt × Kt.	P × Kt.
8. Q × P. Loses a Piece.	

viz:

8. . . .	P to QB4.
9. Q to Q5.	B to K3.
10. Q to B6 Ch.	B to Q2.
11. Q to Q5.	P to B5.

—a short and easy range of moves.   Or in the Albin Counter Gambit,

White	*Black*
1. P to Q4.	P to Q4.
2. P to QB4.	P to K4.
3. P × KP.	P to Q5.
4. P to K3 is unwise, because of 4 . . .	B to Kt5 Ch.
5. B to Q2.	P × KP.
and then if:	
6. B × B.	P × BP Ch.
7. K to K2.	P × Kt (making a Kt) Ch.

The reader may also be reminded of the variations given in the paragraph on Gambits.   There is nothing in these that normal vision should find opaque.

For the rest, it should be obvious that traps, properly or improperly so called, are not peculiar to the opening.   If the reader will refer back to the Fenton and Potter ending, he will appreciate that if, in that line of play, White promotes to a Queen, he is falling into a trap of sorts.   That actually happened in the game.   It was Lasker who discovered the winning move.   But, as has been pointed out, where Black's play is the best in any event (as here) the word trap is out of place.   More consciously a trap is the effort to procure a Stalemate in the following position where the player with the inferior force does not adopt the logical defence, which, as it happens, fails, but plays so as to give his opponent an opportunity for an error that is not hard to make.   Traps of this type, whether coincident with the best play, or justified by desperation, are the only traps that a good player can be said to set. The proper Chess attitude is that one makes the move that is most adequate in the light of all variations.

(BLACK)

(WHITE)

A TRAP
In answer to 1. R to R8 Ch. Black's normal move is K to B2, which, however, loses. He therefore tries 1. ... K to R2. If, then 2. P = Q, R × Q. 3. R × R gives Stalemate.

White's best plan is:

1. K to R4.
2. P to Kt4.
3. P to B5.

LEARNING TO SEE.

The reader has now been shown a great number of clevernesses. He may have observed that some of these are, if not exactly similar to, yet suggestive of others. Ideas echo each other. The next diagram for example shows a different manoeuvre from the Bernstein-Kotov cleverness in Chapter II ; but the suggestion is that a player who has experienced a manoeuvre of one type will be ready to apprehend cognate ideas. Study, from examples, and more particularly by experience in play, of the peculiar geometry of the Chess Board makes one familiar with it ; and, given a general factor of perspicacity, the student can become adept at recognising and appreciating the unexpected possibilities. Hard concentration will also bring into being a certain receptivity and at that stage the player will find himself seeing ideas quite a long way ahead.

About the long variations that the reader has seen, there should be no despair. Very few pieces of Chess are as difficult as the Tarrasch Trap. Moreover not all games of Chess involve the same degree of strain. Some games are less combative than others, less closely contested at all stages, less dependent for their outcome on fine points finally perceived. We shall see more of this aspect of the Chess mind in later

Chapters. Meanwhile let it be said that since the processes of Chess are always rational, always explicable, there is nothing, even in the cleverest moves, to make them the prerogative of genius. Or, to put it another way, genius in Chess is not a revelation of mysteries, but a degree of clarity; achieved, as the saying goes, by perspiration as well as inspiration. To regard Chess vision as the manifestation of an innate faculty is to make the error of confusing the simple with the easy,

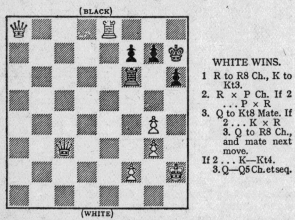

(BLACK)

(WHITE)

WHITE WINS.

1 R to R8 Ch., K to Kt3.
2. R × P Ch. If 2 ...P × R
3. Q to Kt8 Mate. If 2 ...K × R 3. Q to R8 Ch., and mate next move.
If 2 ... K—Kt4. 3. Q—Q5 Ch. et seq.

the logical with the innate. The mind does not work as directly as its mature capacities seem to indicate. To think that it does, whether in Chess or other processes, is to forget about the variety of forces that underlie the surface of the waterfall.

CHAPTER IV

INTRODUCTION TO STRATEGY AND TECHNIQUE

[The reader is advised to read this chapter in conjunction
with the Illustrative Games]

Obviously a great number of games of Chess are lost by
accident (gross oversight), or by mistake (e.g., the failure to see
a tactical point). And obviously there are many degrees of
error ranging from blunders, through failures of anticipation,
to the failure to discover some really fine, subtle possibility
or method of exploitation available to one side or the other.
At the higher level, one is inclined to say not that a player
has lost through a mistake, but that he has been outplayed
by an opponent whose interpretation of the positions that
arose in the game was better, and whose control of an intrac-
table material was subtler.

Even at that stage, it must be remarked that not all errors
lose. A normal game of Chess very rarely amounts to one
single movement of exploitation. The attack ebbs as well as
flows ; advantages are held and wrested. If that is so, then
why is it predictable, as it is, that the better equipped Chess
player will almost invariably win against the less well equipped,
even at a level where not many mistakes of tactics are likely
to be made ?

One answer consists in a type of error that we have not so
far considered, the strategic error—or, at a higher level, the
failure of one player to control a game dominated and made
difficult by the superior strategy of his opponent. Thus when
we find a position such as we have in the next diagram where
White can win easily, breaking open the position with B × RP, it
is clear that the whole method of play of one of the players
has been better than that of the other. It may conceivably
be the result of a long series of tactical manoeuvres, but it is
more likely that Black's idea of his method of defence has
been generally wrong, rather than that he has made particular
oversights.

In the companion diagram the situation is different. White
is attacking his opponent's King's side with a formidable
array of Pieces, but Black's position is well integrated and
tenable. It is evident that in order to accumulate material
for the attack White has allowed Pawns to be taken—he

WHITE WINS

B × RP

If 1. ... Kt × B
    2. R × KtP.
if 1. ... P × B.
    2. R × Kt Ch.
if 1. ... B × R.
    2. B to B4 Dis. Ch.

INSUFFICIENT ATTACK.

KB to B5 is met by Kt to Kt5.

sacrificed them for what may have seemed gains of tempo—but the expenditure has been ill advised, because when the attack is beaten off the opponent will have a superior endgame. Here again the strategy of one player has been better than that of the other. Of course he had to see a lot of specific tactical points well in advance. As has been said above, tactics and strategy are not separable. The coefficient of strategy runs through series of tactical manœuvres. But given a general plan which is sound, a general framework or layout of the game which is adequate to the processes, then one is not likely easily to become the victim of the kind of attack shown in the first diagram, or of the illusion of attack shown in the second diagram. It is also clear from the diagrams that the question is not one of being on the aggressive or being on the defensive. Both policies can be right and both policies can be wrong. It may be a good strategic decision to prepare an attack; it may equally be a good strategic decision to invite the attack. The question is particularly likely to arise when a tactical operation is being considered. Thus it may be wise to seize a Pawn and endeavour to hold it (or the equivalent) in the teeth of attack; or it may be fatal to do so. Sometimes that decision can be arrived at through clear analysis of all the variations. Sometimes it is a decision made mainly on general principles. But whether it is made for tactical reasons, or made on general principles, it is a strategic decision, because it governs the general pattern of the game as well as the tactical possibilities.

The next two diagrams show the different consequences

(BLACK)

(WHITE)

MIESES—THOMAS.
Black plays R x P and loses.

that can follow Pawn-winning excursions. The first is from a game between that famous attacking player Mieses, and Sir George Thomas, one of the leading English Masters of his day. In the diagram position (arising from the Scotch opening) White has the kind of initiative that is normal in the King's Pawn attacks, but Black is sufficiently well co-ordinated not to fear any disaster. However, in order to acquire something out of the opening, so as to compensate for the slight inferiority of general development, or acting in the belief that he had nothing to fear, Black played 10. . . . R × P ignoring the superstition of the fatality that attaches to the QKtP. Also the move has some tactical point, because if White replies 11. Kt to R4 Black has the following pretty piece of play 11. . . . Kt × BP, 12. R × Kt, B × R Ch. 13. K × B, R to Kt5, forking two Pieces and probably winning. However, White had other ideas, and the play went as follows :—

White	*Black*
10. . . .	R × P.
11. Kt to K2. En route for Q4.	P to KR4.
12. Q to B1.	R to QKt1. Perhaps inferior to R to QKt3.
13. P to QB3. White has judged that he can afford time to prepare.	B to Q2. In answer to the threat to the QBP, which will arise whether the Kt is left on Q4 or exchanged.
14. Kt to Q4.	Kt to R3. To protect the square KB4—which White may wish to occupy. Note that for the last few moves Castling has been dangerous for Black, because the Knight could always be driven to R3 and captured. Note the tremendous effect that is flowing from 12. Q to B1.
15. R to K1.	K to B1. Endeavouring to escape.
16. P to K6. A typical " break ing-up " move. It would have been better for Black to play 15 . . . B × Kt, followed by B to K3, blockading this dangerous Pawn. But then his Queen side Pawns would rapidly have fallen without compensation.	
16. . . .	P × P.
17. Kt × P Ch.	B × Kt.
18. R × B. A heavy Piece, using the open lines, is now in the attack. Black's open file is irrelevant.	Q to Q2. A desperate effort to stop the immediate gain of a Pawn (at least) by B × Kt ; also the move defends the QBP.
19. R × Kt. Sometimes the Exchange does not matter to a good player.	P × R.
20. B × P Ch.	K to K1.

White	*Black*
21. Q to B4. A beautiful quiet move bringing the Rook into play. Not every move in an attack has to be Check.	Q to K3. The only move to save material. B to Q3, e.g., would lose the Rook in two moves by B to Kt6 Ch., etc. The next move holds everything for a very short moment and actually threatens to win a Piece.
22. Q × P. Very fine. If in reply R to QB1, then B to Kt6 Ch. picks up two Rooks.	B × P Ch. Ingenious but inadequate. White is not obliged to take the Bishop and expose his King to R to Kt7 Ch.
23. K to R1.	R to Kt7. As good as any. If R to Q1, B to KKt5 is fatal.
24. B to KKt5. Threatening Q to Kt7 followed by B to Kt6. Notice that Q to B2 for Black is met now by B to Kt6, a pretty pin.	K to B1.
25. R to KB1. Immobilizing another Black Piece and, indeed, Black's entire force. Among other things B to R4 is threatened.	K to Kt1. Unpinning the Bishop.
26. B to B1. A very pretty clearance of a square that may be required for the Queen.	R × RP. The only move that does not lose the Bishop. R to K7 fails after a series of Queen Checks.
27. Q to Q8 Ch.	K to Kt2.
28. Q to Kt5 Ch.	K to B2.
29. B to K3.	Q to B3.
30. Q × Q Ch.	K × Q.
31. B to Q4 Ch. Resigns.	

It is not claimed that Black's capture of the Knight's Pawn on move 10 made this debacle inevitable. But clearly Black was involved thereafter in difficulties. Had he succeeded in solving all his problems and surviving the attack without surrendering material, then Black could have claimed that the strategic decision was right. In view of what happened (the process was logical in a high degree) it may be said that the strategic decision was wrong. It was not so much a failure to see, because the distance was too far for normal Chess vision : it was rather a wrong choice of terrain, an ill-advised invitation to combat ; in other words a wrong strategic decision.

The next diagram shows a position from the second game between Lasker and Marshall, in which Lasker captures a Knight's Pawn and holds off the ensuing attack. That may have been an act of vision by Lasker, who, in his day, was capable of seeing very great lengths of tactical process. But however the decision was arrived at, it illustrates the possibility that the capture of a Knight's Pawn can in some settings be a good decision. If and when the tactical consequences are not immediately discernible, the decision has to be a strategic one. Again it is a decision to invite combat, or not to invite it, in a particular situation. That is typical of strategy as distinguished from tactics.

(BLACK)

(WHITE)

**LASKER—
MARSHALL**

White goes in for Q to Kt4 Ch., winning K Kt P, but after R to KKt1 (forcing Q to R6) survives the attack.

The next diagram shows the revenge of Thomas against Mieses, a decade later. This is less spectacular, but

(BLACK)

(WHITE)

MIESES—THOMAS.

21. ... Q to R6 puts pressure on White's centre while he is attacking the King's side.
22. KR to K2, R × P.
23. P × R, Q × B, breaks up White's game.

There followed:

24. P to Q5, Q × BP.
25. P × P, P × P.
26. R × P, B to B4 Ch.
27. K to R1, Q to KKt5, with great advantage.

illustrates the exploitation of a wrong strategic decision. Mieses has committed himself to a King side attack. Thomas demonstrates that this was insufficient justification for leaving certain gaps in the position.

THE FUNCTION OF STRATEGY

Strategy is hard to define, because, as we have seen, the Chess player cannot divide his activities with a clear cut separation between the strategic and the tactical. The strategic decision is hard to abstract from specific lines of play, because no player is content to make a move on the strength of a general principle—if indeed there are any general principles concrete enough to be useful in Chess. It follows that strategy in abstraction is vague; and the word is only meaningful to the player who has used his vision and found that vision is not enough.

At this stage the student will have discovered, from his experience of the Board, that vision in Chess is restricted by more than human stupidity. The reader has seen enough to realise that good players are not likely to exhaust the Board in their tactical analyses, because the nature of the Board is such that lines of play are apt to end in, or pass through, positions which are either too hard to analyse, or else seem not to require analysis. Psychologically, the foreground of clear vision fades into, is indeed suffused in parts by, the hazier blend of seeing and thinking which is judgment. The effort of concentration gives perhaps a wrong impression of the clarity of the human mind. As the limits of concentration are reached one becomes conscious that the mind economises its efforts; indeed, that its operations are never as simple as they appear to be when clarity is achieved. When this is realised, then one appreciates that there is scope for, and there takes place, in Chess, activity other than, though impossible to isolate from, what we call pure vision. If any thought can be stated in general terms to help or guide vision, then that guidance gives us strategy to reinforce our tactics.

This aid is necessary, because of the difficulties of the Board, and because so often it would be wasted labour to try and work further through a position where one is reasonably satisfied that there is no danger, or too much danger, in that position, or that progress thereafter will be easy, or too difficult, as the case may be. And nearer to any immediate move there is scope for thinking, judging, and applying strategic notions in positions where clear tactical processes are not yet available. One function at least of strategy is that it equips a player to know what to do when there is nothing immediate to be done. Then one prepares ; then one " over-protects " points likely to require defence later on ; then one has regard to the general shape of the game ; and the strategian differs from the unstrategic player in that he does not, at such a point, endeavour to force processes into the game for which the position is insufficiently developed, or is otherwise inadequate. Whereas the tactician knows what to do when there is something to do, it requires the strategian to know what to do when there is nothing to do.

Strategy, of course, has always existed in Chess and been known to good players. The difference between the players of today and previous generations of Chess players is that now the scope of strategy is known to be wider.

What may be called primitive, or elementary, strategy consists mainly in playing with a view to the endgame ; thinking of the general frame of the game as constituted by the Pawn position, and so playing that the tactical efforts shall not result, after conflict, in a hopeless endgame. Modern players have more experience of the endgames, and of the methods and technique that the Masters have perfected. Consequently their appraisal of the endgame from a distance is better. But the difference is one of degree. Where the modern player is mainly superior is in his appreciation of the strategy of the earlier game, the opening and the early middle-game attack.

In the middle nineteenth century, when the Chess world was rich in players of great vision and tactical genius, this strategy of the early game was relatively unnoticed. It existed in a degree, but was particularly hard to isolate, or think about, because, in the kind of game that was played then, with rapid attacks succeeding through great gains of tempo achieved by sacrifice, or through the unbalancing of the position, the strategic skill that was required went naturally, and unobserved, with the capacity for gaining tempo, for achieving an unbalance, and for exploiting these things brilliantly. In that kind of play, the play of the more violent King's Pawn openings, the kind of development that was necessary was always seen as tactical necessity. Only when a greater number of players achieved tactical experience of a high order did the Chess world become aware of other factors in the game. It was the success of Steinitz against the more brilliant Anderssen and Zukertort that made the Chess world strategy-conscious.

SOME PRINCIPLES OF STRATEGY

The first principle of opening and middle-game strategy laid down by Steinitz illustrates excellently well what strategy is. This is the principle of the necessity for adequate development. The principle is that, given the capacity on the part of the players to see what is going on tactically over a reasonably good range, so that they do not make oversights, then tactical operations depend for their ultimate success upon the adequacy of preparation or development. The player whose Pieces are relatively well developed in comparison with his opponent's Pieces is more likely to succeed in an attack than his opponent, and much less likely to fail, when attacked, in achieving a satisfactory defence.

This is really a principle of causation. It amounts to the proposition that there are no miracles in Chess. The majority of successful and devastating attacks that appal their victims and dazzle the spectators are not thunders from a clear sky. It is a condition of their coming into being that adequate forces are available to be used. That does not mean that there should be plenty of Pieces lying about the Board. The Pieces must be functionally well placed ; and, incidentally, modern theorists have improved upon Steinitz by achieving a better notion of development ; effective placing rather than bringing the Pieces away from the back rank. A Piece on the back rank may be functionally better developed than a Piece in the centre of the Board. But, that being said, Steinitz was clearly right. If your Pieces are not adequately mobilised, then you cannot reinforce any expedition that you send out ; nor can you organise, when called upon, your own defence. This principle is easier to adopt in theory than to act upon in practice. The following short line illustrates the facility and speed with which a player who sees some of the tactical points of the game can be led by his ideas into disastrous ventures.

	White	*Black*
1.	P to K4.	P to K4.
2.	B to B4.	KKt to B3.
3.	P to Q4.	P to QB3. Not a good move. It aims at over ambitious play in the centre.
4.	P × P.	Kt × P.
5.	Kt to K2.	Kt × BP. Greedy. Of course the King does not re-take because of Q to R5 Ch. ; but there is a very good alternative.

	White	*Black*
6.	O–O.	Kt × Q. A mistake. Necessary was B to B4, to which White can reply with B × P Ch. with advantage. The conclusion of the game is an object lesson in the unwisdom of a tactical excursion from an undeveloped position.
7.	B × P Ch.	K to K2.
8.	B to KKt5 Mate.	

A worse tactician than the opponent of the late Captain Mackenzie (the brilliant blind player who was White in this short game) would not have fallen into such trouble. A better strategian could never have allowed himself to embark on such a venture, however clear or obscure his vision of tactical possibilities. But if the reader will refer to the chapter of illustrative games he will find a more surprising example, where the great strategian himself, no less than Steinitz, suffered, at the hands of the English Master Bird, the consequences of departure from his own principles. Steinitz, a brilliant tactician himself, was capable of the kind of Chess in which the coefficient of strategy seems almost to disappear (see his game against Von Bardeleben among the illustrative games) and was capable of being misled into the pursuit of clever tactical possibilities, in disregard of his own teaching.

And here let it be explained that the principle of development is not a sort of copy book rule ; nor did Steinitz, in stating it, invent something new. There were great players before, and after, Steinitz, players like Morphy and Capablanca, whose command of the Board was so great that their development was always adequate. To suppose from this that they acted upon rules is to make the mistake which Macaulay ridicules, of supposing that great orators build their speeches on the rules of grammar and rhetoric. The rules are regulative principles, laboriously extracted by analysts from their study of the great performances. What Steinitz imported into Chess was a discipline, and himself was sufficiently great a player at times to dispense with it, yet not great enough to do so with impunity.

SPECIFIC PRINCIPLES

The principle of development being stated, it still remains a question how to develop. Here too, Steinitz's researches have been of the greatest utility. He laid it down that the essence of a good development is control of the centre. Lasker put the matter epigrammatically when he commented on a certain game that "this player is not well developed enough in the centre to be able to attack on the wings". And the converse was proved true by Steinitz, when, repeatedly in his match with Zukertort, he allowed his opponent to accumulate forces against his castled King, while himself engaged in other undertakings (the creation of weaknesses elsewhere in his opponent's position) knowing that his centralised forces would be adequate to beat off his opponent's eventual onslaught. Zukertort, be it mentioned, was sufficient of a strategian to appreciate the aggressive merits of the centre, (see his game v. Blackburne), but he tended to underestimate its defensive possibilities.

Modern theory and technique have modified and subtilised the conception of the centre ; but it remains true that a sound centre, of whatever type, is a safeguard for the wings. Thus, if you have a Knight situated at Q4, you are proof against the Greek gift sacrifice, the point being that the Knight can return to KB3 to control R7. That same Knight can work its way via K2, or KB5 to KKt3, in case the attack is upon the Knight's Pawn. Similarly a Queen at Q4 enjoys a big defensive range. So does a Bishop on Q3. There are usually squares to which these Pieces can go in order to defend wings. Moreover from the centre they can counter-attack the wings. And, again, a good centre means that the opponent's manœuvring space is limited, either because the holder of the centre is containing most of the opponent's forces in the opponent's half of the Board, or because, when the centre is blocked, the opponent cannot penetrate the closed lines. Then squares like KB4, QB4, etc., are good outposts for defensive and counter aggressive Pieces.

Now once the fact is grasped that reasonably good positions with well centralised Pieces cannot be stormed, then the tactician has to abandon his ideas of quick mating attacks, and must seek other objectives. The slow penetration of the centre is one such objective ; e.g., the pushing through of a Pawn to K5 or Q5 with threats, and the opening up of diagonals. Similarly the establishment of Knights on good squares from which they cannot be driven, is a good purpose to play for. K5 is a good point , K6 or Q6 even better if the Knight stationed there can be held in position.

Other objectives are the obtaining of open files for Rooks. If a Rook controls an open file it becomes very useful in the middle-game, and can be very destructive in the endgame. And there are lesser objectives of importance. Steinitz, and his pupil and conqueror Lasker, were exponents of the aggregation of minute advantages. These advantages might consist in such small matters as the doubling of opponent's Pawns, the isolation of Pawns, the acquisition of a little extra mobility for a Piece, etc. For these they campaigned tactically, leaving the major attack to wait, in the belief that after minor advantages had been acquired the major attack was more likely to be successfully carried out.

Again let it be made clear that Master play is not so slow that laborious undertakings at great length for small advantages occupy the whole of the play. The game is so well integrated that the major attack is always in contemplation. But the logic of the game now is that the attacker's threats include positional movements as well as attacks on Pieces and Pawns; and the defender is more conscious of the concessions he may be making in moving Pawns. Consequently, more then ever now, the Pawn structure is important; and the possibilities of the endgame are more constantly present to the majority of players than they were. It follows that only a player who is convinced that his middle-game attack is going to succeed, for strategic and tactical reasons, will disregard the endgame. On the other hand the game is too dynamic for players not to compromise their endgame framework. On the same reasoning a player cannot hope to control every stage of the game, holding only strategic advantages, and having no strategic defects. Players must accept as a postulate of the game the belief that advantage sets off advantage. There is a principle of compensation in Chess. You may have a Bishop against a Knight; on the other hand you may have some Pawn weaknesses. You have an open file; your opponent also has an open file. Tactically you must see whether or not you can achieve some exploitation, or can be the victim of some exploitation; but failing the perception of these things, you must be content if the disadvantages are shared.

Most players achieve a feeling for the balance of the position. This helps to form the judgment. One knows whether one has lost time relatively to one's opponent. One knows, or judges, whether one is generally more restricted or less restricted in movement than one's opponent. If both sides are not wasting time, i.e., not going in for manoeuvres that are irrelevant to the progress of the game, or not letting themselves be forcibly retarded in development, by the awkward placing of Pieces; and if one's own development and one's own power of movement, and one's own few technical advantages, seem to be not less than one's opponent's and not more, then there is in being a balance of position which means that the issue of the game is still open. And on consideration, it is logical, in the light of the margin of draw described in the first chapters, to expect that two sets of forces interpenetrating should bring about and maintain a permanent, though unstable, equilibrium.

When the forces are seriously unbalanced in favour of one side, then there is victory. Thus, given a bigger control of space and a saving of tempo, and no noticeable defect in material, you are justified in expecting to win the game by the exercise of reasonable pressure. A great many Chess victories are strategically explicable in those terms. One player has his forces well organised, mobile, with plenty of squares at his disposal; the other has not used his time so well. His Pieces are cramping each other, are short of space ; and he has too many difficulties of development, for purely defensive purposes, to be able to establish any kind of attacking formation. But in a well balanced game it will probably be the case that each player is exerting some pressure against his opponent. If the strategy has been wise, and the tactical play equally good, it is improbable that either side can achieve anything decisive. Then, as material gets exchanged, the game may resolve itself into a Pawn endgame, where each side has to prevent the other from promoting Pawns, or when, alternatively, neither side can be prevented from promotion. Results as far ahead as this are hard to predict in the middle-game ; but in general good Chess produces a large percentage of draws.

Victories are achieved in good Chess when the unbalance proves to be decisive, either in the middle-game or the endgame. Very fine points indeed may be sufficient to make a middle-game attack decisive. There may just be available a combinative possibility, which is either carried out, or which, being apprehended by the opponent, compels him to abandon his own projects in order to defend. Then he will have lost time, and his position will be relatively disintegrated. Similarly a very fine point may determine whether the endgame into which the position ultimately resolves itself gives winning chances to one side or the other. On the whole, it may safely be said that if there are winning chances, either in the middle-game or the endgame, it will be because better tactics and/or better strategy have given one player a better control of the total situation. If in the play neither opponent has missed any important tactical point, and if neither player has allowed the other to consolidate any really dangerous strategic advan-

tage—i.e., if neither position suffers a serious weakening—
then a draw should be the result.

In the old days when players relied more on their capacity
to exploit a slight gain of tempo or a slight advantage in space,
then the typical battle was of the Anderssen-Dufresne—
or (better balanced) the Zukertort-Blackburne type (see illustrative games). Each player was planning something and
carrying it out. The winner was he whose plan could be carried
out the more quickly. That kind of Chess is also played to-day,
for the reader must appreciate that in every period the styles
and talents of players differ, and even at a more advanced
stage players recapitulate in their own development, and as
part of the development of the Chess world, stages typical of
earlier periods ; and always, of course the tactical possibilities
may cause any player to depart from the accepted strategy of
his period. But allowing for all that, it may be said that the
modern player does not embark so easily on his own attack in
disregard of his opponent's attack. There tends to be a better
general preparation of the whole position ; and the result
usually is that neither side achieves a striking preponderance
early in the game. When battle is joined it is because one
player or the other is determined to complete his development,
to make himself free, to occupy a square important in the
integration of his game. Then the attack and counter-attack
is likely to flare up.

Again the old game was more combative in that players
were not only ready to embark on attack quickly, but they
were also prepared to face an attack in order to hold sacrificed
material. That was a strategy of sorts ; and the strategy of
the more cautious players of the older period was to prevent
themselves from being attacked. That method was apt to
provide advantages, as well as to create dangers, for the good
attacking player. Nowadays, strategic experience makes most
players chary of undergoing a heavy sacrificial attack in order
to maintain the material sacrificed. But they will defend
themselves against an attack of reasonable weight in exchange
for very slight compensating advantages, if they are satisfied
with their general development. That is part of the tendency
to attack and to defend, in order to achieve or maintain the
smaller advantages. And this again is part of the general
recognition that in good Chess overwhelming victories cannot
be expected ; that the game is a war rather than a single
battle. With that goes the recognition of the Steinitzian
truth that what matters in the long run is the framework of
the game. Defects in the Pawn structure that seem slight

in the middle game bring about defeat in the end game more certainly than an aggressive formation brings about victory in the middle game. What may be added to this is that the framework of the game, even in the middle-game, is more of a factor in victory than the capacity to produce clever tactical threats which, if seen by the opponent, can be refuted. An excellent example of victory, through the better placing of Pawns and Pieces in the frame of the game, is to be found in the game Szabo-Denker in the illustrative games. Some winning attacks can be analysed in order to show that victory followed the lines that a strategian or tactician could expect; the Szabo-Denker game shows victory more consciously and intentionally gained by technique. Even more striking is the game Nimzowitch-Sämisch; while for a more understandable strategy the game Lasker-Alekhine (New York 1924) is hard to improve upon.

TECHNIQUE.

If Steinitz made Chess players conscious of the general physics of Chess, modern Masters have developed its methods of engineering; and in doing that they have also shown the physics of the game to be subtler than was thought by Steinitz's immediate successors. Thus two developments have taken place in Chess in this century. Players have become more conscious of the method of obtaining and holding small advantages. But, more important, they have acquired a better conception of the nature of some advantages and disadvantages. In consequence they have developed important specific methods of playing; methods which are too concrete to be classed as general principles, and yet, since they belong to the frame of the game, are not apprehended the same way as tactical perceptions. They constitute what, for want of a better word, can be called points of technique. Technique is a middle term between strategy and tactics. It cannot be said that modern Chess has become technological. The vision of modern players is too rich for that. But certainly the modern player is better equipped with knowledge of the technical processes of the game, even if he is no more expert than his predecessors in carrying them out.

POINTS OF MODERN STRATEGY AND TECHNIQUE—
THE CENTRE

From the days of Zukertort onwards players have consciously valued the centre. The King's Gambit itself, the most violent of the openings, starts by gaining a better control

of the centre; and Zukertort saw the possibilities of the
Queen's Gambit for that purpose. For many years, and at
the opening of the twentieth century (after the death of
Steinitz) the conception of the good centre was the centre held
by one's two centre Pawns. Evidently the unrestrained control of the centre by two Pawns can be very effective. Thus
a King's side attack can be launched by the advance P to K5,
opening a line for the Bishop or Queen against R7, driving
the defending Knight from its KB3, and often allowing the
attacker to sacrifice a Piece on that important square in order
to establish a Pawn there as part of a mating attack, or in
order to open the Knight's file, etc. Similarly, the advance
of a Pawn to Q5 can open another diagonal against the King's

(BLACK)

ATTACK ON THE
CENTRE.

(WHITE)

side and can give difficulties to other defending Pieces. Also
the Pawns can be deadly in a central attack, as in the Bird-
Steinitz example. All this is true. But it is not the whole
of the story. Notice for example that if a Pawn goes to K5 a
defending Piece can occupy its Q4. That may create a diagonal
attack; or a Knight may be able to settle there, and to move
from there to its KB5, K6, QKt5, etc. (Incidentally, these
excursions of Knights are quite a feature of modern opening
play, making the game look wilder than it is.) Similarly, the
advance of the P to Q5 gives the defender a square at his K4.
Now if the possession of two centre Pawns has been achieved
through the exchanging of Pawns so that the player with the
central Pawns is lacking one or two Bishop's Pawns, then the

occupancy of the interstitial square is likely to be permanent. If, on the other hand there are Bishop's Pawns in being, then if they move to drive out, say, an occupying Knight, that Knight can, at KKt5 or QKt5, embarrass Bishops at K3 or Q3 respectively, and can have other attacking chances (against B7, R7, etc.). And it requires a great deal of preparation before this can be prevented. Moreover, moves like P to KR3 and P to QR3 in distant support of the centre may also create weaknesses or lose time.

In other words a centre formidable in appearance can be hollow. Modern openings calculated to exploit the potential hollowness of the centre include the Grunfeld Defence and the King's Indian Defence. These are given in the next

(BLACK)

HOLLOW CENTRE
(Grunfeld's Defence).

(WHITE)

chapter. And it will also be seen that the centre can become hollow in many other openings such as the Moller, the King's Gambit Declined, etc. Conscious of this, many players play slower forms of the Queen's Pawn openings, delaying the pressure on the centre. Then there comes a struggle for K4; and that square may have to be occupied by a Piece, which may be good, or the Pawn on K4 may be blocked by the opponent's P to K4, and that in turn introduces notions that will require to be separately considered.

The idea of blocking the centre is one instance of the general idea of *Blockade*. A dynamic Pawn, that is to say a Pawn that can advance dangerously, like Bird's centre Pawns, or like Steinitz Queen's Pawn which advanced against Von

Bardeleben, or Zukertort's Pawn that advanced to open a diagonal, or a Pawn that can sacrifice itself on a square where it can cause a restriction of the opponent's movement or force the opening of a line, etc., a Pawn like this requires to be blocked. It is important for the opponent to have a

(BLACK)

(WHITE)

NEED FOR BLOCKADE.

If Black does not play B to Q4, P to Q5 gives White an attack and freedom.

Pawn or a Piece (preferably a light Piece) on the square immediately in front of it. That is a Blockade. And the line of thought can be carried further. The blockade of an isolated Pawn is very good preparation for an attack on that Pawn. Otherwise it can advance and sell itself dearly. The modern technician will therefore not hasten to attack an isolated Pawn. If the attack is not immediately decisive he will prepare by putting a Knight or a Bishop on the square in front of it, especially if it is a centre Pawn. Later he will double Rooks behind the Knight, perhaps develop a Bishop on the diagonal of the Pawn. He may even add defences to the square that the blockader is occupying. Later, when the blockader moves, the attack on the isolated Pawn is likely to be decisive.

The notion of blockade, which can be generalised to include the obstruction of the paths of other Pieces (e.g., a chain of Pawns on the same diagonal as a hostile Bishop, or blockade by a Pawn, blocking a diagonal), is very important in Chess—but is particularly relevant to the theory of the Centre. If the opponent's Pawns can be anchored by an interstitial Pawn or Piece, in the position K4Q5, or Q4K5, then though they have their strength, which may be considerable if there is an attack available, yet they also have their weaknesses. They allow the occupancy of the adjacent square on the Bishop's file. Thus, if your opponents Pawns are at Q5 and K4, and you have a Pawn on K4 guarded by a Pawn at Q3, you may be able with the aid of a move like P to QR4 (the tactical effect of which has been seen) to establish a Knight at QB4

(BLACK)

(WHITE)

A STUDY IN BLOCKADE.
Black's Knight and KP are holding White immobilized.
Black wins. B to KR3 wins a Pawn at least.

(BLACK)

(WHITE)

BLOCKADE
The Knight on Q4 blockades the isolated Pawn.

which is a very good square. Also you can break up the centre by an eventual P to KB4, incidentally opening your KB file. You can also break the centre by P to QB3, a well-known method of winding up a hostile Pawn chain. You may create by this a weakness at your Q3. Whether that is bad depends on the position. If P×QBP you may be able to liquidate your own QP by a later advance. If the opponent leaves you to capture, then his advanced Pawn is doing both good and harm to your backward QP, but your KP is then very good and with the aid of P to KB4 you will achieve an aggressive centre. (Break-up points can be on any file.)

(BLACK)

(WHITE)

A BLOCKED
CENTRE
(Favourable to Black)

The blocked centre and the hollow centre are alike vulnerable to Bishops on the long diagonals. In the case of the blocked Pawn or Pawns it is quite surprising that a Bishop behind its own blocked Pawn is nearly as strong as a Bishop directed against a hostile blocked Pawn. Thus suppose you have a Pawn on Q4, and your Bishop on QKt2. If you later manage to place a Pawn or a Knight on K5 and that is captured, your Bishop's diagonal is lengthened and then there may be a tactical operation possible against your KB6. Also there are other ways in which a diagonal is likely to open: exchanges on your QB4, etc. That is one of the reasons why Fianchetto Openings are quite popular. The Bishop's action on the long diagonal can be directly good; but if it is delayed it may also be good; and if the diagonal becomes hopelessly blocked, then the Bishop can find another diagonal.

Incidentally, that involves another feature of modern strategy. The modern player is more apt to recognise when tempo has ceased to be of the essence of the game, i.e., when the position has crystallised and a re-grouping of Pieces is more important than the time consumed in carrying out the re-grouping, and not likely to be penalised. That principle also makes it possible for players to go in for manoeuvres such as the following; allowing the Knight at QB3 or KB3 to be driven back on to the back rank so as to re-emerge in a different direction. Thus, the KKt may go to K1 and emerge at KKt2. The QKt may go to Q1 and then KB2, or back to QKt1 and out via Q2 to K4 or QB4. Modern strategy accepts this process of *Reculer pour mieux sauter*, and it is part of the technical equipment of all good players.

(BLACK)

(WHITE)

A FLUID CENTRE.

Another treatment of the centre that is worth noting is not to try to occupy it with Pawns but to keep a control over it with Bishops and Knights. Typical is the Queen's Indian Defence, or the Nimzo-Indian, in which Black plays Kt to KB3, P to K3, B to QKt5 (pinning the QKt and perhaps exchanging it) then P to QKt3 and B to Kt2, and possibly thereafter Kt to K5 followed by P to B4. Then, even without any blocking movement, the control is a good one. This is a fluid centre for the defender; and of course a centre can be fluid both aggressively as well as defensively.

Aggression usually involves Pawn pressure as well as Piece pressure in the centre. But Nimzowitch has taught the Chess world not to regard Pawns in the centre with Fetichism. Nimzowitch has shown that an attack can be good, particularly against the French Defence, if you allow your Pawn on Q4 to fall, and then allow your Pawn on K5 to be exchanged. All that matters is to have the control of the square K5 by some Piece or other. And that control is very helpful in the mounting of a King's side attack. Of course, it should be added that this, too, can become unimportant in the light of other tactical considerations.

(BLACK)

(WHITE)

A GOOD CENTRE for White's attacking purposes.

In general, then, modern technique, and modern improvements in the strategic equipment, have made a great change in the appearance of the Chess Board during the opening and early middle game. Often the centure is left completely vacant while Fianchetto developments are taking place, and approaches to the centre are made by the Bishop's Pawns before the centre Pawns. Eventually centre Pawns tend to be thrown forward, even if only to be exchanged. But more regard is had to the eventual disposition of Pieces; and Pieces tend to be placed where they are useful functionally, on squares where they have the most scope (not necessarily immediate threats) or where they can exercise a pressure that is relatively permanent. Again, as has been said, modern players do not object to re-grouping. Indeed, in a famous game, Bogoljubow, who had his Bishop on KB1 and Pawn on K3, with an outlet on the diagonal to QR6, played P to KKt3 in order to have his Bishop on the longer diagonal, even though while doing that he enabled his opponent to pin his Knight on KB3 against the Queen, and, generally, seemed to be wasting time. The important thing was the re-grouping and it was one of a series of manœuvres which brought him victory in that game and in an important tournament.

But in case the reader receives any false impression let it be emphasised that, in general, time is too important to use in giving scope for alternative developments. Before you use time like that you must be clear on all the opponent's tactical possibilities.

Tactics are still the essence and reality of the game. Nor do modern developments make tactics less important. What has happened has been the diminution of uncontrolled play characterised by excessive reliance on isolated threats which, however clever, are not sufficient to determine the game if the opponent sees them.

But at the same time the development of strategy involves the need for good tactical equipment, because strategic purposes can involve some quite extraordinary placings of Pieces, giving scope for tactical exploitation and combative Chess. How two sound strategians can find themselves quite early engaged in speculative combat is illustrated in the game between Capablanca and Fine played in the Avro Tournament (see illustrative games). There White has sacrificed a certain amount of King's side development in order to achieve an early strategic advantage (a Rook well placed on the seventh rank). Against this Black finds the only resource—one cannot judge how far ahead he saw it—which introduces combative Chess of a high order. The moral of such a masterly draw is that, given reasonable strategic ground work, then, when the combat is joined, good tactical ability enables the player to do justice to himself, and not to lose against the strongest opposition.

SACRIFICIAL ATTACK IN THE MODERN GAME

Strategic, or technical, Chess does not, be it emphasised, exclude the combative, the speculative, or any tactical process involving vision. Only the approach is different. The modern Chess player tends to think first in terms of the framework of the game.

Typical terms are; Open Lines; Outposts; Strongpoint; Blockade, etc. The analyst, looking at a game in which a brilliant combination has been made, finds that there has been an exploitation of these strategic and technical factors. It does not follow that strategy and technique carry with them the capacity for combination ; but a sound strategy and technique is the condition *sine qua non* for the coming into being of a sound combination. That is true. But if one thinks further, it becomes clear that strategy and technique are terms somewhat too abstract in this context. The open lines that matter, the Outposts that matter, the Strongpoints that matter, the Blockades that matter, these are only determinable in the light of combative and combinative possibilities. (The first Diagram on page 161 affords an excellent example of an aggregate of technical advantages—Black has the open lines that matter.)

There was a stage in Chess when players were content to make sure that they had at least as much space as their opponents. This was the period dominated by the geniuses of Capablanca and Rubinstein, players who could exploit very fine shades of advantage on an open Board, or in an end-game, and of course, showing plenty of combinative ability for the exploitation of their strategic advantages.

Later, under the influence of Tartakower, Reti, Nimzowitch, and Alekhine, the conception of space in Chess was altered, as we have seen. And that a more functional type of play could give excellent results was demonstrated in such a game as Samisch-Nimzowitch (see illustrative games).

But that is not the end of the matter. In the new struggle for position there was a greater interpenetration of positions.

The modern openings can, therefore, lend themselves to highly combative complexes. Before the position is crystallized, so that the time factor ceases to be all important, tempo in the struggle for the attainment of the right structure can be as important as it was in the days when Anderssen and Zukertort were annihilating quite strong opponents. Thus there has been a strange reversion in modern times. After Capablanca had declared that he had made Chess safe for, so to speak, the Chess Proletariat, a generation of players arose to make the game as dangerous as it was before. And the Chess of recent generations has been highly combative. Modern Russian Masters with their flair for interesting experiment have completed the refutation of the belief that the resources of the Chess Board have been exhausted. The last game in this book shows that Capablanca realized this himself

It still remains true, however, that much of the combination and sacrifice that has enriched the æsthetic content of Chess has been occasioned by bad strategy. A player allows his opponent to seize important points, to develop on open lines, to put pressure on the defences without there being counter pressure. Then the resulting attack, however beautiful, may even be unnecessary. The intrusion of ideas effects an economy of longer processes of thought and preparation. To win quickly is better than to win slowly, because it reduces the chances of error due to fatigue. Thus it is quite certain that Morphy would have won his game against Paulsen without the beautiful sacrifice seen in the previous chapter, because, from a strategic standpoint Morphy was much better placed. On the other hand, his process of winning without the sacrifice would have been long and laborious and not easy to ascertain. From another standpoint the combination is part of the game, because, without it, Paulsen's previous move would have done much towards relieving the pressure.

(BLACK)

(WHITE)

ALEKHINE—
GRUNFELD.
CREATIVE CHESS.
28. ... Kt to Q6
29. R × R, Q × R.
30. P to B3, R × Kt.
31. P × P, Kt to B5.
32. P × Kt, Q to B5.
33. Q × Q, R × R Ch.
34. Q to B1, B to Q5 Ch., with Mate next move.
Note, if
31. P × R, B × P Ch.
32. K to B1, Kt to B5.
33. Q × P, Q to B5 Ch.
34. K to K1, Kt × P Ch.
35. K to Q2, B to K6 Ch. etc.

According to modern standards sacrifice in Chess is meritorious when it is the determinant that makes the difference between victory and equality. The sacrifice that matters is that which enables whatever strategic advantage exists to be demonstrated. Indeed, the game may be so close, and the strategy so well balanced, that only rich tactical possibilities make the play of one opponent better than that of the other. Makaganov's victory against Reshevsky and Kotov's win against Yudovitch are excellent examples of this (see illustrative games) and Alekhine has enriched Chess with an Art Gallery of beautiful ideas against opponents who were playing so well that only great subtlety and richness of vision in the stategic tactical complex could have achieved victory. The accompanying examples, showing combinations by Alekhine against Grunfeld and Reti, illustrate excellently the exploitation (if not the creation) of the possibilities that condition victory.

(BLACK)

(WHITE)

ALEKHINE—RETI.
White has allowed P to QB5, although he cannot capture the Rook.
Now comes :
19. B × P. If then P × B.
20. Q × R, B to Kt2.
21. QR to Kt1, Q × R.
22. Q × R Ch., K × Q.
23. R × Q wins.;
and if—
19. ... B to Kt2.
20. Q to K5 Ch., P to B3
21. Q to K7 Ch., etc. It was hard to see this at the stage when Black assumed that White could not allow his Bishop to be imprisoned.

There is no advantage in attempting a classification of combinative exploitations. The reader may, however be reminded of some varieties, of which examples are given in this book. We have seen the exploitation of a wrong decision made in a fairly level game (e.g., in the Mieses-Thomas examples). We have also seen exploitations of many types where a clear advantage, whether in the middle game or end game, already exists. In some cases the combination was necessary in order to exploit (if not create) the advantage ; in other cases it was unnecessary. There may be added to this a reference to the frequency of combinative exploitation of defective opening play. This is particularly likely to arise in two sets of circumstances, both illustrated in the illustrative games. One kind of situation arises when one player plays insufficiently incisively, allowing his opponent to prepare a strong attack (Botwinnik-Vidmar and the Morphy examples). The other, more interesting, situation is when one player plays too compromisingly. The game between Botwinnik and Fine is as good an example as any.

Further, interesting combinative play can take place whenever, at any stage, a player endeavours to do too much, gets out of his depth so to speak. In Chess players are destroyed, not only by decapitation as Von Bardeleben by Steinitz, not only by strangulation, as the Duke of Brunswick by Morphy, but by simple drowning. A good example of this is the game between Alekhine and Sterk—an amusing example of a gallant failure to live up to a name (see illustrative games).

(BLACK)

(WHITE)

CLEVER EXPLOITATION OF AN EXISTENT ADVANTAGE

A WIN BY TARTAKOWER.

1. QB7 Ch., Kt × Q.
2. PK6 Ch., Q × P.
3. KtB5 Ch., KQ1.
4. Kt × Q Ch., KQ2.
5. KtB5 Ch., KQ1.
6. KtKt7 Ch., KQ2.
7. BR3 Ch. wins.

But, more frequent than the actual exploitations, and more important even, are the infinite number of combinations which do not take place. These are the unheard melodies of Chess, the variations that are not played. In an infinite number of Chess positions there are lines of play which can lead to a brilliant exploitation, but, being seen, are avoided. They are part of the tactical strategic complex. A good example is furnished by the position in the game between Makaganov and Reshevsky, where a Queen's sacrifice is contemplated but not actualized. In many games we find clever threats that do not come as near to actuality as this; but their possibility may operate to influence the play over many moves. The onlooker who applauds spectacular moves may never know how near he was to seeing say a Kt's sacrifice on Q5, etc.

Conversely, very often the combination that is played in Chess is a variation that could be avoided. Sometimes, in the best games it is not avoided because it cannot be avoided without some other type of loss developing. Sometimes it is not avoided because it is not seen by the defender. But it is part of the game. It is part, and not the whole. On the other hand it is a much more important part than is believed by those theorists who hold that Chess can be reduced to something like a geometry.

The true approach to Chess is a fusion of the tactical and strategic approaches. One cannot isolate individual lines from the framework, because it is unwise to do so. One cannot isolate the framework from the lines of play because it is impossible to do so. Players looking at the Board are analysing lines of play. When they are playing strategically as well as tactically, their choices of move, and of variations to analyse, are conditioned by their conception of the frame of the game.

(BLACK)

(WHITE)

CLEVER EXPLOITATION OF ADVANTAGE
LEVITSKY— MARSHALL.
Marshall plays Q to KKt6, and wins.

If they are lacking in Chess genius their strategic technical equipment will preserve them from a certain amount of danger. If the strategic equipment is not allowed to thwart the speculative mind, then very fine Chess results. In Chess as in the arts one must not strive after effects, but the difficulties of exploitation can be so great that the mind must always be open to the reception and appreciation of constructive, even brilliant, possibilities.

Various Exploitations of Strategic Advantage

The non-combinative method can be as hard as, if not harder than, the imaginative. Rubinstein was a great master of both kinds of exploitation. The diagrams show situations where neat tactical processes are required to turn the accrued strategic advantage into a win : also a few quieter lines.

(BLACK)

(WHITE)

NEAT CAPTURE

White (Rubinstein) wins.
1. B × P, R (either) × B.
2. R × R, R × R.
3. R × P Ch., K to R4.
4. P to B3 wins.

(BLACK)

(WHITE)

SACRIFICIAL EXPLOITATION.

Black (Rubinstein) cannot play R to KR3, because of Q to K7. Therefore
1. .... P to Q7.
2. Q × P, R to KR3, and Q × Kt Ch. is a fatal threat.
(instead)
If 2. R to Q1 R to QB1 wins.
After 2. Q × P, R to KR3. 3. K to Kt1, Q to Kt6 Ch. 4. K to B1, R × Kt. 5. R × R, B to Q6 Ch. forces a win.

RUBINSTEIN—JANOWSKI.

1. B × RP Ch., K × B.
2. P to Kt6 Ch., K to Kt1.
3. Kt × Kt, P × Kt.
4. P to R6, P to KB3.
5. P × KtP, P × Kt
6. R to R8 Ch., K × P.
7. R to R7 Ch., K to Kt1.
8. Q to B5, P to B6.
9. R × Q wins.

A TACTICAL POINT.

White has played B to Q6 and Black gains advantage with K to B2. After R × RP, R to Q6 and, after K to B2, B to B5, the KBP must fall. Then the Black centre Pawns win.

(BLACK)

(WHITE)

SEIZURE OF ADVANTAGE.

White plays B to Kt3 and Black (Rubinstein) plays P to QKt4, eventually forcing the B at B3 from the defence of Q4.

But by contrast the next diagram shows the same player avoiding what appears to be the most vigorous line and doing a great deal of preparation in order to make his strategic advantage greater.

(BLACK)

(WHITE)

SLOW EXPLOITATION (by Rubinstein).

Not the obvious ... P to QB4 because of 2. P × P, Kt × P 3. P to Q4, P × P. 4. P to K5 and White has a little freedom. Black plays first B to K1!

The style of the soundest Chess Masters tends to consist in the avoidance of a combinative variation except in two sets of circumstances. The first requisite is that it shall be exact and completely reliable. The second requirement is that it shall be necessary. More precisely, if the combination is sound and not necessary, the adoption of it is a matter of style. If, however, the combination constitutes something of a strain on the vision, the professional player tends not to rely on it unless this is the only way of establishing a winning advantage. Of this last type, Rubinstein's com-

(BLACK)

(WHITE)

RUBINSTEIN—
CAPABLANCA.

1. B × Kt, Q × B.
2. Kt × QP, Q to R3.
3. K to Kt2, QRQ1.
4. Q to QB1 wins.
The Knight is miraculously unpinned, and still guarded (by the B).

bination against Capablanca at San Sebastian is noteworthy. There, two far sighted players were involved in an early middle game manoeuvre. Capablanca's very interesting counterplay, or resource, fails against a move which, several moves previously, must have been incredibly difficult to anticipate.

But a great number of games of Chess are won uncombinatively by the nursing of small advantages. Sometimes highly complicated tactical lines have to be considered. On other occasions it is only a question of reasonably logical play and the avoidance of obvious risks.

The next diagram shows an interesting study in the disintegration of a game through the quite clever exploitation by the opponent of a strategic feature. This piece of play, by Keres, shows at once the importance of small strategic features and the skill required in the exploitation; it also shows the emergence, in the middle-game, of endgame considerations.

(BLACK)

(WHITE)

DISADVANTAGE.
White's only advantage is that, owing to the placing of Black's QBP, he is tying Black's Bishop to a short diagonal. It follows that the B. is not a good guard for the Rook. R to QKt1 is played and Black cannot play R × R followed by RQ1. Therefore, a White Rook reaches the 7th rank

TRANSITION TO THE ENDGAME

Possibly the hardest of all phases of Chess occurs at that stage when one has a good position, perhaps with slight material advantage or some space, and it is a question of reducing material, or of some tactical engagements in which material becomes reduced. The most typical transition involves the Pawn chase. Each player with his Rook or Rooks can win one or two of his opponent's Pawns. It can often happen that though you emerge victorious in the Pawn hunt, or without loss, yet your opponent has some compensations. It is particularly important not to leave a compensating advantage on one side of the Board in exchange for an increase in your advantage on the other side of the Board. Thus your opponent's lone Pawn guarded by a Rook can even counter-balance your own united passed Pawns on the other wing. Much of course will depend on the relative position of the Kings; but Kings are surprisingly mobile in the endgame. Rather, then, than liquidate, it is advisable to keep the middle game in being, if you can, and hope that the advantage that ultimately crystallizes will be a solider one, not offset by counter thrusts. The ideal endgame position is one in which only your advantage matters. Then it is a question of forcing the promotion of a Pawn. It can be an advantage then to have blocked Pawns on the other wing, so long as yours are safe. In case you cannot Queen the Pawn that you are working on, you may just gain sufficient tempo in order to win on the other wing after the battle for promotion has caused the disappearance of all other material.

These matters require for their handling a technique of endgame play, which is the subject matter of a later chapter.

Meanwhile the reader is reminded that some at least of the technique and strategy of middle game Chess consists in the accumulation of endgame advantages. These can be hard to assess.

One that is clear is the cutting off of one's opponent King from your own important Pawn or Pawns. If you can emerge into the ending with your own King among the Pawns, and your Rook keeping your opponent's King away, you should win. The defender's task is to bring his King across under cover of the Rook, if he can afford Rook exchanges. If the Pawn is not too far, or if a Pawn that is blocking it occupies time in its removal, this manœuvre can be effected. But in general the cut-off King is an unmitigated disadvantage to the player whose King is the victim.

Other advantages include the superiority of joined Pawns to isolated Pawns facing them. When they are on opposite sides of the Board, the advantage is not so great, because isolated Pawns can hold a King as effectively as joined Pawns. The technique has been shown.

Another well known advantage is present when your opponent has two Pawns held by one of yours. If your Pawn at Q5 holds your opponents at his Q3 and QB2, for example, then he has a bad form of "hanging pawn." There may, however, be a situation where a hanging Pawn has its uses. It can sacrifice itself to remove the Pawn that is obstructing its more advanced companion. Quite a well known endgame situation exists whenever hanging Pawns are obstructed by one Pawn only. If the hanging pawns are blocked by an interstitial Pawn, they are quite strong, because the forward member of them is passed and guarded.

The reader must remember that every Chess construction depends on its context. Groupings of Pieces are ambiguous in their functions. In point is one of the well known Chess advantages, the remote passed pawn. Assume three Pawns facing each other on the King's side with Kings near to them. Now one player has a QBP the other a QRP. The player with the QRP should win, because his opponent's King has to travel further to stop it than his own King has to travel to stop the QBP. Then, when the attack on the Pawn masses comes, the nearer King wins. But to show the difficulty of assessment, Rook-play or a well placed King can offset this advantage. The diagram shows Rubinstein winning against a remote passed Pawn. Similar reflections apply to the " hanging Pawns " (Pawns say at K4Q5, with an interstitial opposition Pawn). This can be a weak formation, because it can be broken up by an undermining of the defending Pawn. On the other hand it can constitute a very strong threat if the forward member of the hanging pawn chain holds the King within the Queening square.

(BLACK)

(WHITE)

BLACK WINS.

40. ... R to R1.
41. R to B3, R to R5.
42. R to Q3 (a typical cramp),
    ... K to K2.
43. K to Kt3, K to K3.
44. K to B3, K to Q4.
45. K to K2, P to Kt4.
46. R to QKt3, P to B3.
47. K to K3, K to B5.
48. R to Q3, P to Q4.
49. K to Q2, R to R1.
50. K to B2, R to R2. (Tempo play.)
51. K to Q2, K to K2.
52. R to B3 Ch., K ×P, and now Black is much better placed and wins.

These matters, be it repeated, are hard to assess. What emerges is the necessity for the player of any middle game to be well equipped for the endgame. Endgame technique is so important that appreciation of it may enable you to choose a winning middle game line which otherwise you would not adopt because of your own uncertainty. The technique of endgame play is sufficiently important to require separate treatment.

PART III

CHESS LEARNING

CHAPTER V

THE GROUND WORK OF THE OPENINGS

The history of the development of Chess is the history of development in Chess. The brilliant players of the middle part of the last century, of whom Morphy was the greatest virtuoso, and Anderssen and Zukertort were great types, were not lacking in any of the capacity for Chess vision that has been possessed by the outstanding players of this century. The only defect in their play consisted in the fact that they were more reliant on vision than are modern players. If one examines their best performances one finds usually that either they won their great victories against bad players—and, incidentally a victory can be brilliant even against a bad player ; or else they won their victories in very unbalanced positions. In point, are efforts like that of Morphy against Isouard, a much weaker player, and that of Anderssen against so strong a player as Kieseritsky. They played openings of a combative type, openings in which the game became quickly unbalanced. Skirmishing was early ; each player endeavoured to force the pace or to force his opponent to commit himself decisively. Such openings included the King's Gambit, the Evans Gambit, the Scotch Gambit and (later) the Max Lange, Moller, etc. And these openings, from which the play is really quite controllable, tended to be played at too fast a tempo. From them players won by achieving more than their opponents anticipated. But often they lost through trying to do too much.

The generation of Steinitz, having perceived the logical principles that could be extracted from the play of such a one as Morphy, proceeded to make Chess self-consciously strategic where previously strategy had been the unexpressed discipline of the best vision. From the end of the nineteenth century onwards the evolution has been logical. First an emphasis on space, rather than time, on mobilization rather than attack ; then, in attack, to play for the centre and lesser objectives rather than, with violences, to attempt to gain considerable material, or bring about mate. Thus we have the period of the Queen's Pawn and the Ruy Lopez, following upon the period of the King's Gambit and the Evans. Then, as we have seen, came a subtilisation. Two tendencies became manifest here. First the majority of players became sufficiently well equipped to appreciate the deeper strategy of Steinitz and Lasker, viz., the merits of defence, and the possibility of planning the movements of Pieces without a slavish adherence to the conventional notions of good development. Second was the change in the notion of the centre. These two tendencies give us "ultramodern" Chess, characterised by the Nimzowitch, Tartakower, Alekhine experimentalism, and the Fianchetto Defences. Those treatments, having been heresy, are now orthodox. The present phase is an acceleration of tempo in the new orthodox modes of development. There is also a tendency to go back to older openings and play them in the light of a maturer strategy. That last fact suggests the thought that the student of Chess is unwise to become obsessed with the pursuit of opening learning. Given a reasonable tactical-strategic equipment it may be said that no opening, rationally played, can be bad.

The King's Pawn Openings

The advantage of P to K4 as the first move is reasonably clear. It gives access to the board, immediately, to two pieces, the Queen and the Bishop, and gives an immediate control over the centre squares. Pressure on the centre from squares like K4 and Q4, or, to a lesser degree from KB4 or QB4, implies that the player exerting the pressure has a certain amount of manoeuvring space, behind the Pawn or Pawns, in which he can mobilize. Also the majority of the King's Pawn Openings attack, more or less directly, the weakness at White's KB7.

There are many answers to 1. P to K4.

There is 1. . . . P to K3, which is the French Defence.

    1. . . . P to QB4, Sicilian Defence.

    1. . . . P to QB3, The famous, and difficult,
           Caro-Cahn. Much used by Botwinnik.

    1. . . . P to Q4, The Centre Counter.

    1. . . . Kt to KB3, Alekhine's Defence.

to say nothing of other quite playable irregular opening moves such as 1. . . . Kt to QB3, 1. . . . P to KKt3, 1. . . . P to QKt3. But one of the most frequent, and perhaps the best—though it is not now so popular as it was—is the simple move 1. . . . P to K4. After the opening moves 1. P to K4, P to K4, White and Black are exercising equal pressure in the centre, but White has the slight advantage of tempo. If the game is well played by Black that advantage will disappear. If Black plays more weakly than White, White's initiative will increase. Meanwhile White sets the pace because he can make the first threat, or the first act of aggression. White can thrust against the centre on the second move, either with a Pawn or with a piece. His choice will be determined by the speed with which he desires to attack his opponent's King's side.

Nineteenth century players favoured the immediate 2. P to KB4, the King's Gambit. To understand this, and several other aspects of the King's Pawn openings, the reader must appreciate that Black, who is being attacked, has his greatest weakness at KB2 (White's KB7). White can bring to bear against it a Bishop placed at QB4, a Knight coming quickly to KKt5, a Queen possibly developing itself, after one or two Pawn moves, at QKt3. The advantage, then, of a move like P to KB4 is that it adds to this force the Rook that will arrive on KB1 when White Castles. Further, if White secures control of K5 so as to be able to push a Pawn there at will, he will be able to drive away such a piece as Black's Knight from Black's KB3. For the rest, the control of the K5 square by the P at Q4 is an aggressive feature.

That is the simple basis of White's strategy. Of course Black has plenty of counterplay ; but, since in Chess it is important to make one's moves with a purpose, and preferably a purpose characterized by incisiveness, the type of attacking development that is being described is as good a way of starting the game as any, subject only to the consideration that this kind of attack, against good defence, is likely to burn itself out too quickly, leaving the game a little arid.

There are two main types of Pawn attack on the centre. There is, as we have seen, 2. P to KB4. There is also 2. P to Q4, the Centre Game or Gambit, which can be followed up so as to turn it into the lively but risky Danish Gambit (P to K4, P to K4 ; 2. P to Q4, P×P ; 3. P to QB3) or which can be transposed into the Scotch Gambit and several varieties of later developing attack, such as the Max Lange, etc. In modern times the most frequent second move for White is Kt to KB3. This is an immediate attack on Black's King's Pawn. It is not, as we have seen in an earlier chapter, a terribly serious attack ; but Black has nothing better available, by way of development, than to defend the Pawn with Kt to QB3, or P to Q3 ; or to counter-attack with Kt to KB3.

At this point, it should be observed that a move like 2. . . . B to Q3 is bad. For obvious reasons the Bishop at Q3 is not as good a defender as the Pawn would be (against, e.g., an immediate P to Q4). But, what is more important, the B at Q3 is doing much less than it could do at K2 or QB4, and it is blocking the QP, and with it the Queen's side Pieces. The move then, B to Q3, though it cannot be called an immediate cause of loss, is unsatisfactory. In the opening stages it is desirable to play moves which facilitate further development rather than retard it. That indeed is the whole art of opening play. Certain openings do admittedly give what appears to be a cramped game (e.g., Alekhine's Defence), but it will be found that those openings are really based on a plan for later development which cannot be prevented. A move like B to Q3, that we have just considered, retards development without any compensation.

In answer to 2. Kt to KB3, the moves Kt to KB3 (Petroff's Defence) or P to Q3 (Philidor's Defence), will be considered later. The most usual and popular is 2. Kt to QB3.

Then, on the third move, White has a choice of plans of campaign. In the spirit of the King's Pawn's openings is the move B to B4, pointing to KB7. This can be met by 3. . . . B to B4, after which the game can settle down into the Giuoco Piano (slow game) or can be enlivened by 4. P to QKt4 into the Evans Gambit. An alternative move, 4. P to Q4 is an interesting sacrifice, which is not quite sound, but which can yield a promising game (4. P to Q4, B×P; 5. Kt×B, Kt×Kt; 6. P to KB4, P to Q3; 7. 0–0, Kt to K3). But P to Q4 is stronger on move 3, and can either be played as the Scotch Game (recapture of the Pawn) or as the Scotch Gambit—one variety of which can form the Max Lange. Alternatively, Black on the third move (after 1. P to K4, P to K4. 2. Kt to KB3, Kt to QB3. 3. B to B4), can play Kt to KB3 (the Two Knights Defence) which offers White a choice of attacking lines. According to the best opinion the immediate thrust of Kt to Kt5, winning a Pawn (because Black is compelled to play P to Q4 immediately), gives Black good counterplay, if not the eventual advantage. On the other hand a form of Scotch Gambit can now be immediately initiated by 4. P to Q4, or prepared by 4. 0–0, to be followed by P to Q4. In this way again, the Max Lange or the Moller can develop. These are formidable attacks which can, however, be successfully defended. Let it be added that there is no opening attack in Chess which can be said to give ultimate superiority against good defence. That explains why players tend these days to play openings in which the attack can be delayed.

Typical of these is the Ruy Lopez. This develops when

White, on his third move, plays not B to B4 but B to Kt5. This initiates a long process of pressure against the centre and is one of the hardest openings to defend correctly. Also, if defended correctly, it becomes one of the hardest openings for the attack. Hence its popularity among players who believe themselves capable of exploiting, either for White or Black, the finer points of the Chess struggle.

It is not possible in an introductory volume to give anything like an exhaustive analysis of any particular opening. But the following pages contain some pieces of play from which it is hoped the reader will obtain a grasp of the kind of attacks that develop from the main King's Pawn and Queen's Side Openings.

THE KING'S GAMBIT

After the opening moves, 1. P to K4, P to K4. 2. P to KB4 Black has the option of accepting the Gambit or declining it, 2. . . . P×P constitutes the acceptance of the Gambit. When that is done White usually plays 3. Kt to KB3. The disadvantage of this move is that Black can immediately throw back the Pawn with 3. . . . P to Q4.

In this position Black gets a fairly free development whether or not White captures the Pawn or advances his King's Pawn. The game is quite good, with plenty of scope for both players, but is not characterised by the interesting dangers of the various lines that develop if Black tries to hold the Pawn with 3. . . . P to KKt4.

It is worth remarking at this point, and the reader will be wise to bear in mind, that Black's power to play P to Q4, freeing his game, is the test of equality in most of the King's Pawn Openings. This does not apply, always, in the Ruy Lopez or the Four Knights, where the centre has to be more subtly treated. But in many openings where the attack is against the King's side, e.g., in the Scotch, Giuoco, etc., P to Q4 for Black spells freedom from anxiety. That follows from the general strategic truth that a good control of the centre ensures that one is not likely to be overwhelmed by any attack against either of the wings. On the other hand a good attack in the centre can make possible a quick attack against either of the wings without very much additional preparation.

Sometimes, in order to mitigate the effect of a possible P to Q4 White plays 3. B to B4, instead of Kt to KB3. This is called the King's Bishop's Gambit. In it Black can be tempted into a rapid attack against the King with 3. . . . Q to R5 Ch., followed by Kt to KB3 with chances of bringing that Knight via R4 to Kt6 forking the King (which will have moved to KB1) and the Rook. Suffice it to say that Black's attack can be beaten off. At the proper moment Q to K1 can be played, and the P at B4 captured by the Bishop. White is then left with the kind of centre control that usually occurs when an attack has been successfully beaten off. Black, therefore, is not well advised to pursue his counter-attack too quickly. The move 3. Q to R5 Ch. is not bad ; but after that general development should not be neglected.

That proposition about general development is important in the King's Gambit. Both White and Black have got to consider not only the realities of a sharp attack, and the desirability of keeping material advantage, but the situation that is developing on the parts of the board that are not directly under attack, because they may become important both in connection with the attack, and as the game that remains if and when the attack is beaten off.

Typical of the older forms of the King's Gambit are the following three variations. These constitute respectively, the Allgaier Gambit, the Muzio Gambit and the Kieseritski Gambit.

	White	*Black*
ALLGAIER		
1.	P to K4.	P to K4.
2.	P to KB4.	P × P.
3.	Kt to KB3.	P to KKt4.
4.	P to KR4.	P to Kt5.
5.	Kt to Kt5.	P to KR3.
6.	Kt × P.	K × Kt.
7.	B to B4 Ch. (PQ4 is also playable.)	P to Q4.
8.	B × P Ch.	K to Kt2.
9.	P to Q4. With a lively game. The dangers, to both players, need no stressing.	

	White	*Black*
MUZIO		
1.	P to K4.	P to K4.
2.	P to KB4.	P × P.
3.	Kt to B3.	P to KKt4.
4.	B to B4.	P to Kt5.
5.	0–0.	P × Kt.
6.	B × P Ch. This is the Double (popular) form of the Muzio. Q × P is quite good instead.	K × B.
7.	Q × P.	Q to B3.
8.	P to K5.	Q × P.
9.	P to Q4.	Q × P Ch.
10.	B to K3 with a formidable attack. If White is giving odds of QKt this attack wins quickly !	

White	*Black*

KIESERITZKI

1. P to K4.
2. KP to B4.
3. Kt to KB3.
4. P to KR4.
5. Kt to K5.
6. Kt × KtP. With a sounder position than in the other variations.

1. P to K4.
2. P × P.
3. P to KKt4.
4. P to Kt5.
5. P to Q3.

In modern play Black does not try to hold the Pawn.

White	*Black*

P to K4.
P to KB4.
Kt to KB3.

P to K4.
P × P.
P to Q4 with a free development.

4. P × P followed by P—QB4 (if the Pawn is left) seems good for white.

VIENNA OPENING

A form of King's Gambit can develop on the third move, when White's second move is Kt to QB3 (The Vienna). If Black plays unincisively this attack can be even more vigorous than the normal King's Gambit. The usual play is as follows :—

White	*Black*

1. P to K4.
2. Kt to QB3.
3. P to KB4.
4. P × KP.

P to K4.
Kt to KB3.
P to Q4.
Kt × P.

and here White has the option of proceeding with either 5. Q to B3 or 5. Kt to B3. In the former case Black can simplify with Kt × Kt followed by P to Q5, after which White maintains something of an attack, but nothing decisive.

Let the reader take note that in this, as in all other openings, an attack is not the same thing as a winning attack. An attack is something to be treated with respect, but very often amounts to little more than a slight initiative allowing the player to develop, and to determine the direction of the game for a few moves, but not for sufficient moves, or to sufficient effect, to prevent a more far seeing opponent from eventually winning.

The alternative line 5. Kt to B3 can be met by more or less any move of the King's Bishop, and there are many other moves available.

Other aspects of the Vienna are worth considering.

The following is a very interesting piece of Chess 1. P to K4 P to K4 2. Kt to QB3 Kt to KB3 3. B to B4 Kt × P. Obviously this is only the loan of a piece because if 4. Kt × Kt P to Q4; and if, instead, one treats the B as Desperado with 4. B×P Ch. K×B 5. Kt×Kt P to Q4, the exposure of Black's King is more than compensated by his open development.

There may however, be played (after 1. P to K4 PK4 2. KtQB3 KtKB3 3. B to B4 Kt×P)

White	Black
4. Q to R5.	Kt to Q3.
5. B to Kt3.	Kt to QB3. Modern opinion seems to recommend B to K2.
6. Kt to Kt5.	P to KKt3.
7. Q to B3.	P to B4.
8. Q to Q5.	Q to K2. Q to B3 also has its points.
9. Kt×P Ch.	K to Q1.
10. Kt×R.	P to Kt3.

and Black, although temporarily a Rook down, has a promising counter-attack in the course of which he will regain some of his material. White will have to play exceedingly well to avoid the many dangers that will develop; but he too will have his chances.

Again, there still sometimes occurs the old fashioned line :—

White	Black
1. P to K4.	P to K4.
2. Kt to QB3.	Kt to QB3.
3. B to B4. Not so good as P to B4.	B to B4.
4. Q to Kt4.	K to B1 ; and Black, although he has moved his King, is at no disadvantage.

For the rest, after 2. . . . KtQB3, the delayed King's Gambit 3. P to KB4, can be quite effective. If it takes Allgaier form it is called Hampe-Allgaier.

KING'S GAMBIT DECLINED

In this century the King's Gambit has lost some of its appeal because it can quite reasonably be declined.

The usual declining move is 2. . . . B to B4 (Black's Pawn can obviously not be taken immediately because of the check at R5) ; and this is followed by moves like P to Q3, Kt to QB3 etc. White can then proceed to try and force P to Q4, or else, with the Queen's Knight, to get rid of Black's Black square Bishop, so as to be able to Castle. Black has counterplay with B to KKt5.

It can then happen, as in other King's Pawn openings, that White's centre proves to be less formidable than it looks.

The King's Gambit Declined is an excellent example of the principle that developing move for developing move, coupled with a guard against immediate attacks, constitutes adequate opening play.

A more aggressive continuation for Black is the Falkbeer Counter Gambit :—

White	*Black*
1. P to K4.	P to K4.
2. P to KB4.	P to Q4.
3. P × QP.	P to K5.

and Black can make it difficult for White to develop for quite a time, e.g. (to quote one of several reasonable lines) :

White	*Black*
4. P to Q3.	Kt to KB3.
5. P × P.	Kt × KP.
6. Kt to KB3.	B to QB4.
7. Q to K2.	B to B4.
8. Kt to B3.	Q to K2. With a good development, though not perfect.

The Giuoco Piano and Varieties of Centre Game

If it is desired to point one's pieces quickly towards Black's King's side, a usual method is the following :—

White	*Black*
1. P to K4.	P to K4.
2. Kt to KB3.	Kt to QB3.
3. B to B4.	

Now Black has the choice of two principal methods of defence; either 3. ... B to B4 or 3. ... Kt to KB3.

Evans Gambit

In answer to 3. ... B to B4, White's 4. P to QKt4 introduces a magnificent specimen of combative Chess, the Evans Gambit. This lost its popularity for some years for a variety of reasons. First, it is rather a strain on both players; second, it has been analysed so carefully that well informed players can be expected to cope with its difficulties; and third, because, as we have seen in a previous chapter, it can be quite successfully declined. Latterly, it has been revived because it is known to be capable of slower treatment, yielding good development.

The reader has already seen the Evergreen Game. That developed from an Evans Gambit ; and it may be studied as an excellent example of the possibilities and dangers of that opening.

1. P to K4   P to K4 2. Kt to KB3   Kt to QB3 3. B to B4 B to B4

4. P to QKt4 B × P 5. P to QB3 B to B4 (or R4) 6. P to Q4 P × P 7. 0–0 P × P 8. Kt × P with a good game.

The general plan of a safer defence to the Evans (the

Accepted Gambit) is for Black to play B to R4, refuse the 2nd Pawn, and endeavour to get in the moves, P to Q3. B to QKt3, B to KKt5 and 0-0. There is always a tactical danger of the loss of a piece by the pin of the QKt and the move P to Q5 ; but Black can prevent this if he keeps a steady eye on the possibility of Q to R4 while his B is at R4.

THE MOLLER ATTACK

If White wishes to attack without sacrificing the Knight's Pawn, a good method commences with 4. P to QB3.

The following is the typical form of the Moller attack.

White	Black
1. P to K4.	P to K4.
2. Kt to KB3.	Kt to QB3.
3. B to B4.	B to B4.
4. P to QB3.	Kt to KB3.
5. P to Q4.	P × P.
6. P × P.	B to Kt5 Ch.
7. Kt to B3.	Kt × KP.
8. 0-0.	B × Kt.
9. P to Q5.	Kt to K4 ; B to B3 is playable.
10. P × B.	Kt × B.
11. Q to Q4, with a strong attack.	QKt to Q3.
12. Q × KtP.	Q to B3.
13. Q × Q.	Kt × Q.
14. R to K1 Ch., etc.	

But Black can avoid this kind of attack in two ways :—

On move 7. he can Castle, leaving White with a hollow centre.

Or earlier, on move 4, he can play Q to K2 ;* and in answer to P to Q4 play B to Kt3 following with P to Q3, Kt to KB3, 0-0, etc.—a Giuoco Piano with advantage to Black. Whites development against this involves P—QKt4 and P—QR4.

In contrast, this opening which produces such excitements, can also produce very slow Chess—as the name Giuoco Piano suggests, e.g. :—

White	Black
1. P to K4.	P to K4.
2. Kt to KB3.	Kt to QB3.
3. B to B4.	B to B4.
4. Kt to QB3.	Kt to KB3.
5. P to Q3.	P to Q3.
6. B to K3.	

It is interesting to note that on White's move 6 the apparently safe move of Castles gives Black something of an attack with B to KKt5. In this type of opening that move is bad if played before the opponent Castles, because if the

*This is better than BKt3, because in some variations it gives Black the option of P—QR3 before P—Q4 is played by White.

Bishop is attacked with P to KR3, Black's answer B×Kt can be replied to with P×B, and the opponent has the open King's Knight's file for his Rook, while he Castles on the Queen's side.

The student should also be warned that if he has Castled and the Bishop comes to KKt5, he should not automatically try to drive it with P to KR3 followed by P to KKt4, because it may be that Black will sacrifice the Knight with Kt×KtP, in exchange for a considerable attack.

An interesting pitfall in the Giuoco Piano is the following :—

White	*Black*
1. P to K4.	P to K4.
2. Kt to KB3.	Kt to QB3.
3. B to B4.	B to B4.
4. Kt to QB3.	Kt to KB3.
5. P to Q3.	0–0 (playable because B to Kt5 can be met by B to K2).
6. Kt to KR4.	

This move, which is not very good, is directed towards the occupation of KB5. What is interesting is that Black cannot win a Pawn by Kt×KP because after

White	*Black*
7. Kt×Kt.	Q×Kt.
8. B to KKt5. Wins the Queen.	

What makes 6. Kt to KR4 inferior is

White	*Black*
6. . . .	P to Q4 (the old " Touchstone ").
7. P×P.	Kt×P.
8. Kt×Kt.	Q×KKt., etc.

THE MAX LANGE

If Black on the third move plays Kt to KB3 instead of B to B4 we have seen that the immediate attack by 4. Kt to KKt5 is illusory. But 4. P to Q4 can produce some interesting attacks, of which one is (or can transpose into) the famous Max Lange (which can also arise from the Scotch Gambit).

White	*Black*
1. P to K4.	P to K4.
2. Kt to KB3.	Kt to QB3.
3. B to B4.	Kt to KB3.
4. P to Q4.	P×P (the best).
5. 0–0.	B to B4. An alternative is Kt × KP, after which may follow—
	6. R to K1. P to Q4.
	7. B×P. Q×B.
	8. Kt to QB3. (Canal's attack, which is embarrassing, though defensible.)
6. P to K5.	P to Q4.
7. P×Kt.	P×B.

White	Black
8. R to K1 Ch.	B to K3.
9. Kt to Kt5.	Q to Q4. **Very important. If**

instead—
9. Q to Q2.
10. Kt × B wins a piece by reason of the Check at R5.

If again—
9. . . .   Q to Q3.
10. Kt to K4 wins, e.g., if Q to K4.
11. P to KB4.   P to Q6Ch.
12. K to R1.   P × P.
13. Q × P.

If then—
13 . . . Q to KB4. 14. Kt to Q6 Ch. wins;

If instead—
13 . . . Q to KR4. 14. P × P wins;
If, at 11. Black plays Q to KB4 there can follow—
12. P to KKt4.   Q × P.
13. Q × Q.   B × Q.
14. Kt × B Ch., etc.

White	Black
10. Kt to QB3.	Q to KB4.
11. QKt to K4.	. . . and White has a very fine attack which is defeasible only by the very best play. With the best play Black threatens to win, because he is likely to emerge with a Pawn superiority.

Although much analysed, this opening is still of the greatest interest and eminently playable. Relatively safe is 11. . . . 0–0–0, and a hard game results from this. Interesting also is—

White	Black
11. . . .	B to B1.
12. Kt × BP	K × Kt.
13. Kt to Kt5 Ch.	K to Kt1 (or Kt3)

and White's attack may not be so dangerous as it looks.

If, in this variation,

White	Black
12. P × KtP.	B × P.
13. P to KKt4.	Q × P.
14. Q × Q.	B × Q.
15. Kt to B6 double Ch.	K to Q1.
16. Kt × B.	P to KR4 wins back the Piece.

THE SCOTCH GAME

After the opening moves, 1. P to K4, P to K4. 2. Kt to KB3, Kt to QB3 ; White often plays 3. P to Q4. If then Black plays P × P, White can play B to B4, probably arriving at the Max Lange. He can, however, play 4. Kt × P and this constitutes the Scotch game. (The refusal to recapture

makes it the Scotch Gambit.)   The Scotch game can lead
to very logical Chess, e.g.—

White	*Black*
1. P to K4.	P to K4.
2. Kt to KB3.	Kt to QB3.
3. P to Q4.	P × P.
4. Kt × P.	Q to B3. 4. . . . Kt to KB3 is
	also playable (and after Kt ×
	QKt, KtP × Kt).
5. B to K3.	B to B4.
6. P to QB3.	Kt to K2.
7. B to Kt5.	P to Q3 (not 0–0). If 7. B to K2
	P to Q4 with equality.

An interesting, but unconvincing attack can develop in this
variation (one of the many Blumenfeld attacks) by—

White	*Black*
6. Kt to Kt5.	B × B.
7. P × B.	Q to R5 Ch.
8. P to KKt3.	Q × KP.
9. Kt × P Ch.	K to Q1.
10. Kt × R.	Kt to KB3, to take the edge off
	Q to Q6.

THE CENTRE GAME

1. P to K4, P to K4. 2. P to Q4, P×P. 3. Q×P, Kt to
QB3. 4. Q to K3 with later 0–0–0 is too logical to require
detailed analysis. A by-product is the Danish Gambit.

This is an attempt to gain manoeuvring space and development in exchange for irrelevant Pawns in the following (not
very reliable) attack.

White	*Black*
1. P to K4.	P to K4.
2. P to Q4.	P × P.
3. P to QB3.	P × P.
4. B to B4.	P × KtP.
5. B × P.	B to Kt5 Ch.

Kt to QB3⎫
Kt to Q2. ⎬ with a dangerous formation.
K to B1.   ⎭

In the teeth of danger Black must endeavour to develop and
centralise with P to Q4; also to Castle.

Finally, there should be mentioned the fact that White
can play B to B4 on the second move, before the Knights
develop.   There is no particular advantage in this, except
that it preserves the option of a King's Gambit for one move.

The reader should avoid adventures like, 1. P to K4, P to
K4. 2. P to Q4, P×P. 3. B to B4, B to B4. 4. B×P Ch.,
K×B. 5. Q to R5 Ch., P to KKt3. 6. Q×B with dis-
advantage.

RUY LOPEZ

The feature common to most of the openings considered so far is that in them White aims at a quick attack against the King's side, and the slight advantage of tempo that White enjoys is sufficient to cause Black to play carefully and to face difficulties. But in the long run, given good play, the initiative diminishes—even passes, and Black is left with, at least, equality. Consequently, modern players who want to maintain as long as possible White's initiative (granted that this is not a vain undertaking) are more likely to elect for the Ruy Lopez. In this they are reverting to something that was popular before the Masters of the middle nineteenth century introduced a period of quick attack. In Chess, as in many other departments of intellectual activity, there can happen a reversion to the period before last. The relatively immature strategy of the pre-Morphy epoch produced games nearer to some modern styles, with their advanced strategy, than to the intervening stage of tactical brilliance. However, the Ruy Lopez has survived in Chess because of its merits from any standpoint, and continues to exist as modern, notwithstanding its great age. Here indeed, when we consider Russian analyses of the old Spanish opening, are we reminded of the transition of culture from Iberia to Siberia.

The first three moves of the Lopez are already familiar to the reader, 1. P to K4, P to K4. 2. Kt to KB3, Kt to QB3. 3. B to Kt5, with, as we have seen, a sort of attack on the King's Pawn.

At this stage Black has two main methods of defence or counter play. One of these is based on P to Q3 (the Steinitz Defence), the other on Kt to KB3 (the Berlin Defence). Both of these are playable, but nowadays, whichever choice is adopted, Black usually precedes it with 3. . . . P to QR3. This is due to the discovery that White has little to gain, either tactically or strategically, by the immediate exchange the Bishop for the Knight. He retains the initiative for a short time, and has a slightly better Pawn formation, but Black will eventually get equal play. Consequently White usually retreats with 4. B to R4. If, after that, Black plays 4. . . . P to Q3 we have the Steinitz Deferred. If, instead, Black plays 4. . . . Kt to KB3 we have the Morphy Defence, perhaps the most popular, and reminiscent of the fact that a great master of attack was also a great master of defence.

These lines of play have been the subject matter of much experiment, much trial and error. The most popular is the Morphy Defence, because, notwithstanding early difficulties,

Black's eventual counter chances and strategic compensations are evident to those experienced in the opening.

Here is the main line :

	White	*Black*
1.	P to K4.	P to K4.
2.	Kt to KB3.	Kt to QB3.
3.	B to Kt5.	P to QR3.
4.	B to R4.	Kt to B3.
5.	O—O.	Kt × P.

Here Black has a very important alternative, B to K2, which leads to a rather different type of game, considered below.

6. P to Q4.

This, the product of much experiment gives a more lasting attack than the plausible 6. R to K1. Viz :

6.	R to K1.	Kt to B4.
7.	B × Kt.	QP × B.
8.	P to Q4.	Kt to K3.

9. P × P and although White has a positive strategic advantage for the endgame, Black has sufficient intervening play to compensate. This plan may be improved by the playing of 6. Q to K2 instead of 6. R to K1.

. In this variation incidentally, there is an interesting pitfall—

6.	R to K1.	Kt to B4.
7.	Kt to QB3.	Kt × B.
		A bad move.
8.	Kt × KP.	B to K2.
		Virtually forced.
9.	Kt to Q5.	O—O.
10.	Kt × Kt.	P × Kt.
11.	Kt × B Ch.	K to R1.
12.	Q to R5.	Kt to B4.
13.	R to K3.	Kt to K3.
14.	Q × RP Ch.	K × Q.
15.	R to KR3 Mate.	

It is to be observed that the play from move 12 is not completely forced, but Black is in great difficulties ; e.g., if 12. . . . B to K3. 13. R × B is playable, with quick recapture of the exchange and an excellent game.

To revert to the main line :

	White	*Black*
6.	P to Q4.	P to QKt4. (For P × P see p. 29.)
7.	B to Kt3.	P to Q4.
8.	P × P.	B to K3.
9.	P to B3.	

This is in order to enable White to preserve his very important

White

White-square Bishop in the event of Black playing Kt to QR4. The Russian Master Smyslov has, however, achieved successes with 9. Q to K2 (threatening R to Q1 and P to B4). Against this Kt to QR4 is not immediately playable because of 10. Kt to Q4. Best is 9 ... B to K2. If 10. R to Q1, then Kt to QR4, after which 11. Kt to Q4 can be met by O–O.

9. . . .

Black

B to K2.
Again the result of much experiment. Recently there has been a revival of the old-fashioned 9 ... B to QB4, which has certain tactical advantages (e.g., the pressure on White's KB2), also some defects, including the strategic danger that after the Bishop is forced to retreat Black will be left with a backward QBP against which White can exert a great deal of pressure.

After 9. . . . B to K2 White has a choice of several moves, including possibilities such as P to QR4 and R to K1. In practice Lopez experts usually play, on the tenth move of this variation, either B to K3 or QKt to Q2. Both are very good. In answer to 10. B to K3 Black endeavours to improve his position with 0–0 and Kt to QR4, followed, if the White Bishop moves, by P to QB4, after which he has to defend very carefully on the King's side, standing quite a considerable attack, before his endgame superiority becomes a feature of the game.

The most popular move (after a period in which it was rather critically regarded) is nowadays 10. QKt to Q2.

The following is a typical sequence :—

White	Black
10. QKt to Q2.	0–0.
11. R to K1. B to B2 is also good: best in reply is either P to KB4 or BB4.	Kt to B4.
12. B to B2.	P to Q5.
13. P × P.	Kt × QP.
14. Kt × Kt.	Q × Kt.
15. Q to R5.	P to Kt3.
16. Q to R6.	Q to KR5, with an equal game.

Within the extent of these few moves there is tremendous scope for variation. White has possibilities like 11. Q to K2 ; instead of R to K1. It is not advisable for White to exchange Knights on move 11, because after

	White	*Black*
11.	Kt × Kt.	P × Kt.
12.	B × B.	P × Kt.
13.	B to Q5.	Black can sacrifice the exchange with Kt × KP, obtaining a very good game.

If on move 9 of this variation of the Lopez Black plays B to B4, he is making it more difficult to straighten out his Pawns with eventual P to QB4. He is, however, making possible some counter-attack, of which some interest attaches to the possible sacrifice of two minor pieces for a Rook, Pawn, and the attack, e.g. :—

	White	*Black*
9.	. . .	B to B4.
10.	QKt to Q2.	Kt × KBP.
11.	R × Kt.	P to KB3, with good attacking chances.

This variation, which was much played among Lancashire "Skittlers" in the 1920's was later analysed by a Manchester player named Dilworth, and has become known as the Dilworth Variation. The Russian masters have analysed its sequences to the 36th move.

It is quite impossible in an introductory book to do justice even to a small part of so big an opening as the Lopez. The reader should however, learn the alternative treatment of the Morphy Defence, observing that in this, as contrasted with the line just analysed, Black's problem of developing his QBP is more easily solved. In the last chapter it has been explained that this can be a very important consideration, since a backward Pawn is a target for Rooks. In the quicker form of the Lopez, one possible process is for White to play Kt to Q4 at a proper time (not too early as in the unsound Breslau attack) and recapture on that square with the BP —then develop Rooks on the open file. This should be prevented.

Slower form of Morphy Defence (sometimes called the Tchigorin: and the other the Tarrasch).

	White	*Black*
1.	P to K4.	P to K4.
2.	Kt to KB3.	Kt to QB3.
3.	B to Kt5.	P to QR3.
4.	B to R4.	Kt to B3.
5.	0–0.	B to K2. The divergence that gives a less combative but quite difficult game.
6.	R to K1. (Q to K2, the Worrall attack is playable.)	P to QKt4.
7.	B. to Kt3.	P to Q3. At this point, Black with Castles followed by P to Q4 can introduce the sacrificial Marshall attack which can give

White

Black

White some difficulty, and should not lose, but is not popular in modern first class play.

(7. . . .   0–0.
 8. P to B3.   P to Q4.
 9. P × P.   Kt × P.
10. Kt × P.   Kt × Kt.
11. R × Kt.   P to QB3,
followed by B to Q3, etc.).

White	*Black*
8. P to B3.	Kt to QR4.
9. B to B2.	P to QB4.
10. P to Q4. White often plays P to KR3 here in order to prevent B to KKt5. Black's answer is 0–0.	. . . and now Black has the choice of Q to B2 or Kt to QB3, or (perhaps best) the difficult B to Kt5. He may, incidentally, initiate that manoeuvre earlier if he refrains from pursuing the White Bishop.

In this variation, too, there are countless possibilities. It has been discovered by the Russians that Black can dispense with P to QKt4 and can play P to Q3, B to K2, and later B to Kt5, as a variation of Steinitz Deferred. (The possibility of an early Kt to Kt5 has been mentioned.) If in the slow Morphy Defence Black does not get in an early B to KKt5, then White develops with P to KR3, QKt Q2, R to K1, Kt to KB1, P to KKt4, Kt to Kt3, K to R2, R to Kt1, Kt to KB5, a strong attack. Black defends with 0–0, Kt to K1, P to KKt3, B to KB3, Kt to Kt2, etc.

Of other variations the Steinitz Deferred is too logical to require detailed treatment here.

White	*Black*
1. P to K4.	P to K4.
2. KtK to B3.	Kt to QB3.
3. B to Kt5.	P to QR3.
4. B to R4.	P to Q3.
5. P to B3. (A good alternative is B × Kt Ch., followed by 6. P to Q4 with good development. Black can reply 6. . . . QP × P or (better) P to KB3).	B to Q2.
6. P to Q4.	Kt to KB3.

With a sound game.

On move 5 of this line . . . P to KB4 for Black gives the Siesta variation which is playable.

There are many other defences to the Lopez. Quite hard to refute is the impudent looking " Schliemann's Defence "—

White	*Black*
P to K4.	P to K4.
Kt to KB3.	Kt to QB3.
B to Kt5.	P to KB4.

Best then is Kt to QB3.

If 4. P to Q4, this may happen :—

White	Black
4. . . .	P × KP.
5. Kt × KP.	Kt × Kt.
6. P × Kt.	P to QB3.

winning a Pawn through the check at QR4. (But the Q is misplaced.)

Another line in the Lopez upon which it is impossible to pronounce is :—

White	Black
1. P to K4.	P to K4.
2. Kt to KB3.	Kt to QB3.
3. B to Kt5.	Kt to Q5.
4. Kt × Kt.	P × Kt.

with no perceptible middle-game disadvantage, but doubled Pawns. (This is Bird's Defence).

So far we have considered King's Pawn Openings giving an Open Game—either with defence of the centre, or unbalance of the centre by acceptance of Gambits. Now there must be considered one or two lines in which Black fights for the centre, but avoids the Ruy Lopez pressure; and some other openings in which Black yields centre space, in the hope of later exploiting the hollowness of White's game—or the tempo he has used in building the centre.

PHILIDOR'S DEFENCE

This is a difficult defence based on P to Q3 instead of Kt to QB3. It only retains its popularity these days among those players whose style it is to invite pressure so as to achieve a subtler kind of development, or an eventually better development, when White has over-expanded.

White	Black
1. P to K4.	P to K4.
2. Kt to KB3.	P to Q3.
3. P to Q4.	QKt to Q2. Better than Kt to QB3, after which White could gain tempo by exchanges, including exchange of Queens, leaving Black with his King on Q1.
4. B to B4.	B to K2.
5. 0–0.	P to QB3 or KtKB3.

If the latter, White can go for a quick attack by

White	Black
6. B × P Ch.	K × B.
7. Kt to Kt5 Ch.	K to Kt1.
8. Kt to K6.	Q to K1.
9. Kt × BP.	Black should eventually emerge with a slightly better game, since the Knight, having captured the Rook cannot escape. The variation has something in common

White	Black
	with an attack that was seen in the Vienna. An alternative method of playing this attack is—
	6. Kt to KK5. 0–0.
	7. B × P Ch. R × B.
	8. Kt to K6, etc.

White, however, has no need for these adventures, and can gain a good game by castling and development on both wings. A possibly safer approach to the Philidor is the Author's— i.e. P—QB3 on the first move—then PQ3, QKt Q2 etc.

PETROFF'S DEFENCE

A variation which avoids the Ruy Lopez, but is not easy.

White	Black
1. P to K4.	P to K4.
2. Kt to KB3.	Kt to KB3.
3. Kt × P.	P to Q3.
4. Kt to KB3.	Kt × P.
5. P to Q4.	P to Q4.
6. B to Q3.	B to Q3.
7. 0–0.	0–0.
8. P to B4, and White has a slight initiative.	

Another approach is—

White	Black
1. P to K4.	P to K4.
2. Kt to KB3.	Kt to KB3
3. P to Q4.	Kt × P.
4. B to Q3.	P to Q4.
5. Kt × P.	B to Q3.
6. 0–0.	0–0.
and if now—	
7. P to QB4.	Kt to QB3, gives Black the attacking chances.

FOUR KNIGHTS

This can develop from the Petroff, if White on move 3 plays Kt to QB3 and Black plays Kt to QB3 ; or it can develop instead of the Lopez if after 2. Kt to KB3 Kt to QB3 White plays 3. Kt to QB3 and Black replies Kt to KB3.

The normal form of this opening (of which there are many variations) is the double Ruy Lopez.

White	Black
1. P to K4.	P to K4.
2. Kt to KB3.	Kt to QB3.
3. Kt to QB3.	Kt to KB3.
4. B to Kt5.	B to Kt5. Instead Kt to Q5 gives the interesting but difficult Rubinstein Defence.
5. 0–0.	0–0.
6. P to Q3.	B × Kt.
7. P × B.	P to Q3.
8. B to Kt5.	Q to K2.
9. R to K1.	Kt to Q1. This is the Metger Defence and there are many others.

Observe that White's moves 5 and 6 cannot be transposed, because of 5. P to Q3   Kt to Q5!

DEFENCES TO THE KING'S PAWN OTHER THAN P TO K4

The notion of a subtler treatment of the centre, contemplating the moulding of Black's development on squares left weak in the White field accounts for the prevalence of answers to White's first move P to K4 in the form of 1. . . . P to Q4 (Centre Counter, seen in another Chapter) 1. . . . P to K3, (French Defence), 1. . . . P to QB4 (Sicilian Defence), 1. . . . P—QB3 (Caro-Cahn). 1. . . . Kt to KB3 (Alekhine's Defence). These, between them, cover more than half the King's Pawn openings that are played in modern tournaments. The Sicilian is the most stable of them. The French Defence and Alekhine's Defence give scope to attacking play by White; and Black may wait for White to develop his attack before countering; or else play a flanking attack against the centre. Then it can happen that White's attack breaks down and Black is left with superiority. But the play is far too close to permit of any compendious pronouncement on the merits.

The reader should always remember that it is the player who wins or loses, not the opening. The strategic strength or weakness of any formation is, by itself, usually insufficient to determine the result of a struggle in which there is always scope for ability.

FRENCH DEFENCE

The main variations of this opening commence on the third move :—

White	Black
1. P to K4.	P to K3.
2. P to Q4.	P to Q4.

These moves are the most reasonable and usual and now White has the choice of 3. P × P (the Exchange variation), a deceptively simple looking opening ; or 3. P to K5 developing quickly a pressure which is not easy to maintain ; or 3. Kt to QB3, the most usual line.

Very frequently seen is the following :—

White	Black
1. P to K4.	P to K3.
2. P to Q4.	P to Q4.
3. Kt to QB3.	Kt to KB3. An alternative that is popular nowadays, after a period of disfavour, is 3 . . . B to Kt5. (See below.)
4. B to Kt5. (B to Q3 is playable on this or the next move, but is out of fashion : Lasker played it.)	B to K2. 4. . . . B to Kt5 gives the McCutcheon Defence.
5. P to K5.	KKt to Q2.
6. P to KR4. Alekhine's attack.	

And now Black can hardly play to win the Pawn by B × B because White gains considerable space and tempo. Black can play P to KB3, which gives White the opportunity of a dangerous sacrificial attack commencing B to Q3, which Russian analysis has failed either to establish or refute.

The normal method of defence is to aim at counterplay by P to QB4, etc. This move is usually preceded by P to QR3 to prevent an attack (which may look more dangerous than it is) by Kt to Kt5.

If safely played the game resolves itself into a testing of the weakness of White's apparently good centre.

In this and other variations of the French Defence (e.g., when White plays P to K5 on move 3—Nimzowitch's favourite—or on move 4) White allows his Queen's Pawn to fall to Black's QBP but maintains a Pawn or a Piece on K5 and a Bishop on Q3 maintaining a constant threat against the King's side.

A good deal of interesting play can also arise from White's early abandonment of some centre control by P × QBP when the opportunity affords.

WINAWER'S VARIATION

This alternative system is an old defence revived.

White	Black
	P to K3.
1. P to K4.	P to Q4.
2. P to Q4.	B to Kt5.
3. Kt to QB3.	

This was thought to be refuted by :—

4. P × P, a form of exchange variation in which Black's Bishop does not appear well placed and White appears to have a freer development. That this is not the case was, however, demonstrated by Alekhine in the famous first game of his match with Capablanca. Since that game most players adopt as the fourth move for White P to K5. Then Black can play safely Kt to K2, or, more dangerously, P to QB4— a line much favoured by the Russian Master Botwinnik.

White can then attack with :—

5. Q to Kt4; and it is then doubtful how much attention Black should give to White's King's side attack at the expense of his own Queen's side attack. This is a variation which very often produces exciting Chess of a combative type. Black can, if he wishes, make the game safe with K to B1 at a proper time, but that has not been the usual treatment. Another (typical) sequence is the following:—

White	Black
1. P to K4.	P to K3.
2. P to Q4.	P to Q4.
3. Kt to QB3.	B to Kt5.
4. P to K5.	P to QB4.
5. P × P.	Kt to QB3.
6. Kt to B3.	KKt to K2.
7. B to Q3.	P to Q5.
8. P to QR3.	B to R4.
9. P to QKt4.	Kt × KtP.
10. P × Kt.	B × P.
11. B to Kt5 Ch.	B to Q2.

The reader's attention is directed to the game Fine-Botwinnik (1938) in the illustrative games.

Another good line in the French arises when Black plays 3. ... P×KP. Then White can make a Gambit of it with P to KB3.

A different, and playable, system is introduced by Whites' 3. Kt to Q2 reserving the option of P to QB3.

THE CARO-CAHN

The defect of the French Defence from the point of view of many players is that Black closes out of play his Queen's Bishop. This is not a complete account of the matter, because if eventually the Bishop develops on QKt2, behind the Pawns, it is in play strategically, on the assumption that White's centre cannot last for ever, and the diagonal will be opened ; and there are other possibilities for the Bishop— e.g. via Q2 and K1 to the King's wing.

Nevertheless this difficulty has made many players favour the Caro-Cahn, which also invites pressure in the centre, but gives more scope to Black's Queen's Bishop.

White	*Black*
1. P to K4.	P to QB3.
2. P to Q4.	P to Q4.

and now White can proceed with 3. P to K5, answered by B to B4 ; alternatively he can exchange Pawns and follow up with 4. P to QB4, getting the kind of game which can arise from the Slav Defence to the Queen's Pawn. White has an initiative and some pressure, but Black should not lose. In general, it may be said that the Caro-Cahn is not an opening to be recommended to anyone beginning Chess ; but, if mastered, can constitute a useful weapon against the KP openings.

SICILIAN DEFENCE

The reader may by now have apprehended a general notion about the King's Pawn Opening ; that is, the possibility and desirability for Black of counterplay against White's centre. If White is operating against KB7, P to Q4 seems to be a desirable move for Black at some stage ; if White is operating against KR7, or occupying K5 strongly, Black seems to need P to QB4 at some stage. Indeed, both the Queen's Pawn and the Queen's Bishop's Pawn seem to become aggressive for Black sooner or later. The strategic motif is the difficulty for White of any wing attack unless his control of the centre is unchallenged and unimpeded.

That kind of thinking has been responsible for the increase, in modern times, in the popularity of the Sicilian Defence. In answer to 1. P to K4, Black plays 1. . . . P to QB4. According to the best opinion this is the only first move for Black that stands comparison with 1. . . . P to K4. Development appears easy for White—deceptively easy ; Black on the other hand, though not perfectly free, can build his game up on logical lines ; and will eventually generate some threats on the Queen's wing.

The two best known systems of development for Black in the Sicilian are the Paulsen Variation and the Dragon Variation. The former, involving P to K3, lets the King's Bishop develop on K2. The latter, involving P to Q3 and P to KKt3, gives the King's Bishop a Fianchetto Development, a method very popular these days, and giving the game some of the characteristics of the modern Queen's Pawn structure. There is a third of some importance called the Scheveningen Variation, in which Black plays P to Q3 as in the Dragon and P to K3 as in Paulsen's Variation. The line is eminently playable. [However the Sicilian be played, Black, at some stage, is wise to play P—QR3, for defence and attack.]

PAULSEN'S VARIATION

White	Black
1. P to K4.	P to QB4.
2. Kt to KB3.	P to K3.
3. P to Q4.	P × P.
4. Kt × P.	Kt to KB3. This move is very important. If it is not done immediately, White can play P to QB4 giving the Maroczy attack—a pressure against the centre, and restrictive of Black's space. The same danger has to be avoided also in the Dragon Variation, or indeed, in any way that the Sicilian is played. The loss of space is not fatal ; but Black is much better not to allow the deprivation to take place.
5. Kt to QB3. Some players endeavour, in this and the other main variations to keep the Queen's Bishop Pawn moves open by playing 5. P to KB3. This can lead to highly speculative play after P to K4, sooner or later, by Black.	
5. . .	P to Q3.
6. B to K2.	Kt to B3.
7. O–O.	B to K2.

White	*Black*
8. K to R1. White manoeuvres so as to develop his Queen's Bishop on the line from KKt1 to QR7 and to be able, at the same time to avoid any possible exchange of Bishop for Knight that may be threatened. As he also wants to throw forward his KBP, the text both avoids Check and makes KKt1 available for the Bishop.	
8. ...	P to QR3.
9. P to QR4.	Q to B2.
10. P to B4.	0-0.
	And both players have plenty of scope for manoeuvre.

The Scheveningen can give the same position by transposition of moves, viz. :

White	*Black*
1. P to K4.	P to QB4.
2. Kt to KB3.	Kt to QB3.
3. P to Q4.	P × P.
4. Kt × P.	Kt to KB3.
5. Kt to QB3.	P to Q3.
6. B to K2.	P to K3, etc.

Paulsen's line only differs from the Scheveningen when Black plays (as he can in some lines) B to QKt5.

In the above variations, as in the next—possibly safer—Black must try, either for P—Q4, or to make the Pawn safe at Q3.

THE DRAGON VARIATION

White	*Black*
1. P to K4.	P to QB4.
2. Kt to KB3.	Kt to QB3. This move can also be played on the second move of the Paulsen.
3. P to Q4.	P × P.
4. Kt × P.	Kt to KB3.
5. Kt to QB3.	P to Q3.
6. B to K2. (Kt × Kt ; P × Kt, P to K5 is interesting, but unsound.)	
6. ...	P to KKt3.
7. B to K3.	B to Kt2.
8. 0-0.	0-0.
9. Kt to Kt3.	In order to avoid a long and hard to calculate series of exchanges that might be initiated by Black's 9. .... KtKKt5.
9. ...	B to K3.
10. P to B4.	Kt to QR4.
11. P to B5.	B to B5.
12. B to Q3.	And White has a slight advantage.

A good deal of variation is possible in the previous play. Some experiment has been made with 6. B to KKt5, Richter's attack, in order to impede the Dragon formation, but the effort does not appear to justify itself conclusively.

The most modern experimentalists are shifting the emphasis of the opening to an early P—QR3 for Black. The great Anderssen used it as a first move for White!

WING GAMBIT.

White has a sacrificial method of side-tracking the Sicilian in order to get control of the centre, reminiscent of the Danish Gambit, but safer—

White	Black
1. P to K4.	P to QB4.
2. P to QKt4.	P × P.

The traditional way of proceeding is 3. P to QR3, which, however, leads eventually to advantage for Black. The author, however, has had some success with

White	Black
3. B to Kt2.	P to Q4.
4. P × P.	Q × P.
5. Kt to KB3. Or 5. P to QB4, speculative, but good.	

3. P—Q4 is also eminently playable.

ALEKHINE'S DEFENCE.

Of all the openings based on the strategy of retarded development Alekhine's Defence is the most extreme; and its playability, although it is not recommended to the beginner, demonstrates the richness of strategic resource available on the Chess Board.

White	Black
1. P to K4.	Kt to KB3.
2. P to K5.	Kt to Q4.
3. P to QB4.	Kt to Kt3.
4. P to Q4.	P to Q3. The counterplay begins.
5. P to B4.	P × P.
6. BP × P.	Kt to B3.
7. B to K3.	An interesting point. White waits for the Black Bishop to commit itself before moving the King's Knight. If, e.g., White plays 7. Kt to KB3, Black can pin that Knight without loss of tempo.
7. . . .	B to B4.
8. Kt to QB3.	P to K3.
9. Kt to B3.	Kt to Kt5.
10. R to B1.	P to B4. And Black has recovered some of the mobility of which the opening appeared to deprive him.

Of course White is not obliged to play this opening at a fast tempo. White can play e.g. 3. P to Q4 and develop quietly.

Alternatively, White can chase the Knight with 3. P to QB4 and 4. P to QB5 and 5. Kt to QB3. Thus Kt × Kt then gives a remarkable position in which Black will have used up half a dozen moves with a Knight, while White has opened up his game. Yet Black does not necessarily lose.

The Queen's Side Openings

The reader will have observed, while studying the more combative openings, that it is very easy for the player, either of the attack or of the defence, to become pre-occupied with tactical interests on one side of the Board or another to the detriment of general development. He will also have observed that a quick attack is quite likely to burn itself out too quickly.

For practical purposes then it seems desirable to play a type of Chess in which a more general preparation takes place and in which the attack, when it eventually becomes incisive, has more strategic weight behind it. Now there is no opening in Chess in which a good player will find it impossible to develop strategically. Even the varieties of King's Gambit can be played in a balanced way and a subtler way than they were in the past. But they still offer temptations to impetuosity. Consequently there is a tendency on the part of the many to avoid them. That accounts for the immense popularity in modern Chess of the Queen's Gambit and other varieties of Queen's Pawn opening. These (which are far from new), also have their excitements and their speculative excesses ; but, on the whole the Queen's Pawn gives, to White at least, a steadier, less hectic type of game than those openings in which the tactical threats are more quickly generated. The move 1. P to Q4 is not quite so good a developing move, or so incisive an attack on the centre, as 1. P to K4 ; nevertheless it " contains " the centre, and creates space in which White can mobilise ; and even exerts a pressure that Black cannot ignore, and which can become formidable.

There are perhaps more playable replies to P to Q4 than there are to P to K4. Several Pawns, and both the Knights can move in reply, though 1. . . . Kt to KB3 is a very much better reply than 1. . . . Kt to QB3, the reason being, not only that Black is afraid of pursuit, but that in the Queen's Pawn generally Black's Queen's Bishop's Pawn should be free to move either to QB3 or QB4. Notwithstanding the play-ability of other moves, Black's normal reply to 1. P to Q4 is either 1. . . . P to Q4 or, with a view to one of the modern defences, 1. . . . Kt to KB3. 1. . . . P to KKt3 is also playable.

THE QUEEN'S GAMBIT

The danger of the Queen's Pawn opening, from White's stand point, is that Black can equalise more easily than in the King's Pawn. It therefore behoves White to play with such incisiveness as a relatively slow opening allows. That is why the Queen's Gambit is the normal development, and much more frequent among Queen's Pawn openings than the King's Gambit is among King's Pawn openings. As much as the King's Gambit, the Queen's Gambit is a logical way of generating a pressure on the centre.

In contrast to the King's Gambit, the Queen's Gambit is more usually declined than accepted. Once White is inhibiting Black's P to K4, it is important for Black to inhibit White's P to K4. In the King's Gambit the converse does not hold, because Black can move his King's Pawn away from the centre and still be able to play P to Q4. In modern times there has, indeed, developed a tendency to accept the Queen's Gambit. That entails something of the subtle modern strategy that aims at breaking up White's centre later on, and gaining the occupancy of important squares round the centre. Before considering other lines the reader is well advised to study the orthodox form of the Queen's Gambit declined.

White	*Black*
1. P to Q4.	P to Q4.
2. P to QB4.	P to K3. There is an alternative, 2. ... P to QB3, which aims at a deferred acceptance after Black has brought some pressure on White's K4. Also playable is 2. ... P to K4 (Albin's Counter Gambit: see p. 140).
3. Kt to QB3. More incisive than 2. Kt to KB3, which is good but contemplates a slower development.	
3. ...	Kt to KB3.
4. B to Kt5. Again the incisive line and popularised by the famous Pillsbury. White achieves a good, but different, type of game by keeping his Black square Bishop behind his Pawns.	
4. ...	QKt to Q2. The reader has already seen that this move does not lose a Pawn. The only advantage of this move over 4 ... B to K2 consists, not in the trap, but in the option of developing the Bishop on other squares.
5. P to K3.	B to K2.
6. Kt to B3.	0–0.

At this point White has a variety of moves. He is not well advised to exchange Pawns, because that develops Black. He has some slow moves such as P to QR3, or even P to QKt3, which are not unplayable. But they give Black counterplay. White's normal choice is between 7. R to B1 and 7. B to Q3. 7. Q to B2 used to be played, and was indeed used in the Lasker-Capablanca match. It is still good ; but less popular than 7. R to B1 because R to B1 prevents Black's immediate 7. . . . P to QB4, which 7. Q to B2 does not prevent but indeed invites. Of course if after 7. R to QB1 Black plays P to QB4 White can either win a Pawn or gain positional advantage at Black's option :—

White	Black
7. R to QB1.	P to B4.
8. P × BP.	P × P.
9. P to B6.	Kt to Kt3.
10. Q × Q.	R × Q.
11. Kt to K5.	

Alternatively :—

White	Black
7. R to B1.	P to B4.
8. P × BP.	Kt × P 8. . . . B × P is obviously no better.
9. P × P.	P × P.
10. Kt × P.	Kt × Kt.
11. R × Kt with a distinct advantage.	

In answer to 7. R to B1 Black usually plays P to B3. At that point White frequently plays the logical B to Q3 and Black, at that point, can take the Gambit Pawn with gain of tempo, and secure sufficient counterplay to neutralise any advantage White may have in the centre thus :—

White	Black
7. R to B1.	P to B3.
8. B to Q3.	P × P.
9. B × P.	Kt to Q4. KtQKt3 is also playable.
10. B × B.	Q × B.
11. 0–0.	

Perhaps the best reply to that is 11. . . . R to Q1 but the following line of play has become popular :—

White	Black
11. . . .	Kt × Kt.
12. R × Kt.	P to K4.
13. P × P.	Kt × P.
14. Kt × Kt.	Q × Kt.
15. P to B4.	Q to K5. And Black should be able to perfect his development.
16. B—Q3 intruduces highly speculative chess.	

To Rubinstein is attributable another popular departure. On

move 8, instead of B to Q3, White plays Q to B2, adding a threat of sorts to the move B to Q3 when it is made.

Against 8, Q to B2, Black has no particularly incisive counterplay, 8. . . . Kt to K5 being of doubtful validity after 9. B×B Q×B 10. Kt×Kt P×Kt 11. Kt to Q2. In answer to 8. . . Kt to K5 the Author also favours P to KR4.

The normal play for Black against Q to B2 is as follows :— P to KR3, followed by P to QR3. Sooner or later, Black will free the Queen's side with the moves P×BP, P to QKt4, and P to B4.

It is worth mentioning that the attacking possibilities of the Q.G.D. were known to Zukertort. He, however, used to play 7. P to QB5, in order to avoid the loss of tempo after B to Q3. Steinitz refuted this by showing how it makes possible P to K4.

The move P to QB5 is playable, however, at about move 11 if Black plays P to QR3 as well as P to QB3.

As for the loss of tempo when the Bishop goes to Q3, this is relatively unimportant. Indeed, Black can play P×P before BQ3 without disadvantage, as was shown in a game Naegeli v. Alekhine.

The above is the orthodox treatment of the Queen's Gambit. But, as in the Ruy Lopez (which corresponds to it among King's Pawn Openings) so here, there is a big variety available to Black. He has at his disposal for example the Cambridge Springs Defence (introduced by Marshall at the Cambridge Springs Tournament, 1904).

	White	*Black*
1.	PQ4.	PQ4.
2.	PQB4.	PK3.
3.	KtQB3.	KtKB3.
4.	BKt5.	QKtQ2.
5.	PK3.	PQB3.
6.	KtKB3.	QR4.

and now White cannot play

7. BQ3 because of 7 . . . . KtK5.

Nevertheless, White has good play after 7. B×Kt or 7. B to K2, or 7. P×P, etc. The Defence has been played in World Championship games, but seems to have lost its popularity.

Interesting is the author's treatment of it.

	White	*Black*
7.	B×Kt.	Kt×B.
8.	B to Q3.	B to Kt5.
9.	0–0 sacrificing a Pawn for the attack.	

LASKER'S METHOD

Another useful idea that can be adopted against the Queen's Gambit (B to Kt5 variation) is the following : to play the Bishop to K2 on the fourth move, follow with P to KR3 (this is good because it prevents a counter by P to KR4, but is not strictly necessary) and later Kt to K5. White cannot then win a Pawn on his K4 after the exchange of Bishops because of Black's threat to check with the Queen at QKt5, regaining a Pawn and considerable freedom, thus :

White	Black.
1. P to Q4.	P to Q4.
2. P to QB4.	P to K3.
3. Kt to QB3.	Kt to KB3.
4. B to Kt5.	B to K2.
5. P to K3.	P to KR3.
6. B to R4 (B × Kt is also good).	QKt to Q2.
7. Kt to KB3.	Kt to K5.
8. B × B.	Q × B.
9. Kt × Kt.	P × Kt.
10. Kt to Q2.	Kt to B3.
11. Q to B2.	P to K4 with equality.

A better method for White is, on Move 9, to play not Kt × Kt but P × P. This forces Black to play Kt × Kt ; and after the recaptures of Knight and Pawn, White can play B to Q3 with the initiative.

8. P to KR4 (played by the Author) is also worth considering.

THE SLOWER FORM OF THE QUEEN'S GAMBIT; AND SLAV DEFENCE.

The modern orthodox form of the Queen's Gambit Declined has been popular since the days of Pillsbury Before his period the development of the Queen's Bishop at KKt5 was not popular. And subsequently to Pillsbury's time there has been a revival of the Slow form, as it is called, of the Queen's Gambit on the part of players who feel that the tempo of the Pillsbury attack is too fast. They prefer to leave the Queen's Bishop behind the Pawns, in order to develop it eventually on QKt2 or on the K-wing after the KP has moved to K4. This incidentally suggests another point of strategy already mentioned, and of which modern players are more conscious than were there predecessors, namely, that a Bishop on a long diagonal behind Pawns is a well developed Bishop. If, e.g., White has Pawns on Q4 and K5 or a Pawn on Q4 and a Knight on K5 the Bishop is supporting them. Moreover, the Pawns will eventually be liable to liquidation by exchanges and eventually the Bishop is likely to be in the sole control of the diagonal. This, it must be understood, is a possibility that has to be judged in the light of the tactical dynamics of the particular game. In general however, it may be said that, in the modern openings, both for White and Black, the Fianchetto of one Bishop or two Bishops is normal. *Inter alia* it has the advantage of preserving the Bishops against exchanges by Knights. That player gives up his Bishops for Knights who can block the Fianchettoed Bishops successfully,

Notwithstanding its advantages, the voluntary adoption of the slow form of the Queens is rare.

White	Black
1. P to Q4.	P to Q4.
2. P to QB4.	P to K3.
3. Kt to QB3.	Kt to KB3.
4. Kt to KB3.	B to K2.
5. P to K3.	P to QB3. Preparing for the possibility of the Meran counter attack. A good alternative is Castles.

The reason why players do not play the voluntary form of the slow Queens is that most of them do not wish to facilitate P to QB4 for Black. Consequently we find that the slow form of the Queen's is usually played when Black has committed himself to the move P to QB3. This may happen in the following way :

White	Black
1. P to Q4.	P to Q4.
2. P to QB4.	P to K3.
3. Kt to QB3.	P to QB3.

If now White plays Kt to KB3 in order to preserve the option of B to Kt5 he runs the risk of the deferred acceptance of the Gambit by the following

White	Black
4. Kt to KB3.	P × P.
5. P to K3.	P to QKt4.
6. P to QR4.	B to Kt5.
7. B to Q2.	P to QR4.
8. P × P.	B × Kt.
9. B × Kt.	P × P.
10. P to QKt3.	B to Kt2. Obviously P to Kt5 is unplayable for the moment.
11. P × P.	P to Kt5.
12. B to Kt2.	Kt to KB3. With a good game. (Black's play from 5 onwards is known as Abrahams' Defence.)

If on move 4, White plays P to K3, Black can play P to KB4 —the Stonewall Defence—which has never been refuted

White	Black
1. PQ4.	PQ4.
2. PQB4.	PK3.
3. KtQB3.	PQB3.
4. PK3.	PKB4.
5. KtKB3.	BQ3.
6. BQ3.	KtKR3. (In order to ensure that BP × P can be met by KP × P.)
7. QB2.	0–0, etc.

The Slav Defence introduces P to QB3 for Black on the second move, viz:

White	Black
1. P to Q4.	P to Q4.
2. P to QB4.	P to QB3.

This is very popular nowadays. It has the advantage of giving Black's Queen's Bishop more freedom than in the orthodox Q.G.D. Thus

White	Black
3. Kt to QB3.	Kt to KB3.
4. Kt to KB3.	B to B4: or 4. ... P×P a playable variation of Queen's Gambit Accepted; but the main line is popular, because it is wise for Black to control White's K4.

However, there are dangers in the quick development of Black's Queen's Bishop. White, with or without the exchange of Pawns, can get a quick development on the Queen's side, with some endgame advantages. e.g., by P×P, followed by Q to Kt3. Also White can, after much preparation, force P to K4 with advantage.

Consequently, and rather paradoxically, Black frequently abandons that particular advantage of the Slav and on the fourth move plays not B to B4 but P to K3.

At this point B to Kt5 for White is not generally recommended, because again Black can carry out the deferred acceptance of the Gambit by 5 ... P×P—a difficult game for both sides. Normal, therefore, is the following main play:

White	Black
1. P to Q4.	P to Q4.
2. P to QB4.	P to QB3.
3. Kt to QB3.	Kt to KB3.
4. Kt to KB3.	P to K3.
5. P to K3.	And we have the Slow form of the Queen's, which is a very good opening.

Play may continue as follows:

White	Black
5. ...	QKt to Q2.
6. B to Q3.	B to Q3. Many authorities regard B to K2 as safer against the possible 7. P to K4; but it is now generally thought that 7. P to K4 is a drawing line. That may or may not be a reason for allowing it.
7. O—O	O—O.

White	Black
8. P to K4.	P × BP. Not, however :

8. . . .	P × KP.
9. Kt × P.	Kt × Kt.
10. B × Kt.	P to K4.
11. P × P.	Kt × P.
12. Kt × Kt.	B × Kt.
13. B × P Ch.	K × B.
14. Q to R5 Ch. wins a Pawn.	

9. B × P.	P to K4. With a tolerable game

THE MERAN COUNTER-ATTACK

At move 6 in this variation (which can be reached by transposition from the (voluntary slow Queen's) Black has the option of P × P, and that can be followed up by the Meran counter-attack.

White	Black
6. . . .	P × P.
7. B × P.	P to QKt4.
8. B to Q3.	P to QR3.
9. P to K4.	P to B4.
10. P to K5.	P × P.
11. Kt × KtP.	Kt × KP. Better, perhaps, is

	11. . . . P × Kt.
	12. P × Kt. Q to Kt3.

White	Black
12. Kt × Kt.	P × Kt.
13. Q to B3.	B to Kt5 Ch.
14. K to K2.	R to QKt1 with many excitements to come.

Complete analysis of this and other variations is of course beyond the scope of an introductory volume. Enough has been shown, however, for the reader to realise that even in the so called slow openings there is scope for tactical lines that raise the tempo and style of the game from piano to forte.

Modern strategians, both as Black and White, are quite likely to take early steps to prevent the game from reaching crescendo too early. This accounts for the modern popularity of the Catalan System for White. After 1. P to Q4. P to Q4. 2. P to QB4. P to K3 (or P to QB3), White instead of playing Kt to QB3 plays Kt to KB3. This move, in answer to P to K3 makes the eventual B to KKt5 a little more difficult because it is unsupported by the attack on the Queen's Pawn; and Black with P to KR3 can virtually force an exchange of pieces. (1. P to Q4 P to Q4 2. P to QB4 P to K3 3. Kt to KB3 Kt to KB3 4. B to Kt5 P to KR3. If 5. B to R4 P to KKt4 6. B to Kt3 Kt to K5 7. P to K3 P to KR4 with advantage.) But when White plays 3. Kt to KB3 he can elect not for eventual B to KKt5 but for P to

KKt3 followed by B to KKt2 and he can combine that with
P to QKt3 and B to QKt2. In this way White gets a good
control of the centre squares, but Black, playing carefully, can
prevent White's attack from becoming too strong. At the
proper time Black will have to play vigorously in the centre
in order to free his game.

White	Black
1. P to Q4.	P to Q4.
2. P to QB4.	P to K3.
3. Kt to KB3.	Kt to KB3.
4. P to KKt3.	B to K2.
5. B to Kt2.	0–0.
6. Kt to B3.	And now Black has to prepare P to K4 or P to B4 in order to get counterplay in the middle of the board.

If Black has started with a Slav, the Catalan is better for
White because P to B4 for Black will waste a tempo. In that
case Black has to play for the possibility of P × BP followed
by P to K4.

RETI-ZUKERTORT. ENGLISH OPENING, ETC.

The Catalan leads us logically away from the Queen's Gambit
to the set of openings loosely known as the Queen's Pawn
Openings. These include some openings in which the move
of the Queen's Pawn is long delayed, so that they might more
properly be called Queen's side openings or Slow openings
than Queen's Pawn openings.

Typical is the Reti-Zukertort system. The combination
of names—a classical master and a modern master—indicates
that old experiments have been perfected in modern strategy.
White's first move is Kt to KB3. Whether Black replies with
Kt to KB3 or P to Q4 White's second move can be P to QB4.
(If P to QB4 is White's first move—and it is eminently playable—we get the English opening, which, achieving continental
appearances, comes to resemble the Reti-Zukertort). If
Black plays slowly against the Reti-Zukertort, what happens
may be as follows—

White	Black
1. Kt to KB3.	Kt to KB3.
2. P to QB4.	P to QB4.
3. Kt to QB3.	P to KKt3.
4. P to K4.	P to Q3.
5. P to Q4.	P × P.
6. Kt × P.	

And White has the Maroczy Attack in the Sicilian. If
Black plays more vigorously with 1. . . . P to Q4, White, as has been

pointed out can play P to QB4. If then Black plays P to Q5 he is engineering a premature attack. If he plays P to K3, we have the English by transposition (P to QB4, P to K3, Kt to KB3, P to Q4). At that point, or later, White can adopt the P to KKt3 system.

It is even possible for White to play P to KKt3, or P to QKt3, on the second move (Kt to KB3 being the first). This method, which would in the past (late 19th century) have been regarded as dreadfully unenterprising, is now quite orthodox.

MODERN VARIATIONS OF THE QUEEN'S PAWN

From the point of view of Black, particularly, it is in the Queen's Pawn rather than the King's Pawn Openings that most of the experiments of modern opening strategy have taken place; because, since the tempo of White's attack in the Queen's Pawn is slower at the outset of the game, Black has got more leisure in which to carry out his own purposes.

There are many aspects of modern theory—which must not be thought of as a simple formula. One of these aspects consists in the recognition that a centre development is not a good thing in itself, Grunfeld's Defence illustrates this truth.

GRUNFELD'S DEFENCE

The reader will appreciate that after the moves 1. P to Q4, P to Q4. 2. P to QB4, Kt to KB3 is not a very good move for Black. That is to say that Black cannot immediately recapture on his Q4 (in the event of White playing 3. P×P) because of the immediate loss of tempo.

Now consider the Grunfeld system—

White	*Black*
1. P to Q4.	Kt to KB3.
2. P to QB4.	P to KKt3.
3. Kt to QB3.	P to Q4. The following will show why this is playable.
4. P×P.	Kt×P.
5. P to K4.	Kt×Kt.
6. P×Kt.	

And now Black with B to Kt2 and P to QB4, etc., gets excellent command of the diagonal, or forces White to weaken the centre (The Hollow Centre) by advancing one of the Pawns leaving weak squares around it for Black to occupy.

On reflection the reader will recognise that this is precisely the reasoning that takes away value from some of the Giuoco

Piano lines ; the apparently formidable centre turns out to be insubstantial.

In the Grunfeld, White is well advised not to attempt to play any quick Pawn advance in the centre. The best treatment is as follows :—

White	Black
4. B to B4.	B to Kt2.
5. P to K3.	0—0.
6. Kt to B3.	P to QB4.
7. B to K5.	And White's development is solid as well as aggressive. Notice that now White is threatening to win a Pawn.

King's Indian Defence

At first sight this is a more surprising system than the Grunfeld because it permits White more activity in the centre.

White	Black
1. P to Q4.	Kt to KB3.
2. P to QB4.	P to KKt3.
3. Kt to QB3.	B to Kt2.
4. P to K4.	P to Q3.
5. P to B4.	0—0
6. Kt to B3.	P to B4. Black commences to weaken the centre.

If now White captures the Pawn, Black gets a good free game with Q to R4. If, instead, White advances the Queen's Pawn then Black has several strategic possibilities to consider. With moves like P to K3 and Pawn exchanges followed by Q moves he can exploit White's weak Queen side and weak diagonals, while White attempts a King's side attack. Alternatively, the Pawn position now being crystallized, Black can prepare to play P to QKt4 or P to K4 and P to KB4 liquidating or undermining the centre. White has counterplay to this; but both sides have chances.

Here, again, the better practice for White is not to over-develop the centre. Instead of 5. P to KB4 there is much to be said for P to KB3 or Kt to KB3. The former leads to a development with P to KKt4, Kt to Kt3, etc., not unlike a possible development for White in the slow form of the Morphy Defence to the Ruy Lopez.

The reader may be reminded by this opening of the temptation given to White to develop the centre excessively against Alekhine's Defence.

Also playable is 5. B to K2 followed by 6. P—KR4 (the Author's method).

THE NIMZOVITCH SYSTEM

One of the most popular modern methods, backed by the authority of one of the greatest players of this century, consists in a different method of undermining, or blocking the centre.

White	Black
1. P to Q4.	Kt to KB3.
2. P to QB4.	P to K3.
3. Kt to QB3.	B to Kt5. This obviously prevents P to K4 ; and against it P to K4 is surprisingly hard to force, P to KB3 being slow.

One popular reply is 4. P to QR3, which is replied to by B×KtCh. White loses a tempo, and gets a development in which the Pawn at QB4 is not very helpful. On the other hand he has strengthened the defensive aspect of his centre and got rid of one of Black's good pieces. It is not advisable, thereafter, to try and force P to K4 because Black can occupy his own K4 (P to Q3 being played first) blocking the centre.

Other methods of treating the Nimzovitch Defence consist in 4. Q to B2 which can be replied to with P to Q4 giving Black a not unsatisfactory form of the Queen's Gambit.

Also White can play 4. Q to Kt3 to which Black can reply P to QB4 coupled with eventual Kt to QB3. This is typical of the system ; and the following line is instructive :

White	Black
1. P to Q4.	Kt to KB3.
2. P to QB4.	P to K3
3. Kt to QB3.	B to Kt5.
4. Q to Kt3.	P to QB4.
5. P×P.	Kt to QB3.
6. Kt to KB3.	Kt to K5.
7. B to Q2.	Kt×QBP.
8. Q to B2.	0—0.
9. P to QR3.	B×Kt.
10. B×B.	P to QR4.
11. P to KKt3.	

White can also elect to ignore Black's 3rd move, assuming that the Black Bishop is not placed on its best possible square. Thus 4. P to K3. This is sometimes coupled with 5. K KtK2, and P to KB3, a slow process, because it does not avoid the need for P to QR3. Reasonable is P to KKt3 at move 4 or 3.

Exciting is the Budapest—1. P to Q4 KKt to B3, 2. P to QB4 P to K4, 3. P×P Kt to Kt5 (or K5) with play. In answer to 3. . . . Kt to K5 4. P to QR3 is recommended.

QUEEN'S INDIAN DEFENCE

In order to control a fluid centre it is quite a desirable thing for Black to develop his Queen's Bishop at Kt2. This is most usually played when White develops his King's Knight before his Queen's Knight. Black's first three moves are usually Kt to KB3, followed by P to K3 and P to QKt3. To dispense with the second of these is possible ; but if P to K3 is played, then Black can combine his B to QKt2 with B to QKt5. He must be careful about order if White on the third move plays the Queen's Knight to B3. Thus,

White	*Black*
1. P to Q4.	Kt to KB3.
2. P to QB4.	P to K3.
3. Kt to QB3.	P to QKt3.
4. P to K4.	B to Kt5.
5. P to K5.	Kt to K5.
6. Q to K4.	Kt × Kt. Black is in trouble.
7. P × Kt.	B × P Ch.
8. K to Q1.	K to B1 (best).
9. B to R3 Ch.	K to Kt1.
10. R to QKt1.	B to Kt2.
11. R to Kt3.	B to R4.
12. Q × KtP Ch. with a mating attack.	

However, if the Bishop is played to Kt2 before B to Kt5 this situation cannot come about. Nor does the danger exist if White's third move is Kt-KB3. Normally the Queen's Indian is played without B to QKt5. If B to QKt5 is played it is with the intention of exchanging that Bishop, because evidently the Pawn formation is incompatible with the comfort of the Bishop on the Queen's wing.

The Queen's Indian and the Nimzo-Indian (Q.I. with B to Kt5) are too logical to require detailed treatment. They are usually met by a King's Fianchetto on the part of White. White will eventually endeavour to play P to K4 and Black will play to block the centre with P to Q3 and K4, the Black Queen's Knight being developed at Q2.

OTHER Q.P. OPENINGS

Of other openings that are worth mentioning, not least is the Dutch Defence 1. P to Q4, P to KB4.

White also can open with 1. P to KB4, but it is not so advantageous to White as to Black, since, early in the game, the move is defensive rather than aggressive.

The Dutch Defence can be met by a Gambit 2. P to K4, (or even P to KKt4) which requires no special treatment. Otherwise it is likely to transpose itself into the Stone Wall Defence.

In conclusion, it may be said of the Queen's Pawn Openings generally, that once their strategy is grasped they do not require learning. That consideration, together with the less intense nature of the early struggle accounts for the preferences that are shown among modern players for the Queen's Pawn over the King's Pawn systems.

It may also be added, as a final note on the Openings, generally—

1. That even good openings do not win games. All they create is an initiative—which passes as both sides develop.

2. It is therefore, important for Black not to regard himself as at any disadvantage. If truth be told, he may even have the advantage.

3. It is more important to concentrate on seeing good moves than on learning them.

4. There are fashions in Opening choices. These may produce surprise, but should not produce alarm. In point is a recent (1961) resuscitation of an old move—1. . . . P to KKt3 in answer to 1. P to K4 (or Q4) and the impressive label Kotov-Robatsch. But this is precisely the kind of play that gives to the player that meets it every opportunity for doing well on his own resources.

After the Opening

As you emerge from the opening you will find, if you are playing intelligently, that you have no occasion to ask yourself, What shall I think about now ? As the game proceeds, two processes are going on. You are developing your pieces, and you are attacking or defending. These processes are really one process. You will find that no attack on a specific object is worth while if it involves you in difficulties of development, and no defence is good, if it cramps your development. Again you will also find that if your pieces are coming into play, e.g., Rooks getting on to Open Files, etc., then you are also generating plenty of specific threats and parrying threats. Your opponent is, from his side, doing likewise. The problem for both of you is to secure Control and Freedom. As the two sets of forces integrate the position itself will indicate to you the proper direction of your thoughts. Then the important thing will be to miss as little as possible of what the Board reveals to those who can interpret it.

CHAPTER VI

SOME RESOURCES AND REFINEMENTS IN THE ENDGAME.

We have seen that the endgame is the beginning of Chess. It is also the end—the latest stage and the most advanced. It calls for vision in the highest degree, and in addition to vision, or in necessary support of it, a considerable technique.

Of basic elementary endgame technique, the reader has already been told a great deal in the second and subsequent chapters. In an introductory volume, it is not possible or desirable to undertake an exhaustive account. All that is aimed at here is the demonstration of a few of the resources and refinements that characterise the ending. The appreciation of these should help to equip the reader for the endgame, as acquaintance with some of the tactical processes may have equipped him for the middle-game.

(BLACK)

(WHITE)

AN ERROR.

White can lose.

1. R to Kt8 Ch., K to K2.
2. R to Kt8, K to B3.
3. R to B8 Ch., K to K4.
4. R to B7, K to B5! and White cannot avoid Mate.

Fundamental to the endgame is, of course, vision. In the endgame it is possible to lose by an oversight as easily as at any other stage. The first diagram illustrates an easy error to make.

That is an error of vision at a reasonably elementary level. But it is much easier to go wrong, through, for example, missing points of tempo. Here is a great endgame player (Spielmann) missing the best move in the diagram position. He can win by 1 . . . K to B6. He actually played 1 . . . K × P and there followed 2. P to Kt6, K to Q6. 3. R to Q7, P to Q5. 4. P to Kt7, R to Kt3. 5. K to Kt2, R to Kt8. 6. K to Kt3. Black was wrong to allow the White Pawn to advance to Kt6, because after that he cannot move his King usefully without allowing a Rook threat followed by P to Kt7, and then Black's

(BLACK)

(WHITE)

Black to play.

Rook is relatively immobilized, so that nothing can be forced. Had Black not been greedy and played 1 . . . K to B6 he would have won as follows : 1. . . . K to B6, 2. R to B7 Ch. K × P. Now 3. R to KKt7 is forced because if 3. R to QKt7 there follows R × P, 4. R × P Ch. K to B6 winning the Rook or mating. Therefore, 3. R to KKt7 (Black has already gained a tempo) K to B6, 4. R to B7 Ch., K to Q6 (another gain of tempo), 5. R to KKt7, P to Q5. 6. P to KKt6, R to QB7 Ch. 7. K to Kt1 (the effect of K to Q1 is worse) R to B3. 8. R to Kt8, K to B6 (cleverly protected against the tempo gaining check) 9. P to Kt7, R to B2 and White must move and lose.

It was said earlier in the book that strategy consists, in some part, in the preparation for the endgame, in so playing as to have a good endgame structure. That is true, but "negatively" true. You must rather play so as not to have a bad endgame structure. But to guarantee the endgame structure for victory is an impossible requirement. One enters the actual endgame fighting ; and at that stage the Board is full of resource.

A very fine example is furnished in a game of Alekhine's (Reshevsky-Alekhine, 1938). Black drew this apparently hopeless ending by play involving a brilliant manoeuvre.

(BLACK)

(WHITE)

RESHEVSKY—
ALEKHINE (1938).
Black draws.

	White	*Black*
44.	. . .	R to Q6.
45.	R × P.	P to R5.
46.	P to Q5 (R to R5 is **not** demonstrably better).	P to R6.
47.	R to R7 Ch.	K to B3.
48.	R to R7.	K to K4.
49.	R to R5.	R to Q7 Ch.
50.	K to B3.	R to Q6 Ch.
51.	K to K2.	R to QKt6.
52.	K to B2.	R to Kt7 Ch.
53.	K to Kt3.	R to Kt6 Ch.
54.	K to Kt4.	R to Kt7.
55.	K to R3.	P to R7.
56.	P to Q6. Ch.	K × P.
57.	P to Kt4.	K to B3.
58.	K to Kt3.	K to Kt3.
59.	R to R8.	K to Kt4.
60.	P to R3.	K to Kt5.
61.	K to B4 (threat was R **to** Kt6 Ch. and R to R6).	R to QB7—threat repeated.
62.	R to Kt8 Ch.	K to B6.
63.	R to B8 Ch.	K to Kt5.
		Draw by repetition of moves.

And here is a position reached between Botwinnik and Euwe at a tournament in 1946 in which the Russian Master gained a draw resourcefully in a position where his opponent had a clear endgame advantage.

(BLACK)

(WHITE)

BOTWINNIK
—EUWE.

Black to play.
37. ... P to B5.
38. P×P, P×P.
39. P to R4, P to R3.
40. P to Kt5, P to R4.
41. K to K3 ! K to K4.
42. R to B2 ! P to B6.
43. K to Q3, R to Q1 Ch. (K to B5 is probably better.)
44. K to K3, R to Q5.
45. R×P, R×P Ch.
46. K to B3, R×P.
47. R to B6! R to B5. Ch.
48. K to K3, R to K5 Ch.
49. K to B3, K to B4.
50. R to B6 Ch., K×P.
57. R×P Ch. Drawn.

A number of diagrams at the end of this chapter illustrate something of the infinite variety of clever Chess that the endgame affords. Meanwhile it may be useful to mention a few points of endgame technique that are sufficiently difficult for an intelligent player to have difficulty in discovering them unaided.

(BLACK)

(WHITE)

OPPOSITION PLAY
1. If P to B6 Ch. P×P Ch.
2. K to B5. If 2 ... K to B1.
3. K×P Wins. If 2 .. K to Q1.
3. K to Q6 wins. Therefore 1 ... K to B1.
2. K to Q6 K to Kt1.
3. K to Q7 P×P!
4. K×P K K to B1 draws.
To win, White plays
1. K to K5 K to B3 (best).
2. K to Q4 K to Q2.
3. K to Q5 with Opposition.

The reader has already seen the technique of play by King and Pawn against King (see Chapter II). The basis of that is the move in hand that the player with the Pawn must try to keep. Thus, if a King is situated at K1 opposite a King at K1 and the Pawn is at K2, the technique is to play the King to Q2, K3, K4 as quickly as possible, preserving the Pawn moves. The Pawn move preserves the opposition to the dominant King, so that eventually the position that is reached is King at K6, Pawn at K5, opponent's King it matters not where, and the player with the Pawn must win. This is tempo play and opposition play, of which other examples have been given. Let the reader now work out why K at K5, P at K4 : Black K at K2 is not a win if White to move.

Incidentally, two Pawns against one are more favourable to the attacker than a lone Pawn. He may be able to choose his time to exchange.

(BLACK)

(WHITE)

DISTANT OPPOSITION

(Modern analysts describe this, also, as a study in RE-LATED SQUARES)

More difficult is the *distant opposition*. There are Pawns on both sides and possibly on both wings. The Kings are distant from each other, but when they approach each other, the opposition will determine which player (if any) breaks through in order to capture the Pawns. How then to gain the opposition at a distance ? This is not always possible ; but the diagram illustrates the problem tackled. White has to keep the King in such a position relatively to the other that when they approach there shall be a distance of three squares between them, and the King to move shall have to leave the square of the same colour as the opposing King, or else retreat. In either case the dominant King will penetrate the Pawn position.

In the diagram the process is made possible by the configuration of the Pawns, which is slightly favourable to White.

Obviously if the White King tries to go straight through, either on the Queen's wing or on the King's wing, he will find the Black King barring his entry ; and this inevitability is only removed by ensuring that the Black King will not have the opposition when the two Kings are next square but one to each other. It so happens that White can take advantage of the restriction in the Black King's space. 1. K to Kt1, K to Kt2. 2. K to B1, K to B2. 3. K to Q1, K to Q2. 4. K to B2, K to Q1. 5. K to B3, K to B2. 6. K to Q3 ; and now if Black plays K to Q2 in apparent opposition, White plays K to B4. [If at move 4. ... K to B1. 5. K to Q2, K to Q2 (or 1). 6. K to B3!]

If, however, in the diagram position it were Black's turn to move, Black could draw by 1. ... K to Kt2. 2. K to Kt1, K to R2. If then the White King goes to Kt2, Black plays K to R1 ; if 3. K to B1, K to Kt2 ; if K to B2, K to Kt1 ; and Black's King can always remain an odd number of squares away from the White King on the same colour squares.

In an elementary book all the variations cannot be analysed ; but the student is invited to experiment for himself. A very simple method of learning how to handle the distant opposition is the following : place the two Kings each on their KR1. Let White then endeavour to reach either of two squares for victory, QR8 or QB8. The process is 1. K to R2, K to Kt1. 2. K to Kt2, K to B1. 3. K to B2, K to K1. 4. K to K2, K to Q1. 5. K to Q2, K to B1. 6. K to B2, K to Kt1. 7. K to Kt2, K to R1. 8. K to B3. (The last two moves amount to triangulation ; White still has the distant opposition.) 8. ... K to Kt2. 9. K to Kt3, K to R2. 10. K to B4, K to Kt3. 11. K to Kt4, K to R2. 12. K to B5, K to Kt2. 13. K to Kt5, K to R2. 14. K to B6, K to Kt1. 15. K to Kt6, K to R1. 16. K to B7, K to R2. 17. K to B8.

More practically important than the distant opposition is the notion of triangulation which we saw in that example. The King with three squares to manoeuvre on can defeat the King with two squares. This kind of manoeuvre is seen in the position in the next diagram. Black has fewer squares. Yet if White were to play immediately, K to K3, Black would reply K to K4 with advantage. But White can waste a move with K to Q2 or K to B2. Then if Black plays K to K4 White becomes dominant with K to K3, and if Black plays K to B3 or Q2, instead, White simply wins the Pawn with K to K3.

The opposition and the distant opposition can be the occasion of neat play of a tempo-losing character. Thus imagine Pawns at R4 and R5, and an opposition Pawn at Kt2; Kings facing each other among Pawns elsewhere on the Board. Then White forces Black to move by playing P to R6 P×P 2. P to R5. It is noteworthy that, whereas in the middle game one usually wishes to gain tempo, in the

(BLACK)

(WHITE)

Purposive Loss of Tempo.

WHITE WINS (by Triangulation).
1. K to Q2 (not K to K3).
If 1. . . . . K—K4, then 2. K—K3.

endgame one often requires to lose tempo. This is the only phase at which Chess technique resembles that of Draughts.

When other Pieces are present with King and Pawn or King and Pawns the possibilities become too great for compendious description.

Some points are worth observing.

Observe the power of a Knight to sacrifice itself for a Pawn. Thus if you have a Pawn at say KB7, and a hostile Knight is guarding the Queening square, you can never force the Pawn home with the aid of your King. Thus suppose your King goes to K7 attacking the Knight on its Q2, the Knight goes to its K4. Then, if you Queen the Pawn, Kt to Kt3 forks King and Queen. Again if you attack the Knight with K to K6 the Kt plays to its B1. If then K to K7, Kt to Kt3; and so forth. Therefore it can come about that King, Pawn and Knight can draw with King, Rook and Pawn. With your Pawn on the seventh you hold the hostile Rook, and with the Knight you play against the King and Pawn. The Knight sacrifices itself for the Pawn, and you win the Rook in exchange for your own dangerous Pawn. That of course assumes a fortunate placing of the Pieces ; but it is a feature to be borne in mind.

Another important feature of endgame play is the virtual impossibility of winning with a Pawn majority when each side has a Bishop, and the Bishops are of opposite colour. The reasoning is that given a King barring the path of one or two Pawns, those Pawns cannot be forced (with B check) to a square not controlled by their Bishop. Alternatively if the position reduces itself far enough, the Bishop cannot be prevented by the opposing Bishop from sacrificing itself for the Pawn. The most favourable situation in these circumstances is to have a majority of two Pawns and for Pawns to be on both wings. Then you may be able with the aid of the King to force the Bishop to sacrifice itself for one or two of your Pawns while you still have a Bishop and a guarded Pawn on the Board. Then (usually) Bishop, King and Pawn will defeat King and Pawn.

And this brings us to another consideration, which is of the first importance in endgame play ; that Bishop and, Rook's Pawn cannot win if the defending King can place itself in front of the Pawn and if the Bishop does not control the final Queening square. This, be it emphasized, only applies to the Rook's file. On any other file the King can arrive at a seventh square adjoining the Pawn ; this cannot be done when the hostile King is on a Rook's file and the Pawn is the Rook's Pawn, because stalemate occurs first.

However, there is a special case. If you can get your Bishop on R7 and your Pawn on R6, the King cannot reach its R1—and can be headed off by your King, while the Pawn gets promoted.

ROOK AND PAWN ENDGAMES

But far and away the most important feature of endgame technique is the play of the Rooks against the Pawns. The reader has already seen that two or three well-placed Pawns can defeat a Rook. That is a tactical occurrence which is relatively easy to see. What causes difficulty is the fact that a majority of endings are characterised by Rook or Rooks on each side, and a Pawn majority on one side. The keystone of this type of ending is the situation where King, Rook and one Pawn are against King and Rook. This can be extremely difficult.

To emphasise the difficulty let it be mentioned that King, Rook and two Pawns do not necessarily win against King and Rook. The diagram shows such a position. Obviously here Black cannot attack and capture the Bishop's Pawn because the backward King could not stop the Knight's Pawn. But similarly White can do nothing. If he checks, the King can then capture the Pawn, because it so happens that White cannot thereafter save the Knight's Pawn. On the same reasoning the White Rook cannot leave his rank. Even if he goes to R8 and subsequently defends the Pawn from QKt8, it will fall.

(BLACK)

(WHITE)

DRAW.
1. R to R8 K × P.
2. P to Kt5 K to B5.
3. P to Kt6 R to K2!
   (not the 'normal'
   R to QKt8 because
   of the check on the
   file).
4. R to QKt8 K to B4
5. K to K6 R to KR2.
6. P to Kt7 K to Kt3
   Draws.

The diagram position is unusually favourable to Black. It is more favourable to the defender when the two Pawns are Rook's Pawn and Knight's Pawn on the same side of the Board ; and there can also be great difficulty when the Pawns are separated by one file or even two files. When they are separated by more the likelihood is that the defending King will prove inadequate to the task of co-operating in the gain of one Pawn and then in the stopping of the other.

Fundamental in the last diagram position is the fact that when one Pawn falls the other cannot be Queened. But that need not be the case. It follows that the fundamental consideration for endgame play is the possibility of Queening a Pawn with the aid of a Rook against a Rook.

Now obviously the most favourable circumstances exist when the King is playing a causative part in the Queening of the Pawn. A typical position is the Lucena position in the diagram. Here White wins neatly by playing R to B5. The threat is then R to K5 Ch. followed by K to B7. If then R to B7 Ch. K to Kt6 and after R to Kt7 Ch. R to Kt5. The Rook has, as it were, built an arch under which the King can operate. If the Black King were less dominant than in the diagram, obviously the process would be easy, because a Rook is not adequate to controlling a King that is helping a Pawn to Queen (except in the solitary case of the Rook's Pawn, where perpetual check is possible). But even where

(BLACK)

(WHITE)

WHITE WINS
The Lucena Position
1. R to B5 (See Text)
   If 1. . . . K to K2.
2. R to K5 Ch. K to B3.
3. K to B8 wins.
(1. R—K1 Ch. followed by R—K4 also creates an archway for the King.)

the Pawn is a Rook's Pawn, then if the hostile King is sufficiently far away the dominant Rook can execute the kind of protective manœuvre that we have just seen.

That line of thought amounts to one reason among others why it is an advantage to cut the hostile King off from the critical Pawn context; and it is not easy to keep a King cut off. The King can always pass a file with the aid of a Rook, provided that he has time after the exchanges of Rooks to prevent the promotion of the Pawn.

In short then, if both Kings are on the scene of action the win is unlikely. This with one reservation; that if the defending King is on the back rank faced by Pawn with adjacent King, then mating threats become a factor, and it is very important that the defending Rook shall be able to drive away the threatening King.

Most difficult of all is where the attacking King has an option. At K6 it is facing a King on its K1. The Pawn is at Q5. If the King is checked on the rank the Pawn may be able to advance, creating a mating threat; if the King is checked on the file its position when it goes to Q6 is dominant, because then it is probable that the defending King can be driven from the back row, and the Lucena position may easily come into being.

The second main class of Rook and Pawn against Rook endings is when the Kings are not in the battle but the Rooks are.

Then if the dominant Rook is behind its Pawn and the Pawn is sufficiently advanced, the defending Rook, in front of it, is at a great disadvantage; and it is a question of which King can arrive at the scene of action first. It is quite likely that the freer Rook can cut off the defending King along the rank for sufficiently long to enable the attacking King to arrive in time to force the Queening of the Pawn. This class of position is relatively easy. More difficult is the situation where the attacking Rook is in front of its Pawn, and the Pawn is on the sixth or the seventh. Then the position is delicate indeed. Then it may not pay the defending King to be too near. Obviously on the third rank the defending King is at a clear loss because it cannot keep out of Check. Let White King be at K3, R at QR8; P at QR7; Black Rook at KR2, King at Q3. Black's only available move is R to Q2. There follows 2. K to K4. If then R to K2 Ch. White plays either K to Q4 or K to Q3. 3. ... R to Q2 is then forced and White plays K to B4 and cannot be stopped from taking a decisive part; thus K to B4, R to B2 Ch. 5. K to Kt5, R to B4 Ch. 6. K to Kt4, winning.

If the Black Rook were not on the second rank Black's situation would be worse.

(BLACK)

(WHITE)

White to move, wins. If the Black King were on the third rank (other than QB3 QKt3 or QR3) the win would be even more obvious.

The Diagram on the opposite page is of great technical interest. White to move wins and Black to move draws. White has only to play R to KB8 or KKt8, or KR8 ; and obviously the Pawn cannot be captured or stopped. It follows that unless the Black King can move a square nearer to the Pawn it is worse off than if it were further away. Now further down the file is no use because of the file checks, giving a tempo for Queening. The correct position, and one rather hard to find by the light of nature, is the position in the following diagram.

(BLACK)

(WHITE)

DRAW.

If the Black King stays on its KKt2 or KR2 the game is a draw. The Black King is proof there against file checks or rank thrusts. The White King can never be useful because it can be driven away by an endless series of checks. Therefore, it is useless for the White King to work its way to QKt2 and then up the file. Similar technique applies even if the Pawn is not on the Rook's file. More difficult is the position when the Pawn is at R6. If at the moment the defending King is near enough to reach its QB2 then the game is a draw because the Pawn is forced on to R7 and the King reaches QB2 and QKt2. But if the King is at that moment on the King's file it must rush back to KKt2, because of the threat of P to R7. However, the White King can be prevented, by a combination of file and rank threats, from reaching R7 while the Rook is still at R8. There are checking possibilities on the QB file to cope with the situation.

If, however, the Pawn instead of being at R6 were at Kt6

with the two Rooks at their respective Kt8, then the situation would be uncontrollably difficult for Black, though it would require the greatest delicacy for White to win. The reader is left to work out the process for himself.

Enough has now been said to give the student an idea of the nature of endgame technique and to communicate to him a few of its important principles. To do more would require a

(BLACK)

(WHITE)

WHITE WINS.
(An ending by Kubbel)

1. Kt to K3 Dis. Ch., K to Kt6.
2. Q to Kt4 Ch., K to B7.
3. Q to B4 Ch., K to K7 (best).
4. Q to B1 Ch., K to Q7.
5. Q to Q1 Ch., K to B6.
6. Q to B2 Ch., K to Kt5.
7. Q to Kt2 Ch., Kt to Kt6.
8. Q to R3 Ch., K ×Q.
9. Kt to B2, Mate.

(BLACK)

(WHITE)

WHITE WINS.

1. Kt to K2, K ×Kt.
2. B to Q1 Ch., K ×B.
3. P = Q wins, by 4Q to Kt1 Ch.
If 2. . . . K to K6, etc.
3. B to B3, K ×B.
4. P = Q wins by 5Q to R8 Ch.
[After 5. . . . K to Kt7 the Q. wins because Black's other pawns prevent stale-mate.]

much larger, indeed a special, volume. To conclude the chapter here are a number of endgame compositions by famous composers—and a few from play. Between them they illustrate several of the resources of the Chess Board and some of its beauties.

WHITE WINS.
1. P to Kt7, R to QKt4.
2. P to K7, K to B2.
3. P to K8 Ch., K × Q.
4. B to R4, wins.

WHITE WINS.
1. R to K1.

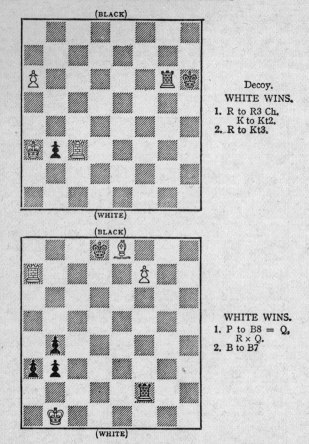

Decoy.
WHITE WINS.
1. R to R3 Ch.
　　K to Kt2.
2. R to Kt3.

WHITE WINS.
1. P to B8 = Q,
　　R × Q.
2. B to B7

A NOTE ON CHESS PROBLEMS, CHESS COMPOSITIONS AND
THE AESTHETIC IN CHESS

It is not proposed in this book to consider the rather special
aspect of Chess which is the Chess problem. At one time
problems were studies in difficulty, and were solved by
unexpected captures and spectacular sacrifices. Nowadays
the problem that is seen in the newspapers and the magazines
is a special thing. It is characterised by a certain difficulty :

but normally, the essence of the problem is that the solution and the variations illustrate and express some geometric theme which is intellectually satisfying and may be quite beautiful. The interest, however, is specialized. For the purposes of the student of Chess it should be said, then, that problems are not very helpful. Nevertheless they are not valueless.

In the typical two move or three move problem you have to Mate in the specific number of moves. Usually the position given would not be difficult to win. But to Mate in two or three moves can, from that position, be extraordinarily difficult. The problem may be what is called a Waiter. That is to say if Black moved you could Mate him, but any move you make seems to take away your capacity to Mate him. You therefore have to find an ingenuity which preserves the possibilities, or substitutes possibilities for those that it takes away (Change Mate). Alternatively, you may have to find a way of mating that is unexpected, and threaten it—or prevent a defence to a threat that is in being. These are Threat problems. Very neat can be those in which the defence to one threat reciprocally interferes with the defence to another threat. In the case of three moves the processes involved may be really difficult, and there may be clever Chess in the very short range over which you are thinking ; but they, too, are specialized. The utility of problems for a Chess player consists in this, that in solving them you have to visualize the Mate or the manœuvre that the composer has in mind ; to do that is an exercise of imagination, and imagination is the soul of Chess. The reader is therefore well advised to endeavour to solve problems. In doing so he is well advised to remember that it is not a question of winning but of doing a special task ; and the solution is not likely to be a forceful move such as check or a capture. And when he comes from solving problems to practical play he must not spend his time imagining possible Mates too improbable to be important.

Here in notation are two well known Chess problems to illustrate what ideas Chess problems express and to show how the problem mind works.

6K1, 8, 4p 1 k p, 7p, 4PR 1P, 8, 6 B1, 8.

MATE IN THREE—

	White		*Black*

Solution :

1. B to B1.	P to K4.
2. B to Q3.	P × R.
3. P to K5 Mate.	

The Mate is pretty, and that Mating idea has to be conceived for the problem to be solved.

Harder and even prettier is the following :—
8. 7Q, 4k 3, 4P3, 8. 2Kt 1 p Kt 2, K7, 8.

MATE IN THREE

White   *Black*

Solution :
  1. Kt to QR4 (threatening Kt
     to Kt6 followed by QQ7).
  1. ...   K to Q4.
  2. Q to KB7 Ch.
  2. ...   K to K5.
  3. Kt to B5 Mate.
If 2. ...   K to B3.
  3. Kt to Q4 Mate.

These show clever mating ideas. Problems can also express decoys, batteries, avoidance of stalemate, etc., etc., but with the idea abstracted from the reality of the game.

The reader will also have noticed other compositions, especially in the last chapter, which can only be described as elegant. These (endgame compositions) are much more useful than problems because they show not only elegances of the Board, but interesting methods of play, and resources that may be of practical value.

Again the reader has seen some combinations in actual play that can be described as beautiful. These suggest the reflection that Chess is not only a Science, but may also possess the appeal to the spectator, real or imaginary, which is the essence of art. Nevertheless, let it always be remembered that the beauty of a piece of Chess is accidental, relatively to its effectiveness. Chess is a science and the good Chess move is the effective Chess move, as the good scientific process is the one that carries a result. The formal beauty of an idea is as irrelevant in Chess as, in Science, the aesthetic pleasure provided by colours that may occur in chemical experiments. Yet perhaps Chess gives something greater than the aesthetic. If the student of Chess comes to a stage where he can see a neat, elegant, or beautiful idea, and reject it because there is a better move available, then he has arrived at a high stage of Chess, and is approaching the attainment of that intellectual integrity which is the contribution of any science to culture.

CHAPTER VII

ILLUSTRATIVE GAMES

White MORPHY	*Black* DUKE OF BRUNSWICK
	P to K4.
1. P to K4.	
2. Kt to KB3.	P to Q3. Philidor. A good move, but one that involves the need for very careful play very early.
3. P to Q4.	B to Kt5. A mistake, of which the worst consequences are hard to see. Black is losing tempo ; best is Kt to Q2 which enables Black reply to P×P with P×P. Black would subsequently develop with P to QB3, B to K2, Kt to B3.
4. P×P.	B×Kt. Almost forced. Black has to fear— 4. ... P×P. 5. Q×Q Ch. K×Q. 6. Kt×P. 4. ... Q to K2 is playable, but "difficult." P×P.
5. Q×B.	Kt to KB3. Black is already in difficulties. The text gives him an immediate defence on which Morphy puts great pressure. Possibly better was 6 ... Q to B3 followed by 7. Q to Kt3, Kt to Q2 losing (or sacrificing) a Pawn but getting some counterplay.
6. B to B4 with immediate pressure.	
7. Q to QKt3 with double attack.	Q to K2. The best available effort.
8. Kt to QB3. Not Q×KtP because then 8 ... Q to Kt5 Ch. forces exchanges of Queens and Black has a little freedom to compensate for his Pawn.	P to B3. Defending the Kt Pawn, but leaving the game very cramped. Better was Kt to Q2, letting the Pawn go.
9. B to KKt5. Maintaining the pressure. At this point the game is not yet lost for Black, but his disadvantage is clear. If, e.g., he plays P to KR3 there might follow— B×Kt P×B. and later, the establishment of a Kt on KB5.	P to QKt 4. A desperate effort for freedom which fails disastrously. Black has not seen all that his opponent can do.
10. Kt × KtP.	P×Kt.
11. B × KtP Ch.	QKt to Q2.
12. 0-0-0.	R to Q1. Apparently good enough.

White	*Black*
13. R × Kt, showing how little the values of the Pieces matter when there is a decisive process available.	R × R.
14. R to Q1.	Q to K3, necessary in order to enable the Kt to recapture.

At this point White can win simply by B × KKt and if then, P × B either B × R ch. or Q to R4, but the win will not be such a rapid one.

What Morphy does is immediately decisive, and very pretty—

White	*Black*
15. B × R Ch.	Kt × B.
16. Q to Kt8 Ch.	Kt × Q.
17. R to Q8 Mate.	

Observe that White's entire force is B and R against Q, R, B and Kt.

A companion study in strangulation is afforded in Modern Chess, where players are better equipped strategically than was the Duke of Brunswick, but where a keen player still surpasses a dull player, and does so the more strikingly in that what he has to see may be the exploitation of a finer difference in development than was usually exploited in the past.

White (ALEKHINE)	*Black* (BÖÖK)
1. P to Q4.	P to Q4.
2. P to QB4.	P × P. The Queen's Gambit Accepted. A difficult opening.
3. Kt to KB3.	Kt to KB3.
4. P to K3.	P to K3. Slow.
5. B × P. White achieves this without losing the tempo that is usually lost in the Q.G.D.	P to B4
6. 0–0.	Kt to QB3. Awkward. The Kt should go to Q2—the reason appears later. The point of the text is to try and get in Kt to Kt5 after the B has been driven.
7. Q to K2. Offering a Pawn.	P to QR3, (Safer than P × P).
8. Kt to B3. Better than R to Q1, which is met by 8.... P to QKt4. 9. B to Kt3, P to B5. 10. B to B2, Kt to Kt5.	P to QKt4.
9. B to Kt3.	P to Kt5. Bad because it is a premature attack. More specifically bad, because it does not cope with the (admittedly brilliant) tactical possibilities that Alekhine finds. Better (but not very good) was P to QB5 followed by B to Kt2, losing, at least, no tempo.
10. P to Q5. Vigorous and good. White is commencing on excellent combination.	Kt to QR4. If ... P × Kt, B to R4 is excellent for White. If P × P, Kt × P followed by R to Q1 etc.

White	Black
11. B to R4 Ch.	B to Q2.
12. P×P.	P×P. B×B would lose at least a Pawn by P×P Ch. K×P Kt×B, but is playable.
13. R to Q1. Pinning the Bishop and attacking in a way reminiscent of the Morphy game.	P×Kt.
14. R×B. This and the following moves had to be seen quite clearly, at the latest on move 13, but in order to make move 10 sound, it had to be seen then.	Kt×R.
15. Kt to K5.	R to R2.
16. P×P. This gives the game its hall-mark. White had to see when he sacrificed that, after this quiet move, Black has nothing to stop the attack.	K to K2. A horrible expedient, but it has to be done sooner or later, because of the number of Pieces that White can mobilize against the pinned Kt. If P to Kt3, e.g., 17. Q to Q3 stops any idea of Castling.
17. P to K4. White has seen that he can still attack if the Kt is temporarily unpinned.	Kt to KB3.
18. B to KKt5.	Q to B2. Attempting to get in P to K4.
19. B to B4	Q to Kt3. The brilliance of the attack may be judged on the assumption that White had seen 19. . . . Q to Kt2. 20. R to Q1, Kt×P. 21. Q×Kt, Q×Q. 22. B to Kt5 Mate. Easier to see but less decisive is 19. . . . Q to Kt2. 20. R to Q1, Q×P. 21. Q to Q2, Kt to Q4. 22. B to Kt5 Ch., with a prolonged and convincing attack.
20. R to Q1.	P to Kt3.
21. B to KKt5.	B to Kt2.
22. Kt to Q7.	R×Kt.
23. R×R-Ch.	K to B1.
24. B×Kt.	B×B.
25. P to K5.	Resigns. After all the simplification, Black cannot escape.

A splendid example of strangulation carried out on other than the weakest.

The next example is of quick suffocation, occasioned by a great master's decision to incur pressure.

RUY LOPEZ

White (BIRD)	Black (STEINITZ)
1. P to K4.	P to K4.
2. Kt to KB3.	Kt to QB3.
3. B to Kt5.	Kt to B3. Berlin Defence.
4. P to Q4.	P×P.

White (BIRD)	*Black* (STEINITZ)
5. P to K5.	Kt to K5.
6. Kt × P.	Kt × Kt.
7. Q × Kt.	Kt to B4.
8. 0–0.	B to K2.
9. P to KB4.	P to QKt3. Too aggressive. Black is trying to exploit White's bold 9th move. The idea is ingenious, but unwarranted.
10. P to B5.	Kt to Kt6.
11. Q to K4.	Kt × R.
12. P to B6. At move 9 . . . Black had probably expected 12. Q × R.	B to B4 Ch.
13. K to R1.	R to QKt1.
14. P to K6 wins.	

From the 1890's an example of combative, rather than positional play; typical of the attack based on advantage of tempo, in which the positional differences are hard to state. It is an example of neat decapitation, rather than strangulation. It was played by the winner, when he was past his prime, in the famous Hastings Tournament of 1895.

White (W. STEINITZ)	*Black* (C. VON BARDELEBEN)
1. P to K4.	P to K4.
2. Kt to KB3.	Kt to QB3.
3. B to B4.	B to B4.

These moves constitute the Giuoco Piano (or Italian) opening. The name implies that it is a slow game; but the variation here played does not support that description.

White	*Black*
4. P to B3. Endeavouring to control the centre.	Kt to B3. Counter attacking towards, rather than defending, the centre.
5. P to Q4.	P × P.
6. P × P.	B to Kt5 Ch. A good move giving Black a breathing space in which to attend to the centre, but developing White's game as well. The opening is becoming tactically rich.
7. Kt to B3. The Moller attack. If now Black plays Kt × P, he lies open to a dangerous albeit speculative attack commencing with P to Q5 or Q to Kt3, or 8. 0–0 (followed possibly by B × Kt. 9. P × B, P to Q4. 10. B to R3 with a vigorous game).	P to Q4. Also playing dangerously. Black was anxious to avoid the main lines of the Moller attack and adopts a method of development which requires the most careful handling.
8. P × P.	KKt × P.
9. 0–0.	B to K3. White was threatening to win a Piece; and the best defence was hard to find.

For Black to win a Pawn by Kt×Kt, P×Kt, B×P, would be wrong because of White's Q to Kt3 to follow, initiating a winning attack against the Black King. There were, however, other playable moves, e.g., 9. . . . . B × Kt followed by 0–0 or BK3. Also 9. . . . Kt to KB3 was playable. Both of these moves leave White with the attack; but, given good defence, the attack would not be fatal. The text move, which looks safe, proves, in a subtle way, to have lost tempo.

White	*Black*
10. B to KKt5. Good and unexpected. It was hard for Black to see what a control of the Board this gives his opponent.	B to K2. At this point choices are becoming limited. If e.g., 10. Q to Q2 there follows 11. B × Kt, B × B. 12. R to K1 Ch. with a considerable attack. If, on the other hand 10 . . . P to KB3. 11. R to K1 is disruptive. If 10 . . . KKt to K2, 11. P to Q5 seems to win a Piece. If 10 . . . QKt to K2, a variation similar to the text ensues. In any event, it was hard for Black to see, through the exchanges, how formidable White's attack was going to prove.
11. B × Kt.	QB × B. If KB × B there might follow B × B, P × B, Q to Kt3 winning at least a Pawn.
12. Kt × B. Continuing the forcing sequence.	Q × Kt. If B × B White has options like Kt × B forcing Q × Kt(Q4) R to K1 Ch. K to B1; or Kt × BP Ch., winning a Pawn but not fatal; or R to K1 Ch. with similar pressure on the King's file to what happens, but with Black having lost a tempo less.
13. B × B. Much better than R to K1, P to B3. Simplification that helps the attack.	Kt × B. Had Black anticipated the resources that White was to call out of the position, he might have played K × B, which gives him a better chance of eventually mobilizing his Rooks. The position is more critical than Black imagines.
14. R to K1. Stopping Black from immediate Castles, and as it turns out, from ever Castling.	P to KB3. Evidently the move on which Black had relied in order to emancipate himself from the pin and in order to mobilize the Rook.
15. Q to K2. More force being exerted.	Q to Q2.
16. QR to B1. A subtle move, inducing a weakness.	P to B3. Black was afraid that after K to B2, there might follow 17. Q × Kt Ch., etc

White

17. P to Q5. A brilliant sacrifice a Pawn in order to obtain a square.

18. Kt to Q4.

19. Kt to K6. White obtains, with this move, a wonderful command of the squares on which he wishes to attack.

20. Q to Kt4. Threatening Mate among other things.

21. Kt to Kt5 Ch.

22. R × Kt. Ch. Taking excellent advantage of the fact that the Queen is tied. But Steinitz has also seen that the King cannot take. If the King could take, White would be left the exchange and a Pawn to the bad. Moreover, it was also necessary for Steinitz to see the effect of Black's refusal of the exchange because, after Black's next move, every Piece of White's is under attack and White is threatened with Mate.

23. R to B7 Ch.

24. R to Kt7 Ch. An idea that White must have entertained for a long time. This Rook cannot be captured by the Queen because Black will be left a Piece down at least, whereas the King's capture allows Q × Q Ch.

25. R × P Ch. And wins.

Black

giving White at least two Pawns for the exchange. That, however, would not have been so destructive.

P × P.

K to B2. Evidently necessary.

KR to QB1. To prevent, among other things, R to B7. The King's Rook is chosen to avoid the possibility that the Black King may be compelled to go to the back rank, shutting off KR square.

P to Kt3. White's next move shows why Kt to Kt3 was impossible.

K to K1. In order to save the Queen. That Queen, incidentally, is now in an awkward position because it is guarding the Rook rather than the Knight.

K to B1. If K × R, there follows, 23. R to K1 Ch. If, then, K to Q1, Kt to K6 Ch. wins the Queen quickly. If, instead, K to Q3. 24. Q to Kt4 Ch., K to B2, Kt to K6 Ch. K to Kt1, Q to KB4 Ch. wins.

K to Kt1. Obviously this Rook could not be captured. Black's reply still leaves White with the problem arising from the attack on his Pieces.

K to R1. If K to B1, 25. Kt × P Ch. is fatal, because if K × R, Q × Q Ch. and if K to K1, Kt × BP Ch. etc.

At this point Von Bardeleben is reported to have made no comment but to have put on his hat and quietly walked home, leaving his opponent to win by effluxion of time. That was a

Teutonic way of showing that he knew what was coming. If, now, K to Kt1, there follows R to Kt7 Ch. Now the King cannot go to B1 or take the Rook for reasons that we have seen. But in answer to 26. ... K to R1, there follows a beautiful and long mating process, viz. :

	White	*Black*
26.	. . .	K to R1.
27.	Q to R4 Ch.	K × R.
28.	Q to R7 Ch.	K to B1.
29.	Q to R8 Ch.	K to K2.
30.	Q to Kt7 Ch.	K to K1. (Best.)
31.	Q to Kt8 Ch.	K to K2.
32.	Q to B7 Ch.	K to Q1.
33.	Q to B8 Ch.	Q to K1.
34.	Kt to B7 Ch.	K to Q2.
35.	Q to Q6 Mate.	

The reader will observe that White is still threatened with R × R Mate.

The next example shows the significance of a clear superiority in development.

A good specimen of exploitation of a cramped game. Stabbing the insufficiently agile. Giuoco Piano (in effect).

	White (HERMANN)	*Black* (HUSSONG)
1.	P to K4.	P to K4.
2.	Kt to KB3.	Kt to QB3.
3.	B to Kt5.	P to QR3.
4.	B to B4. Changing to Giuoco Piano with loss of a move.	Kt to B3.
5.	P to Q3. The Pianissimo Variation.	B to B4.
6.	B to K3.	P to Q3.
7.	QKt to Q2.	B to K3.
8.	B × KB.	P × B.
9.	B × B.	P × B. These exchanges are not to White's advantage. The doubled Pawns are not easy to exploit without Bishops.
10.	Kt to B4.	Kt to Q2.
11.	P to QR4.	Q to B3.
12.	P to B3.	0–0.
13.	0–0.	QR to Q1.
14.	P to R5.	Kt to K2. Starting a long trek to the King side.
15.	Q to Kt3.	Kt to KKt3.
16	Q × P. Unwise.	Kt to B5.
17.	Kt to K1. From excessive rashness to excessive caution. Kt to K3 was better.	Q to Kt4.
18	K to R1.	R to B3.
19.	Kt to K3.	QR to KB1. (If R to R3 21. Kt to B3).
20.	Q × BP. Nero in reincarnation !	QR to B2.
21.	Q to B8 Ch.	Kt to B1.

White (HERMANN)	Black (HUSSONG)
22. Q × BP.	Q to R4. Black's agressive formation is excellent. White's next move perfects it and allows a pretty finish, which is the better because of White's counter sacrifice.
23. R to KKt1.	Q × P Ch.
24. K × Q.	R to R3 Ch.
25. K to Kt3.	Kt to K7 Ch.
26. K to Kt4.	R to B5 Ch.
27. K to Kt5.	R to R7.
28. Q × Kt Ch.	K × Q.
29. Kt to B3.	P to R3 Ch.
30. K to Kt6.	K to Kt1.
31. Kt × R.	R to B4.
Resigns.	

A game in which both sides fight well, and a stroke of genius decides the issue.

ENGLISH OPENING.

White (ZUKERTORT)	Black (BLACKBURNE)
1. P to QB4.	P to K3.
2. P to K3.	Kt to KB3.
3. Kt to KB3.	P to QKt3.
4. B to K2.	B to Kt2.
5. 0–0.	P to Q4.
6. P to Q4.	B to Q3. B to K2 is safer for Black in this type of game.
7. Kt to B3.	0–0.
8. P to QKt3.	QKt to Q2.
9. B to Kt2.	Q to K2.
10. Kt to QKt5—gaining a slight advantage.	Kt to K5.
11. Kt × B.	P × Kt.
12. Kt to Q2.	QKt to B3. Black plays boldly to invite White's attack. Safer was P × P followed by P to Q4 and Kt to Q3.
13. P to B3.	Kt × Kt.
14. Q × Kt.	P × P.
15. B × P. Strategic decision.	P to Q4.
16. B to Q3.	KR to B1. The interest of this game derives from the fact that Black as well as White has an aggressive plan.
17. QR to K1.	R to B2.
18. P to K4.	QR to QB1. Kt to QB1.
19. P to K5.	Kt to K1.
20. P to B4. A typical King's side attack of the QP order.	P to Kt3.
21. R to K3.	P to B4. (In defence of R2).
22. P × P e.p.	Kt × P.
23. P to B5. One of the points of move 17.	Kt to K5. White has seen the distant consequences of this.
24. B × Kt.	
	P × B.

White (ZUKERTORT)

25. P × KtP.

26. P × P Ch.
27. P to Q5 Ch.

28. Q to Kt4. One of the best moves in the history of Chess, and certainly the only one to win here.

29. R to B8 Ch. An additional beauty.

30. Q × P Ch.
31. B × P Ch.
32. B to Kt7 Ch. Pretty finish.

33. Q × Q.

Black (BLACKBURNE)

R to B7. Black's attack is also looking formidable, in view is a possible R × Kt P Ch.

K to R1.
P to K4. Apparently, a sound defence.
QR to B4. If Q × Q—
   39. B × P Ch. K × P.
   30. R to R3 Ch. K to Kt3.
   31. R to B6 Ch. K to Kt4.
   32. R to Kt3 Ch. K to R4.
   33. R to B5 Ch. K to R3.
   34. B to B4 Ch. and Mate next move.

K × P. If Q × R. 30. B × P Ch. initiates a rapid winning process.

K to Kt2.
K × R.
K to Kt1. Of course, if Q × B. Q to K8 Mate.

Resigns.

The other pole of Chess. A study in position play—" Judo " rather than " All-in."

White (SÄMISCH)

1. P to Q4.
2. P to QB4.
3. Kt to KB3.

4. P to KKt3.
5. B to Kt2.
6. Kt to QB3. Good now that the Black Bishop has committed itself.

7. 0–0.

8. Kt to K5.
9. P × P. Not the best. White ought to prevent Black from choosing his own method of liquidating the centre. A better move for White was probably P to QKt3.

Black (NIMZOWITCH)

Kt to KB3.
P to K3.
P to QKt3. The Queen's Indian. this move cannot be played if White plays 3. Kt to QB3, because then, P to K4 is playable for White with advantage.

B to Kt2.
B to K2.
0–0.

P to Q4. Black now feels the necessity of putting a stronger hold on the centre. The fact that this Pawn is on the line of the Bishop does not amount to a limitation on the Bishop according to the modern conception. This point is made more striking by Black's next move.

P to QB3.
BP × P. A very shrewd choice. Many players would play KP × P and eventually push the QBP forward. Black sees a better method.

White (Sämisch)

10. B to KB4.

11. R to QB1.

12. Q to Kt3. Not a good move in the light of subsequent play. Better was an immediate challenge by P to QR4.

13. Kt × Kt.

14. P to KR3. With a view to King's side development. This is inconsistent with White's 12th move. There is no good Knight move available for White. Nevertheless, Kt to K4 is better than the text.

15. K to R2. P to KKt4 is better.

16. B to Q2. In order to prevent an unfavourable exchange.

17. Q to Q1. With a view to counter play against the King's side which proves to be inadequate.

18. Kt to Kt1.

19. R to Kt1. Unpinning the Pawn.

20. P to K4. The move on which White had relied in order to save the game. Black refutes this manoeuvre by sacrificing the Knight for two Pawns, or more, and a

Black (Nimzowitch)

P to QR3. This is the beginning of an attempt to seize the square at Black's QB5. The reader will remember earlier comments on the use of the Rook's Pawn.

P to QKt4.

Kt to QB3. A very good move threatening to bring the Knight into play on the Queen's wing. The move is tactically good because Black can reply to the immediate Kt × QP with Kt × QP. (If 13. Kt × KtP Kt to QR4).

B × Kt. Black has gained tempo by this exchange, but White has got rid of one danger.

Q to Q2.

Kt to R4. Black's original intention has been to work this Knight over to the Queen's side, but now that a King's side weakness presents itself he revises his plan.

P to KB4. Black's game being now better integrated, he proceeds to play vigorously into his opponent's territory. The fact that he is leaving a backward Pawn is unimportant in the light of the strength of the attack that he can develop.

P to Kt5. Seizing the opportunity of further immobilizing White's Pieces.

B to QKt4. Bringing pressure to bear on a point that may become weak, and improving the position of the Bishop. Note how the Bishop comes to life on an unexpected diagonal.

B to Q3. Strengthening the attack against the King's side.

BP × P.

White (SÄMISCH)   *Black* (NIMZOWITCH)

considerable attack. The open lines that become available to Black are almost sufficient in themselves to warrant the expenditure of material.

21. Q × Kt.   R × P.
22. Q to Kt5. Because, inter alia,   QR to KB1. This Piece too is
    to move the Bishop would   finding its way into the game;
    cost another Pawn.   also this move prevents
                                     B to KB4.
23. K to R1. In order to prevent   R (B1) to B4.
    QR to KB6.
24. Q to K3.   B to Q6. A most cramping move
                                     from White's point of view,
                                     preventing (at move 26.) B to
                                     B1. Undoubtedly the im-
                                     mediate R to K7 would have
                                     been very good for Black but
                                     it is not conclusive. The text
                                     is conclusive Now R to K7
                                     threatens to win the Queen and
                                     to White's only reply Black has
                                     an extraordinary answer.
25. QR to K1.   P to KR3.
26. Resigns.

Black's 25th move creates one of the most remarkable Zugzwang positions in the history of Chess. White to move must lose. He can delay things with P to QR3 (met by P to QR4) and P to KR4 met by any non-committal move on Black's part, but eventually he has to move a Piece or the Pawn at KKt3.

Now evidently the B on Q2 cannot move because that costs White a Knight (the point of move 24); the King's Rook cannot move without loss of a Piece, the Queen's Rook cannot move because of R to K7 winning the major exchange, and neither the King's Bishop nor the King's Knight Pawn can move because of R to KB6; and that move in any event can be played by Black as soon as he likes because the Queen has no escape (the point of move 25).

As a whole the game is a remarkable example of reliance on positional factors. At all stages there were lines of play to consider; but the difference of degree is remarkable between the emphasis on combinative threats in some of the games that have been shown, and the emphasis on strategic and technical features in this game.

It is an amusing footnote to this game that a greater player, Alekhine, some years later inflicted a remarkable Zugzwang on Nimzowitch himself.

The " Zugger " " Zugged."

FRENCH DEFENCE

White ALEKHINE)	*Black* (NIMZOWITCH)

1. P to K4.   P to K3.
2. P to Q4.   P to Q4.
3. Kt to QB3.   B to Kt5.
4. P to K5.   P to QB4. Safer is Kt to K2, followed, if B to Q2 is played, by P to QR3. The text, however, is playable because the Kt excursion is speculative.

5. B to Q2.   Kt to K2.
6. Kt to Kt5.   B × B Ch.
7. Q × B.   0–0.
8. P to QB3.   P to QKt3. Slow—or else artificial —White's Kt is strengthened on Kt5 by this process, not weakened.

9. P to KB4.   B to R3.
10. Kt to KB3.   Q to Q2.
11. P to QR4.   QKt to B3.
12. P to QKt4.   A move of Alekhinian vigour.   P × KtP.

13. P × P.   B to Kt2. An admission that his policy has been wrong. White has a big control of space now.

14. Kt to Q6.   P to B4. A good move to get in while it can be done, but not helpful to the general situation.

15. P to R5.   Kt to B1.
16. Kt × B.   Q × Kt.
17. P to R6. A restrictive move, made without loss of tempo.   Q to KB2.

18. B to Kt5   KKt to K2. QKt to K2 may be a trifle better, but the pressure is severe.

19. 0–0.   P to KR3. To stop Kt to Kt5 if it be contemplated and with a view to P to KKt4 if Black lasts long enough.

20. KR to B1.   KR to B1.
21. R to B2.   Q to K1. Not good : but there is only a choice of evils, of which Black chooses all. Better was Kt to Q1, but that is met by 22. QR to B1 with tremendous pressure. A possible line would be—

      22. . . .   R × R.
      23. R × R.   R to B1.
      24. R × R.   Kt × R.
      25. Q to B2.

22. QR to QB1.   QR to Kt1. Contemplating move 27 with the R at Kt1, but White does not allow this formation to come into being.

23. Q to K3.   R to B2.

White (ALEKHINE)	Black (NIMZOWITCH)
24. R to B3.	Q to Q2.
25. QR to B2.	K to B1.
26. Q to B1.	QR to B1.
27. B to R4.	P to QKt4.
28. B × P.	K to K1.
29. B to R4.	K to Q1.
30. P to R4. Waiting for a guard to be removed from the R at C7.	Q to K1. Black is in Zugzwang. The next move relieves it by an increase of the pressure to breaking point.
31. P to Kt5.	Resigns.

Now a study in technique.

QUEEN'S INDIAN DEFENCE

White (SZABO)	Black (DENKER)
1. P to Q4.	Kt to KB3.
2. P to QB4.	P to K3.
3. Kt to KB3.	P to QKt3.
4. P to KKt3.	B to Kt2.
5. B to Kt2.	B to K2.
6. O–O.	O–O.
7. Kt to B3.	Kt to K5.
8. Q to B2.	Kt × Kt. This loss of tempo is justified because it makes possible Black's treatment of the centre. An alternative was P to KB4.
9. Q × Kt.	P to Q3.
10. Q to B2. Slow. Threatens KtKt5, but Black's reply meets this and equalizes.	Kt to B3.
11. KR to Q1.	B to B3.
12. P to Q5.	KP × P.
13. P × P.	Kt to Kt5. Typical, in conjunction with the next few moves, of modern technique. Black has much to counterbalance White's apparent gain of space.
14. Q to Kt3.	P to QR4.
15. B to K3.	R to K1.
16. QR to B1.	Kt to R3.
17. Kt to Q4.	Kt to B4. Incidentally, a blockade of the White Rook.
18. Q to B2.	Q to Q2.
19. P to KR4. Sound, but not well followed up.	R to K4. Initiating a King's side attack.
20. B to B4. Kt to B6 is better.	R × QP. Giving the Exchange for good consideration.
21. B × R.	B × B. Note Black's control of the White squares.
22. P to Kt3. Saving a Pawn at too much expense. K to R2 was necessary.	Q to R6.
23. Kt to B3.	B to K5. Note how Black is able to defend his Piece without loss of tempo.

White (SZABO)	*Black* (DENKER)
24. Q to Q2.	Kt to K3. The Kt having done its work on the Queen's side now joins in the King's side attack. P to KKt4 is being prepared.
25. Q to K3.	P to Q4.
26. R × BP Hoping to distract Black from the attack by surrender of the Exchange.	B × P. A neat little combination. If P × B, Q Kt5 Ch. Then B to Kt3 is forced and Kt × R is playable.
27. R to Kt7.	B to Q1.
28. R to QB1.	P to KKt4. Decisive. Obviously, the Pawn cannot be captured.
29. B to B7.	B to B3. B × B followed by P to Kt5 was sound, but unnecessarily complicated. White is deprived by the text of any counterchance.
30. B × QKtP. To get as much material as possible in exchange for what is going to be lost.	P to Kt5.
31. R to Q1.	B to Kt4. Very good. The threat is the 33rd move
32. Q to B3.	P × Kt.
33. P × P.	Kt to B5. P to Q5 also wins, but the text is a more rapid process.
34. P × Kt.	B × P (B6).
35. Q × B.	Q × Q.
36. R to QB1.	B × P.
37. R to K1.	P to Q5.
38. R (K1) to K7.	Q to Kt5 Ch.
39. K to B1.	P to Q6.
Resigns.	

An object lesson in the development of a good attack from technically correct chess.

White (ALEKHINE)	*Black* (STERK)
1. P to Q4.	P to Q4.
2. Kt to KB3.	Kt to KB3.
3. P to B4.	P to K3.
4. Kt to B3.	QKt to Q2.
5. P to K3.	B to Q3.
6. Kt to QKt5. Doubtful, but inexpensive.	B to K2.
7. Q to B2.	P to B3.
8. Kt to B3.	0–0.
9. B to Q3.	P × P.
10. B × P.	P to B4. A good move, since there is not much pressure on the QB file.
11. P × P.	B × P. Perhaps Kt × P is preferable, since PQKt4 creates weakness for White.
12. 0–0.	P to QKt3.
13. P to K4.	B to Kt2.

White (ALEKHINE)	Black (STERK)
14. B to KKt5.	
15. Q to K2.	Q to B1.
16. B to Q3. A clever reply.	B to Kt5.
	B × Kt. Here Black starts going beyond his depth. White's pin of the Bishop is too logical and consistent with development to be escaped combinatively.
17. KR to QB1.	Kt × P.
18. B × Kt.	B × B.
19. Q × B.	Kt to B4.
20. Q to K2.	B to R4. The awkwardness is forced. This is the only move to stop PQKt4.
21. QR to Kt1.	Q to R3. Very ingenious, but inadequate.
22. R to B4. A dominating move.	Kt to R5. Still being ingenious.
23. B to B6. More than ingenious : deep and sound.	If 23. P to QKt4 Kt to B6! KR to QB1.
24. Q to K5. If Black takes the Rook, then after QKt5, there is no escape for the K via B1, K1, Q2, because of White's Kt and Rook.	R to B4.
25. Q to Kt3. If R × R P × B.	P to Kt3.
26. R × Kt.	Q to Q6.
27. R to KB1.	Q to B4.
28. Q to B4.	Q to B7.
29. Q to R6.	Resigns.

A case of drowning in depths.

White (ALEKHINE)	Black (LASKER)
1. P to Q4.	P to Q4.
2. P to QB4.	P to K3.
3. KKt to B3.	KKt to B3.
4. Kt to B3.	QKt to Q2.
5. P × P. Relieving Black of a problem.	P × P
6. B to B4.	P to B3.
7. P to K3.	Kt to R4.
8. B to Q3.	Kt × B. A good exchange.
9. P × Kt.	B to Q3.
10. P to KKt3.	0–0.
11. 0–0.	R to K1.
12. Q to B2.	Kt to B1.
13. Kt to Q1. Aiming at the K side, but the process is slow.	P to B3. A far seeing move. Black wants KB2 for a Bishop.
14. Kt to K3.	B to K3.
15. Kt to R4.	B to QB2. Slow, but effective. The Bishop is directed against a weakness at White's Q4.
16. P to QKt4.	B to Kt3.
17. Kt to B3.	B to KB2. And this Bishop can operate from KR4. Black has arranged his Bishops so as to exercise their maximum functions.

	White (ALEKHINE)	Black (LASKER)

18. **White:** P to Kt5. Logical counter-play—a "minority attack" to reduce Black's Q side Pawn advantage. **Black:** B to KR4. Well timed. The QBP is guarded by the potential R to QB1.
19. P to Kt4.   B to KB2.
20. P × P.   R to B1.
21. Q to Kt2.   P × P. Better than R × P for tactical reasons (e.g., defence of QP).
22. P to B5.   Q to Q3.
23. Kt to Kt2. To prevent Q to B5.   B to B2.
24. KR to K1. White is on the defensive and wishes to reduce material.   P to KR4. The point of many previous moves.
25. P to KR3.   Kt to R2.
26. R × R Ch.   R × R.
27. R to K1.   R to Kt1. One of the points of move 21.
28. Q to B1.   Kt to Kt4. This Knight's path into this game is a study in the exploitation of weak squares.
29. Kt to K5. A desperate endeavour to close lines.   P × Kt. Black can afford now to give up his Kt.
30. Q × Kt.   P to K5.
31. P to B6. Hoping to cause Queen exchanges.   P to Kt3.
32. P to B4.   RP × P. Avoiding unnecessary difficulties.
33. B to K2.   P × P.
34. B to R5.   R to Kt7.
35. Kt to R4.   Q × P.
36. Q × Q.   B × Q.

Resigns.

Very rarely has a great master been so outplayed and so deprived of control. The game is a study in the use of open lines and useful squares.

FRENCH DEFENCE (WINAWER VARIATION)

White (FINE)	Black (BOTWINNIK)

1. P to K4.   P to K3.
2. P to Q4.   P to Q4.
3. Kt to QB3.   B to Kt5.
4. P to K5.   P to QB4.
5. P × P. A method which relies on the strength of White's King's side, and allows some weakness on the Queen's side.   Kt to K2.
6. Kt to B3. Better than P to KB4 ("always too early") which leaves the centre hollow.   QKt to B3.
7. B to Q3.   P to Q5.
8. P to QR3.   B to R4.
9. P to QKt4.   Kt × KtP. Attempting too early to take advantage of a tactical complex.

White (FINE)	Black (BOTWINNIK)
10. P × Kt.	B × P.
11. B to Kt5 Ch.	Kt to B3. B to Q2 is better, because after exchanges, B × B, Q × B White cannot play R to R4.
12. B × Kt Ch.	P × B.
13. R to R4. A development worth the material invested.	B × Kt Ch.
14. B to Q2.	P to B3. A desperate attempt to loosen White's grip.
15. 0–0.	0–0.
16. B × B.	P × B.
17. Q to K1. White has control of much more of the board than his opponent.	P to QR4.
18. Q × P.	B to R3.
19. KR to R1.	B to Kt4.
20. R to Q4.	Q to K2.
21. R to Q6. A good restrictive move.	P to R5. An attempt to exploit Black's only counter-chance.
22. Q to K3.	R to R2.
23. Kt to Q2. In this type of game the Knight finds a big choice of squares (K4, Q4 etc.).	P to R6
24. P to QB4.	B to R5.
25. P × P.	Q × P.
26. R × RP.	R to K1. Q to Kt7 leads to nothing after Q × P Ch. and R to K3.
27. P to R3.	QR to R1.
28. Kt to B3.	Q to Kt7.
29. Kt to K5. Much better play than the capture of the KP.	Q to Kt8 Ch.
30. K to R2.	Q to B4.
31. Q to KKt3.	Resigns. R to KB3 cannot be prevented. Black is only half a Pawn down, but White can carry out any attack he wishes to prepare, e.g.—

31.		R to R2.
32. R to KB3.		Q to R4.
33. Kt to Q7.		K to R1.
34. R × KP,		R × Kt.
35. Q to Kt5 et seq.		

Q.G.D. (in effect)

White (BOTWINNIK)	Black (VIDMAR)
1. P to QB4.	P to K3.
2. Kt to KB3.	P to Q4.
3. P to Q4.	Kt to KB3.
4. B to Kt5.	B to K2.
5. Kt to B3.	0–0.
6. P to K3.	QKt to Q2.
7. B to Q3.	P to B4.
8. 0–0.	BP × P.
9. KP × P.	P × P.
10. B × P.	Kt to Kt3.
11. B to Kt3.	B to Q2.

White (BOTWINNIK)	*Black* (VIDMAR)
12. Q to Q3.	QKt to Q4.
13. Kt to K5.	B to B3.
14. QR to Q1.	Kt to QKt5. Up to this point Black has developed quite soundly, though without embarrassing White. The text is, however, unwarrantable, losing tempo.
15. Q to R3.	B to Q4. Unnatural.
16. Kt×B.	QKt×Kt.
17. P to B4. White has a definite advantage now.	R to B1.
18. P to B5.	P × P?
19. R×P.	Q to Q3. Missing a point.
20. Kt×KBP. A fine exploitation, the analysis of which is not easy.	R × Kt.
21. QB×Kt.	B×B. If Kt×B, R×Kt is good enough. Observe R " hanging."
22. R×Kt.	Q to B3.
23. R to Q6. Pretty.	Q to K1.
24. R to Q7.	Resigns.

An excellent exploitation of uninspired play.

Q.G.A.

White (KOTOV)	*Black* (YUDOVITCH)
1. P to Q4.	P to Q4.
2. Kt to KB3.	Kt to KB3.
3. P to B4.	P to K3.
4. B to Kt5.	B to Kt5 Ch.
5. Kt to B3.	P×P.
6. P to K4.	P to B4.
7. B×P.	P×P.
8. K×tP.	Q to R4.
9. B×Kt.	B×Kt Ch.
10. P×B.	P×B. A tribute to the land where midnight oil is unrationed. It is hard to see that Q×P Ch. loses. After K to B1. Q×B Ch. K to Kt1. P×B. R to B1 is decisive. If, instead of 12. . . . P×B 0–0 is played, White has a strong King's side attack.
	Kt to Q2.
11. 0–0.	
12. K to R1. Preparation for opening of lines that may never be opened.	Kt to Kt3. If Q × BP 13. Kt to Kt5.
13. B to Kt3.	B to Q2.
14. Q to B3.	K to K2.
15. Q to K3.	QR to QB1.
16. QR to B1.	Kt to B5. Planless.
17. Q to K2.	Kt to Kt3.
18. Q to Q3.	R to B4.
19. P to KB4.	KR to QB1.
20. P to B4.	B to K1 with a view to P to K4.

White (KOTOV)   *Black* (YUDOVITCH)

21. P to K5. Initiating a brilliant piece of play.   P×P.
22. P×P.   R×KP.
23. QR to Q1.   Q to B4. To guard Q3.
24. Q to Kt3.   R to K5. To stop Q to R4 Ch.
25. R to B5. A stroke of genius.   P×R.
26. Kt×P Ch.   K to B3.
27. R to Q6 Ch.   K×Kt.
28. Q to B3 Ch.   R to B5.
29. Q to R5 Ch.   K to K5.
30. B to B2 Ch.   K to K6.
31. R to Q3 Ch.   Resigns. If K to B7 or K to K5, R to Q2 Ch. is fatal.

GRUNFELD DEFENCE (in effect).

White (MAKAGONOV)   *Black* (RESHEVSKY)

1. P to Q4.   Kt to KB3.
2. P to QB4.   P to KKt3.
3. Kt to KB3.   B to Kt2.
4. Kt to B3.   P to Q4.
5. Q to Kt3.   P to B3.
6. B to B4.   P×P.
7. Q×BP.   B to K3.
8. Q to Q3.   Kt to Q4. Misconceived. Better, either at move 7, or here, was QKt to Q2 aiming at QKt3, Q4, etc.
9. Kt×Kt.   Q×Kt.
10. P to K4.   Q to R4 Ch.
11. B to Q2.   Q to Kt3.
12. B to B3.   O-O. Now White has very slightly the advantage, but Black has counterplay.
13. B to K2.   R to Q1.
14. O-O.   P to QR4. A far fetched idea for developing the QKt. Nevertheless White's reply comes as a surprise.
15. Kt to Kt5. A beautiful move, involving a long and clever line of thought. White is sacrificing his Queen.   B×QP.
16. Kt×B.   P×Kt. Observe, Black can win the Queen with—

         16. ...   B×P Ch.
         17. R×B.   R×Q.
         18. B×R.   P×Kt.
     But there follows :
         19. B to B4.   P to B4.
         20. QR to KB1.   Kt to Q2.
         21. R to B7.   Kt to B3.
         22. R×KP and wins easily.
     One of the "unheard melodies" of Chess.

17. Q to R3. Now White, having had his sacrifice refused, has a big advantage.   P to B4.

	White (MAKAGONOV)	*Black* (RESHEVSKY)
18.	B to KKt4.	K to R1.
19.	B × KP.	Kt to R3.
20.	K to R1.	Kt to B2.
21.	B to KKt4.	P to R5.
22.	P to R3.	B × B.
23.	P × B. An interesting decision implying an aggresive intention on the QKt file.	P to B5.
24.	QR to QKt1.	Q to B4. The most vigorous.
25.	R × P.	R (R1) to Kt1.
26.	R × R.	R × R.
27.	Q to Kt3.	R to Kt6. Loss of tempo.
28.	R to Q1.	R to Kt3. To defend the Kt on B2, if necessary, and so as not to let the B in at K6.
29.	R to Q8 Ch.	K to Kt2.
30.	P to R4.	R to Q3.
31.	R to QB8.	P to K4.
32.	P to R5.	R to Q6.
33.	Q to R4.	P to R3.
34.	P × P.	Q to Q3.
35.	R to KR8. Another move of great beauty, notwithstanding that there were many good alternatives.	Q × KtP.
36.	B to B5.	Resigns, because White has a decisive attack.

Finally, a fighting draw.

Q.P. (Nimzowitch D.)

	White (CAPABLANCA)	*Black* (FINE)
1.	P to Q4.	Kt to KB3.
2.	P to QB4.	P to K3.
3.	Kt to QB3.	B to Kt5.
4.	Q to B2.	P to Q4.
5.	P × P.	Q × P. Counter aggressive; choosing a Queen's Fianchetto for the Bishop. The disadvantage is the loss of B for Kt on move 7 to save tempo.
6.	Kt to B3.	P to B4.
7.	B to Q2.	B × Kt.
8.	B × B.	Kt to B3. Kt to K5 would be met by P × P, winning a Pawn.
9.	R to Q1.	0–0.
10.	P to K3.	P to QKt3.
11.	P to QR3.	B to Kt2.
12.	P × P.	Q × P.
13.	P to QKt4.	Q to KR4.
14.	B × Kt. An interesting decision. Logical was B to Q3 or B to K2. The text is an attempt to cash an immediate advantage. Black's brilliant counterplay shows that the posi-	P × B.

White (Capablanca)   *Black* (Fine)

tion was not ready for it. On the other hand, given slower play, Black would have equalized with QRQl.

15. R to Q7.

QR to B1. Defending the Bishop indirectly, viz:
    16. R×B   Kt×KtP.
with a formidable counter-attack.

16. Q to Kt2.

KR to Ql. This, in conjunction with the following moves, amounts to a brilliant defence.

17. R×B.

Kt to K4. Of course, Kt cannot take Kt because of the Mate at White's Ql.

18. B to K2.

Kt×Kt Ch.

19. B×Kt.

Q to K4.

20. Q×Q.

R to B8 Ch.

21. B to Q1.

QR×B Ch.

22. K to K2.

QR to Q7 Ch.

23. K to B3.

P×Q.

24. R×RP. After a combinative middle-game, a typical transition to endgame.

P to K5 Ch.

25. K to Kt3.

R to R7.

26. R to R6.

KR to Q7.

27. R to KB1.

KR to Kt7. A typical endgame situation. White cannot hold his Pawn.

28. R×P.

R×RP.

29. P to Kt5.

K to Kt2. There is no hurry for the attack on the Pawn.

30. P to R4.

QR to Kt6.

31. K to B4.

R×KtP.

32. R×R.

R×R.

33. P to Kt4. Obviously if K× P. R to Kt5 Ch.

R to Kt5.

34. R to B1.

R to Kt7.

35. K to Kt3.

K to B3. A mistake.

36. R to B4.

K to K4.

37. R to B8. The point.

K to B3.

38. R to KKt8. A strong move which should win. The King is "cut off".

P to R3.

39. P to Kt5 Ch.

P×P.

40. R×P (P to R5 appears to win easily).
If 40. .... R to Kt8
    41. K to Kt2, etc.

R to Kt5.

41. K to R3. If R moves along the rank, the Black K can place itself at Kt3. If R moves on the file, then R to Kt8 for Black embarrasses White: if then K to Kt2. R to Kt4 and so to KR4.

P to K4.

White (CAPABLANCA)	*Black* (FINE)
42. R to Kt1.	K to B4. Keeping the White King out of the game. The Rook alone cannot force the Pawn forward. If now 43. P to R5, R to Kt3, or R to Kt1 or even P to B3 draws.

Drawn.

A well-fought game, rich in examples of attack and counter-attack.

LIST OF GAMES

[Some very short games are to be found on pp. 29, 46, 136, 138, 151.]

Anastasia

Anastasia herself has stated that this book consists of words and phrases in combinations *which have a beneficial effect on the reader.* This has been attested by the letters received to date from tens of thousands of readers all over the world.

If you wish to gain as full an appreciation as possible of the ideas, thoughts and images set forth here, as well as experience the benefits that come with this appreciation, we recommend you find a quiet place for your reading where there is the least possible interference from artificial noises (motor traffic, radio, TV, household appliances etc.). *Natural sounds,* on the other hand — the singing of birds, for example, or the patter of rain, or the rustle of leaves on nearby trees — may be a welcome accompaniment to the reading process.

THE RINGING CEDARS SERIES · BOOK ONE

Anastasia

Vladimir Megré

Translated from the Russian by **John Woodsworth**
Edited by **Dr Leonid Sharashkin**

RINGING
CEDARS
PRESS

KAHULUI · HAWAII · USA

Glasgow Life
Glasgow Libraries

IB

C 005543024		
Askews & Holts	21-Dec-2011	
130 / CL	£9.95	

Publisher's Cataloging-In-Publication Data

Megre, V. (Vladimir), 1950-
[Anastasi´i`a. English.]
   Anastasia / Vladimir Megré ; translated from the Russian by John
Woodsworth ; edited by Leonid Sharashkin. — 2nd ed., rev.

   p. : ill., maps ; cm. — (The ringing cedars series ; bk. 1)

   ISBN: 978-0-9801812-0-3

   1. Spirituality. 2. Nature—Religious aspects. 3. Human ecology. I.
Woodsworth, John, 1944- II. Sharashkin, Leonid. III. Title. IV. Title:
Anastasi´i`a. English. V. Series: Megre, V. (Vladimir), 1950- Ringing cedars
series, bk. 1

GF80 .M44 2008
304.2   2008923346

Contents

Translator's Preface

When I opened my on-line Slavic-languages bulletin one day in early September 2004 and first learnt about a book in the *Ringing Cedars Series* that was seeking a translator into English, little did I realise the kind of literary adventure that was awaiting me. But as I became acquainted with the details of Vladimir Megré's[1] fascinating work (I read through the first three books in the series before beginning the actual translation), it gradually dawned on me that much of my previous translation experience, especially in *poetry* (from Pushkin to Anna Akhmatova to modern bards) and *poetic prose* (as with the stories of contemporary Russian writer Mikhail Sadovsky), not to mention my own religious background (emphasising Man's unique status as the image and likeness of the Creator), had been preparing me specifically for this particular task. Megré's work was simply the next logical step, it seemed, in the progression of my career. Indeed, I found myself taking to it not only with the enthusiasm that comes with the prospect of facing a new professional challenge but even more with the thought of feeling very much at home in this new literary environment.

Some of my friends and colleagues have asked: "What kind of book are you translating?" — no doubt wondering whether they could look forward to reading a novel, a documentary

---

[1]*Vladimir Megré* — pronounced *vla-DEE-meer mi-GREH* (capitalised syllables stressed). In fact, the pronunciation of the surname is not unlike that of its French counterpart, *Maigret*. The word *Anastasia* in Russian is sounded as *a-na-sta-SEE-ya* — i.e., not too different from "On a star see ya!".

account, an inspirational exegesis on the meaning of life, or even a volume of poetry.

But even after completing the translation of *Anastasia*, I still do not have a definitive answer to give them. In fact, I am still asking myself the same question.

My initial response was a rather crude summary of a gut impression — I would tell them: "Think of *Star Trek meets the Bible.*" My feelings about the book, however, go far beyond this primitive attempt at jocularity. Of the four disparate genres mentioned above, I would have to say *Anastasia* has elements of all four, and then some.

First — the book *reads* like a novel. That is to say, it tells a first-person story in a most entertaining way, bringing out the multi-faceted character of both the author and the title personage in a manner not unlike what readers of novels might expect. It tells a tale of adventure in the raw Siberian wilds where even sex and violence make an occasional appearance, though with a connection to the plot-line quite unlike their counterparts in any work of fiction I have read.

Secondly — the book gives the *impression* of a documentary account of real-life events, even if one's powers of belief are sometimes stretched to the limit. I am glad that my linguistic experience has given me access not only to the book itself, but also to a host of Russian-language texts on the Internet that have enabled me to corroborate from independent sources a great many of the specifics the author saw fit to include in his narrative (names of individuals, institutions, scientific phenomena etc.) — all of which turned out to be genuine, thereby contributing an additional measure of credence to what otherwise might seem utterly fantastic. Much of the corroborative information so gleaned I have attempted to pass on to the English-speaking reader in the footnotes, with the help of additional commentary by the editor. And yet there is a significant area of the author's description where authenticity must still be judged by the individual reader (which to me is one of the hallmarks of a work of *literature*, in contrast to a merely academic or journalistic report).

Thirdly, the book *penetrates one's thinking and feelings* with the gentle force of a divinely-inspired treatise — a treatise on not only the meaning of human life, but much more. *Anastasia* offers a tremendous new insight into the whole interrelationship of God, Man, Nature and the Universe. I would even go so far as to call it a revelation in science and religion.

One 'nutshell' description that comes to my mind is *a chronicle of ideas* — ideas on (a) the history of humanity's relationship to everything outside itself, (b) the clouds (not only dark and foreboding but even the fluffy and attractive variety) of mistaken belief that have, over the years, hid this relationship from our sight and comprehension and (c) where to begin — once we have caught a glimpse of this relationship — the necessary journey to reclaiming the whole picture. Deeply metaphysical in essence, the chronicle is set forth with both the supporting evidence of a documentary account and the entertainment capacity of a novel. In other words, it can be read as any of these three in isolation, but only by taking the three dimensions together will the reader have something approaching a complete picture of the book. And all three are infused with a degree of soul-felt inspiration that can only be expressed in poetry.

Indeed, one must not overlook the *poetry*. As a matter of fact, I learnt right at the start that experience in poetic translation was one of the qualifications required of a Ringing Cedars Series translator. And not just on account of the seven sample poems by readers at the end of Chapter 30.[2] Much

---

[2]These poems were written by readers with varying degrees of poetic experience. Every effort was made to reproduce the poetic features of the original (or, on occasion, their absence) on a poem-by-poem basis.

of the book's prose (especially when Anastasia is speaking) exudes a poetic feel, with rhyme and metre running a background course through whole paragraphs at a time; hence a particular challenge lay in reproducing this poetic quality, along with the semantic meaning, in English translation. Such poetic prose is even more evident in subsequent books in the series.

Another challenge has been to match, as closely as possible, Vladimir Megré's progressive development as a writer. According to his own admission, Megré began this whole literary project not as a professional writer, but as a hardened entrepreneur for whom writing was the farthest activity from his mind.[3] I smiled when one of the test readers of the translation, after finishing the first few chapters, described the author's style as "choppy". Megré himself talks about the initial rejection notices he received from publisher after publisher, telling him his language was too "stilted".[4] And yet his rendering of some of Anastasia's pronouncements toward the end of Book i waxes quite lyrical indeed — especially in the poetic passages referred to above. The author's development in literary style (which he attributes to Anastasia's direct and indirect guidance) becomes even more pronounced as the series progresses. It will be up to the English-speaking reader to judge whether this transformation is also conveyed in the translation.

There were two Russian words, of frequent occurrence throughout the book, that presented a particular translation challenge. One of them was *dachniki* (plural of *dachnik*), referring to people who own a *dacha,* or a country cottage, situated

---

[3]See especially Chapters 15: "Attentiveness to Man" and 26: "Dreams — creating the future".

[4]See Chapter 30: "Author's message to readers".

on just 600 square metres of land obtainable free of charge from the Russian government. But there is little comparison here to most Western concepts of *cottagers*.[5] While Russian dachas may be found in forested areas, or simply on open farmland, one almost invariable feature is a plot (*uchastok*) on which are grown fruits and vegetables to supply the family not only for their dacha stays but right through the year.[6] Given that the word *dacha* is already known to many English speakers (and is included in popular editions of both Oxford and Webster), it was decided to use the Russian word designating its occupants as well, with the English plural ending: *dachniks*.

The question that entailed the most serious difficulty, however — one that formed the subject of dozens of e-mails between editor and translator before it was finally resolved[7] — was the rendering into English of the Russian word *chelovek*. It is the common term used to denote a human being of either gender, the equivalent of German *Mensch* as well as of English *man* in the familiar Bible verse "God created man in His own image" (Genesis 1: 27).

The problem with the term *human* (as in *human being*) is that it not only suggests a formation of the species from matter, or earth (compare: *humus* — the organic constituent of

[5]I am thinking especially here of the example I am most familiar with — namely, the 'cottage country' in the Muskoka Lakes region of Ontario, north of Toronto, dotted by vacation cottages with nothing but trees around and (in some cases) a view of a lake.

[6]According to official statistics, since entitlement to dachas was legalised in the 1960s, 35 million families (amounting to approximately 70% of Russia's total population!) have acquired these tiny parcels of land. The produce grown on these plots makes an enormous contribution to the national economy — for example, over 90% of the country's potatoes come from privately tended plots like these.

[7]Reaction from readers on this point since the publication of the first English edition has been mixed; the explanation which follows has been revised to take certain readers' concerns into account.

soil), but is associated with lowly concepts (from *humus* come words like *humble, humility* etc.); besides, the word *human* is essentially an adjective, not a noun, even though commonly used as a noun in today's English.

On the other hand, *chelovek* is derived from two Old Russian words indicating 'mind' or 'thinking' (*chelo* < *lob*) and 'eternity' or 'time' (*vek*). And, interestingly enough, the English word *man* has a similar derivation, in this case from the Proto-Indo-European root *men-*, signifying 'mind', 'thinking' or 'intelligence' (cf. our contemporary English word *mental*). It was not until approximately the eleventh century C.E.[8] that the word *man* in Germanic languages became narrowed in focus to denote primarily an adult male; by the late thirteenth century it had all but squeezed out the earlier term for 'male' — *wer* (cf. Latin *vir,* echoed in modern words like *virile*).[9]

On the basis of Anastasia's sayings as presented by the author in the whole series, it may be seen that a constriction of overall human thought has been reflected in a narrowing of the meaning of *man,* which originally — like Russian *chelovek* and German *Mensch* even today[10] — designated all humanity, both men and women, as *thinking, intelligent beings.*

At one point, realising that some readers would take exception to the use of *man* (on the grounds that, in today's usage,

[8]*C.E.* — Common Era (otherwise designated A.D.).

[9]A similar displacement has happened in other languages; offshoots from the root *men-* have resulted in Russian *muzhchina* and German *Mann,* both denoting an adult male (also Russian *muzh* — 'husband' and *muzhik* — denoting a peasant man or a strong and sturdy male). There are at least two traces of *wer* in modern English: (a) the noun *werewolf* (also spelt *werwolf*), signifying literally 'man-wolf' and (b) the noun *world,* which is derived from the roots *wer-* and *-eld* (originally meaning 'age', but later extended to include 'place of habitation').

[10]Russian and German do have a related problem, however: the words *chelovek* and *Mensch* are *grammatically* masculine, even though their *meaning* is not confined to a single gender.

at least, it seems to exclude half the total number of sentient, thinking beings on the planet), we contemplated using the word *chelovek* in transliteration for this purpose. However, we decided this alternative was outweighed by (a) the feeling of exclusion many readers would experience at being described by a *foreign* word appearing so frequently throughout the book (almost one per page, on average) and (b) the opportunity to rediscover the *original meaning* of an English word whose usage has been constricted and corrupted over the past ten centuries.

It is interesting to note that from the eleventh to nineteenth centuries in Russia the word *chelovek* itself suffered the same fate as the English word *man* — largely confined to designating male human beings (often male servants or slaves in particular). It was only in the twentieth century that its original, universal sense made a comeback of sorts among the population at large to refer to — in most contexts, at least — both men and women equally. This offers hope that in time its English counterpart *man* may meet with a similar restoration of its original sense.

Hence it was decided to translate *chelovek*, wherever appropriate to the context, by the term *Man* with a capital *M*, not only in an effort to retain the association of the term with a divine (as opposed to a material, earthly) origin, but also to draw upon the original, uncorrupted meaning of the word *man* as a manifestation of 'eternal Mind' — implied in the etymology of the Russian term *chelovek*. So let *all* readers of this book be put on notice: whenever you see *Man* with a capital *M*, this includes *you*.

There are other discrepancies between Russian and English concepts behind respective translation equivalents, but their explanation is best left to individual footnotes.

In conclusion, I must express my gratitude to my editor, Leonid Sharashkin, first for entrusting me with the privileged task of translating such a monumental work as the Ringing Cedars Series and, secondly, for the tremendous support he has given me throughout this initial project, namely, in illuminating aspects of Vladimir Megré's — and Anastasia's — concepts of God, Man, Nature and the Universe that my previous experience with Russian literature could not possibly have prepared me for. These shared insights have made a significant difference in how particular nuances of the original are rendered in the translation, and especially in making allowances for the considerable geographical, social and philosophical distances that all too often separate English-speaking readers from the vast cultural treasures accessible to those with a knowledge of Russian.

I now invite you all to take your seats in the familiar exploration vehicle known as the English language as we journey together to examine a previously inaccessible Russian treasure of momentous significance for all humanity (including the planet we collectively inhabit) — an experience summed up in one beautiful word: *Anastasia.*

Ottawa, Canada
January 2005 / October 2007   John Woodsworth

CHAPTER ONE

The ringing cedar

In the spring of 1994 I chartered three riverboats, on which I carried out a four-month expedition on the River Ob in Siberia, from Novosibirsk to Salekhard and back. The aim of the expedition was to foster economic ties with the regions of the Russian Far North.

The expedition went under the name of *The Merchant Convoy*. The largest of the three riverboats was a passenger ship named the *Patrice Lumumba*. (Western Siberian riverboats bear rather interesting names: the *Maria Ulyanova,* the *Patrice Lumumba,* the *Mikhail Kalinin,*[1] as if there were no other personages in history worth commemorating.) The lead ship *Patrice Lumumba* housed the expedition headquarters, along with a store where local Siberian entrepreneurs could exhibit their wares.

The plan was for the convoy to travel north 3,500 kilometres,[2] visiting not only major ports of call such as Tomsk,

---

[1] *Maria Ulyanova* — a name borne by two historical figures: *Maria Alexandrovna Ulyanova* (*née* Blank, 1835–1916) — mother to Vladimir Ilich Ulyanov (a.k.a. Vladimir Lenin, founder of the Soviet Union), and *Maria Ilinichna Ulyanova* (1878–1937) — Lenin's sister; the ship has since been re-named the *Viktor Gashkov.* *Patrice Emery Lumumba* (1925–1961) — Communist leader of the *Mouvement National Congolais*, who formed the first elected government of the Democratic Republic of the Congo; the ship is now known as the *Paris.* *Mikhail Ivanovich Kalinin* (1875–1946) — Chairman of the Soviet National Executive Committee (the USSR's first titular Head of State) from the 1920s until his death; the *Kalinin* still retains its original name.

[2] *3,500 kilometres* (= approx. 2,100 miles) — The metric system of measures is used throughout the book. One kilometre equals approximately six tenths (0.6) of a mile.

Nizhnevartovsk, Khanty-Mansiysk and Salekhard, but smaller places as well, where goods could be unloaded only during a brief summer navigation season.

The convoy would dock at a populated settlement during the daytime. We would offer the wares we had brought for sale and hold talks about setting up regular economic links. Our travelling was usually done at night. If weather conditions were unfavourable for navigation, the lead ship would put into the nearest port, and we would organise on-board parties for the local young people. Most places offered little in the way of their own entertainment. Clubs and community centres (so-called 'Houses of Culture') had been going downhill ever since the collapse of the USSR, and there were almost no cultural activities available.

Sometimes we might go for twenty-four hours or more without seeing a single populated place, even the tiniest village. From the river — the only transportation artery for many kilometres around — the only thing visible to the eye was the taiga³ itself. I was not yet aware at the time that somewhere amidst the uninhabited vastness of forest along the riverbank a surprise meeting was awaiting me — one that was to change my whole life.

One day on our way back to Novosibirsk, I arranged to dock the lead ship at a small village, one with only a few houses at best, dozens of kilometres distant from the larger population centres. I planned a three-hour stopover so the crew could have shore leave and the local residents could buy some of our goods and foodstuffs, while we could cheaply pick up from them both fish and wild-growing plants of the taiga.

---

³*taiga* — the Russian name given to the boreal forest that stretches across much of Siberia and northern Canada. The word *Siberia* is derived from an Old Tungus word *sivir* meaning 'land', 'world' or 'tribe'.

During our stopover time, as the leader of the expedition I was approached with a really weird request by two of the local senior citizens (as I judged at the time) — one of them appeared to be somewhat older than the other. The elder of the two — a wisened fellow with a long grey beard — kept silent the whole time, leaving his younger companion to do the talking. This fellow tried to persuade me to lend him fifty of my crew (which numbered no more than sixty-five in total) to go with them into the taiga — a trek of twenty-five kilometres from the dock where the ship was berthed. They would be taken into the depths of the taiga to cut down a tree they described as a 'ringing cedar'.[4] On top of that, the cedar, which he said reached forty metres in height,[5] needed to be cut up into pieces which could be carried by hand to the ship. We must, he said, definitely take the whole lot.

The old fellow further recommended that each piece be cut up into smaller pieces. Each of us should keep one for himself and give the rest to relatives, friends and anyone who wished to accept a piece as a gift. He said this was a most unusual cedar. The piece should be worn on one's chest as a pendant. Hang it around your neck while standing barefoot in the grass, and then press it to your exposed chest with the palm of your left hand. It takes only a minute or so to

---

[4]*cedar* (Russian *kedr*) — in this case (as elsewhere) referring either to the Siberian pine (Siberian cedar, *Pinus sibirica*) or to the Lebanese cedar (*Cedrus libani*). Like the south European stone pine (*Pinus pinea*) and North American pinyon pines (*Pinus monophylla* and other species), the Siberian pine produces edible pine nuts. This tree is quite distinct from the Eastern red cedar (*Juniperus virginiana*) and the Western red cedar (*Thuja plicata*) of North America, the Australian red cedar (*Toona ciliata*) or many other 'cedars'. In keeping with the Russian usage and the tree's Biblical associations, however, we are translating the name of this tree as *cedar* throughout the Series.

[5]*forty metres* — about 131 feet. The *metre* is the basic unit of length in the metric system, equal to 3.28 feet.

feel the pleasing warmth emanating from the piece of cedar, followed by a slight shiver running through the whole body. From time to time, whenever desired, the side of the pendant facing away from the body should be rubbed with one's fingertips, the thumbs pressed against the other side. The old fellow confidently assured me that within three months the possessor of one of these 'ringing cedar' pendants will feel significant improvement in his sense of well-being, and will be cured of many diseases.

"Even AIDS?" I asked, and briefly explained what I had learnt about this disease from the press.

The oldster confidently replied:

"From any and all diseases!"

But this, he considered, was an easy task. The main benefit was that anyone having one of these pendants would become kinder, more successful and more talented.

I did know a little about the healing properties of the cedars of our Siberian taiga, but the suggestion that it could affect one's feelings and abilities — well, that to me seemed beyond the bounds of probability. The thought came to me that maybe these old men wanted money from me for this 'unusual cedar', as they themselves called it. And I began explaining that out in 'the big wide world', women — in an effort to please men — were used to wearing jewellery made of gold and silver and wouldn't pay a dime for some scrap of wood, and so I wasn't going to lay out any money for anything like that.

"They don't know what they're wearing," came the reply. "Gold — well, that's dust in comparison with one piece of this cedar. But we don't need any money for it. We can give you some dried mushrooms in addition, but there's nothing we need from you..."

Not wanting to start an argument, out of respect for their age, I said:

"Well, maybe someone will wear some of your cedar pendants. They certainly would if a top wood-carving craftsman agreed to put his hand to it and create something of amazing beauty!"

To which the old fellow replied:

"Yes, you could carve it, but it would be better to polish it by rubbing. It will be a lot better if you do this yourself, with your fingers, whenever your heart desires — then the cedar will also have a beautiful look to it."

Then the younger of the two quickly unbuttoned first his old worn jacket and then his shirt and revealed what he was wearing on his chest. I looked and saw a puffed-out circle or oval. It was multi-coloured — purple, raspberry, auburn — forming some kind of puzzling design — the vein-lines on the wood looked like little streams. I am not a connoisseur of *objets d'art,* although from time to time I have had occasion to visit picture galleries. The world's great masters had not called forth any particular emotions in me, but the object hanging around this man's neck aroused significantly greater feelings and emotions than any of my visits to the Tretyakov Gallery.[6]

"How many years have you been rubbing this piece of cedar?" I asked.

"Ninety-three," the old fellow responded.

"And how old are you?"

"A hundred and nineteen."

At the time I didn't believe him. He looked like a man of seventy-five. Either he hadn't noticed my doubts or, if he had, he paid no attention to them. In somewhat excited tones he started in trying to persuade me that any piece of this cedar,

---

[6]*Tretyakov Gallery* — the foremost collection of Russian art in the world, located in the centre of Moscow. The original collector, Pavel Tretyakov, donated his extensive collection to the City of Moscow in 1892; it has been steadily increasing ever since.

polished by human fingers alone, would also look beautiful in just three years. Then it would start looking even better and better, especially when worn by a woman. The body of its wearer would give off a pleasant and beneficial aroma, quite unlike anything artificially produced by Man!

Indeed, a very pleasant fragrance was emanating from both these old men. I could feel it, even though I'm a smoker and (like all smokers) have a dulled sense of smell.

And there was one other peculiarity...

I suddenly became aware of certain phrases in the speech of these strangers that were not common to the residents of this isolated part of the North. Some of them I remember to this day, even the intonations associated with them. Here is what the old fellow told me:

"God created the cedar to store cosmic energy...

"When someone is in a state of love they emit a radiant energy. It takes but a split second for it to reflect off the planets floating overhead and come back to Earth and give life to everything that breathes.

"The Sun is one of those planets, and it reflects but a tiny fraction of such radiance.

"Only bright rays can travel into Space from Man on the Earth. And only beneficial rays can be reflected from Space back to Earth.

"Under the influence of malicious feelings Man can emit only dark rays. These dark rays cannot rise but must fall into the depths of the Earth. Bouncing off its core, they return to the surface in the form of volcanic eruptions, earthquakes, wars etc.

"The culminating achievement of these dark rays is their direct effect on the Man originating them, invariably exacerbating this Man's own malicious feelings.

"Cedars live to be five hundred and fifty years old. Day and night their millions of needles catch and store the whole spectrum of bright energy.[7] During the period of the cedars' life all the celestial bodies which reflect this bright energy pass above them.

"Even in one tiny piece of cedar there is more energy beneficial to Man than in all the man-made energy installations taken together.

"Cedars receive the energy emanating from Man through Space, store it up and at the right moment give it back. They give it back when there is not enough of it in Space — and, consequently, in Man — or in everything living and growing on the Earth.

"Occasionally, though very rarely, one discovers cedars that have been storing up energy but not giving back what they have stored. After five hundred years of their life they start to ring. This is how they talk to us, through their quiet ringing sound — this is how they signal people to take them and cut them down to make use of their stored-up energy on the Earth. This is what the cedars are asking with their ringing sound. They keep on asking for three whole years. If they don't have contact with living human beings, then in three years, deprived of the opportunity to give back what they have received and stored through the Cosmos, they lose their ability to give it back directly to Man. Then they will start

---

[7]Trees indeed capture a wide range of radiation beyond visible light. Man-made antennas are but an imitation of branching pattern in trees. Both the structure of trees and the materials composing them betray natural wave-receptors. Tree sap is a great conductor of electricity (this is why a tree hit by a lightning virtually explodes), and static electricity was first received from *amber* — a fossil resin from conifer trees. For details please see Dr Philip Callahan's books, including *Tuning in to nature* and *Ancient mysteries, modern visions: The magnetic life of agriculture*. Viktor Schauberger (see footnote 1 in Chapter 16: "Flying saucers? Nothing extraordinary!") referred to trees as "bioelectric condensers". This statement is corroborated by Dr Georges Lakhovsky (see footnote 2 in Chapter 26: "Dreams — creating the future"), a pioneer explorer of energy fields as the foundation of all life on a cellular level.

burning up the energy internally. This torturous process of burning and dying lasts twenty-seven years.

"Not long ago we discovered a cedar like this. We determined that it had been ringing for two years already. It was ringing very, very softly. Perhaps it is trying to draw out its request over a longer period of time, but still, it has only one year left. It must be sawed up and given away to people."

The old man spoke at length, and for some reason I heard him out. The voice of this strange old *Sibiriak*[8] would sound at first quietly confident, then very excited, and each time he got excited, he would rub the piece of cedar with his fingertips as though they were lightly tripping over some kind of musical instrument.

It was cold on the riverbank. An autumn wind was blowing across the river. Gusts of wind ruffled the hair on the old men's capless heads, but the spokesman's jacket and shirt remained unbuttoned. His fingertips kept rubbing the cedar pendant on his chest, still exposed to the wind. He was still trying to explain its significance to me.

Lidia Petrovna,[9] an employee of my firm, came down the gangplank to tell me that everyone else was already on board and ready for departure, waiting for me to finish my conversation. I bade farewell to the oldsters and quickly climbed aboard. I couldn't act on their request — for two reasons: delaying departure, especially for three days, would mean a significant financial loss. And besides, everything these old fellows said seemed to me, at the time, to be in the realm of pure superstition.

---

[8] *Sibiriak* — the Russian word denoting a resident of Siberia.

[9] *Lidia Petrovna* — *Petrovna* here is a patronymic, derived from her father's first name (*Petr*, pronounced 'Piotr'). The combination of the first name plus the patronymic is the standard form of formal address among business colleagues and acquaintances.

The next morning during our usual company meeting I suddenly noticed that Lidia Petrovna was fingering a cedar pendant of her own. Later she would tell me that after I'd gone aboard she stayed behind for a while. She noticed that when I started hurrying away from them, the oldster that had been talking with me stared after me with a perplexed look, and then said excitedly to his older companion:

"Now how can that be? Why didn't they understand? I really don't know how to speak their language. I couldn't make them believe, I simply couldn't! I got nowhere with them... Nowhere! Why? Tell me, Father!"

The elder man put his hand on his son's shoulder and replied:

"You weren't convincing enough, son! They didn't comprehend."

"As I was going up the gangplank," Lidia Petrovna went on, "the old man that was talking with you suddenly rushed up to me, grabbed me by the arm, and led me back down to the grass below.

"He hurriedly pulled out of his pocket a string, and attached to it was this piece of cedar wood. He put it around my neck, and pressed it against my chest with the palm of both his hand and mine. I even felt a shiver go through my whole body. Somehow he managed to do all this very quickly, and I didn't even get a chance to say anything to him.

"As I was walking away, he called after me: 'Have a safe journey! Be happy! Please come again next year! All the best, people! We'll be waiting for you! Have a safe journey!'

"As the ship pulled away from the dock, the old fellow kept on waving at us for a long time, and then all at once sat down on the grass. I was watching him through a pair of binoculars. The old man that talked with you and later gave me the pendant — I saw him sit down on the grass, and his shoulders were trembling. The older one with the long beard was bending over him and stroking his head."

Amidst the flurry of my subsequent commercial dealings, account-keeping and end-of-voyage farewell banquets I completely forgot about the strange Siberian oldsters.

Upon my return to Novosibirsk I was afflicted with sharp pains. The diagnosis: a duodenal intestinal ulcer and osteochondrosis of the thoracic spine.

In the quiet of the comfy hospital ward I was cut off from the bustle of everyday life. My deluxe private room gave me an opportunity to calmly reflect on my four-month expedition and to draw up a business plan for the next one. But it seemed as though my memory relegated just about everything that had happened to the background and for some reason the old men and what they said came to the forefront of my thought.

I requested to have delivered to me in the hospital all sorts of literature on cedars. After comparing what I read with what I had heard, I became more and more amazed and began to actually believe what the oldsters had said. There was at least some kind of truth in their words... or maybe the whole thing was true?!

In books on folk medicine there is a lot said about the cedar as a healing remedy. They say that everything from the tips of the needles to the bark is endowed with highly effective healing properties. The Siberian cedar wood has a beautiful appearance, and is used with great success by both masters of artistic wood-carving and cabinet-makers, as well as in producing soundboards for musical instruments. Cedar needles are highly capable of eliminating airborne germs and purifying the surrounding atmosphere. Cedar wood has a distinctive, pleasant balsam fragrance. A small cedar chip placed inside a house will keep moths away.

In the popular-science literature I read it was said that the qualitative characteristics for the northern cedars were significantly higher than for those growing in the south. Back in 1792 the academician P.S. Pallas[10] wrote that the fruits of the Siberian cedar were effective in restoring youth and virility and significantly increasing the body's resilience — its ability to withstand a number of diseases.

There is a whole host of historical phenomena directly or indirectly linked to the Siberian cedar. Here is one of them.

In 1907 a fifty-year-old semi-literate peasant named Gregory Rasputin,[11] who hailed from an isolated Siberian village in an area where the Siberian cedar grows, found himself in St Petersburg, the capital, and soon became a regular guest of the imperial family. Not only did he amaze them with his predictions, but he possessed incredible sexual stamina. At the time of his assassination, onlookers were struck by the fact that despite his bullet-ridden body he continued to live. Perhaps because he had been raised on cedar nuts in a part of the country where cedars abound?

[10]*P.S. Pallas* — a reference to Peter Simon Pallas (1741–1811), a German zoologist, paleontologist, botanist and ethnographer, born in St Petersburg. As a member of the St Petersburg Academy of Sciences, he was a prominent pioneer explorer of the Siberian taiga.

[11]*Gregory Efimovich Rasputin* (1871?–1916; sources do not agree on the date of his birth) — a monk from the Tiumen region of Western Siberia who appeared to have unusual healing powers. He curried favour with the court of Tsar Nicholas I (especially Nicholas' wife Alexandra Fedorovna) by demonstrating a beneficial influence on their son (and heir to the throne) Alexei, who suffered from hemophilia. For more on Rasputin, see Book 2, Chapter 1: "Alien or Man?". The passage on Rasputin's alleged debauchery is quoted from the 1979 novel *U poslednei cherty* (At the last frontier) by Valentin Pikul (1928–1990) — for further details, please see footnote 16 in Book 2, Chapter 1: "Alien or Man?".

This is how a contemporary journalist described his staying power:

"At age fifty he could begin an orgy at noon and go on carousing until four o'clock in the morning. From his fornication and drunkenness he would go directly to the church for morning prayers and stand praying until eight, before heading home for a cup of tea. Then, as if nothing had happened, he would carry on receiving visitors until two in the afternoon. Next he would collect a group of ladies and accompany them to the baths. From the baths he would be off to a restaurant in the country, where he would begin repeating the previous night's activities. No normal person could ever keep up a régime like that."

The many-time world champion and Olympic champion wrestler Alexander Karelin, who has never been defeated so far,[12] is also a Siberian, also from an area where the Siberian cedar grows. This strongman also eats cedar nuts. A coincidence?

I mention only those facts which can be easily verified in popular-science literature, or which can be confirmed by witnesses. Lidia Petrovna, who was given the 'ringing cedar' pendant by the Siberian oldster, is now one of those witnesses. She is thirty-six years old, married with two children. Her co-workers have noticed changes in her behaviour. She has become kinder and smiles more often. Her husband, whom I happen to know, told me that their family has now been experiencing a greater degree of mutual understanding. He also remarked that his wife has somehow become younger-looking, and is starting to arouse greater feelings in him — more respect and, quite possibly, more love.

But all these multitudinous facts and evidences pale in comparison to the main point, which you can look up for

---

[12] *Alexander Alexandrovich Karelin* (1967–) — a Russian, European, Olympic and world champion wrestler many times over, undefeated in international competition from 1987 to 2000 (for most of this time not even giving up a point).

yourself — a discovery which has left me with not a trace of doubt — and that is the *Bible*. In the Book of Leviticus in the Old Testament (Ch. 14, vs. 4), God teaches us how to treat people, and even decontaminate their houses, with the help of... the *cedar*!!!

After comparing all the facts and data I had gleaned from various sources, I was confronted by such a remarkable picture that all the wonders of the world faded before it. The great mysteries that have excited people's minds began to pale into insignificance in comparison with the mystery of the ringing cedar. Now I could no longer have any doubts about its existence. They were all dispelled by the popular-science literature and the Old Vedic scriptures I was reading.

Cedars are mentioned forty-two times in the Bible, all in the Old Testament.[13] When Moses presented humanity with the Ten Commandments on stone tablets, he probably knew more about them than has been recorded in the Old Testament.

We are accustomed to the fact that in Nature there are various plants capable of treating human ills. The healing properties of the cedar have been attested in popular-science literature and by such serious and authoritative researchers as Academician Pallas, and this is consistent with the Old Testament scriptures.

And now, pay careful attention!

When the Old Testament talks about the cedar, it is just the cedar alone; nothing is said about other trees.[14] Doesn't this suggest the inference that the cedar is the most potent

[13]In the *Authorised (King James) Version* of the English Bible, in fact, the word *cedar* (or *cedars*) appears 75 times, from Leviticus to Zechariah. But see footnote 4 above.

[14]There are, of course, separate references in the Bible to a number of trees (e.g., fir, oak, juniper), but not in conjunction with cedars.

medicine of any existing in Nature? What is this, anyway? A whole medicine kit? But how is it to be used? And why, out of all the Siberian cedars, did these strange old fellows point to a single 'ringing cedar'?

But that's not all. Something immeasurably more mysterious lies behind this story from the Old Testament:

King Solomon built a temple out of cedar wood. In return for the cedar from Lebanon, he gave another king, Hiram, twenty cities of his kingdom. Incredible! Giving away twenty cities just for some kind of building materials?! True, he got something else in return. At King Solomon's request he was given servants that were "skilled in felling timber".[15]

What kind of people were these? What knowledge did they possess?

I have heard that even now, in the far-flung reaches of the taiga there are old people with an uncanny ability to select the right trees for construction. But back then, over two thousand years ago, everybody might have known this. Nevertheless, specialists of some sort were required. The temple was built. Services began to be held there, and... "the priests could not stand to minister because of the cloud".[16]

What kind of a cloud was that? How and from where did it enter the temple? What could it have been? Energy? A spirit? What kind of phenomenon, and what connection did it have with the cedar?

The old fellows talked about the ringing cedar as storing up some kind of energy.

Which cedars are stronger — the ones in Lebanon or those in Siberia?

---

[15] I Kings 5: 6 (*New International Version*).

[16] I Kings 8: 11 (*Authorised King James Version*).

Academician Pallas said that the healing properties of the cedars increased in proportion to their proximity to the forest tundra. In that case, then, the Siberian cedar would be the stronger.

It says in the Bible: "...by their fruits ye shall know them."[17] In other words, again the Siberian cedar!

Could it be that no one has paid any attention to all this?

Has no one put two and two together?

The Old Testament, the science of the past century and the current one — are all of the same opinion regarding the cedar.

And Elena Ivanovna Roerich[18] notes in her book *Living ethics:* "...a chalice of cedar resin figured in the rituals of the consecration of the kings of the ancient Khorassan. Druids also called the chalice of cedar resin the Chalice of Life. And only later, with the loss of the realization of the spirit, was it replaced by blood. The fire of Zoroaster was the result of burning of the cedar resin in the chalice."[19]

So, then, how much of our forebears' knowledge of the cedar, its purpose and properties, has been passed down to the present day?

Is it possible that nothing has been preserved?

What do the Siberian oldsters know about it?

And all at once my memory harked back to an experience of many years ago, which gave me goosebumps all over. I didn't pay any attention to it back then, but now...

---

[17]Matth. 7: 20 (*Authorised King James Version*).

[18]*Elena Ivanovna Roerich [Rerikh]* (1879–1955) — Russian religious thinker. Travelling through Asia with her husband, the prominent Russian artist Nikolai Konstantinovich Roerich, she became fascinated with Oriental religions and devoted her life to studying and writing about them. In 1920 she and her husband founded the Agni Yoga Society, a non-profit educational institution in New York.

[19]This translation is taken from an English version of Roerich's *Leaves of Morya's Garden, Book 2: Illumination* (1925) — 2.4.18.

During the early years of *perestroika* I was president of the Association of Siberian Entrepreneurs. One day I got a call from the Novosibirsk District Executive Council (back then we still had Communist Party committees and 'Executive Councils'), asking me to come to a meeting with a prominent Western businessman. He had a letter of recommendation from the government of the day. Several entrepreneurs were present, along with workers from the Executive Council secretariat.

The 'Western businessman' was of a rather imposing external appearance — an unusual person with Oriental features. He was wearing a turban, and his fingers were adorned with precious rings.

The discussion, as usual, centred around the possibilities for co-operation in various fields. The visitor said, among other things: "We would like to buy cedar nuts from you." As he spoke these words, his face and body tightened, and his sharp eyes moved from side to side, no doubt studying the reaction of the entrepreneurs present. I remember the incident very well, as even then I wondered why his appearance had changed like that.

After the official meeting the Moscow interpreter accompanying him came up to me. She said he would like to speak with me.

The businessman made me a confidential proposal: if I could arrange a steady supply of cedar nuts for him — and they had to be fresh — then I would receive a handsome personal percentage over and above the official price.

The nuts were to be shipped to Turkey for processing into some kind of oil. I said I would think it over.

I decided I would find out for myself what kind of oil he was talking about. And I did...

On the London market, which sets the standard for world prices, cedar nut oil fetches anywhere up to five hundred dollars per kilogram![20] Their proposed deal would have given us approximately two to three dollars for one kilogram of cedar nuts.

I rang up an entrepreneur I happened to know in Warsaw, and asked him whether it might be possible to market such a product directly to customers, and whether we could learn the technology involved in its extraction.

A month later he sent me a reply: "No way. We weren't able to gain access to the technology. And besides, there are certain special-interest groups in the West so involved in these issues of yours that it would be better just to forget about it."

After that I turned to my good friend, Konstantin Rakunov,[21] a scholar with our Novosibirsk Consumer Co-operative Institute. I bought a shipment of nuts and financed a study. And the laboratories of his institute produced approximately 100 kilograms of cedar nut oil.

I also hired researchers, who came up with the following information from archival documents:

Before the Revolution (and even for some time afterward) there was in Siberia an organisation known as the *Siberian Co-operator*. People from this organisation traded in oil, including cedar nut oil. They had rather swanky branch offices in Harbin, London and New York and rather large Western bank accounts.[22] After the revolution the organisation eventually collapsed, and many of its members went abroad.

---

[20] *kilogram* — metric measure of weight, equal to approximately 2.2 pounds.

[21] *Konstantin Petrovich Rakunov* (1954–) — With a post-graduate degree in economics, Rakunov holds the rank of *docent* (equivalent to Associate Professor) in the Management Department at what is now the Novosibirsk Consumer Co-operative University; he is the author of a number of scholarly publications on consumer co-operatives.

[22] In fact, prior to the 1917 revolution Russian exports of cedar nut oil generated 10% of all foreign-trade revenues, rivalling such commodities as grain, timber and furs.

A member of the Bolshevist government, Leonid Krasin,[23] met with the head of this organisation and asked him to return to Russia. But the head of the *Siberian Co-operator* replied that he would be of more help to Russia if he remained outside its borders.

From archival materials I further learnt that cedar oil had been made using wooden (only wooden!) presses in many villages of the Siberian taiga. The quality of the cedar oil depended on the season in which the nuts were gathered and processed. But I was unable to determine, either from the archives or the institute, exactly which season was being indicated. The secret had been lost. There are no healing remedies with properties analogous to those of cedar oil. But perhaps the secret of making this oil had been passed along by one of the émigrés to someone in the West? How was it possible that the cedar nuts with the most effective healing properties grow in Siberia, and yet the facility for producing the oil is located in Turkey? After all, Turkey has no cedars like those found in Siberia.

And just what 'Western special-interest groups' was the Warsaw entrepreneur talking about? Why did he say it would be better just to forget about this issue? Might not these groups be 'smuggling' this product with its extraordinary healing properties out of our Russian-Siberian taiga? Why, with such a treasure here at home with such time-tested effective properties — proved over centuries, millennia, even — do we spend millions and maybe billions of dollars buying up foreign medicines and swallow them up like half-crazed people? How is it that we keep losing the knowledge known to our forebears? Our recent forebears yet — the ones who lived

---

[23]*Leonid Borisovich Krasin* (1870–1928) — an early Bolshevik and Communist Party activist. During the 1920s he served as Foreign Trade minister as well as the new government's trade representative in London and Paris.

in our century — let alone the Bible's description of that extraordinary happening of over two thousand years ago?

What kind of unknown forces are trying so earnestly to erase our forebears' knowledge from our own memories? "Oh, you'd better stick to minding your own business!" we're told. Yes, they *are* trying to wipe it out. And, indeed, they are succeeding!

I was seized by a fit of anger. To add insult to injury, I discovered that cedar oil *is* sold in our pharmacies, but it is sold in foreign packaging! I bought a single thirty-gram vial and tried it. The actual oil content, I think, was no more than a couple of drops — the rest was some kind of diluting agent. Compared to what was produced in the Consumer Co-operative Institute — well, there was simply no comparison. And these diluted couple of drops cost fifty thousand roubles![24]

So what if we didn't buy it abroad, but sold it ourselves? Just the sale of this oil would be enough to raise the whole of Siberia above the poverty level! But how did we ever manage to let go of the technology of our forebears?! And here we are snivelling that we live like paupers...

Well, okay, I thought I'd come up with something all the same. I'd produce the oil myself — and my firm would only get wealthier.

I decided I would try a second expedition along the Ob — back up north, using only my headquarters ship, the *Patrice Lumumba.* I loaded a variety of goods for sale into the hold, and turned the film-viewing room into a store. I decided to hire a new crew and not invite anyone from my firm. As things stood, my firm's financial situation had worsened while I was distracted with my new interest.

---

[24]*fifty thousand roubles* — approximately 16 US dollars at the November 1994 exchange rate — equivalent to 20% of the average Russian's monthly income.

Two weeks after leaving Novosibirsk my security guards reported they had overheard conversations about the ringing cedar. And, in their opinion, the newly hired workers included some 'pretty strange people', to put it mildly. I began summoning individual crew members to my quarters to talk about the forthcoming trek into the taiga. Some of them even agreed to go on a volunteer basis. Others asked for an extra-large bonus for this operation, since it was not something they had agreed to when signing up for work. It was one thing to stay in the comfortable conditions aboard ship — quite another to trek twenty-five kilometres into the taiga and back, carrying loads of wood. My finances at the time were already pretty tight. I was not planning to sell the cedar. After all, the oldsters had said it should be given away. Besides, my main interest was not the cedar tree itself, but the secret of how to extract the oil.[25] And of course it would be fascinating to find out all the details connected with it.

Little by little, with the help of my security guards, I realised that there would be attempts made to spy on my movements, especially during any time I spent ashore. But for what purpose was unclear. And who was behind the would-be spies? I thought and thought about it, and decided that to be absolutely certain, I would somehow have to outsmart everyone at once.

---

[25]Note that the fruit of the *Siberian* cedar, translated in this Series as *cedar nuts*, is known to most English speakers under the name *pine nuts*, and the oil pressed from these nuts is better known as *pine nut oil*. It does not refer to the 'oil' (or resin) from the North American red cedar, which is not edible. See footnote 4 above.

Chapter Two

Encounter

Without a word to anyone, I arranged to have the ship stop not far from the place where I had met the old men the previous year. Then I took a small motorboat and reached the village. I gave orders to the captain to continue along the trade route.

I hoped I would be able, with the help of the local residents, to look up the two old fellows, see the ringing cedar with my own eyes and determine the cheapest way of getting it back to the ship. Tying the motorboat to a rock on the shore, I was about to head for one of the little houses close by. But spotting a woman standing alone atop the steep riverbank, I decided to approach her.

The woman had on an old quilted jacket, long skirt and high rubber galoshes of the kind worn by many residents of the northern backwoods during the spring and fall. On her head was a kerchief tied so that the forehead and neck were fully covered. It was hard to tell just how old this woman was. I said hello and told her about the two old men I had met here the previous year.

"It was my grandfather and great-grandfather who talked with you here last year, Vladimir," the woman replied.

I was amazed. Her voice sounded very young, her diction was crystal clear. She called me by my first name and right off used the informal form of address.[1] I couldn't remember

---

[1] *informal form of address* — in Russian this means using the pronoun *ty* (and its grammatical variants) in place of the more formal *vy* (much the same as using *tu* instead of *vous* in French).

the names of the oldsters, or whether we had introduced ourselves at all. I thought now we must have done so, since this woman knew my name. I asked her (deciding to continue in the same informal tone):

"And how do you call yourself?"

"Anastasia," the woman answered, stretching out her hand toward me, palm down, as though expecting me to kiss it.

This gesture of a country woman in a quilted jacket and galoshes, standing on a deserted shore and trying to act like a lady of the world, amused me no end. I shook her hand. Naturally, I wasn't going to kiss it. Anastasia gave me an embarrassed smile and suggested I go with her into the taiga, to where her family lived.

"The only thing is, we shall have to make our way through the taiga, twenty-five kilometres. That is not too much for you?"

"Well, of course, it's rather far. But can you show me the ringing cedar?"

"Yes, I can."

"You know all about that, you'll tell me?"

"I shall tell you what I know."

"Then let's go!"

Along the way Anastasia told me how their family, their kin, had been living in the cedar forest generation after generation — as her forebears had said, over the course of several millennia. It is only extremely rarely that they find themselves in direct contact with people from our civilised society. These contacts do not occur in their places of permanent residence, but only when they come into the villages under the guise of hunters or travellers from some other settlement. Anastasia herself had been to two big cities: Tomsk and Moscow. But only for one day each. Not even to stay the night. She wanted to see whether she might have been mistaken in her perceptions about the lifestyle of city people. She had saved the money for the trip by selling berries and dried mushrooms. A local village woman had lent her her passport.[2]

Anastasia did not approve of her grandfather and great-grandfather's idea of giving away the ringing cedar with its healing properties to a whole lot of people. When asked why, she replied that the pieces of cedar would be scattered among evildoers as well as good people. In all probability the majority of the pieces would be snatched up by negative-thinking individuals. In the final analysis they might end up doing more harm than good. The most important thing, in her opinion, was to promote the good. And to help people through whom the good was accomplished. If everyone were benefited at random, the imbalance between good and evil would not be changed, but would stay the same or even get worse.

After my encounter with the Siberian oldsters I looked through a variety of popular-science literature as well as a host of historical and scholarly works describing the unusual properties of the cedar. Now I was trying to penetrate and comprehend what Anastasia was saying about the lifestyle of the cedar people and thinking to myself: "Now what if anything can that be compared to?"

I thought about the Lykovs[3] — a true story many Russians are familiar with from the account by Vasily Peskov of another family that lived an isolated life for many years in the taiga. They were written up in the paper *Komsomolskaya Pravda* under the headline: "Dead-end in the taiga", and were the subject

---

[2]*passport* — in this case, an internal identity document required for any kind of travel within the Russian Federation (or the former Soviet Union).

[3]*the Lykovs* — a family of 'Old Believers' that lived in self-imposed isolation in the taiga unknown to the outside world through most of the Soviet period. They were discovered by a party of geologists in 1978. Their story is told by *Komsomolskaya Pravda* journalist Vasily Peskov in his book *Lost in the taiga* (available in English translation).

of television programmes. I had formulated for myself an impression of the Lykovs as people who knew Nature pretty well, but had a rather fuzzy concept of our modern civilised life. But this was a different situation. Anastasia gave the impression of someone who was perfectly acquainted with our life and with something else besides that I couldn't fathom at all. She was quite at ease discussing our city life, which she seemed to know first-hand.

We walked along, getting deeper into the woods, and after about five kilometres stopped to rest. At this point she took off her jacket, kerchief and long skirt, and placed them in the hollow of a tree. All she was wearing now was a short, light-weight frock. I was dumbstruck at what I saw. If I were a believer in miracles, I would put this down to something like extreme metamorphosis.

For now here before me stood a very young woman with long golden hair and a fantastic figure. Her beauty was most unusual. It would be hard to imagine how any of the winners of the world's most prestigious beauty contests could rival her appearance, or, as it later turned out, her intellectual prowess. Everything about this taiga girl was alluring, simply spellbinding.

"You are probably tired?" asked Anastasia. "Would you like to rest for a while?"

We sat down right on the grass, and I was able to get a closer look at her face. There were no cosmetics covering her perfect features. Her lovely well-toned skin bore no resemblance to the weather-beaten faces of people I knew who lived in the Siberian backwoods. Her large greyish-blue eyes had a kindly look, and her lips betrayed a gentle smile. As indicated, she wore a short, light-weight smock, something like a night-shirt, at the same time giving the impression that her body was not at all cold, in spite of the 12–15-degree temperatures.[4]

I decided to have a bite to eat. I reached into my bag and took out sandwiches, along with a travel bottle filled with good cognac. I offered to share it with Anastasia but she refused the cognac and for some reason even declined to eat with me. While I was snacking, Anastasia lay on the grass, her eyes blissfully closed, as though inviting the Sun's rays to caress her. The rays reflected off her upturned palms with a golden glow. Lying there half-exposed, she appeared absolutely gorgeous!

I looked at her and thought to myself: *Now why have women always bared to the limit either their legs, or their breasts, or everything at once, with their mini-skirts and décolletage? Is it not to appeal to the men around them, as if to say: "Look how charming I am, how open and accessible!" And what are men obliged to do then? Fight against their fleshly passions and thereby denigrate women with their lack of attention? Or make advances toward them and thereby break a God-given law?*

When I had finished with my refreshment, I asked:

"Anastasia, you're not afraid of walking through the taiga alone?"

"There is nothing I have to fear here," replied Anastasia.

"Interesting, but how would you defend yourself if you happened to encounter two or three burly men — geologists, or hunters, let's say?"

She didn't answer, only smiled.

I thought: *How is it that this so extraordinarily alluring young beauty could not be afraid of anyone or anything?*

What happened next still makes me feel uncomfortable, even to this day. I grabbed her by her shoulders and pulled her close to me. She didn't offer any strong resistance, although

---

[4]*12–15 degree temperatures* — the Celsius (Centigrade) scale common throughout Russia, Europe and Canada, is used throughout the book. 12–15 degrees Celsius equals 54–59 degrees Fahrenheit. To convert a Celsius temperature to Fahrenheit, multiply it by 1.8 and add 32.

I could feel a considerable degree of strength in her resilient body. But I couldn't do anything with her. The last thing I remember before losing consciousness was her saying: "Do not do this... Calm down!" And even before that I remember being suddenly overcome by a powerful attack of fear. A fear of what, I couldn't grasp — as sometimes happens in childhood when you find yourself at home all alone and suddenly become afraid of something.

When I woke up, she was on her knees, bending over me. One of her hands lay upon my chest, while the other was waving to someone up above, or to either side. She was smiling, though not at me, but rather, it seemed, at someone who was invisibly surrounding us or hovering above us. Anastasia seemed to be literally gesturing to her invisible friend that there was nothing amiss going on. Then she calmly and tenderly looked me in the eye:

"Calm down, Vladimir, it is over now."

"But what was it?" I asked.

"Harmony's disapproval of your attitude toward me, of the desire aroused in you. You will be able to understand it all later."

"What's 'harmony' got to do with it? It's you! It's only that you yourself began to resist."

"And I too did not accept it. It was offensive to me."

I sat up, and pulled my bag over toward me.

"Come on, now! 'She didn't accept me! It was offensive to her...' Oh you women! You just do everything you can to tempt us! You bare your legs, stick out your breasts, walk around in high-heeled shoes. That's very uncomfortable, and yet you do it! You walk and wriggle with all your charm, but as soon as... 'Oh, I don't need that! I'm not that way...' What do you wriggle for then? Hypocrites! I'm an entrepreneur and I've seen a lot of your sorts. You all want the same thing, only you all act it out differently. So why did you, Anastasia, take off your outer clothes? The weather's not that hot! And then you lolled about on the grass here, with that alluring smile of yours..."

"I am not that comfortable in clothing, Vladimir. I put it on when I leave the woods and go out among people, but only so I can look like everyone else. I just lay down to relax in the sun and not disturb you while you were eating."

"So you didn't want to disturb me... Well, you did!"

"Please forgive me, Vladimir. Of course, you are right about every woman wanting to attract a man's attention, but not just to her legs and breasts. What she wants is not to let pass by the one man who can see more than just those things."

"But nobody's been passing by here! And what is this 'more' that must be seen, when it's your legs that are front and centre? Oh you women, you're so illogical!"

"Yes, unfortunately, that is the way life sometimes turns out... Maybe we should move along, Vladimir! Have you finished eating? Are you rested?"

The thought crossed my mind: *is it worth going on with this philosophising wild woman?* But I replied:

"Fine, let's go."

Chapter Three

Beast or Man?

We continued our journey to Anastasia's home, her outer clothes left behind in the tree hollow, her galoshes too. She was still wearing the short, light-weight frock. She herself picked up my bag and offered to carry it. Barefoot, she walked ahead of me with an amazingly light and graceful step, waving the bag about her with ease.

We talked the whole time. Talking with her on any subject was most interesting. Perhaps because she had her own strange ideas about everything.

Sometimes Anastasia would whirl about while we were walking. She would turn her face to me, laughing, and keep on walking backwards for a while, quite absorbed in the conversation without so much as a glance down at her feet. How could she walk like that and not once stumble, or prick her bare feet against the knot of a dry branch? We didn't seem to be following any visible path; on the other hand, our way was not hindered by the tangled undergrowth so common in the taiga.

As she walked she would occasionally touch or quickly brush by a leaf or a twig on a bush. Or, bending over without looking, she would tear off some little blade of grass and... eat it.

"Just like a little creature," I thought.

When berries were handy, Anastasia would offer me a few to eat as we walked. The muscles of her body didn't seem to have any unusual features. Her overall physique appeared quite average. Not too thin and not too plump. A resilient, well-fed and very beautiful body. But, from what I could tell, it possessed a goodly degree of strength and extremely sharp reflexes.

Once when I stumbled and started to fall, my arms outstretched in front of me, Anastasia whirled around with lightning speed, quickly placing her free hand under me, and I landed with my chest on her palm, her fingers spread wide. I fell, but my hands did not touch the ground. There she was, supporting my body with the palm of one hand, helping it regain its normal position. During all this time she went on talking, with not the slightest sign of strain. After I had straightened up with the help of her hand, we continued on our way, as though nothing whatever had happened. For some reason my mind momentarily rested on the gas pistol I had in my bag.

With all the interesting conversation I hadn't realised how much ground we had actually been covering. All at once Anastasia stopped, put my bag down under a tree and joyfully exclaimed:

"Here we are at home!"

I looked around. A neat little glade, dotted with flowers amidst a host of majestic cedars, but not a single structure to be seen. No kind of shelter at all. In a word, nothing! Not even a primitive lean-to! But Anastasia was beside herself with joy. As though we had arrived at a most comfortable dwelling.

"And where is your house? Where do you sleep, eat, take shelter from the rain?"

"This *is* my house, Vladimir. I have everything here."

A dark sense of disquiet began to come over me.

"Where is this 'everything'? Let's have a tea-kettle, so we can at least heat up some water on the fire. Let's have an axe."

"I do not have a kettle or an axe, Vladimir. And it would be best not to light a fire."

"What are you talking about? She doesn't even have a kettle?! The water in my bottle is all gone. You saw when I ate. I even threw the bottle away. Now there's only a couple of swallows of cognac left. To get to the river or the village is a good day's walk, but I'm so tired and thirsty right now. Where do you get water from? What do you drink out of?"

Seeing my agitation, Anastasia herself showed signs of concern. She quickly took me by the hand and led me through the glade into the forest, admonishing me along the way:

"Not to worry, Vladimir! Please. Do not get upset. I shall take care of everything. You will have a good rest. You will get a good sleep. I shall take care of everything. You will not be cold. You are thirsty? I shall give you something to drink right away."

Not more than ten or fifteen metres from the glade, beyond a clump of bushes, we came across a small taiga lake. Anastasia quickly scooped up a small quantity of water in her cupped hands and raised it to my face.

"Here is some water. Drink it, please."

"What, are you crazy? How can you drink raw water out of some puddle in the woods? You saw how I was drinking *borzhomi*.[1] On board ship even for washing we pass the river water through a special filter, chlorinate it, ozonise it."

"It is not a puddle, Vladimir. This is pure, living water! Good water! Not half-destroyed water, like yours. You can drink this water — it is just like mother's milk! Look."

Anastasia raised her cupped hands to her lips and took a drink.

I blurted out:

"Anastasia, are you some kind of beast?"

---

[1]*borzhomi* — a popular kind of mineral water from the Caucasus mountains in Georgia, famous for its health-giving properties.

"Why a beast? Because my bed is not like yours? There are no cars? No appliances?"

"Because you live like a beast, in the forest, you haven't any possessions, and you seem to enjoy that."

"Yes, I enjoy living here."

"There, you see, you just made my point."

"Do you consider, Vladimir, that what distinguishes Man from all other creatures living on Earth is his possession of manufactured objects?"

"Yes! But even more precisely — his civilised living conditions."

"And do you consider your living conditions to be more civilised? Yes, of course, you do. But I am not a beast, Vladimir.

"I am Man!"[2]

[2]The word *Man* (with a capital *M*) is used throughout the book to refer to a human being of any gender. For details on the word's usage and the important distinction between *Man* and *human* please see the Translator's Preface.

CHAPTER FOUR

Who are they?

Subsequently, after spending three days with Anastasia and observing how this strange young woman lives all by herself in the remote Siberian taiga, I began to understand a little something of her lifestyle, and to be confronted by a number of questions regarding our own.

One of them still haunts me to this day: Is our system of education and bringing up children sufficient to comprehend the meaning of existence, to arrange every individual's life-priorities in the correct order? Does it help or hinder our ability to make sense of Man's essence and purpose?

We have set up a vast educational system. It is on the basis of this system that we teach our children and each other — in kindergarten, school, university and post-graduate programmes. It is this system that enables us to invent things, to fly into Space. We structure our lives in accordance with it. Through its help we strive to construct some happiness for ourselves. We strive to fathom the Universe and the atom, along with all sorts of anomalous phenomena. We love to discuss and describe them at great length in sensational stories in both the popular press and scholarly publications.

But there is one phenomenon which, for some reason, we try with all our might to avoid. Desperately try to avoid! One gets the impression that we are afraid to talk about it. We are afraid, I say, because it could so easily knock the wind out of our commonly accepted systems of education and scientific deductions and make a mockery of the reality of our experience! And we try to pretend that such a phenomenon does not exist. But it does! And it will continue to exist, however much we try to turn away from it or avoid it.

Isn't it time to take a closer look at this and, just maybe, through the collective effort of all our human minds together, find an answer to the following question? If you take all our great thinkers, without exception — people who have formulated religious teachings, all sorts of teachings which the vast majority of humanity are following — or at least endeavouring to follow — why is it that, before formulating their teachings, they became recluses, went into solitude — in most cases, to the forest? Not to some super academy, mind you, but to the forest![1]

Why did the Old Testament's Moses go off into a mountain-top forest before returning and presenting to the world the wisdom set forth on his tablets of stone?

Why did Christ Jesus go off, away from his disciples, into the desert, mountains and forest?

Why did a man named Siddhartha Gautama, who lived in India in the sixth century B.C. spend seven years alone in the forest? After which this recluse came out of the forest, back to humanity, complete with a set of teachings — teachings which even to this day, many centuries later, arouse a multitude of human minds. And people build huge temples and call these teachings Buddhism. And the man himself eventually came to be known as Buddha.[2]

And what about our own not-so-ancient forebears (now acknowledged as historical figures) — men such as Serafim

---

[1]Incidentally, even the word *academy*, translated from Greek, means *groves!*

[2]*Buddha* or *Siddhartha Gautama* (623–544 B.C.) — a member of the Imperial Shakya family, who (according to tradition, at least) rejected the wealthy circumstances of his family upbringing and devoted his life to alleviating human suffering. He is occasionally referred to as *Shakyamuni* — 'a recluse (*lit.* departer) from the Shakyas'.

Sarovsky[3] or Sergiy Radonezhsky?[4] Why did they too go off to become recluses in the forest, and how were they able, after a short period of time there, to so fathom the depths of wisdom that the kings of this world made the long journey through uncharted wilderness to seek their advice?

Monasteries and majestic temples were raised at the locations of their respective solitudes. Thus, for example, the Trinity-Sergiev Monastery in the town of Sergiev Posad near Moscow today attracts thousands of visitors each year. And it all started from a single forest recluse.

Why? Who or what enabled these people to obtain their wisdom? Who gave them knowledge, who brought them closer to understanding the essence of life? How did they live, what did they do, what did they think about during their forest solitude?

These questions confronted me some time after my conversations with Anastasia — after I had started reading everything that I could lay my hands on regarding recluses. But even today I haven't found answers. Why has nothing been written about their solitude experiences?

The answers, I think, must be sought through a collective effort. I am trying to describe the events of my three-day stay

---

[3] *Serafim Sarovsky* (*né:* Prokhor Sidorovich Moshnin, 1759–1833) — a monk of the Sarovsky Hermitage near Tambov, who had a gift for healing and foretelling the future. He was particularly concerned about improving the situation of women and in the 1820s helped establish what would become the Holy Trinity Serafimo-Diveevo Women's Monastery. Canonised in 1903, he is now one of the most revered saints of the Russian Orthodox Church.

[4] *Sergiy* (*né: Varfolomei*) *Radonezhsky* (1314?–1392) — a monastic reformer from the Rostov area, who devoted his life to the principle of brotherly love and meeting the practical needs of the less fortunate; he also mediated disputes between warring princes. In the 1330s he founded a monastery deep in the Radonezh Forest north of Moscow (now the site of the town of Sergiev Posad, until recently called Zagorsk). He was canonised in 1452.

in the Siberian taiga forest and my impressions from my experience with Anastasia, in the hopes that someone will be able to fathom the essence of this phenomenon and put together a clearer picture of our way of life.

For now, on the basis of all that I have seen and heard, only one thing is crystal clear to me: people who live in solitude in the forest, including Anastasia, see what is going on in our lives from a point of view completely different from our own. Some of Anastasia's ideas are the exact opposite of what is commonly accepted. Who is closer to the truth? Who can judge?

My task is simply to record what I have seen and heard, and thereby give others an opportunity to come up with answers.

Anastasia lives in the forest altogether alone. She has no house to call her own, she hardly wears any clothes and does not store any provisions. She is the descendant of people who have been living here for thousands of years and represents what is literally a whole different civilisation. She and those like her have survived to the present day through what I can only term the wisest possible course of action. Very likely the only correct course of action. When they are among us they blend in with us, trying to appear no different from ordinary people, but in their places of habitual residence they merge with Nature. It is not easy to find their habitual dwelling-places. Indeed, Man's presence in such places is betrayed only by the fact that they are more beautiful and better taken care of, like Anastasia's forest glade, for example.

Anastasia was born here and is an integral part of the natural surroundings. In contrast to our celebrated recluses, she did not go off into the forest simply for a time, as they did. She was born in the taiga and visits our world only for brief periods. And what seemed at first glance to be a mysterious phenomenon — the strong fear that overwhelmed me and made me lose consciousness when I attempted to possess

Anastasia — turned out to have an altogether simple explanation: just as we tame a cat, a dog, an elephant, a tiger, an
eagle, and so on, here *everything* around has been 'tamed'.[5]
And this *everything* cannot permit anything bad to happen to
her. Anastasia told me that when she was born and while she
was still under a year old, her mother could leave her alone
on the grass.

"And you didn't die from hunger?" I asked.

The taiga recluse first looked at me in surprise, but then
explained:

"Food should be absolutely of no concern to Man. One
should eat just as one breathes, not paying attention to nutrition, not distracting one's thought from more important issues. The Creator has left that task up to others, so that Man
can live as Man, fulfilling his own destiny."

She snapped her fingers, and right away a little squirrel
popped up beside her, hopping onto her hand. Anastasia
lifted the creature's muzzle up to her mouth, and the squirrel passed from its mouth into hers a cedar nut seed, its shell
already removed. This did not seem to me anything out of
the ordinary. I remembered how, back at the academic complex near Novosibirsk,[6] a lot of squirrels were quite used to
people and would beg for food from passers-by, and even get
angry if they weren't given anything. Here I was simply observing the process in reverse. But this *here* was the taiga,
and I said:

"In the normal world, our world, everything's arranged differently. You, Anastasia, could try snapping your fingers at

[5]*'tamed'* — in this case meaning 'brought into an interrelationship with Man'.

[6]*academic complex* — just outside Novosibirsk there is a whole town known
as *Akademgorodok* (lit. 'Academic town') — home of the Siberian branch of
the Russian Academy of Sciences as well as Novosibirsk State University —
where the professors and researchers live as well as work.

a privately-run kiosk,[7] or even beat on a drum, and nobody would give you anything, yet here you're saying the Creator has decided everything."

"Who is to blame if Man has decided to change the Creator's creative design? Whether it is for the better or for the worse, that is up to you to divine."

This is the kind of dialogue I had with Anastasia on the question of human sustenance. Her position is simple — it is sinful to waste thought on things like food, and she does not think about it. But for us in our civilised world, as it happens, we are obliged to give it thought.

We know from books, reports in the press and TV programmes, of a multitude of examples of infants who have found themselves out in the wilds and ended up being fed by wolves. In this case, however, generations of people have made their permanent residence here, and their relationship to the animal kingdom is different from ours. I asked Anastasia:

"Why aren't you cold, when here I am in a warm jacket?"

"Because," she replied, "the bodies of people who wrap themselves in clothing and shelter themselves from the cold and heat, more and more lose their ability to adapt to changes in their environment. In my case this capacity of the human body has not been lost, and so I really have no need of any clothing."

[7]*privately-run kiosk* — a small enclosed stand selling food and many other items under private (as opposed to State) control. Such kiosks began proliferating during the latter days of *perestroika* and are still popular today.

CHAPTER FIVE

A forest bedroom

I wasn't at all equipped to spend a night in the wilds of the forest. Anastasia put me to bed in some kind of cave hollowed out of the ground. Exhausted after my wearying trek, I soon fell fast asleep. When I woke up, I felt a sense of bliss and comfort, as though I were lying in a magnificently comfortable bed.

The cave, or dugout, was spacious, the floor covered with small feathery cedar twigs and dried grass which filled the surrounding space with a fragrant aroma. As I stretched and spread my limbs, one hand touched a furry pelt and I determined at once that Anastasia must be something of a hunter. I moved closer to the pelt, pressing my back to its warmth, and decided to have another little snooze.

Anastasia was standing near the entranceway to my forest bedroom. Noticing I was awake, she said at once:

"May this day come to you with blessings, Vladimir. And I invite you, in turn, to greet *it* with your blessing. Only, please, do not be frightened."

Then she clapped her hands, and all at once the 'pelt'... I was horror-struck at the realisation that this was no pelt. Out of the cave a huge bear began to gingerly crawl. Receiving a pat of approval from Anastasia, the bear licked her hand and began lumbering off into the forest. It turned out that she had placed some belladonna herbs by my head and made the bear lie down beside me so I wouldn't get cold. She herself had curled up outdoors in front of the entranceway.

"Now how could you do such a thing to me, Anastasia? He could have torn me to shreds or crushed me to death!"

"First of all, it is not a *he,* but a *she*-bear. She could not possibly have done anything to harm you," Anastasia responded. "She is very obedient. She really enjoys it when I give her tasks to carry out. She never even budged the whole night — just nuzzled her nose up to my legs and kept blissfully still, she was so happy. Only she did give a little shudder whenever you waved your arms about in your sleep and slapped her backside!"

CHAPTER SIX

Anastasia's morning

Anastasia goes to bed at nightfall in one of the shelters hollowed out by the creatures of the forest, most often in the bear's dugout. When it is warm, she can sleep right on the grass. The first thing she does upon waking is offer an exuberant outburst of joy to the rising Sun, to the new sprouts on all the twigs, to the new shoots of growth popping up from the earth. She touches them with her hands, strokes them, occasionally adjusts something into place. Then she runs over to the little trees and gives them a thump on their trunks. The tree-tops shake and shower down on her something resembling pollen or dew. Then she lies down on the grass and spends about five minutes blissfully stretching and squirming. Her whole body becomes covered with what appears to be a moist cream. Then she takes a run and jumps into her little lake, splashes about and dives down. She's a terrific diver!

Her relationship with the animal world around her is very much like people's relationships with their household pets. Many of them watch Anastasia as she does her morning routine. They don't approach her, but all she has to do is look in the direction of one of them and make the tiniest beckoning gesture, and the lucky one jumps up on the spot and rushes to her feet.

I saw how one morning she clowned around, playing with a she-wolf just as one might play with the family dog. Anastasia clapped the wolf on the shoulder and dashed off at full tilt. The wolf gave chase, and just as she was about to catch up with her, Anastasia, still on the run, suddenly jumped in the air, repelled herself with both feet off the trunk of a tree, and dashed off in another direction. The wolf couldn't stop but kept on running past the tree, finally making an about-turn and chasing after the laughing Anastasia.

Anastasia gives absolutely no thought to feeding or clothing herself. She most often walks about nude or semi-nude. She sustains herself with cedar nuts, along with varieties of herbs, berries and mushrooms. She eats only dried mushrooms. She never goes hunting for nuts or mushrooms herself, never stores up any kind of provisions, even for the winter. Everything is prepared for her by the multitude of squirrels dwelling in these parts.

Squirrels storing up nuts for the winter is nothing out of the ordinary — that's what they do everywhere, following their natural instincts. I was struck by something else, though: at the snap of Anastasia's fingers any squirrels nearby would compete to be the first to jump onto her outstretched hand and give her the kernel of an already shelled cedar nut. And whenever Anastasia slaps her leg bent at the knee, the squirrels make some sort of sound, as if signalling the others, and they all start bringing dried mushrooms and other supplies and piling them up before her on the grass. And this they do, it seemed to me, with a good deal of pleasure. I thought she had trained them herself, but Anastasia told me that their actions were, so to speak, instinctive, and the mother squirrel herself teaches this to her little ones by example.

"Perhaps one of my early forebears once trained them, but most likely this is simply what they are destined to do. By the time winter has set in, each squirrel has stored up several times as many supplies as it can use for itself."

To my question "How do you keep from freezing during the winter without the proper clothing?" Anastasia replied with a question of her own: "In your world are there no examples of people able to withstand the cold without any kind of clothing?"

And I remembered the book by Porfiry Ivanov,[1] who went around barefoot and wearing only shorts no matter how cold the weather. It tells in the book how the fascists, wanting to test the endurance abilities of this extraordinary Russian, poured cold water over him in a minus-twenty-degree frost and then made him ride naked in a motorcycle side-car.

In her early childhood, in addition to her mother's milk Anastasia was able to draw upon the milk of many different animals. They freely allowed her access to their nipples. She makes absolutely no ritual of mealtime, never sits down just to eat, but picks berries and sprouts of plants as she walks and continues on with her activities.

By the end of my three-day stay with her I could no longer relate to her as I had done at our first encounter. After all I had seen and heard, Anastasia had been transformed for me into some kind of being — but not a beast, since she has such a high degree of intelligence, and then there's her memory! Her memory is such that she, of course, forgets nothing of what she has seen or heard at any moment in time. At times it seemed that her abilities are well beyond the comprehension of the average person. But this very attitude toward her is something that greatly distressed and upset her.

In contrast to certain people we all know with unusual abilities — people who wrap themselves in an aura of mystery and exclusivity, she constantly tried to explain and reveal the

---

[1] *Porfiry Korneevich Ivanov* (1899–1983) — a famous proponent of healthy living through closeness to Nature. In his thirties he cured himself of cancer through self-exposure to extremely cold temperatures and spiritual cleansing. After decades of experimentation he formulated a set of twelve ethical and practical principles for health and harmonious relationship with Nature in his popular *Detka* (literally, 'Baby'), and gained a substantial following.

mechanism underlying her abilities, to prove that there was nothing supernatural to Man in them or in her — that she was Man, a woman, and she repeatedly asked me to bear that in mind. I did attempt to keep it in mind after that, and try to find an explanation for these extraordinary phenomena.

In our civilisation one's brain works to develop a life for one's self, obtain food to eat and satisfy one's sexual instincts. In Anastasia's world no time is spent on these things whatsoever. Even people who find themselves in a situation like the Lykovs'² are obliged to constantly give thought to how to feed and shelter themselves. They don't get help from Nature to the same extent as does Anastasia. There are all sorts of tribes living far from civilisation that are not blessed with this kind of contact. According to Anastasia, it is because their thoughts are not pure enough. Nature and the animal world feel this.

²See footnote 3 in Chapter 2: "Encounter".

CHAPTER SEVEN

Anastasia's ray

I think the most unusual, mystical phenomenon I witnessed during my time in the forest was Anastasia's ability to see not only individuals at great distance but also what was going on in their lives. Possibly other recluses have had a similar ability.

She did this with the help of an invisible ray. She maintained this was something everybody has, but people don't know about it and are unable to make use of it.

"Man has still not invented anything that is not already in Nature. The technology behind television is but a poor imitation of the possibilities of this ray."

Sine the ray is invisible, I didn't believe in it, in spite of her repeated attempts to demonstrate and explain how it worked, to find some proof or plausible explanation. And then one day...

"Tell me, Vladimir, what do you think daydreams are? And are many people able to dream of the future?"

"Daydreaming? I think a lot of people are able to do that. It's when you imagine yourself in a future of your own desire."

"Fine. So, you do not deny that Man has the capacity to visualise his own future, to visualise various specific situations?"

"That I don't deny."

"And what about intuition?"

"Intuition... It's probably the feeling one has when, instead of analysing what might happen of why, some sort of feelings suggest the right thing to do."

"So, you do not deny that in Man there exists something besides ordinary analytical reasoning that helps him determine his own and others' behaviour?"

"Well, let's say that's true."

"Wonderful! Good!" exclaimed Anastasia. "Now, the night-dream. The night-dream — what is that? The dreams almost all people have when they are asleep?"

"The night dream — that's... I really don't know what that is. When you're asleep, a dream is simply a dream."

"All right, all right. Let us call it just a dream. But you do not deny it exists? You and other people are aware that someone in a dream state, when his body is almost beyond the control of a part of his consciousness, can see people and all sorts of things going on."

"Well that, I think, is something nobody will deny."

"But still, in a dream people can communicate, hold conversations, empathise?"

"Yes, they can."

"And what do you think, can a person control his dream? Call up in the dream images and events he would like to see? Just like on ordinary television, for example."

"I don't think that would work out for anyone. The dream, somehow, comes all by itself."

"You are wrong. Man can control everything. Man was created to control everything.

"The ray I am telling you about consists of all the information, concepts, intuitions, emotional feelings one possesses, and, as a result, of dream-like visions consciously controlled by Man's will."

"How can a dream be controlled within a dream?"

"Not within a dream. Wide awake! As if pre-programmed, and with absolute accuracy. You only experience this in a dream and it is chaotic. Man has lost most of his ability to control, to control natural phenomena and himself. So he has decided that a night-dream is simply an incidental by-product of his tired brain. In fact, almost everybody on the Earth can... Well, if you like, I can try helping you see something at a distance right here and now?"

"Go ahead."

"Lie down on the grass and relax, let go, so that your body draws less energy. It is important that you are comfortable. Nothing standing in the way? Now think about the person you know best — your wife, for example. Recollect her habits, how she walks, her clothing, where you think she might be right now, and turn the whole thing over to your imagination."

I remembered my wife, knowing that at that moment she might be at our country home. I imagined the house and some of the furnishings and things. I remembered a great deal, and in some detail, but I didn't see anything. I told Anastasia about all this, and she replied:

"You are not able to let go all the way, as though you were going to go to sleep. I shall help you. Close your eyes. Stretch out your arms in different directions."

Closing my eyes, I felt her fingers touch mine. I began to immerse myself in a dream, or a wakeful doze...

...There was my wife standing in the kitchen of our country home. Over her usual dressing gown she was wearing a knitted cardigan. That meant it was cool in the house. Again some kind of trouble with the heating system.

My wife was making coffee on the gas stove. And something else, in the small crock-pot, 'for the dog'. My wife's face was gloomy and unhappy. Her movements were sluggish. All at once she turned her head, tripped over to the window, looked out at the rain and smiled. The coffee on the stove was spilling over. She picked up the pot with its overflowing liquid but didn't frown or get upset as she usually did. She took off the cardigan...

I woke up.

"Well? Did you see anything?" asked Anastasia.

"I did indeed. But maybe it was just an ordinary dream?"

"How could it be ordinary? Did you not *plan* on seeing your wife in particular?"

"Yes, I did. And I saw her. But where is the proof that she was actually there in the kitchen at the moment I saw her in the dream?"

"Remember this day and hour, Vladimir, if you want to have proof. When you get home, ask her. Was there not something else out of the ordinary that you noticed?"

"Can't think of anything."

"You mean to say you did not notice a smile on your wife's face when she went over to the window? She was smiling, and she did not get upset when the coffee spilled."

"That I did notice. She probably saw something interesting out the window which made her feel good."

"All she saw out the window was rain. Rain which she never likes."

"So, why was she smiling?"

"I too was watching your wife through my ray and warmed her up."

"So, *your* ray warmed her up — what about mine? Too cold?"

"You were only looking out of curiosity, you did not put any feeling into it."

"So, your ray can warm people up at a distance?"

"Yes, it can do that."

"And what else can it do?"

"It can gather certain kinds of information, or transmit. It can cheer up a person's mood and partially take away someone's illness. There are a lot of other things it can do, depending on the energy available and the degree of feeling, will and desire."

"And can you see the future?"

"Of course."

"The past too?"

"The future and the past — they are pretty much the same thing. It is only the external details that are different. The essence always remains unchanged."

"How can that be? What can remain unchanged?"

"Well, for example, a thousand years ago people wore different clothes. They had different instruments at their disposal. But that is not what is important, by any means. Back a thousand years ago, just like today, people had the same feelings. Feelings are not subject to time.

"Fear, joy, love. Just think, Yaroslav the Wise,[1] Ivan the Terrible[2] and the Egyptian pharaohs were all capable of loving a woman with exactly the same feelings as you or any other man today."

"Interesting. Only I'm not sure what it means. You say every person can have a ray like this?"

"Of course everyone can. Even today people still have feelings and intuitions, the capacity to dream of the future, to conjecture, to visualise specific situations, to have dreams while they sleep — only it is all chaotic and uncontrollable."

"Maybe some kind of training's necessary. Some exercises could be developed?"

---

[1] *Yaroslav the Wise* (Russian: *Yaroslav Mudry*; 978?–1054) — a Grand Prince of Kiev who managed to impose a degree of unity on the warring princes of what was then Kievan Russia, consolidate its southern and western borders and establish dynastic liaisons with a number of European nations.

[2] *Ivan the Terrible* (Russian: *Ivan Grozny*, also known as *Ivan IV*; 1530–1584) — the first Russian Grand Prince to proclaim himself *Tsar of all the Russias*. His reign was marked by bloody repressions of political rivals and wealthy aristocrats, stronger ties with England, political and social reforms at home and an expansion of the Russian Empire eastward.

"Some exercises might help. But you know, Vladimir, there is one absolute condition that must be met before the ray can be controlled by the will..."

"And what condition is that?"

"It is absolutely necessary to keep one's thoughts pure, as the strength of the ray depends on the strength of radiant feelings."

"Now there you go! Just when everything was starting to get clear... What on earth have pure thoughts got to do with it? Or 'radiant feelings'?"

"They are what power the ray."

"That's enough, Anastasia! I'm already losing interest. Next you'll be adding something else."

"I have already told you what is essential."

"That you most certainly did, but you've got too many darn conditions! Let's talk about something else. Something a little simpler..."

All day long Anastasia engages in meditation, visualising all sorts of situations from our past, present and future life.

Anastasia possesses a phenomenal memory. She can remember a multitude of people she has seen in her imagination or through her ray, and what they have been going through mentally. She's a consummate actress — she can imitate the way they walk and talk, and even think the way they do. She embodies in her thought the life experience of a great many people in the past and present. She uses such knowledge to visualise the future and to help others. This she does at a great distance by means of her invisible ray, and the ones she helps through suggestion or decision, or the ones she heals, haven't the slightest idea that she is helping them.

It was only later that I found out that similar rays invisible to the eye, only of different degrees of strength, emanate from every individual. The academician Anatoly Akimov[3] photographed them with special devices and published his results in 1996 in the May issue of the magazine *Chudesa i prikliuchenia* (Wonders and Adventures). Unfortunately, we are unable to use these rays as she does. In scientific literature there is a phenomenon similar to this ray, known as a *torsion field*.

Anastasia's world-view is unusual and interesting.

"What is God, Anastasia? Does He exist? If so, why hasn't anyone seen Him?"

"God is the interplanetary Mind, or Intelligence. He is not to be found in a single mass. Half of Him is in the non-material realm of the Universe. This is the sum total of all energies. The other half of Him is dispersed across the Earth, in every individual, in every Man. The dark forces strive to block these particles."

"What do you think awaits our civilisation?"

---

[3] *Anatoly Evgenevich Akimov* — Director of the International Institute of Theoretical and Applied Physics of the Russian Academy of Natural Sciences.

"In the long term, a realisation of the futility of the technocratic path of development and a movement back to our pristine origins."

"You mean to say that all our scholars are immature beings who are leading us into a dead end?"

"I mean to say that they are accelerating the process, thereby bringing you closer to the realisation that you are on the wrong path."

"And so? All the machines and houses we build are pointless?"

"Yes."

"You're not bored living here alone, Anastasia? Alone, without television or telephone?"

"These primitive things you mention, Man has possessed them right from the very beginning, only in a more perfect form. I have them."

"Both television and telephone?"

"Well, what is television? A device through which certain information is served up to an almost atrophied human imagination and scenes and story-plots are acted out. I can, through my own imagination, outline the plot of any story, and act out the most improbable situations — even take part in them myself, just like having an influence on the outcome. ...Oh dear, I suppose I have not been making myself too clear, eh?"

"And the telephone?"

"Every Man can talk with any other individual without the aid of a telephone. All that is needed is the will and desire of both parties and a developed imagination."

CHAPTER EIGHT

Concert in the taiga

I proposed that she herself come to Moscow and appear on TV.

"Just think, Anastasia, with your beauty you could easily be a world-class fashion or photomagazine model!"

And at this point I realised that she was no stranger to earthly matters — like all women, she delighted in being a beauty. Anastasia burst out laughing.

"A world-class beauty, eh?" She echoed my question and then, like a child, began to frolic about, prancing through the glade like a model on a catwalk.

I was amused at her imitation of a fashion model, placing one foot in front of the other in turn as she walked, showing off imaginary outfits. Finding myself getting into the act, I applauded and announced:

"And now, ladies and gentlemen, your attention, please! Performing before you will be that magnificent gymnast, second-to-none, that incomparable beauty: Anastasia!"

This announcement tickled her fancy even more. She ran out into the middle of the glade and executed an incredible flying somersault — first forward, then backward, then to the side, both left and right, then an amazingly high leap into the air. Grasping a tree-branch with one hand, she swung herself around it twice before flinging her body over to another tree. After yet another somersault, she began to bow coquettishly to my applause. Then she ran off out of the glade and hid behind some thick bushes. Anastasia peeped smilingly out from behind them, as though they were a theatre-curtain, impatiently awaiting my next announcement.

I remembered a videotape I had of some of my favourite songs being performed by popular artists. I would watch it occasionally in the evening in my cabin aboard ship. I had this tape in mind (but not with the thought that Anastasia would actually be able to reproduce anything from it) as I announced:

"Ladies and gentlemen, I now present to you the star singers of our current stage, in a performance of their top hits. Your attention, please!"

Oh, how wrong I had been in my estimate of her abilities! What happened next I could not possibly have predicted. No sooner had Anastasia made her entrance from behind her improvised curtain, than she launched into the authentic voice of Alla Pugachova.[1] No, it wasn't just a parody or an imitation, but Alla herself, effortlessly conveying not only her voice, but her intonations and emotions as well.

But an even more amazing feature was to come. Anastasia accentuated particular words, adding something of her own, infusing the song with her own supplemental attenuations, so that Alla Pugachova's own performance, which before, it seemed, nobody else could even begin to surpass, now called forth a whole new range of additional feelings, illuminating the images even more clearly.

In a magnificently executed overall performance of the song:[2]

---

[1] *Alla Borisovna Pugachova* (also spelt: *Pugacheva,* 1949–) — one of the most popular Russian stage and screen singers of the twentieth century, the recipient of a number of national and international awards. Pugachova, known as a 'national Russian legend', has toured extensively abroad, including Canada and America. Her *Alla* entertainment company grew out of *Alla Pugachova's Theatre of Song,* which she has headed as Artistic Director since 1988.

[2] *The song* — *A million red roses* (Russian: *Million alykh roz*), with words by prominent Russian poet Andrei Voznesensky (1933–) and music by Latvian composer Raymond Pauls (1936–) — was one of the greatest hits of Soviet pop-music stage of the 1980s and is said to be based on a real-life story.

> *Once lived an artist alone,*
> *Canvases all through his home.*
> *He loved an actress, he thought,*
> *Flowers were* her *love, fresh-grown.*
> *He went and sold his big home,*
> *Sold every canvas he owned,*
> *And with the money he bought*
> *Whole fields of flowers, fresh-grown.*

Anastasia put particular emphasis on the word "canvas". She screamed out this word in fright and surprise. A canvas is an artist's most prized possession — without it he can no longer create — and here he is giving up the most precious thing he owns for the sake of his loved one. Later, as she sang the words *Then she went off on the train,* Anastasia tenderly portrayed the artist in love, looking longingly after the departing train which was carrying off his loved one forever. She portrayed his pain, his despair, his perplexed state of mind.

I was too shaken by everything I had seen and heard to applaud at the end of the song. Anastasia bowed, anticipating the applause and, hearing none, launched into a new song with even more enthusiasm. She performed all of my favourite songs, in the same order they had been recorded on the videotape. And every single song, which I had heard so many times before, was now even clearer and more meaningful in her rendition.

Upon completing the last song on the tape, still hearing no applause, Anastasia retreated 'backstage'. Too dumbfounded to speak, I remained seated in silence, still feeling an extraordinary impression from what I had just witnessed. Then I jumped up, began applauding and cried:

"Terrific, Anastasia! Encore! Bravo! All performers on stage!"

Anastasia gingerly stepped forth and gave a bow. I kept on shouting:

"Encore! Bravo!" — clapping my hands and stamping my feet. She too livened up. She clapped her hands and cried:

"*Encore* — does that mean 'Again'?"

"Yes, again! And again! And again!... You did it so marvellously, Anastasia! Better than the singers themselves! Even better than our top stars!"

I fell silent and began attentively studying Anastasia. I thought how multifaceted her soul must be if she could infuse her singing performance with so many new, splendid, clear features. She too stood motionless, silently and enquiringly looking at me.

"Anastasia, do you have any song of your own? Couldn't you sing something of your own, something I haven't heard before?"

"I could, but my song does not have any words. Would you still like to hear it?"

"Please sing your song."

"Fine!"

And she started in singing her most unusual song. First Anastasia screamed like a newborn baby. Then her voice started sounding quiet, tender and caressing. She stood beneath a tree, her hands clasped to her breast, her head bowed. It was like a lullaby, gently caressing a little one with her voice. Her voice spoke to him of something very tender. Her soft voice, amazingly pure, caused everything around to grow silent — the birds' singing, the chirping of the crickets in the grass. At that point Anastasia seemed to take absolute delight in the little one waking from sleep. The sound of rejoicing could be heard in her voice. The incredibly high-pitched sounds soared above the Earth before taking flight into the heights of infinity. Anastasia's voice first pleaded, then went into battle, and once again caressed the little one and bestowed joy upon all around.

I too felt this all-pervading sense of joy. And when she finished her song, I joyfully exclaimed:

"And now, my dear ladies and gentlemen, comrades, a unique and never-to-be-repeated number by the top animal trainer in the world! The most agile, brave, charming trainer, capable of taming any beast of prey on the Earth! Behold and tremble!"

Anastasia positively squealed with delight, leapt into the air, clapped her hands in rhythm, shouted something, started in whistling. Something I could never have imagined began taking place in the glade.

First the she-wolf made her entrance. She leapt out of the bushes and stopped at the edge of the glade, giving a puzzled look around. In the trees around the perimeter of the glade, squirrels sprang from branch to branch. Two eagles circled low overhead, while some kind of little creatures rustled in the bushes. With the sharp crackle of dry twigs as he broke and crushed the bushes, a huge bear lumbered out into the glade and stopped, as though embedded in the ground, just short of Anastasia. The wolf began growling at him disapprovingly, since the bear had approached so close to Anastasia without an invitation.

Anastasia ran up to the bear, playfully stroking his muzzle, then grabbed him by his front paws and stood him upright. Judging by the fact that she didn't seem to be exerting much physical effort in this, the bear himself must have been carrying out her commands according to how much he understood and how he interpreted them. He stood stock still, trying to understand what was desired of him. Anastasia took a running leap and, grabbing hold of the thick scruff of the bear's neck, did a handstand on his shoulders, jumping off again with a somersault on her way down. Then she took the bear by one paw and started to bend over, pulling the bear after her — creating the impression that she was tossing him over her shoulder. This trick would have been impossible if the bear had not been able to do it himself. Anastasia simply guided him. It looked at first as though the bear was going to fall on top of Anastasia, but at the last moment he reached out a paw to the ground and broke his fall. He was no doubt doing everything he could so as not to harm his mistress or friend. In the meantime the wolf was becoming more and more concerned — she could no longer hold still, but thrashed about from side to side, growling or howling with displeasure.

At the edge of the glade there appeared several more wolves, and when Anastasia was on the point of yet another routine 'toss' of the bear over her shoulder, the bear, attempting to do the trick properly, fell over on his side and remained motionless.

At last the wolf, now at her wits' end, and with a malicious grin, made a leap in the bear's direction. With lightning speed Anastasia placed herself in the wolf's path. The wolf braked with all fours, somersaulted over her back, bumping into Anastasia's legs. Immediately Anastasia put one hand on the back of the wolf, who obediently crouched to the ground. With her other hand she began waving, as she had done that first time with me when I had tried to embrace her without her consent.

The forest around us began to make a rustling sound — not threateningly, but with some agitation. The agitation was felt as well in all the big and little creatures jumping, running and hiding. Anastasia began to relieve the agitation. First, she stroked the wolf, slapped her on the back and sent her off out of the glade as though she were a pet dog. The bear was still lying on his side in an uncomfortable pose, like some kind of stuffed animal. He was probably waiting to see what else was required of him. Anastasia went over to him, made him stand up, stroked his muzzle and sent him out of the glade like the wolf.

Anastasia, blushing and cheerful, ran over and sat down beside me, breathed in deeply and slowly exhaled. I noticed that her breathing all at once became even, as though she hadn't been carrying out any extraordinary exercises at all.

"They do not understand play-acting, and they ought not to — it is not entirely a good thing," Anastasia remarked. Then she asked me: "Well, how was I? Do you think I could find any kind of work in your life?"

"You're terrific, Anastasia, but we already have all that, and our circus trainers show us a lot of interesting tricks with animals, so you don't have a hope of breaking through all the red tape to even get started. There are so many formalities and machinations to deal with. You don't have any experience in that."

The remainder of our play consisted in going over possible alternatives: where could Anastasia get a job in our world and how would she overcome the formalities in the way? But no easy alternative presented itself, since Anastasia had neither a residence permit nor proof of education, and nobody would believe the stories about her origins on the basis of her abilities, no matter how extraordinary they might be. Suddenly turning serious, Anastasia said:

"Of course I would like to visit one of the big cities again, maybe Moscow, to see how accurate I was in visualising certain situations from your life. For one thing, I am at a complete loss to understand how the dark forces manage to fool women to such a degree that they unwittingly attract men with the charms of their bodies, and thereby deprive them of the opportunity of making a real choice — to choose someone close to their heart. And then they themselves suffer for not being able to create a real family, since..."

And once again she launched into deep and poignant discussions about sex, family and the upbringing of children, and I could only think: *The most incredible thing in all I have seen and heard is her ability to talk about our lifestyle and understand it in such specific detail!*

CHAPTER NINE

Who lights a new star?

On the second night, fearing that Anastasia would once again assign me her she-bear or concoct up some new device to keep me warm, I categorically refused to go to sleep at all unless she herself lay down beside me. I thought that as long as she was beside me she wouldn't be up to any tricks. And I told her:

"You've invited me as a guest, or so you say. In your home. I imagined there would be at least a few buildings here, but you won't even let me light a fire, and you offer me a beastie to keep me company at night. If you don't have a normal home, what's the point of inviting a guest?"

"All right, Vladimir. Do not worry, please, do not be afraid. Nothing bad is going to happen to you. If you want, I shall lie down beside you and keep you warm."

This time in the dugout cave there were even more cedar branches strewn around, along with neatly arranged dry grasses, and there were also branches stuck on the wall.

I got undressed. I put my sweater and trousers under my head for a pillow. I lay down and covered myself with my jacket. The cedar twigs gave off that same bacteria-killing aroma described in the popular literature as capable of purifying the air. Though here in the taiga the air is already so pure, the air in the cave was particularly easy to breathe. The dried grasses and flowers contributed a still more unusual delicate fragrance.

Anastasia kept her word and lay down beside me. I sensed the fragrance of her body, which surpassed all other odours. It was more pleasant than the most delicate perfume I had ever sensed from a woman's body. But now I had no thought of wanting to possess her. After my attempt to do so on the way to the glade, which had resulted at the time in an attack of fear and loss of consciousness, I no longer felt aroused by fleshly desires, even when I saw her naked.

I lay down and dreamt of the son my wife never bore to me. And I thought: *Wouldn't it be wonderful if my son could be borne by Anastasia! She is so healthy, sturdy and beautiful! The child, then, too would be healthy. He would look like me. Like her too, but more like me. He would be a strong and clever individual. He would know a lot. He would become talented and prosper.*

I imagined our infant son sucking at his mother's nipple and involuntarily put my hand on Anastasia's warm, supple breast. Immediately a shiver ran through my whole body and then dissipated at once, but it wasn't a shiver of fear, but something else, extraordinarily pleasing. I didn't take my hand away, but only held my breath and waited for what might happen. Next thing I noticed was the feeling of the soft palm of her hand on mine. She did not push me away.

I raised my head and began looking into Anastasia's marvellous face. The white twilight of the northern night made it seem even more attractive. I couldn't take my gaze off her. Her greyish-blue eyes looked at me tenderly. I didn't restrain myself, but bent closer and, quickly and carefully, with just the slightest touch, planted a kiss on her half-open lips. Once more a pleasing shiver ran through my body. My face was enshrouded with the fragrance of her breath. Her lips didn't utter, as the last time, "Do not do this!... Calm down!", and I had no fear at all. I was still haunted by the prospect of a son. And when Anastasia tenderly embraced me, stroked my hair and pressed her whole body against mine, I felt something indescribable!

Only upon awaking in the morning was I able to realise that this kind of magnificent feeling, blissful excitement and satisfaction was something I had never once experienced in my entire life. Another peculiar thing: after a night spent with a woman I had always felt a sense of physical fatigue, but here everything was different. In addition, I had the feeling of some kind of great co-creation. My satisfaction wasn't just something physical, but had another dimension I couldn't quite comprehend, one I had never experienced before, extraordinarily lovely and joyful. The thought even flashed through my mind that life was worth living just for this feeling alone. And why had I never experienced anything that even came close to this before, even though there had been all sorts of women — beautiful women, beloved women, women experienced in love?

Anastasia was a girl. A tender, quivering girl. But beyond that there was something in her that belonged not to a single woman I had known. What was it? And where had she gone now? I made my way over to the entrance of the cozy dug-out cave, poked my head out and looked out into the glade.

The glade was situated at a slightly lower level than my night-time resting-place. It was covered by a layer of morning mist a half-metre thick. In this mist I could see Anastasia spinning around with outstretched arms. A little cloud of mist was forming about her. And when it covered her completely, Anastasia sprang lightly into the air, stretched out her legs in a split just like a ballerina, flew over the layer of mist, landed in a different spot and once more, laughing, spun a new cloud around her, through which could be seen the rays of the rising Sun, gently caressing her body. It was a charming and delightful scene, and I cried out with an overflow of emotion:

"Ana-sta-SI-ya![1] Good morning, my splendid forest fairy, Antastasi-ya-ya!"

---

[1] *Ana-sta-SI-ya* — As noted in the Translator's Preface, this reflects the Russian pronunciation of her name, with the stress on the syllable *SI* (pronounced 'see').

"Good morning, Vladimir!" she joyfully called out in response.

"It's so delightful, so wonderful out right now! Why is that?" I cried as loud as I could.

Anastasia lifted up her hands toward the Sun, and began laughing with that happy, alluring laugh of hers, calling out to me (and someone else besides, high above) in a sing-song voice:

"Out of all the beings in the Universe only Man is given an experience like tha-at!

"Only men and women sincerely desiring to have a child between them!

"Only a Man having such an experience lights a new star in the heavens!

"Only a Ma-a-an striving for creation and co-creation!

"Tha-ank yo-o-u!" And, addressing me alone, she quickly added: "Only a Man striving for creation and co-creation, and not for satisfaction of his carnal needs."

And again she went off in trills of laughter, leaping high into the air, stretching her legs into a split as though soaring over the mist. Then she came running over, sat down beside me at the entrance to our night-time resting-place and began combing her golden tresses with her fingers, lifting them up from the bottom.

"So, you don't consider sex to be something sinful?" I asked.

Anastasia stopped dead in her tracks. She looked at me in amazement and responded:

"Was *that* the 'sex' the word implies in your world? And if not, then what is more sinful — to give of yourself so that a Man can come into the world, or to hold back and not allow a Man to be born? A real Man!"

I started thinking. In actual fact, my night-time closeness with Anastasia could not possibly be described by our usual word *sex*. Then what *did* happen last night? What term *would* be appropriate here? Again I asked:

"And why did nothing even approaching that experience ever happen with me before — or, for that matter, I would venture to say, with a great many others?"

"You see, Vladimir, the dark forces are constantly trying to make Man give into base fleshly passions, to prevent him from ever experiencing God-given grace. They try all sorts of tricks to persuade people that satisfaction is something you can easily obtain, thinking only of carnal desire. And at the same time they separate Man from truth. The poor deceived women who are ignorant of this, spend their lives accepting nothing but suffering and searching for the grace they have lost. But they are searching for it in the wrong places. No woman can restrain a man from fornication if she allows herself to submit to him merely to satisfy his carnal needs. If that has happened, their life together will not be a happy one.

"Their conjugal life is only an illusion of togetherness, a lie, a deception accepted by convention. For the woman immediately becomes a fornicator, regardless of whether she is married to the man or not.

"Oh, how many laws and conventions mankind has invented in an attempt to artificially strengthen this false union! Laws both religious and secular. All in vain. All they have done is caused people to play around, accommodate themselves and create an impression that such a union exists. One's innermost thoughts invariably remain unchanged, subject to nobody and nothing.

"Christ Jesus saw this. And trying to counteract it, he said: 'Anyone who looks at a woman lustfully has already committed adultery with her in his heart.'[2]

---

[2]Matth. 5: 28 (*New International Version*).

"Then you, in your not-so-distant past have tried to attach shame to anyone who leaves his family. But nothing, at any time or in any situation, has been able to stop Man's desire to seek out that sense of intuitively felt grace — the greatest satisfaction. And to persist in seeking it.

"A false union is a frightening thing.

"Children! Do you see, Vladimir? Children! They sense the artificiality, the falsity of such a union. And this makes them sceptical about everything their parents tell them. Children sub-consciously sense the lie even in the act of their conception. And that has a bad effect on them.

"Tell me who — what individual — would want to come into the world as a result of carnal pleasures alone? We would all like to be created under a great impulsion of love, the aspiration to co-creation itself, and not simply come into the world as a result of someone's carnal pleasure.

"People who have come into a false union will then look for true satisfaction in secret, apart from each other. They will strive to possess body after body, or make paltry and fateful use of their own bodies, realising only intuitively that they are drifting farther and farther away from the true happiness of a true union."

"Anastasia, wait!", I said. "Can it be that men and women are doomed this way if the first time all that happens between them is sex? Is there no turning back, no possibility of correcting the situation?"

"There is. I now know what to do. But where do I find the right words to express it? I am always looking for them — the right words. I have been looking for them in the past and in the future. But I have not found them. Perhaps they are right in front of me, after all? And then they will appear, new words will be born — words capable of breaking through to people's hearts and minds. New words for the ancient truth about our pristine origins."

"Don't panic, Anastasia! Use existing words to start with, just as an approximation... What else can one possibly need for true satisfaction, apart from two bodies?"

"Complete awareness! A mutual striving to co-create. Sincerity and purity of motive."

"How do you know all this, Anastasia?"

"I am not the only one who knows about it. A number of enlightened thinkers have tried to explain its essence to the world — Veles, Krishna, Rama, Shiva,[3] Christ, Mohammed, Buddha."

"You've what... read about all these? Where? When?"

"I have not read about them, I simply know what they said, what they thought about, what they wanted to accomplish."

"So sex by itself, according to you, is bad?"

"Very bad. It leads Man away from truth, destroys families. An enormous amount of energy is wasted."

"Then why do so many different magazines publish pictures of naked women in erotic poses, why are there so many films with erotica and sex? And all of this is extremely popular. Demand generates supply. So, you're trying to say that our humanity is completely bad?"

"Humanity is not bad, but the devices of the dark forces obscuring spirituality by provoking base carnal desires — these are very powerful devices. They bring people a lot of grief and suffering. They act through women, exploiting their

[3]*Veles* — in the Russian-Slavic tradition: the god of wisdom and Nature, one of the *Triglav* (Trinity) and the incarnation of God the Creator (*Rod*) on Earth. *Krishna* — an earthly incarnation of god Vishnu, one of the *Trimurti* (the three personalities of God in the Hindu tradition), responsible for the maintenance of the world. *Rama* — a god-king and an earthly incarnation of Vishnu (in the Hindu tradition). *Shiva* — one of the *Trimurti* along with Vishnu and Brahma. While Brahma is seen as the creator the world, Shiva is held to be responsible for destroying it at the end of each cosmic cycle.

beauty. A beauty whose real purpose is to engender and support in men the spirit of the poet, the artist, the creator. But, to do that, women themselves must be pure. If there is not sufficient purity, they start trying to attract men by fleshly charms — the outward beauty of empty vessels. In the upshot, the men are deceived and the women must suffer their whole lives on account of this deception."

"So what, then, is the result?" I queried. "Through all the millennia of its existence, mankind has not been able to overcome these devices of the dark forces? That would mean they are stronger than Man. Man hasn't been able to overcome them, in spite of the appeals by spiritually enlightened people, as you put it? So, is it downright impossible to overcome them? Or maybe it's not necessary?"

"It *is* necessary. Absolutely necessary!"

"Who then can do it?"

"Women! Women who have been able to grasp the truth and their own purpose. Then the men will change too."

"Oh, no, Anastasia, I doubt it. A normal man will always be aroused by a pretty woman's legs, her breasts... Especially when you're on a business trip or on holiday far away from your partner. That's the way things are. And nobody here will change anything — they won't do it any other way."

"But I did it with you."

"What did you do?"

"Now you are no longer able to indulge in that harmful sex."

All at once a terrible thought hit me like a flood, and started chasing away the magnificent feeling that had been born in me during the night.

"What have you done, Anastasia? What? I'm now... what — I'm now... impotent?"

"On the contrary, you have now become a real man. Only the usual sex will be repugnant to you. It will not bring what you experienced last night, but what you experienced last night is possible only when you desire to have a child and the woman wants the same from you. When she loves you."

"'Loves'? But under those conditions... That can happen only a few times during one's whole life!"

"I assure you, Vladimir, that is enough for your whole life to be happy. You will understand. Eventually you will feel the same way... People enter many times afresh into sexual interaction only through the flesh — not realising that true satisfaction in the flesh is impossible to attain. A man and a woman who unite on every plane of existence, impelled by radiant inspiration, earnestly aspiring to the act of co-creation, experience tremendous satisfaction. The Creator gave this experience to Man alone. No transitory thing, this satisfaction, no! It never can compare with fleeting, fleshly gratification. As you cherish the feelings from it over time, all planes of being will, with influence sublime, happify your life and the woman too — a woman who can give birth to a creation in the Creator's own image and likeness, His design!"

Anastasia held out her hand toward me, trying to move closer. I quickly darted away from her into a corner of the cave and cried:

"Out of my way!"

She got up. I crawled outside and backed off from her a few steps.

"You have deprived me, quite possibly, of my chief pleasure in life! Everybody strives for it, everybody thinks about it, only they don't talk about it out loud."

"They are illusions, Vladimir, those pleasures of yours. I have helped save you from a terrible, harmful and sinful appetite."

"Illusion or not — doesn't make any difference. It's a pleasure recognised by everyone! Don't even think of trying to save me from any other 'harmful' appetites, as you see them.

Or by the time I get out of here I'll be... — no relations with women, no drinks or appetizers, no smoking! That's not something most people are accustomed to in normal life."

"But what good can there possibly be in drinking and smoking, in the senseless and harmful digestion of such a huge quantity of animal meat, when there are so many splendid plants created especially for Man's nourishment?"

"You go and feed yourself with plants, if you like. But don't get in my way. A lot of us get pleasure out of smoking, drinking, sitting down to a good meal. That's how we do things, d'you understand? *That's how!*"

"But everything you name is bad and harmful."

"Bad? Harmful? If guests come to celebrate at my place, and they sit down at the table and I tell them: 'Here are some nuts to gnaw on, have an apple, drink water and don't smoke' — now *that* would be bad."

"Is that the most important thing, when you get together with friends — to sit right down at the table and drink, eat and smoke?"

"Whether it's the most important thing or not is beside the point. That's how *all* people behave the world over. Some countries even have things like ritual dishes — roast turkey, for example."

"That is not accepted by everyone, even in your world."

"Maybe not by everyone, but I happen to live among normal people."

"Why do you consider the people around you to be the most normal?"

"Because they're in the majority."

"That is not a good enough argument."

"It's not good enough for you, because you will not listen to explanations."

My anger at Anastasia began to pass. I recalled hearing about medical prescriptions and sex therapists and the thought came to me that if she *had* somehow injured me, the doctors would be able to fix it. I said:

"Okay, Anastasia. Let's make peace. I'm no longer angry at you. I thank you for the wonderful night. Only don't you try saving me from any more of my habits. As far as sex goes, I'll fix the situation with the help of our doctors and modern medicines. Let's go for a swim."

I began heading for the lake, admiring the morning woods. Just as my good mood was beginning to come back, she— well, there you go again! Walking behind me, she piped up:

"Medicines and doctors will not help you now. To put everything back the way it was, they will have to erase your memory of everything that happened and everything you felt."

Stunned, I stopped in my tracks.

"Then you put everything back the way it was."

"I cannot either."

Again I was overwhelmed by a feeling of rampant rage — and, at the same time, fear.

"You! You brazen—! You poke your nose in where it doesn't belong and turn my life upside down! So, you played a nasty trick on me! And now you say you can't fix it?"

"I did not play any nasty tricks. After all, you wanted a son so badly. But so many years had gone by, and you still did not have a son. And none of the women in your life would bear you a son. I also wanted a child by you, a son too. And that is something I can do...

"And why are you getting so concerned ahead of time that things are going to go badly for you? Maybe you will still come to understand.

"Please do not be afraid of me, Vladimir, I am certainly not trying to meddle with your mind. This happened all on its own. You got what you wanted.

"And I would very much like to save you from at least one more mortal sin."

"And what's that?"

"Pride."

"You're a funny one. Your philosophy and lifestyle aren't human."

"What do you find in me so inhuman that it frightens you?"

"You live all alone in the forest, and communicate with plants and wild animals. Nobody in our society even comes close to that kind of life."

"How can that be, Vladimir? Why?" Anastasia exclaimed, flustered. "But what about your *dachniks*[4] — they too communicate with plants and animals, only not yet consciously. But they will understand one day. Many have already begun to understand."

"Oh, come on! Now she's a *dachnik*? And this ray of yours. You know a lot, but you don't read books. Sheer mysticism!"

"I shall try to explain everything to you, Vladimir. Only not all at once. I am trying, but I cannot find the right words. Comprehensible words. Please believe me. All my abilities are inherent in Man. It is something Man was given right from the start. Back in the days of his pristine origins. And everyone is capable of doing the same today. Nevertheless, people will certainly go back to their pristine origins. It will be a gradual process after the forces of light triumph!"

"But what about your 'concert'? You sang in all sorts of different voices, you portrayed my favourite artists, and even in the same order as on my videotape."

"That is how it turned out, Vladimir. You know, I once saw that tape of yours. I shall tell you later how it happened."

---

[4]*dachniks* — people who spend time (their days off, especially summer holidays) tending a garden at their *dacha*, or cottage in the country. See further details in the Translator's Preface and the Editor's Afterword.

"And what — you... right off memorised the words and tunes of all the songs?"

"Yes, I memorised them. What is so complex or mystical about that?... Oh dear, what have I gone and done! I have talked too much, I have shown too much! You have become frightened of me! I must be muddle-headed and tactless! My grandfather once called me that. I thought he was just be-ing affectionate. But in fact I probably *am* tactless. Please... Vladimir!"

Anastasia's voice betrayed a very human concern, and this was probably the reason that almost all my fear of her had now left me. My whole feelings were pre-occupied with the prospect of my son.

"Okay, I'm no longer afraid... Only please try to be a bit more restrained. Remember, your grandfather told you that."

"Yes. And grandfather... But here I keep on talking and talking. I have such a strong desire to tell you everything. Am I a chatterbox? Yes? But I shall try. I shall try very hard to restrain myself. I shall try to speak only in terms you will understand..."

"So, you'll soon be giving birth, Anastasia?" I said.

"Of course! Only, it will not be on time."

"What do you mean, it will not be on time?"

"Ideally it should be in the summertime, when Nature can help with the nurturing."

"Why did you make that decision, if it's so risky for you and the child?"

"Do not worry, Vladimir. At least our son will live."

"And you?"

"And I shall try to hold on till the spring, and everything will adjust itself then."

Anastasia said this without a tinge of sorrow or fear for her life. Then she ran off and jumped into the little lake.

The spray of the water in the sunlight took flight, just like fireworks, and landed on the smooth, mirror-like surface of the water. Some thirty seconds later her body slowly began to break the surface. She lay, as it were, on the water, her arms widespread, her palms upturned, and smiled.

I stood on the shore, looked at her and thought to myself: *Will the squirrel hear the snap of her fingers when she lies with her baby in one of her shelters? Will she get help from any of her four-footed friends? Will her body have enough heat to warm up the little one?*

"If my body should cool off and the baby have nothing to eat, he will start crying," she said quietly, coming out of the water. "His cry of displeasure may waken Nature, or at least part of it, before the beginning of spring and then every-thing will be all right. They will nurse him."

"You read my thoughts?"

"No, I just guessed you were thinking about that. That is quite natural."

"Anastasia, you said your relatives are living on the adjacent plots of land. Would they be able to help you?"

"They are very busy, and I must not take them away from their work."

"What are they busy with, Anastasia? What do you do all day long, when in fact you are so completely served by your natural environment?"

"I keep busy... And I try to help people in your world — the ones you call *dachniks* or gardeners."

CHAPTER TEN

Her beloved dachniks

Anastasia enthusiastically explained to me how many new opportunities could open up for people who communicate with plants. There were two major subjects she talked about not only with particular excitement and animation but, I would have to admit, with a kind of love — namely, bringing up children on the one hand, and *dachniks*[1] on the other. According to everything she said about these people and the importance she attached to them, we would all need to literally bow on our knees before them. Just think! According to her the dachniks have not only managed to save the whole nation from famine, but also sown seeds of good in people's hearts, and are educating the society of the future. There are far too many points to enumerate here — one would need a whole book! And Anastasia kept on arguing, trying to demonstrate this:

"You see, the society you are living in today can learn a lot from communication with the plants to be found around dachas. Yes, I am talking about the dachas, where you personally know every individual plant in your garden-plot, and not those huge, impersonal fields cultivated by monstrous, senseless machines. People feel better when they are working in their dacha plots. Many of them end up living longer. They become kinder. And it is these very dachniks that can pave the way for society to become aware of how destructive the technocratic path can be."

[1]See footnote 4 in Chapter 9: "Who lights a new star?".

"Anastasia, whether that's true or not is, for the time being, beside the point. What is *your* role in all this? What kind of help can you offer?"

Taking me by the arm, she led me over to the grass. We lay on our backs, the palms of our hands turned upward.

"Close your eyes, let go, and try to picture to yourself what I am saying. Right now I shall take a look with my ray and locate, at a distance, some of those people you call dachniks."

After a period of silence, she began to say softly:

"An old woman is unwrapping a piece of cheesecloth in which cucumber seeds have been soaking. The seeds have already begun to develop quite a bit, and I can see little sprouts. Now she has picked up a seed. I have just suggested to her that she should not soak the seeds that way — they will become deformed when they are planted, and this kind of water is not good for them — the seed will go bad. She thinks she herself must have guessed that. And that is partially true — I just helped her guess a bit. Now she will share her idea and tell other people about it. This little deed is done."

Anastasia told how she visualises in her consciousness all sorts of situations involving work, recreation and people's interaction — both with each other and with plants. When the situation she has visualised comes closest to reality, contact is established whereby she can see the person and feel what this person is suffering or sensing. She herself then, as it were, steps into the image of the person and shares her expertise with them. Anastasia said that plants react to people, to Man, with love or hate, and exercise a positive or negative influence on people's health.

"And here is where I have an enormous amount of work to do. I keep myself busy with the dacha garden-plots. The dachniks travel out to their plots — their plantings — as though they were going to visit their own children but, unfortunately, their relationship to them is still pretty much on the level of intuition. They still do not have the foundation that comes with a clear realisation of the true purpose behind this relationship.

"Everything — but everything — on the Earth, every blade of grass, every little bug, has been created for Man, and everything has its individual appointed task to perform in the service of Man. The multitude of medicinal plants are a confirmation of this. But people in your world know very little about how to benefit from the opportunities they are presented with — about how to take full advantage of them."

I asked Anastasia to show some concrete example of the benefits of conscious communication — an example that could be seen, verified in practice and subjected to scientific investigation. Anastasia thought for a little while, then suddenly brightened and exclaimed:

"The dachniks, my beloved dachniks! They will prove it all! They will show what is true and confound all your science! Now how is it I did not think of that or understand it before?"

Some kind of brand new idea made her bubble over with joy.

I must say that, the whole time I was with her, not once did I see Anastasia sad. She can be serious, thoughtful and concentrated, but more often than not delighting in something. This time her joy literally bubbled over — she jumped up and clapped her hands, and it seemed to me as though the whole forest had become brighter, and begun to stir, responding to her with the rustling of tree-tops and the singing of birds. She whirled round and round, as though she were doing a kind of dance. Then, all radiant, she once again sat down beside me and said:

"Now they will believe! All on account of them, my dear dachniks. They will explain and prove everything!"

Trying to bring her a little more quickly back to the topic of our interrupted conversation, I noted:

"Not necessarily. You say that every little bug has been created for Man's benefit, but how can people believe that when they look with so much loathing on the cockroaches crawling over their kitchen tables? What — can it be that they too have been created for our benefit?"

"Cockroaches," declared Anastasia, "will only crawl over a dirty table to collect the remains of any food particles lying about — particles too small for the human eye to see. They process them and render them harmless before discarding them in some secluded spot. If there happen to be too many of them, simply bring a frog into the house and the surplus cockroaches will disappear at once."

What Anastasia went on to propose the dachniks do will probably contradict the principles of the plant sciences — and will certainly contradict the commonly accepted methods of planting and cultivating various garden-plot crops. Her affirmations, however, are so colossal that it seems to me they would be worth trying out for anyone with the opportunity to do so — maybe not throughout their whole plot, but at least in one small section of it, especially since nothing harmful and only good could come of it. Besides, much of what she told me has already been confirmed by the experiments of the biological science expert Mikhail Prokhorov.[2]

---

[2]*Mikhail Nikolaevich Prokhorov* — Director of ecological programming for a private firm in Moscow, with a doctoral degree in Biology. The author of numerous studies on the interaction of people and plants, Prokhorov speaks about the possibility of the "*direct* influence of human beings on the growth and development of plants and, in certain situations, on the health and behaviour of animals".

CHAPTER ELEVEN

Advice from Anastasia

The seed as physician

Anastasia has stated:

"Every seed you plant contains within itself an enormous amount of information about the Universe. Nothing made by human hands can compare with this information either in size or accuracy. Through the help of these data the seed knows the exact time, down to the millisecond, when it is to come alive, to grow, what juices it is to take from the Earth, how to make use of the rays of the celestial bodies — the Sun, Moon and stars — what it is to grow into, what fruit to bring forth. These fruits are designed to sustain Man's life. More powerfully and effectively than any manufactured drugs of the present or future, these fruits are capable of counteracting and withstanding any disease of the human body. But to this end the seed must know about the human condition. So that during the maturation process it can satiate its fruit with the right correlation of substances to heal a specific individual of his disease, if indeed he has it or is prone to it.

"In order for the seed of a cucumber, tomato or any other plant grown in one's plot to have such information, the following steps are necessary:

"Before planting, put into your mouth one or more little seeds, hold them in your mouth, under the tongue, for at least nine minutes.[1]

"Then place the seed between the palms of your hands and hold it there for about thirty seconds. During this time it is important that you be standing barefoot on the spot of earth where you will later be planting it.

"Open your hands, and carefully raise the seed which you are holding to your mouth. Then blow on it lightly, warming it with your breath, and the wee little seed will know everything that is within you.

"Then you need to hold it with your hands open another thirty seconds, presenting the seed to the celestial bodies. And the seed will determine the moment of its awakening. The planets will all help it! And they will give the sprouts the light they need to produce fruit especially for you.

"After that you may plant the seed in the ground. In no case should you water it right off, so as not to wash away the saliva which is now covering it, along with other information about you that the seed will take in. It can be watered three days after planting.

"The planting must be done on days appropriate to each vegetable (people already know this, from the lunar calendar). In the absence of watering, a premature planting is not as harmful as an overdue planting.

"It is not a good idea to pull up all the weeds growing in the vicinity of the sprouts. At least one of each kind should be left in place. The weeds can be cut back..."

According to Anastasia, the seed is thus able to take in information about the person who plants it, and then, during the cultivation of its fruit, it will pick up from the Universe and the Earth the maximum amount of energies needed for a

---

[1]Please note that store-bought seeds available in America and elsewhere in the 'civilised world' are often coated with rat poison for ease of storage, and should never be used for planting in the way recommended here. If you wish to follow the planting advice set forth herein, be sure to use your own seeds or procure *organic* seeds from a reputable producer (available from many on-line and mail-order vendors or through health-food stores).

given individual. The weeds should not be disposed of completely, as they have their own appointed function. Some weeds serve to protect the plant from disease while others give supplemental information. During the cultivation time it is vital to communicate with the plant. And it is desirable to approach it and touch it during a full moon at least once during its growth period.

Anastasia maintains that the fruit cultivated from the seed in this manner, and consumed by the individual who cultivated it, is capable not only of curing him of all diseases of the flesh whatsoever but also of significantly retarding the ageing process, rescuing him from harmful habits, tremendously increasing his mental abilities and giving him a sense of inner peace. The fruit will have the most effective influence when consumed no later than three days after harvesting.

The above-mentioned steps should be taken with a variety of plant species in the garden-plot.

It is not necessary to plant a whole bed of cucumbers, tomatoes etc., in this manner; just a few plants each is enough.

The fruit of plants grown like this will be distinguished from other plants of the same species not only in taste. If analysed, it will be seen that they are also distinct in terms of the substances they contain.

When planting the seedlings, it is important to soften the dirt in the excavated hole with one's fingers and bare toes, and spit into the hole. Responding to my question "Why the feet?", Anastasia explained that through perspiration from one's feet come substances (toxins, no doubt) containing information about bodily diseases. This information is taken in by the seedlings. They transmit it to the fruit, which will thus be enabled to counteract diseases. Anastasia recommended walking around the plot barefoot from time to time.

"What kind of plants should one cultivate?"

Anastasia replied:

"The same variety that exists in most garden-plots is quite sufficient: raspberries, currants, gooseberries, cucumbers, tomatoes, wild strawberries, any kind of apple tree. Sweet or sour cherries and flowers would be very good too. It does not make any difference how many plants of each kind there are or how big their area of cultivation is.

"There are a few 'definites', without which it would be difficult to imagine a full energy micro-climate: one of them is sunflowers (at least one plant). There should also be one-and-a-half or two square metres of cereal grains (rye or wheat, for example), and be sure to leave an 'island' of at least two square metres for wild-growing herbs — ones that are not planted manually. If you have not left any of them growing around your dacha, you can bring in some turf from the forest and thereby create an island of natural growth."

I asked Anastasia if it were necessary to plant these 'definites' directly in the plot, if there were already some wild-growing herbs close by — say, just beyond the fence — and this is how she responded:

"It is not just the variety of plants that is significant, but also how they are planted — the direct communication with them that allows them to take in the information they need. I have already told you about one of the methods of planting — that is the basic one. It is essential to infuse the little patch of Nature surrounding you with information about yourself. Only then will the healing effect and the life-giving support of your body be significantly higher than from the fruit alone. Out in the natural 'wilds' (as you call them) — and Nature really is not wild, it is just unfamiliar to you — there are a great many plants that can help us cure all — and I mean *all* — existing diseases. These plants have been designed for that purpose, but Man has lost, or almost lost, the ability to identify them."

Above: map of Russia with the route of Megré's 1994 trade trip.

Right: close-up of the 1994 Merchant Convoy's itinerary: Novosibirsk, Tomsk, Nizhnevartovsk, Surgut, Khanty-Mansiysk, Salekhard and back. See Chapter 1 for details.

Below: the *Mikhail Kalinin*, one of the ships in Vladimir Megré's fleet.

Left: Vladimir Megré (front, at left) with his staff in front of the *Mikhail Kalinin* in the early 1990's.

Right: the Merchant Convoy's stopover in Tomsk. Vladimir Megré in front of the banner reading "WELCOME, TOMSK ENTREPRENEURS!".

Left: Vladimir Megré (second from left) on board ship, with the Ob River and taiga in the background.

Right: one of the stops along the Ob. Vladimir Megré (left) with a member of his crew.

Trip photos from the Internet (photographer unknown).

Above: a taiga lake surrounded by Siberian cedar trees. Photo © 2007 Tatiana Grozetskaya.

Below: young residents of the *Kovcheg* eco-village, Kaluga Region, watch a swarm of bees entering a new beehive of Anastasia-inspired construction. When bees are kept in conditions closely approximating their natural habitat, they become healthy and non-aggressive. Photo © 2007 by Fedor Lazutin, eco-village *Kovcheg*.

Above: A typical dacha settlement along a powerline cutting through the forest. Dacha plot allocations have typically been confined to marginal, non-productive lands. *Below:* a 20 x 30 m dacha garden plot in the spring. Strawberry, greens and vegetable beds, a potato patch, fruit trees, a cold frame and bathhouse in the corner make a typical setting.

"The Earth needs our help. ... The Earth may be large, but it is most sensitive. And it feels the tender caress of even a single human hand. Oh, how it feels and anticipates this touch! ... Russians, yearning for contact with the Earth, took to [their dacha plots] with joyous enthusiasm. ... Because nothing can break Man's connection with the Earth! ... Millions of pairs of human hands began touching the Earth with love. ... And the Earth felt this, it felt it very much. ... And the Earth found new strength to carry on."

— *Anastasia's words from Book 2, "The Ringing Cedars of Russia"*

"*The meaning of life* — that is to be found in truth, joy and love. A nine-year-old child brought up in the natural world has a far more accurate perception of creation than all the scientific institutions of your world..."

— *Anastasia's words from Ch. 13: "A helper and mentor for your child"*

Dachas & community-garden photos © 2003–2006 Leonid Sharashkin

Above: Korean Peace Gardens near downtown Minneapolis. Like Russian dachniks, community gardeners in America and elsewhere delight in creating spaces of beauty and love amid urban wastelands.

"No amount of roaring machines or senseless cataclysms devised by the technocratic world can nullify the embrace of kindness and love from the hearts of its people. ... Through all the bustle and the clamour of roaring machinery they feel its tremendous power and grace."

— *Anastasia's words from Book 3, "The Space of Love"*

Above: A dance by Maria Ignatieva from Kostroma, Russia. This 2006 painting was inspired by Maria's reading of *Anastasia*. True to Anastasia's promise, after reading the book thousands of people have felt a huge creative upsurge, manifested in poetry, songs, artwork and gardening.

A dance © 2006 Maria Ignatieva. Used by permission.

I told Anastasia that we already have many specialised pharmacies which deal in healing herbs, just as there are many physicians and medicine men who make a profession out of herb treatments, and she replied:

"The chief physician is your own body. Right from the start it was endowed with the ability to know which herb should be used and when. How to eat and breathe. It is capable of warding off disease even before its outward manifestation. And nobody else can replace your body, for this is your personal physician, given individually to you by God, and personal only to you. I am telling you how to provide it with the opportunity to act beneficially on your behalf.

"If you make connections with the plants in your garden-plot, they will take care of you and cure you. They will make the right diagnoses all by themselves and prepare the most effective medicine especially designed for you."

Who gets stung by bees?

In every garden-plot there should be at least one colony of bees.

I told Anastasia there are very few people in our society who can communicate with bees. Special training is required, and not everyone is successful.

But she replied:

"A lot of what you do to maintain bee colonies just gets in the way. Over the past millennia there have been only two people on Earth who have come close to understanding this unique life-form."

"And who might they be?"

"They are two monks, who have since been canonised. You can read about them in your books — they can be found in many monastery archives."

"Come on, now, Anastasia! You read church literature too? Where? When? You don't even have a single book!"

"I have at my disposal a much more complete method of retrieving information."

"What kind of method? Again, you're talking in circles! After all, you promised me you wouldn't resort to any mysticism or fantasy."

"I shall tell you about it. I shall even try teaching it to you. You will not understand it right away, but it is simple and natural."

"Well, okay. So, how should bees be kept in a garden-plot?"

"All you have to do is build the same kind of hive for them they would have under natural conditions, and that is it. After that, your only task remaining is to go to the hive and gather part of the honey, wax and other substances they produce that are so useful for Man."

"Anastasia, that's not simple at all. Who knows what that natural hive should look like? Now, if you could tell me how to do it myself with the materials we have at our disposal, then that might be something feasible."

"All right," she laughed. "Then you will have to wait a bit. I need to *visualise* it, I have to see what people in today's world might have on hand, as you say."

"And where should it be placed so as not to spoil the view?" I added.

"I shall look into that too."

She lay down on the grass as she always did, visualising her — or, rather, our — life situations, but this time I began to observe her carefully. As she lay on the grass, her arms were stretched out in different directions, with palms upturned. Her fingers were partly curled, and their tips (specifically, the

tips of the four fingers on each hand) were also positioned so
that their soft parts faced upward.

Her fingers first began to stir a little, but then stopped.

Her eyes were closed. Her body was completely relaxed.
Her face too appeared relaxed at first, but then a faint shadow
of some kind of feeling or sensation moved across it.

Later she explained how seeing at a distance could be practised by anyone with a particular kind of upbringing.

About the beehive, Anastasia had the following to say:

"You need to make the hive in the shape of a hollow block.
You can either take a log with a hole in it and hollow it out
to enlarge the cavity, or use boards from a deciduous tree to
make a long hollow box 120 centimetres long. The boards
should be no less than 6 cm thick and the inside measure-
ments of the cavity at least 40 by 40 centimetres. Triangular
strips should be inserted into the corners where the inner
surfaces meet, to make the cavity somewhat rounded. The
strips can be just lightly glued in place, and the bees themselves will firm them up afterward. One end should be fully
and permanently covered with a board of the same thickness,
with a removable panel at the other end. For this the panel
needs to be cut in such a way so that it fits neatly into the
opening and sealed with grass or some kind of cloth covering
the whole bottom. Make a slit or a series of slits (to provide
access for the bees) along the bottom edge of one of the sides
approximately one and a half centimetres wide, starting 30
cm from the removable panel and continuing to the other
end. This hive can be set on pilings anywhere in the garden-
plot — at least 20–25 centimetres off the ground, with the
slits facing south.

"It is even better, however, to set it up under the roof of
the house. Then people will not interfere with the bees flying out, and will not be bothered by them. In this case the
hive should be aligned horizontally at a 20–30 degree angle,

with the opening at the lower end. The hive could even be installed in the attic, provided there is proper ventilation, or on the roof itself. Best of all, though, attach it to the south wall of the house, just under the eaves. The only thing is, you need to make sure you have proper access to the hive so you can remove the honeycomb. Otherwise the hive should stand on a small platform, with an overhead canopy to protect it from the sun, and can be wrapped with insulation in winter."

I remarked to Anastasia that this type of hive could be rather heavy, and the platform and canopy might spoil the appearance of the house. What to do in that case? She looked at me a little surprised, and then explained:

"The thing is that your beekeepers do not really go about it the right way. My grandfather told me about this. Beekeepers today have concocted a lot of different ways of constructing a hive, but all of them involve constant human intervention in its operation — they move the honeycomb frames around within the hive, or move both the hive and the bees to a different spot for the winter, and that is something they should not do.

"Bees build their honeycombs at a specific distance apart to facilitate both ventilation and defence against their enemies, and any human intervention breaks down this system. Instead of spending their time gathering honey and raising offspring, the bees are obliged to fix what has been broken.

"Under natural conditions bees live in tree hollows and cope with any situation perfectly well on their own. I told you how to keep them under conditions as close to their natural ones as possible. Their presence is extremely beneficial. They pollinate all the plants much more effectively than anything else, thereby increasing the yield. But you must know this pretty well already.

"What you may not know is that bees' probosces open up channels in the plants through which the plants take in supplemental information reflected by the planets — information the plants (and, subsequently, human beings) require."

"But bees sting people, don't you see? How can somebody get a good rest at a dacha if they're constantly afraid of being stung?"

"Bees only sting when people act aggressively toward them, wave them off, become afraid or irritated inside — not necessarily at the bees, but just at anyone. The bees feel this and will not tolerate the rays of any dark feelings. Besides, they may attack those parts of the body where there are channels connecting with some diseased internal organ or where the protective aura has been torn, and so forth.

"You know how effectively bees are already used in treating the disease you call radiculitis, but that is far from being the only thing they can do.

"If I were to tell you about *everything*, especially showing the evidence you are asking for, you would have to spend not just three days but many weeks with me. There is a lot written about bees in your world, all I have done is introduce a few correctives — but please believe me, they are extremely important correctives.

"To establish a colony of bees in a hive like that is very easy. Before dumping a swarm of bees into the hive, put in a little chunk of wax and some honey-plant. You do not need to put in any hand-made frames or cells. Afterward, when there are colonies established on even a few neighbouring dacha plots, the bees will multiply all by themselves; then, as they swarm, they will occupy the empty hives."

"And how should the honey be gathered?"

"Open the panel, break off the hanging honeycomb and retrieve the sealed honey and pollen. Only do not be greedy. It is important to leave part of it for the bees for the winter.

In fact, it is better not to collect any honey at all during the first year."

Hello, Morning!

Anastasia has adapted her morning routine to the conditions of the dacha plot:

"In the morning, preferably at sunrise, walk out to the garden-plot barefoot, and approach any plants you like. You can touch them. This does not have to be done in accord with some sort of schedule or ritual to be strictly followed day after day, but simply as one feels moved, or as one desires. But it should be done before washing. Then the plants will sense the odours of the substances emitted by the body through the pores of the skin during sleep.

"If it is warm and there is a small grassy patch close by (and it would be helpful if there were), lie down there and stretch out for three or four minutes. And if some little bug should happen to crawl onto your body during this time, do not chase it away. Many bugs open up pores on the human body and cleanse them. As a rule, the pores prone to clogging are the ones through which toxins are expelled, thus bringing all sorts of internal ailments to the surface and allowing the person to wash them away.

"If there is any pond water on the plot, you should immerse yourself in it. If not, then you can pour water over yourself as you stand barefoot close to the plants and garden beds or,

even better, between the beds — or, for example, one morning alongside the raspberry bushes, the next by the currant
bushes etc. And after washing you should not dry off right
away. You should shake off the water drops from your hands,
spreading them onto the surrounding plants. And use your
hands to brush off the water from other parts of your body.
After this you can go through the usual procedures of washing
and using any conveniences to which you are accustomed."

Evening routine

"In the evening, before going to bed it is important to wash
your feet, using water with the addition of a small quantity
(a few drops) of juice from saltbush or nettles — or the two
together — but no soap or shampoo. After washing your feet,
pour the water onto the garden beds. Then, if necessary, you
can still wash your feet with soap.

"This evening routine is important for two reasons. As the
feet perspire, toxins come to the surface, removing internal diseases from the body, and these must be washed away to cleanse
the pores. Juices from saltbush or nettles are good at facili-
tating this process. In pouring the remaining water onto the
beds, you are giving supplemental information to the microorganisms and plants about your current state of well-being.

"This is very important too. Only after receiving this information can our visible and invisible world around you work
out and pick up from the Universe and the Earth everything
it needs for the normal functioning of your body."

It will prepare everything by itself

I was still interested in knowing what Anastasia had to say about food. After all, she has a rather unique dietary régime, and so I asked:

"Anastasia, tell me how you think a person should feed himself — what should he eat, how often during the day and in what amounts? Our world pays a great deal of attention to this question. There's a huge quantity of all sorts of literature on this subject, health-food recipes, advice on losing weight..."

"It is difficult to picture Man's lifestyle any other way under the circumstances currently imposed by the technocratic world. The dark forces are constantly trying desperately to take the natural mechanism of this world — the one given to humanity right from the start — and substitute their own cumbersome artificial system which goes against human nature."

I asked Anastasia to put it in more concrete and understandable terms, without her philosophical musings, and she continued:

"You know, these questions of yours as to what, when and how much a person should eat — they are best answered by the individual's own body. The sensations of hunger and thirst are designed to send a signal to each particular individual, indicating when he should take in food. This precise moment is the right one for each person. The world of technocracy, being incapable of affording each individual the opportunity of satisfying his hunger and thirst at the moment desired by his body, has tried to force him into its own schedule based on nothing but this world's own helplessness, and then attempted to justify this compulsion in the name of some sort of 'efficiency'.

"Just think: one person spends half the day sitting down, expending hardly any energy, while another exerts himself with some kind of physical labour, or simply runs and perspires all over, thereby using up many times more energy, and yet both are expected to eat at exactly the same time. A Man should take in food at the moment advised by his body, and there can be no other advisor. I realise that under your world's conditions this is practically impossible, but the opportunity does exist for people at their dachas with their attached garden-plots, and they should take advantage of it and forget about their unnatural, artificial régimes.

"The same applies to your second question: *What* should one eat? The answer is: whatever is available at the moment — whatever is on hand, so to speak. The body itself will select what it needs. I could offer you a bit of non-traditional advice: if you have a household pet like a cat or a dog, keep track of its movements carefully. Occasionally it will find something in the way of grasses or herbs and eat it. You should tear off a few samples of whatever it selects and add it to your diet. This is not something you have to do every day — once or twice a week is sufficient.

"You should also take it upon yourself to gather some cereal grain, thresh it, grind it into flour and then use the flour to bake bread. This is extremely important. Anyone consuming this bread even once or twice a year will build up a store of energy capable of awakening his inner spiritual powers — not only calming his soul but also exerting a beneficial influence on his physical condition. This bread can be shared with relatives and close friends. If shared with sincerity and love, it will have quite a beneficial influence on them as well. It is very helpful to every individual's health to spend three days, at least once each summer, eating only what is grown in his garden-plot, along with bread, sunflower oil and just a pinch of salt."

I have already described Anastasia's own eating habits. While she was telling me all this, she would unwittingly tear off a blade of grass or two, put it in her mouth and chew it, and offer me some too. I decided to give it a try. I can't say the taste was anything to write home about, but neither did it provoke any sense of distaste.

It seems as though Anastasia has left the whole task of nourishment and life-support up to Nature; she never allows it to interrupt her train of thought, which is always busy with some more important issue. Even so, her health is as remarkable as her outward beauty, of which it is an inseparable part. According to Anastasia, anyone who has established such a relationship with the Earth and the plants on his own plot of land, has the opportunity of ridding his body of absolutely every kind of disease.

Disease *per se* is the result of Man distancing himself from the natural systems designed to take care of his health and life-support. For such systems, the task of counteracting any disease presents no problem whatsoever, since this is their whole reason for being. However, the benefits experienced by people who have set up such information-exchange contacts with a little patch of the natural world go far beyond dealing with diseases.

CHAPTER TWELVE

Sleeping under one's star

I have already mentioned how animated Anastasia becomes when talking about plants and people who communicate with them. I thought that, living in Nature as she did, she might have studied Nature alone, but she also possesses information about planetary relationships. She literally feels the celestial bodies. See for yourself what she has to say about sleeping under the stars:

"Once plants have received information about a specific person, they embark upon an information exchange with cosmic forces, but here they are simply intermediaries, carrying out a narrowly focused task involving one's fleshly body and certain emotional planes. They never touch the complex processes which, out of all the animal and plant world on the planet, are inherent only in the human brain and on human planes of existence. Nevertheless, this information exchange they establish allows Man to do what he alone can do — namely, interact with the Intelligence of the Universe or, more precisely, to exchange information with this Intelligence. An altogether simple procedure permits you not only to do this, but also to feel the beneficial effect of such interaction."

Anastasia described this procedure as follows:

"Pick an evening when weather conditions are favourable and arrange to spend the night under the stars. You should situate your sleeping place close to raspberry or currant bushes, or to beds where cereal plants are growing. You should be there alone. As you lie with your face to the stars, do not close your eyes right away. Let your gaze, physically and mentally, wander across the celestial bodies. Do not become tense while thinking about them. Your thought must be free and unencumbered.

"First, try to think about those celestial bodies which are visible to your eye; then you can dream about what you treasure in life, about the people closest to you, people for whom you wish only good. Do not attempt to even think at this point about seeking revenge or wishing evil upon anyone, for that might have a negative effect on you. This uncomplicated procedure will awaken some of the many little cells dormant in your brain, the vast majority of which never wake even once during a person's whole lifetime. The cosmic forces will be with you and help you attain the realisation of your brightest and most unimaginable dreams, will help you find peace in your heart, establish positive relationships with your loved ones, and increase — or call into being — their love for you.

"It is useful to try repeating this procedure a number of times. It is effective only when carried out at the location of your constant contact with the plant world. And you will feel it yourself as early as the next morning. It is especially important to go through this procedure on the eve of your birthday. To explain how all this works would take too long right now, and is not important. Parts of the explanation you would not believe, other parts you would not understand. It can be discussed much more quickly and easily with people who are already trying it and feeling its influence on themselves, since the information, once received and verified, will facilitate the reception of any information that follows."

CHAPTER THIRTEEN

A helper and mentor for your child

In asking Anastasia how a plot of ground with vegetation, even planted in the special manner she described and maintaining close contact with Man, could facilitate the raising of children, I expected to hear an answer something like: 'Children need to be imbued with a love of nature.' However, I was wrong. What she actually said was amazing both in its simplicity of argument and in the depth of its philosophical implications.

"Nature and the Mind of the Universe have seen to it that every new Man is born a sovereign, a king! He is like an angel — pure and undefiled. Through the still soft upper part of his head he takes in a huge flood of information from the Universe. The abilities inherent in each newborn child are such as to allow him to become the wisest being in the Universe, God-like. It takes him very little time to bestow grace and happiness upon his parents. During this period — amounting to no more than nine earth-years — he becomes aware of what constitutes creation and the meaning of human existence. And everything that he needs to accomplish this already exists. Only the parents should not distort the genuine, natural order of creation by cutting the child off from the most perfect works in the Universe.

"The world of technocracy, however, does not allow parents to do the right thing. What does an infant see with his first conscious glance around? He sees the ceiling, the edge of his crib, some patches of fabric, the walls — all attributes and values of the artificial world created by a technocratic society. And in this world he finds his mother and her breasts.

"'This must be the way things are!' he concludes. His smiling parents offer him toys and other objects that rattle and squeak, as though they were priceless treasures. Why? He will spend a long time trying to make sense of this rattling and squeaking. He will try to comprehend them both through his conscious mind and his sub-conscious. And then these same smiling parents will try wrapping him up in some kind of fabric, which he finds most uncomfortable. He will make attempts to free himself, but in vain! And the only means of protest he has at his disposal is a cry! A cry of protest, an appeal for help, a cry of rebellion. And, from that moment on, this angel and sovereign becomes an indigent slave, begging for handouts.

"One after another, the child is presented with the accoutrements of an artificial world. Some new toy or item of clothing is offered to him as the latest *summum bonum*. And the thought is thereby drummed into him that these are the most important objects in the world where he has arrived. In his infancy, despite his status as the most perfect being in the Universe, he is already pandered to and treated as an imperfect creature, and even in those institutions you consider educational, he is constantly reminded of the values of this artificial world. Not until the age of nine does he hear a passing mention of the existence of the world of nature, and then only as an adjunct to that other, more important world of manufactured objects. And most people are never afforded the opportunity to become aware of the truth, even to the end of their days. And so the seemingly simple question 'What is the meaning of life?' goes unanswered.

"*The meaning of life* — that is to be found in truth, joy and love. A nine-year-old child brought up in the natural world has a far more accurate perception of creation than all the scientific institutions of your world or, indeed, many of your prominent scholars."

"Stop, Anastasia! You probably have in mind a knowledge of nature, assuming his life proceeds along the same lines as yours. Here I can agree with you. But think: today's Man is obliged (rightly or wrongly — that is another question) — but he is obliged to live specifically in our technocratic world, as you call it. Someone brought up as you propose will certainly know nature, and have a feeling for it, but in everything else he will be an utter ignoramus. Besides, there are other sciences, like mathematics, physics, chemistry — or simply just knowing about life and its societal manifestations."

"For someone who has learnt at the right time what constitutes creation, those things are mere trifles. If he wants, or considers it necessary to prove himself in some scientific field, he will easily surpass all others."

"And just why would that happen, all of a sudden?"

"Man in the world of technocracy has never yet invented anything that is not already present in nature. Even the most perfect manufactured devices are but a poor imitation of what exists in nature."

"Well, that may be. But you promised to explain how a child could be raised and his capabilities developed in *our* conditions. Only talk about this in a way I can understand, using concrete examples."

"I shall try to be more concrete," replied Anastasia. "I have already visualised situations like this and have tried to hint to one family what they should do, only there was no way they could have grasped the crucial point and started putting *questions* to their child... These parents turned out to have an unusually pure, talented child, who could bring tremendous benefit to people living on Earth.

"So, these parents arrive with this three-year-old child at their dacha plot and bring along his favourite toys. Artificial toys which displace the true priorities of the Universe. Oh, if only they would not do that! Just think, the child could be occupied and inspired with something far more interesting than senseless and even harmful interaction with manufactured objects.

"First of all, you should ask him to help you, only ask him in all seriousness, without any pandering, especially since he will actually be able to offer you assistance. If you do any planting, for example, ask him to hold the seeds in preparation for sowing, or rake out the seedbeds, or have him put a seed into the hole you have prepared. And in the process talk to him about what you are doing, something like this:

"'We will be putting the little seed into the ground and covering it with earth. When the Sun in the sky shines and warms the earth, the little seed will get warm and start to grow. It will want to see the Sun, and a little shoot will poke its head out of the earth, just like this one.' At this point you can show him some little blade of grass. 'If the shoot likes the sunshine, it will grow bigger and bigger and maybe turn into a tree, or something smaller, like a flower. And I want it to bring us tasty fruit, and you will eat it if you like it. The little shoot will prepare its fruit for you.'

"Whenever you arrive with your child at the garden-plot, or when he awakes in the morning, have him look first and see whether any new shoots have come up. If you should notice one, show your delight. When you are putting young plants rather than seeds into the ground, it is just as important to explain to your child what you are doing. If you are planting tomato seedlings, for example, let him hand you the stalks one by one. If he should inadvertently break a stalk, take the broken stalk into your hands and say: 'I do not think this one will live or bear fruit, since it is broken, but let us try planting it anyway.' And plant at least one of the broken ones right along with the others.

"A few days later, when you visit the garden bed again with your child and the stalks have firmed up, point out the broken, withering stalk to your little one and remind him that it was broken during the planting, but do not use any preaching tone of voice in doing so. You need to talk with him as an equal. You should bear in mind the thought that he is superior to you in some respects — in the purity of his thought, for example. He is an angel! If you succeed in understanding that, you can then proceed intuitively, and your child will indeed become a person who will happify your days.

"Whenever you sleep under the stars, take your child with you, lay him down beside you, let him look at the stars, but under no circumstances tell him the names of the planets or how you perceive their origin and function, since this is something you do not really know yourself, and the dogmas stored in your brain will only lead the child astray from the truth. His sub-conscious knows the truth, and it will penetrate his consciousness all by itself. All you might do is to tell him that you like looking at the shining stars, and ask your child which star he likes best of all.

"In general, it is very important to know how to ask your child questions. The next year you should offer your child his own seedbed, fix it up and give him the freedom to do whatever he likes with it. Do not ever compel him by force to do anything with it, and do not ever correct what he has done. The only thing you can do is ask him what he likes. You can offer help, but only after asking his permission to work along with him. When you are planting cereal grains, have him throw some grains on the seedbed for you."

"Okay," I remarked to Anastasia, still not fully convinced. "Maybe this way a child will show interest in the plant world and maybe he'll become a good agronomist, but still, where is he going to get knowledge from in other areas?"

"What do you mean, *where from?* It is not just a matter of having a knowledge and feeling about what grows and how. The main thing is that the child is starting to think, analyse, and cells are awakening in his brain which will operate throughout his life. They will make him brighter and more talented compared to those whose corresponding cells are still dormant.

"As far as 'civilised' life goes — what you call *progress* — he may well turn out to be superior in any field of endeavour — all the more so since the purity of his thought will make him an exceptionally happy person. The contact he has established with his planets will allow him to constantly take in — and *exchange* — more and more information. The incoming messages will be received by his sub-conscious and transmitted to his consciousness in the form of many new thoughts and discoveries. Outwardly he will look like everyone else, but inwardly... This is the kind of Man you call a genius."

CHAPTER FOURTEEN

Forest school

"Tell me, Anastasia, is this the way *your* parents brought *you* up?"

She responded after a brief pause, during which, I gathered, she was recollecting her childhood.

"I remember practically nothing of my Papa or Mama in the flesh. I was brought up by my grandfather and great-grandfather pretty much as I have explained to you. But, you see, I myself had a good feeling very early on for Nature and the animal world around me — perhaps I was not aware of all the details of how it operated, but that is not important when one has a feeling for it. Grandfather and Great-Grandfather would approach me from time to time and ask questions and expect me to answer them. In our culture, older generations treat an infant or young child virtually as a deity, and use the child's responses as a check on their own purity."

I began asking Anastasia to recall some specific question and answer. She smiled, and told me:

"Once I was playing with a little snake. I turned around, and there were Grandfather and Great-Grandfather standing right beside me, smiling. I was very delighted, since it was always interesting being with them. They are the only ones who can ask me questions and their hearts beat in the same rhythm as mine, but with animals it is different. I ran over to them. Great-Grandfather bowed to me, while Grandfather took me on his knees. I listened to his heart beat and I fingered the hairs on his beard as I examined them. Nobody spoke. We were thinking together, and it was good that way. Then Grandfather asked me:

"'Tell me, Anastasia, why do you think my hair grows here and here,' pointing to the top of his head and his beard, 'and not here?' pointing to his nose and forehead.

"I touched his nose and forehead, but no reply was forthcoming. I could not give an unthinking answer — I had to understand it.

"The next time they came, Grandfather again said:

"'Well, I am still thinking, why my hair grows here, and not here,' again indicating his nose and forehead.

"Great-Grandfather looked at me seriously and attentively. Then I thought: perhaps it is really a serious question with him, and I asked:

"'Grandfather, what is it? Do you really want your hair to grow everywhere, even on your nose and forehead?'

"Great-Grandfather began pondering the question, while Grandfather replied:

"'No, not really.'

"'Then that is why your hair does not grow there, because you do not want it to!'

"He reflected on that, stroking his beard, and mused, as though he were putting the question to himself: 'And if it grows here, that means it is because I want it to?'

"I confirmed his thought:

"'Of course, Grandfather, not only you, but I, and the one who thought you up.'

"At this point Great-Grandfather asked me rather excitedly:

"'And who was it that thought him up?'

"'The one who thought everything up,' I replied.

"'But where is he, show me!' Great-Grandfather asked, bowing to me.

"I could not give him an answer right away, but the question stayed with me, and I started thinking about it often."

"And did you eventually give him an answer?" I asked Anastasia.

"I gave him an answer about a year later, and then they started asking me more questions, but up until the time I gave the answer, neither Grandfather nor Great-Grandfather had asked me any new questions, and I began to get very concerned."

CHAPTER FIFTEEN

Attentiveness to Man

I asked Anastasia who taught her to speak and converse, since she had almost no memory of her father and mother and her grandfather and great-grandfather talked with her only rarely. The answers she gave were quite a shock to me, and require interpretation by specialists, and so I shall try to reproduce them as fully as I can. Their meaning has gradually begun to sink in. She responded to my first question with a question of her own:

"Do you mean the ability to speak in different people's languages?"

"How do you mean, 'different'? What, you can speak more than one language?"

"Yes," she replied.

"Including German, French, English, Japanese, Chinese?"

"Yes," she repeated, and then added: "You can see I speak your language."

"You mean Russian?"

"Well, that puts it too generally. I speak, or at least try to speak, using words and phrases you yourself use when you talk. At first it was a little challenging for me, since your vocabulary is not very large and you repeat yourself a fair amount. Nor do you have much expression of feeling. That is not the kind of language which easily lends itself to accurately saying everything one wishes to say."

"Wait, Anastasia — I'm going to ask you something in a foreign language, and you give me an answer."

I said *Hello* to her in English, and then in French. She answered me right off.

Unfortunately I myself have not mastered any foreign language. In school I studied German, but with rather poor marks. I did remember one whole sentence in German, which my schoolmates and I learnt by rote. I recited it to Anastasia:

"*Ich liebe dich, und gib mir deine Hand.*"[1]

She extended her hand to me and answered in German:

"I give you my hand."

Amazed by what I had heard, and still not believing my ears, I asked:

"So then, any person can be taught all languages?"

I had an intuitive feeling that there must be some kind of simple explanation for this extraordinary phenomenon, and I had to know what it was so I could tell others about it.

"Anastasia, so have a go at it: explain this in my language, and try to do it with examples, so that I can understand," I asked somewhat excitedly.

"All right, all right, only calm down and let go, or you will not understand. But let me first teach you to write in Russian."

"I know how to write. You tell me about learning foreign languages."

"I do not mean just handwriting — I shall teach you to be a writer. A very talented writer. You shall write a book."

"That's impossible."

"It *is* possible! It is quite simple."

Anastasia took a stick and outlined on the ground the whole Russian alphabet along with the punctuation marks, and asked me how many letters there were.

"Thirty-three," I replied.[2]

---

[1]"I love you, and give me your hand."

[2]*Thirty-three* — This is the correct number of letters in the modern Russian version of the Cyrillic alphabet. It is believed that Cyrillic was adapted from Greek by the monk St Cyril in the ninth century to introduce the

"You see, that is a very small number of letters. Can you call what I have outlined a book?"

"No," I answered. "It's just an ordinary alphabet, that's all. Ordinary letters."

"Yet all the books in the Russian language are made up of these ordinary letters," Anastasia observed. "Do you not agree? Do you not see how simple it all is?"

"Yes, but in books they're — they're arranged differently."

"Correct, all books consist of a multitude of combinations of these letters. People arrange them on the pages automatically, guided by their feelings. And from this it follows that books originate not from a combination of letters and sounds, but from feelings outlined by people's imagination. The result is that the readers are aroused by approximately the same feelings as the writers, and such feelings can be recalled for a long time. Can you recollect any images or situations from books you have read?"

"Yes, I can," I replied, after a moment's thought.

For some reason I recalled Lermontov's[3] *Hero of our time,* and began to tell the story to Anastasia. She interrupted me:

Gospels to the Slavic-speaking peoples of the Balkan peninsula. It later spread to all Slavic lands (including Russia) where the Orthodox Church predominated. The number of letters in the alphabet varies from language to language. In other areas, under the influence of the Roman Catholic Church, the Latin writing system was adapted to the local Slavic language.

[3] *Mikhail Yurevich Lermontov* (1814–1841) — after Alexander Pushkin, Russia's second most-loved classic poet, who also has several novels and stories to his credit, including *Hero of our time (Geroi nashego vremeni).* A descendant of a Scottish military officer, Captain George Learmont, who had entered the Russian service in 1613, Lermontov (an officer himself) came to prominence especially after writing an inflammatory poetic eulogy on Pushkin when the latter was killed in a duel ("Death of a poet", 1837). Ironically, Lermontov himself was killed in a duel only four years later.

"You see, you can still depict the characters from this book and tell me what they felt, even though quite a bit of time has gone by since you read it. But if I were to ask you to tell me in what sequence the thirty-three letters of the Russian alphabet were set forth in that book, what combinations they were arranged in, could you do that?"

"No. That would be impossible."

"Indeed, it would be very difficult. So, feelings have been conveyed from one Man to another with the help of all sorts of combinations of these thirty-three letters. You looked at these combinations of letters and forgot them right off, but the feelings and images remained to be remembered for a long time.

"So it turns out that if you link emotional feelings directly to these marks on paper without thinking about any conventions, one's soul will cause these marks to appear in just the right sequence and combinations so that any reader may subsequently feel the soul of the writer. And if in the soul of the writer—"

"Wait, Anastasia. Put it more simply, more clearly, more specifically, show me through some kind of an example how languages are to be learnt. You can make me into a writer later on. Come on, tell me first: who taught *you* to understand different languages and how."

"My great-grandfather," replied Anastasia.

"Give me an example," I kept insisting, anxious to understand everything in a hurry.

"All right, but do not be concerned. I shall still find a way to help you understand, and if it is that important to you, I shall try teaching all the languages to you too. It is simple, after all."

"For us it's quite incredible, Anastasia. So do try to explain. And tell me, how much time would it take to teach me?"

She thought for a moment as she looked at me, and then said:

"Your memory is no longer very good, and then there are your domestic problems... You will need a lot of time."

"How long?" I was impatient for an answer.

"For everyday comprehension of phrases such as *Hello* and *Good-bye,* I would say it would take at least four months, possibly six," she replied.

"Enough, Anastasia! Tell me how your great-grandfather did it."

"He played with me."

"How did he play? Tell me."

"Calm down! Take it easy! I cannot understand why you are so impatient!"

And then she quietly went on:

"Great-Grandfather played with me, as though he were joking with me. Whenever he came to me all by himself, without Grandfather, he would always approach me, bow at the waist, and hold out his hand to me, and I would hold out mine to him. He would first shake my hand, then get down on one knee, kiss my hand and say 'Hello, Anastasia!'

"One time he came, he did everything as usual, his eyes looked at me tenderly as usual, but his lips were saying some kind of abracadabra. I looked at him in surprise, and he said something else, equally unintelligible. I could not take it any longer and asked:

"'Granpakins, have you forgotten what to say?'

"'Yes, I have,' Great-Grandfather answered. Then he stepped away from me a few paces, stopped to think about something and came over to me again, extended his hand to me and I held out mine to him. He dropped on one knee and kissed my hand. His look was gentle, his lips were moving, but no sound was coming out at all. I was even a bit afraid. Then I decided a reminder might help.

"'Hello, Anastasia!' I hinted.

"'Correct!' Great-Grandfather confirmed with a smile.

"At that point I realised it was a game — he and I would often play this game together after that. At first it was quite simple, but then the game became more complicated, and more fascinating. It is a game that begins when one is three years old and goes on until the age of eleven, when one undergoes a kind of test. This involves looking attentively at the person you are talking with and being able to understand what they are saying, no matter what language they are expressing it in. This kind of dialogue is far superior to speech — it is more rapid and conveys far more information. You would call it thought-transfer. You think it is abnormal, something out of fantasy, but it is simply an attentive attitude toward Man, drawing upon a developed imagination and a good memory. It involves not just a more efficient method of information exchange, but getting to know a person's soul, along with the animal and plant world, and what constitutes creation as a whole."

"Anastasia," I said, "what can plants growing in a garden-plot possibly have to do with this — what is their role in all this?"

"What do you mean, what have they to do with it? At the same time as the child is getting to know the world of plants as a part of the functioning of the Universe, he is also entering into contact with his planets. With their help and the help of his parents he quickly, very quickly, gets to know the truth and develops intensively in the fields of psychology, philosophy and the natural sciences — your disciplines. But if the game is played using some kind of man-made object from the artificial world as an example, the child will become lost. He will not receive any assistance from the powers of Nature or the Universe."

"I have already noted, Anastasia, that in the final analysis such a child could become an agronomist. Now where would his knowledge come from in other areas?"

But Anastasia maintained that a Man raised in such a manner would show an aptitude for quick learning in any of our scholarly disciplines.

Chapter Sixteen

Flying saucers?
Nothing extraordinary!

Then I asked her to show me an example of her knowledge of technology.

"Do you want me to tell you how all the different machines of your world operate?"

"The kind of thing our prominent scientists are only touching the fringes of. Why don't you make some great scientific discovery, let's say?"

"That is what I have been doing for you the whole time you have been here."

"Not just for me, for the world of science — a discovery they would be prepared to recognise. Go ahead, make a discovery in some technical field which will prove your abilities — like space ships, the atom, automobile fuel — since you say it's all so simple."

"In comparison with what I have been trying to show you, those fields you mention are something like, to use a term from your language, the stone age!"

"That's perfect, then! You may consider it primitive, but at least I'll be able to understand it. You can prove you're right and show evidence that your intelligence is superior to mine. Tell me, for example, what you think of our aeroplanes and space ships — pretty close to perfect machines?"

"No. They are altogether primitive, they only serve to show how primitive the technocratic path of development is."

That remark put me on my guard, since I realised that either her conclusions were those of a madwoman *or* she really knew far more than someone with an ordinary consciousness could ever imagine. I continued my questioning:

"What do you mean when you say our rockets and planes are primitive?"

Anastasia responded after a brief pause, as though allowing time for her words to sink in.

"The functioning of all your machines, every single one of them, is based on the energy of explosion. Not knowing any more efficient natural sources of energy, you resort to such primitive, awkward substitutes with incredible stubbornness. And even the destructive consequences of their use do not stop you. The range of your aeroplanes and rockets is simply laughable — according to the scale of the Universe they rise a wee tiny bit above the Earth, and now this method has practically reached its ceiling, do not you agree? But that is ridiculous! An exploding or burning substance propels some monstrous structure that you call a space ship. And the greater part of this ship is designed precisely to 'solve' this problem of propulsion."

"And what might be an alternative principle of movement through the atmosphere?"

"A flying saucer might be a good example," Anastasia responded.

"What?! You know about flying saucers and their propulsion systems?"

"Of course I know. It is very simple and rational."

I felt my throat go dry, and tried to hurry her up.

"Tell me, Anastasia, quickly... and in a way I can understand."

"All right, only do not get excited — it will be harder to understand when you are excited. The propulsion principle of a flying saucer is based on the energy of generating a vacuum."

"How so? Be more precise!"

"You have a limited vocabulary, yet I am compelled to restrict myself to it so that you can understand me."

"Well!" I blurted out in agitation. "I'll add *jar, lid, tablet, air...*" and I began to quickly name all the words that just popped into my head at that moment, and even let out a few swearwords.

Anastasia broke in:

"You need not bother — I already know all the words you can express yourself with, but there are still others, and besides that, there is a whole different method of conveying information. If I used that, I could explain everything to you in a minute. As things stand now, it may take two hours or more. That is a lot, and I really wanted to tell you about something else, something much more meaningful."

"No, Anastasia. Tell me about flying saucers and their propulsion methods, tell me about energy carriers. Until I understand that, I shan't listen to anything else."

"All right," she acquiesced, and then went on. "An explosion occurs when a solid substance quickly changes under a certain influence into gaseous form, or when, in the course of a reaction, two gaseous substances evolve into something even lighter. Everyone, of course, understands this part."

"Yes," I replied. "If powder is ignited it becomes smoke, and liquid fuel becomes gas."

"Yes, more or less. But if you or your people had purer thoughts and consequently a knowledge of the functionings of Nature, you would have long ago become aware that if there is a substance capable of instant expansion and, through explosion, transformation into another state, the opposite process must also hold true.[1] In Nature there are living microorganisms that transform gaseous substances into solids. All plants do this in fact, only at varying speeds and with varying degrees of firmness and solidity of the resulting substance.

"Take a look around you, and you will see that plants take in liquid from the earth and breathe air, and then process these into a hard and solid body — let us say, wood, or something even harder and more solid, like a nut-shell or a plum-stone. A microorganism smaller than the eye can see does this with fantastic speed, feeding, it would seem, on air alone. It is these same kinds of microorganisms that power flying saucers. They are like the microcells in the brain, only their operation has a very narrow focus. Their sole function is propulsion. But they carry out this function to perfection and they can accelerate a flying saucer to one-nineteenth the speed of the average modern Earth-dweller's thought.

"These microorganisms are located on the inner surface of the upper part of the flying saucer and positioned between its double walls, which are set approximately three centimetres apart. The upper and lower surfaces of the outer walls are porous, with micro-sized pinholes. The microorganisms draw in air through these pinholes, thereby creating a vacuum ahead of the saucer. The streams of air begin to congeal even before contact with the saucer, and as they pass through the microorganisms they are transformed into tiny spheres. Then these spheres are enlarged even more, to approximately half a centimetre in diameter. They lose their firmness, and slide down between the walls into the lower part of the saucer, where they again decompose into a gaseous substance. You can even eat them, if you can do this before they decompose."

"What about the walls of the flying saucer — what are they made of?"

---

[1]Many non-traditional scientists have criticised the generating of energy from explosion or the burning of fuel as unnatural and destructive. One of them, the so-called 'water wizard' Viktor Schauberger (1885–1958), an illustrious Austrian forester and engineer, has spoken — in terms very similar to those used by Anastasia here — of the 'energy of *implosion*' — as a natural alternative to today's destructive technologies. Schauberger has gained deep insights into the workings of Nature and, among other things, was involved in research on the use of implosion (or energy from a vacuum) for propulsion. For a fascinating account of Schauberger's work in eco-technology, forestry, water purification and other areas, see Callum Coats' book *Living energies*.

"They are cultivated — grown."

"How so?"

"Why the surprise? Just give it a little thought, you will figure it out. Many people cultivate a fungus in various kinds of containers.[2] The fungus, by the way, imbues the water in which it is placed with a pleasant, slightly acidic flavour, and takes the shape of the container. This fungus, by the way, is very similar to a flying saucer; it creates a double wall above and below. If another microorganism is added to its water, it produces a congealment, but this so-called microorganism can be produced — or, rather, given birth to — by the power of the will, or the brain, much like a vivid concept or imagery."

"Can you do this?" I asked.

"Yes, but I do not have sufficient power of my own. The action of several dozen people having the same ability is required, and it takes about a year all told."

"And can one find on our Earth everything necessary to make — or grow, as you say — such a flying saucer and these microorganisms?"

"Of course one can. The Earth has everything that the Universe has."

"But how do you get the microorganisms inside the walls of the saucer if they are so small you can't even see them?"

"Once the upper wall is cultivated, it will attract and collect them in huge numbers, just as bees are attracted to cells. But

---

[2]This fungus, famous for its medicinal properties, is known as *kombucha* (*Medusomyces gisevii*). It looks like a pile of pancakes or a flat multi-layered jellyfish (its scientific name is actually derived from the German word for 'jellyfish' — *meduse*), floating on top of the water in the container in which it is placed and eventually assuming the form of that container. The fungus is cultivated in sweetened weak tea. The result is a pleasant-tasting drink used both as a refreshment and as a cure for a great number of diseases. In Russia this fungus is commonly cultivated by people in large glass jars on their kitchen window sills.

this process also requires the collective will of several dozen people. In any case, what is the use of elaborating further, if you cannot cultivate it for lack of people with the right kind of will, intelligence and knowledge?"

"Isn't there some way *you* could help?"

"I could."

"So, do it!"

"I have already."

"What have you done?" I was still perplexed.

"I told you how children should be raised. And I shall tell you more. You will tell this to others. Many will understand, and their children raised in this manner will have the intelligence, knowledge and will which permits them to make not only a primitive flying saucer, but significantly more..."

"Anastasia, how do you know so much about a flying saucer? Don't tell me that, too, comes through your communication with plants?"

"They have been landing here, and I, well, I have helped them repair their ship."

"Are they much smarter than us?"

"Not at all. They have a long way to go to attain the level of Man — they are afraid of us, afraid to approach people, even though they are very curious. At first they were afraid of me. They trained their mental paralysers on me. Put on quite a show. They tried to frighten me, shock me. It was quite a challenge to calm them down and convince them I would only treat them with affection."

"Well, how can they be less smart than us if they can do things Man can't do yet?"

"What is so surprising about that? Bees too make incredible structures out of natural materials, including whole ventilation and heating systems, but that does not mean they are superior to Man in intelligence. In the Universe there is no one and nothing stronger than Man except God!"

CHAPTER SEVENTEEN

The brain — a supercomputer

The possibility of building a flying saucer greatly interested me. If one examines the principle of propulsion just as a hypothesis, it is still a new one. A flying saucer, however, is a complex machine and is not a high-priority item for us earthlings.

For that reason I wanted to hear something that would be understandable right away. I wanted a 'something' that did not require any investigation of scholarly minds, but could be immediately put into practice in our daily lives and benefit everyone. I began asking Anastasia to come up with a solution to a question that our society was being confronted with today. She agreed, but asked:

"Could you at least put it in more specific terms, this question? How can I solve something when I do not know what you have in mind?"

I began thinking: What was the number one problem we faced today, and the following terms came to mind:

"You know, Anastasia, our major cities right now are confronted with a most acute problem — environmental pollution. The air in these cities is so bad it's hard to breathe."

"But you yourselves are the ones polluting it."

"We realise that. Please, hear me out, only don't go philosophising about how we must be purer ourselves, have more trees around and so forth. Just take things as they are today and think up something — for example, how to reduce the pollution in our major cities by fifty percent without costing the treasury — the government, that is — any extra money. And make it so that your plan will be the most logical of all possible alternatives, and that it will be capable of instant implementation so that I and everyone else cannot fail to understand it."

"I shall try at once," Anastasia replied. "Have you specified all the terms?"

I thought I should try and make it even more complex, just in case her mind and abilities really turned out to be truly superior to what our own powers of reasoning allowed. So I added:

"And make whatever you think up to be profit-generating!"

"For whom?"

"For me, and for the country too. You live within the borders of Russia, so make it the whole of Russia."

"Are we talking about money?"

"Yes."

"An enormous amount of money?"

"Profit, Anastasia — well, money — is never an enormous amount. But I need enough money to be able to pay for this expedition and have enough left over for a new one. And as for Russia..."

I thought for a moment... I thought: *What if I managed to get Anastasia just a little interested in the material benefits of our civilisation?* and then asked:

"You wouldn't want anything for yourself?"

"I have everything," she replied.

But all at once an idea came to me — something that might possibly interest her.

"How about this, Anastasia: let's have your plan make enough money to provide free seeds — or at least seeds at a discount — to all your beloved dachniks, or gardeners, throughout Russia!"

"Terrific!" Anastasia exclaimed. "What a wonderful idea! If you have finished, I shall now get to work. How delightful that sounds! Seeds... Or... is there anything else you wish to add?"

"No, Anastasia, that's enough for now."

I felt her inspiration and excitement not only over the task itself, but especially over the free seeds for her dachniks. Yet at that point I still felt convinced that, even with her special abilities, a solution to the problem of air pollution was simply out of the question, else our many scientific institutions would have come up with one long ago.

With a bustle of energy this time, not her usual calm and quiet self, Anastasia lay down on the grass, her arms widespread. Her curled fingers reached their cushioned tips upward, alternating between motion and stillness, while her eyelids trembled on her closed eyes.

She lay there for about twenty minutes, then opened her eyes, sat up and said:

"I have come up with it. But what a nightmare it is!"

"What have you come up with, and what's this about a nightmare?"

"The greatest harm is coming from your so-called automobiles. There are so many of them in the large cities and every one of them is emitting both an unpleasant odour and substances harmful to human bodies. The most frightening thing is that these substances are mixing with earth- or dust-particles, and impregnating them. The movement of the automobiles picks up the impregnated dust, and people are breathing in this horrible mess. It gets swept into the air, and then settles on the grass and the trees, covering everything around. This is very bad. It is very harmful to the health of both people and plants."

"Of course it's bad. Everybody knows it's bad, only nobody can *do* anything about it. We have street-cleaning machines, but they can't keep up. You, Anastasia, have discovered absolutely nothing new, you haven't thought up any original solution to purify our air."

"All I did just now was to determine the basic source of the danger. Now I shall think about it further and analyse it... I need to concentrate for a long time, perhaps as long as an hour, since I have never dealt with a problem like this before. So that you will not be bored, do go for a walk in the forest or—"

"You get on with your thinking. I'll find something to do."

And Anastasia withdrew into herself. Coming back an hour later, after a walk in the forest, I found her, as it appeared to me, in a state of some discontent, and I said:

"You see, Anastasia, you and that brain of yours aren't capable of doing anything either. Only don't worry about it — we've got a lot of scientific institutions working on this question. But they, just like you, can only describe the fact that pollution is going on. They haven't been able to do anything about it yet."

She answered in a somewhat apologetic tone:

"I have gone over in my mind, I believe, all the possible variants, but I do not see any way of quickly reducing the pollution by fifty percent."

My mind was at once set on the alert: she had found some sort of solution after all.

"So, what kind of reduction did you come up with?" I asked.

She sighed.

"Not that much. I managed to achieve... thirty-five to forty percent."

"What?!" I couldn't help exclaiming.

"Pretty poor result, eh?" asked Anastasia.

A lump formed in my throat, I realised she was incapable of lying, exaggerating or downplaying anything she said. Trying to restrain my excitement, I said:

"Let's change the terms of the project — let's say thirty-eight percent. Quick, tell me what you've come up with."

"Your automobiles must be equipped to not only scatter this foul dust, but to collect it as well."

"How can we do that? Talk faster!"

"Those things sticking out in front of the automobiles, what are they called?"

"Bumpers?" I offered.

"All right, bumpers. Inside them or below them should be attached a little box with small holes facing frontwards. There should also be holes on its back side, so that air can escape. While the automobiles are in motion, air laden with this harmful dust will be drawn in through the front holes, purified, and then escape through the back holes, and that air will already be twenty percent less polluted."

"And what about the remaining twenty percent?"

"Right now virtually none of this dust is removed, but with this method there will be a lot less of it in the air, since it will be collected all over the place every day. I have calculated that in one month, with the help of these little boxes, if they are fitted on all automobiles, the amount of polluting dust will decrease by forty percent. Beyond that there will be no reduction, since other factors are at work."

"What size of boxes, and what should they contain? How many holes and at what distance from each other?"

"Vladimir, perhaps you would like me to personally attach them to every single automobile?"

For the first time I perceived that Anastasia had a sense of humour, and I began to laugh at the thought of her attaching her little boxes to all our cars. She laughed too, delighting in my cheerful mood and began whirling her way across the glade.

The principle was really very simple — the rest was merely a question of logistics. Already, without Anastasia's help, I was beginning to imagine how it could all be: orders from administrative heads, motor-vehicle inspection control, turning in old filters for new ones at filling stations, a system of vouchers and so forth. A routine regulation, just like seat-belts.

All it had taken back then was one stroke of the pen, and presto! — seat-belts in every family car. And here too, one stroke of the pen, and, again, presto! — cleaner air! And there would be tough competition among entrepreneurs for orders to supply the boxes, a good deal of work for the manufacturing plants, and the main thing, of course, cleaner air!

"Wait," I said, turning once more to Anastasia, who was still whirling around in a boisterous dance.

"What should be put into those boxes?"

"Into those boxes... into those boxes... You will come up with a little something. It is very simple," she replied, without stopping.

"And where is my money going to come from, and to supply seeds for the dachniks?" came another question.

She stopped.

"What do you mean, where from? You wanted my idea to be the most rational of all — and that is exactly what I have thought up: the most rational solution there can be. It will spread to large cities throughout the world and for this idea they will pay Russia enough to supply the free seeds, and enough to pay you. Only you will receive your payment under certain conditions."

I didn't pay attention immediately to her remark about the 'certain conditions', but began focusing in on something else:

"So, we should patent it? Otherwise who would pay of their own free will?"

"Why would they not pay? They will pay, and I can even set the rates right now. From the production of these boxes, Russia will get two percent, and you will get one hundredth of a percent."

"What's the good of your setting the rates? You do have a few strong points, but when it comes to business you're still a complete ignoramus. Nobody will pay voluntarily. Even when there are signed agreements they don't always pay. If only you knew how many there are in our world that don't![1] Our arbitration courts are overloaded. By the way, do you know what an arbitration court is?"

"I can guess. But in this case they will pay faithfully. Anyone who does not pay will go bankrupt. Only honest people will prosper."

"What will make them go bankrupt? Don't tell me you're in the racket business?!"

"What *are* you imagining now? What gave you that idea?! They themselves — or rather, circumstances themselves will overtake any cheaters and *make* them go bankrupt."

And then the thought dawned on me — given that Anastasia is incapable of lying and, as she herself said, the systems inherent in Nature do not allow her to make a mistake: it means that before stating any conclusions, she must have processed in her brain an enormous amount of information, made zillions of mathematical calculations, and taken into account a whole mass of psychological characteristics of the people who would be participating in her project. In our terms, she not only solved the most difficult question of purifying the air, but also drew up and analysed a business plan, and all that in roughly an hour and a half. I thought I had still better clarify certain details, and so I asked her:

"Tell me, Anastasia, you made some sort of calculations in your head, figuring out the percentage of pollution reduction,

---

[1]Following Russia's liberal economic reforms of 1992 (including abandonment of governmental control over prices and cessation of subsidies to unprofitable industries) the country witnessed run-away inflation and disruption of existing economic ties, resulting in mass unemployment, widespread bankruptcies, delays in salary payments of six months or more, and a crisis of non-payments between enterprises (goods shipped and services rendered from one business to another but not paid for), which plagued the national economy for years.

and the amount of money to be realised from the sale of your car-accessory boxes, filter replacements and so forth?"

"Calculations were made — in the greatest detail — and not just with the help of the brain—"

"Stop! Quiet! Let me tell you what I think... Does this mean you could compete with our top-of-the-line computers — let's say, Japanese or American computers?"

"But I do not find that very interesting," she replied, adding: "It is primitive and somewhat degrading. Competing with a computer — that is tantamount to... oh, how can I find you a good analogy? That is tantamount to hands or feet competing with a prosthesis — and not even with a full prosthesis, but just part of one. With the computer the most vital element is missing. And that most vital element is... *feelings*."

I started to argue the opposite, telling how in our world there are people considered very intelligent, respected in society, that play chess with computers. But when this and other arguments still failed to convince her, I started asking her to agree to do this for me and other people as a proof of the possibilities of the human brain. She finally agreed, and then I made the invitation more specific:

"So, I can officially announce your willingness to take part in a problem-solving contest with a Japanese supercomputer?"

"Why a Japanese?" Anastasia questioned.

"Because they are considered to be the best in the world."

"Well now! It will be better if I do it with all of them at once, so you will not have to ask me again to do such a boring thing!"

"Great!" I exclaimed enthusiastically. "Let's do it with all of them, only you'll have to think up a problem."

"All right," Anastasia reluctantly agreed. "But for a start, so as not to waste time on thinking one up, let them try solving the problem you put to me earlier, and see whether they confirm or refute my hypothesis. If they refute it, let them put forth their own. Let us be judged by life and by other people."

"Great, Anastasia! Good for you! That is most constructive. And how much time, do you think, should be allowed for them to come up with a solution? I think the hour and a half you took will not be enough for them. Let's give them three months."

"Three months it shall be."

"And I suggest the judging be left to anybody who wants to take part. If there're a lot of judges, then no one can influence the outcome for their own ulterior motives."

"So be it, but I would still like to talk with you about raising children..."

Anastasia considered the raising of children paramount and would always delight in talking about it. She wasn't particularly excited about my idea of competing with computers. However, I was very happy to have secured her co-operation. Now I want to invite all firms producing state-of-the-art computers to join a competition to solve the above-stated problem.

I still felt I had to clarify a point or two with Anastasia.

"And what prize should be offered to the winner?" I asked.

"I do not need anything!" she replied.

"Why did you think just of yourself? Are you so absolutely certain you're going to win?"

"Of course. I am Man, after all."

"Well, okay. What can you offer the firm who takes first place after you?"

"Well, I could give them some advice on how to perfect their primitive computer."

"Then it's settled."

Chapter Eighteen

"In him was life; and the life was the light of men"

The Gospel of John

Upon my request Anastasia took me to see the ringing cedar which her grandfather and great-grandfather had talked about. It was not very far from the glade. The tree, approximately forty metres tall, rose slightly higher than its neighbours, but its principal distinguishing feature was the aureole radiating from its glistening crown — similar to the halos around the faces of saints depicted on icons. The aureole was not even — it pulsated, and at its upper tip one could see a thin ray of light beaming into the infinity of the heavens.

The spectacle was dazzling and absolutely charming.

At Anastasia's suggestion I pressed the palms of my hands to its trunk. I could hear a ringing or crackling noise, comparable to what one might hear standing under a high-voltage transmission line, only more resonant.

"It was I who happened to discover a way to send its energy back into Space and then have it distributed here on Earth," Anastasia told me. "You see how its bark has been torn off in various places. That is where the bear was climbing it. It was quite a challenge to get her to carry me up to the first branches. I clung on to the fur on her neck. She would climb and then let out a roar, climb and roar. After reaching the lowest branches, I was able to clamber up from branch to branch, right to the top. I sat there for two days and thought of everything I could to save the tree. I stroked the tree, and shouted up into the sky, but nothing helped.

"Then Grandfather and Great-Grandfather arrived. You can imagine the scene — there they were standing down below, reprimanding me and demanding that I climb down. I in turn demanded that they tell me what could be done with the tree. How to save the ringing cedar, since nobody was cutting it down. They would not tell me. But I felt that they knew the answer. Grandfather, old trickster that he is, tried to lure me down, promising to help me establish a connection with a certain woman I had been unable to reach on my own.

"This was a woman I very much wanted to help. Earlier, Grandfather would only be annoyed by my desire to spend so much time on her instead of doing other things. But I knew that he could not help me, as Great-Grandfather had twice tried to do this behind Grandfather's back, and he failed too.

"At that point Grandfather really began putting up a fuss. He seized hold of a branch, ran around the cedar tree and beat the air with the branch, shouting that I was the most hare-brained member of the family, that I was acting illogically, that I refused to accept sound advice and that he would give my bottom a good whipping. And again he beat the air with the branch. Now that was a real 'humdinger' of a threat, and even Great-Grandfather burst out laughing. I too gave a hearty laugh. In doing so I inadvertently broke a branch at the top, and a glow began emanating from it. And I heard Great-Grandfather's voice, serious, commanding and entreating all at the same time:

"'Do not touch anything more, little one. Come down very carefully. You have already done enough!'

"I obeyed and climbed down. Great-Grandfather silently embraced me. Trembling all over, he pointed at the tree, on which more and more branches were beginning to glow. Then a ray formed, pointing upward. Now the ringing cedar would not burn up — through its little ray it would give everything it had saved up for the past five hundred years to people and to the Earth. Great-Grandfather explained that the ray had formed in the exact spot where I had shouted upward and had inadvertently broken a branch while I was laughing. Great-Grandfather said that if I had touched the ray emanating from the broken branch, my brain would have exploded, as there was too much energy and information in this little ray. That was exactly how my Papa and Mama had perished..."

Anastasia put her hands on the mighty trunk of the ringing cedar she had saved, and pressed her cheek against it. After pausing for a while, she continued her story.

"They, my Papa and Mama, once came upon a ringing cedar just like this one. Only Mama had been doing everything a little differently, since she did not know. She had climbed up into a neighbouring tree, from which she reached out and touched one of the lower branches of the ringing cedar and broke it off, inadvertently exposing herself to the ray which flamed up out of the broken branch. The branch had been pointing downward, and the ray went down into the Earth. It is very bad, very harmful, when such energy falls into the Earth.

"When Papa came, he saw this ray, and saw my Mama, who had been left hanging, one hand still firmly grasping the *ordinary cedar* branch. In the other hand she held the broken branch of the *ringing cedar.*

"Papa, no doubt, had an immediate grasp of everything that had happened. He climbed up the ringing cedar, right to the top. Grandfather and Great-Grandfather saw him break off the upper branches, but they did not glow, while more and more of the lower ones began glowing. Great-Grandfather said that Papa realised that it would not be long before he would never be able to climb down. The upward-beaming ray with its pulsating glow failed to appear. All that was going on was more and more thin rays shining downward. An upward ray did appear when Papa broke off a large branch pointing up. And even though it was not glowing, he bent it and pointed it at himself.

"When it did flame up, Papa still managed to unclasp his hands, the branch straightened and the ray from the branch directed itself toward the sky, and then the pulsating aureole formed.

"Great-Grandfather said that at the last moment of his life Papa's brain was able to take in an enormous flood of energy and information, and that he was able, in some incredible way, to clear his mind of all previously accumulated information, and so was able to gain the time required to unclasp his hands and direct the branch upward just before his brain exploded."

Anastasia once more stroked the cedar trunk with her hands, once more pressed her cheek against it and stood stock still, smiling, listening to the ringing of the cedar.

"Anastasia, that cedar nut oil,[1] are its healing properties stronger or weaker than the pieces of the ringing cedar?"

"The same. Provided the nuts are gathered at the proper time and with the proper attitude toward the cedar. Provided the tree bestows them of itself."

"Do you know how to do that?"

"Yes, I do."

"Will you tell me?"

"All right. I shall tell you."

---

[1] *cedar nut oil* — see footnote 25 in Chapter 1: "The ringing cedar" above.

CHAPTER NINETEEN

The need to change
one's outlook on the world

I asked Anastasia about the woman over whom she had a disagreement with her grandfather. I asked her why she had been unable to establish a connection with her and why she thought this contact was necessary.

"You see," Anastasia began her story, "it is very important, when two people join their lives together, that they have a spiritual attraction to each other. Unfortunately, as a rule, everything starts with the carnal. For example, you see a beautiful girl and desire to possess her. You still have not seen the individual — the Man — or her soul. Very often people join their destinies together only on the basis of carnal attraction. Either that quickly passes or it is transferred to someone else. What then keeps people together?

"To find a kindred spirit with whom one can attain true happiness is not all that complicated. Your technocratic world, however, puts up massive interference. The woman I am trying to reach lives in a large city, and regularly travels to the same place each day — probably to her work. Either there or on the way she finds or meets up with a man who is very close to her spirit, one with whom she could be really happy and, most importantly, one with whom she could bear a child capable of bringing so much good into the world. Because they would co-create this child with the same impulsion as we did.

"But there is no way this man can bring himself to tell this woman that he loves her, and she herself is partly to blame for this. Just think: he looks into her face and sees, as it were, his heart's desire, the apple of his eye, while she, as soon as she feels someone's gaze upon her, perks up right away, and 'unwittingly' tries to lift her skirt higher. And so on. This man is at once carnally aroused, but he does not know her well, and so he then goes to someone he is better acquainted with, someone he feels is more accessible, but still led on by these same carnal desires.

"I want to suggest to this woman what she should do, but I cannot break through to her. Her brain will not open to the awareness of new information, even for a second. It is constantly pre-occupied with issues of day-to-day living. Can you imagine, one time I followed her for a whole twenty-four hours! What a terrible sight! Grandfather then got upset with me for not working enough with the dachniks and for spreading myself too thin, and sticking my nose in where it does not belong.

"When this woman wakes in the morning, her first thought is not to delight in the coming day but how to prepare something to eat. She gets upset over some missing food item, and then gets upset over something you smear on your face in the morning, like face-cream or rouge. She spends her whole time thinking how she is going to get it. She is always late and is constantly on the run, trying not to miss first one form of transport and then the next.

"At her regular destination her brain is overloaded with — how shall I put it — all sorts of *nonsense,* at least from my point of view. On the one hand it is supposed to give her face a business-like expression and fulfil the job tasks she is assigned. All this while she is thinking about one of her girlfriends or acquaintances and getting angry at them. Yet at the same time she is listening to everything going on around her. And, can you imagine, the same routine is repeated day after day like clockwork.

"On her way home, when people notice her, she can put on the appearance of an almost happy woman. But she is continually thinking about problems, or her make-up, or looking at clothes in shop windows — above all, clothes that will expose her alluring charms, supposing that this will result in some kind of miracle, except in her case everything happens the wrong way around. She gets home and starts house-cleaning. She thinks she is relaxing when she watches her television and prepares her meals, but the main thing is, she thinks about good things only for a split second. Even when she goes to bed, she is still mulling over her daily cares and stays in the same mental rut.

"If only she could turn away from her thoughts even just for a moment during the day and think of—"

"Wait, Anastasia! Explain specifically how you see her, her outward appearance and clothing, and tell me what she should be thinking about at the moment when this man is with her. What should she do to make him at least attempt to tell her he loves her?"

Anastasia explained everything in the minutest detail. I shall only mention here what I consider to be the most important points.

"Her dress should come to just below the knee. It should be green with a white collar and no cleavage. She should wear hardly any make-up, and listen with interest to the person talking to her."

"And that's it?" I remarked upon hearing such a simple explanation.

To which Anastasia remarked:

"There is so much underlying these simple elements. In order for her to choose that particular dress, change her make-up and look at that person with genuine interest, she will have to change her whole outlook on the world."

CHAPTER TWENTY

A mortal sin

"I still need to tell you, Vladimir, about the terms under which you will receive money in the bank, when there will be a great deal of money in your accounts."

"Go ahead, Anastasia, it will be a pleasant experience," I replied.

However, I was devastated by what I heard. Judge for yourselves: here is what she set forth:

"In order to withdraw the money from your bank account, you must meet the following conditions: first of all, for three days before receiving it you must not drink anything alcoholic. When you arrive at the bank, the manager must verify, with the help of the devices you have, your compliance with this condition in the presence of not less than two witnesses. If this first condition is met, you may then proceed to carry out the second: you must do no less than nine deep knee-bends in front of the bank manager and the two witnesses present."

When the significance — or rather, the absurdity — of her words finally sunk in, I jumped up, and she stood up as well. I couldn't believe my ears and double-checked:

"First they're going to check my alcohol content, and then I am to do at least nine deep knee-bends in front of witnesses, is that it?"

"Yes," responded Anastasia. "And for each knee-bend they will be able to release from your account no more than one million of your roubles at their present worth."

I was overwhelmed by a sense of rage, anger and annoyance.

"What did you say that for? Well, what for?! I was feeling so good. I believed you. I was starting to think that you were right about a lot of things, that there was logic in your arguments. But you... Now I am absolutely convinced that you're a schizophrenic, a stupid hick, a mad woman! This latest thing you said has wiped out everything else. It's completely devoid of any sense or logic — that's not just my opinion, any sane person would agree with me. Ha! Don't tell me you also want me to write out these conditions in your book?"

"Yes."

"Now you've really gone mad. Do you mean to tell me you were planning to write out instructions to the banks or publish this order?"

"No. They will read it in the book, and they will act accordingly with you. Otherwise they can expect to go bankrupt."

"Oh, my God!!! And I've been listening to this creature three days already? Don't tell me you would like the bank manager to do knee-bends with me too in the presence of witnesses?"

"It would be good for him, as it will be for you. But for them I have not set such strict conditions as I have for you."

"So, you're only doing this for *my* benefit? Do you have the slightest idea what a mockery you've made of me? See what the love of a crazy recluse can spill over into! Only it won't work — not one single bank will ever agree to serve me under those conditions, no matter how much you have visualised such a situation. Now your dreams have gone too far!... Well, you can stand here and do all the deep knee-bends you want, you nincompoop!"

"The banks will agree and, whether you know it or not, will open accounts for you — granted, only those banks which are willing to operate ethically, and people will trust them and come to them," Anastasia went on, not budging an inch from her position.

I found myself becoming increasingly irritated and angry. Angry with myself or angry at Anastasia. Come on now, think how long I've listened to her, trying to understand what she was saying, and here she's turned out to be simply half-crazy. I started laying into her, using, to put it mildly, some pretty coarse language.

She stood there, leaning with her back to a tree, her head just slightly bowed. One hand was clasped to her chest, the other was raised upward, lightly waving.

I recognised that gesture. She used it every time she needed to bring calm to the surrounding natural environment so I wouldn't get fearful of it, and I realised why she needed to calm them down on this occasion.

Every insulting or coarse word directed at Anastasia felt like a whip cracking against her flesh, making her whole body tremble.

I fell silent. I sat down again on the grass, turned away from Anastasia, deciding I'd better calm down myself and head back to the riverbank, and not talk with her any more at all. But when I heard her voice call out behind me, I was amazed that it didn't have the slightest hint of resentment or rebuke:

"You know, Vladimir, everything bad that happens to Man is brought on by Man himself, whenever he disobeys the laws of spiritual being and breaks his connection with Nature.

"The forces of darkness try to distract their attention with the temporary attraction of your technocratic way of life, to make them forget the simple truths and commandments set forth way back in the Bible. And they all too often succeed.

"One of the mortal sins of Man is pride. Most people are subject to it, this sin. I shall not at the moment go into all the terrible, disastrous effects it produces. After you return home and try to make sense of it, you will understand, either on your own or through the help of enlightened individuals who will stand by you. For now I shall just say this: the forces of darkness, which are diametrically opposed to the forces of light, are every moment working to make sure Man does not let go of this sin, and money is one of their basic tools in this campaign.

"They were the ones that thought up this concept of money. Money is like a high-tension zone. The forces of darkness are proud of this invention. They even think themselves stronger than the forces of light for having come up with money. And for being able to use money to distract people from their true purpose.

"This great confrontation has lasted for millennia, and Man is at its centre. But I do not want *you* to be enslaved to this sin.

"I realise that mere explanations are not enough to settle this question. Because in spite of thousands of years of explanations mankind has not understood nor discovered the means of counteracting this sin. It is only natural that you would not be able to discover it either. But I really, very much, want to save you from this mortal danger which can corrupt the spirit. That is why I thought up a special situation just for you, one that would cause this device of the forces of darkness to be broken, or fail, or even work the opposite way, for the extermination of the sin.

"That is why they have become so enraged. Their anger has been implanted in you, and you for your part started shouting your insults at me. They wanted to make me angry at you in return, but I will never do that. I realised that what I thought up would hit the mark precisely, and now it is clear that their system which has worked flawlessly for thousands of years can indeed be broken. Right now I have done this only for you, but I shall think up something for other people too.

"Now what harm is there in drinking less of that alcoholic poison and in becoming less arrogant and stubborn? What were you so upset over? Of course, it was pride that was upsetting you."

She fell silent, and I thought: *Improbable as it is, her brain — or something besides — may have imbued this comic, utterly abnormal situation of doing deep knee-bends in a bank with such a deep meaningfulness that there really could be some logic in it. I'd better think about this a little more calmly.*

All my anger at Anastasia passed and, in its place, arose a feeling of uneasy guilt. However, instead of apologising on the spot, I simply turned to her with a desire for reconciliation. Anastasia, it seemed, could feel my inner state. She at once gave a joyful shudder all over and began talking at top speed.

CHAPTER TWENTY-ONE

Touching Paradise

"Your brain is tired of listening to me, and yet I still have so much I want to tell you. I do so want to... But you need to rest. Let us sit again for a little while."

We sat down on the grass. Anastasia took me by the shoulders and drew me close to her. The back of my head touched her breasts, which gave me a pleasant warm feeling.

"Do not be afraid of me, let yourself go," she quietly said and lay down on the grass so that it would be more comfortable for me to rest. She ran the fingers of one of her hands through my hair, as if combing it, while the fingertips of her other hand quickly touched my forehead and temples. Occasionally she would lightly press down with her fingernails at various points on the top of my head. All this gave me a feeling of tranquillity and enlightenment. Then, putting her hands on my shoulders, Anastasia said:

"Listen now... and please tell me what sounds you hear around you."

I listened, and my hearing caught a wide range of sounds, all different in tonality, rhythm and continuity.

I began naming the sounds aloud: the birds singing in the trees, the chirping and clicking of insects in the grass, the rustle of the leaves, the fluttering and flapping of birds' wings. I named everything I could hear, then fell silent and went on listening. This was pleasant and very interesting for me.

"You have not named everything," Anastasia observed.

"Everything," I replied. "Well, maybe I left out something not very significant or something I didn't catch — not anything important, that is."

"Vladimir, do you not hear how my heart is beating?" asked Anastasia.

Could I really have not been paying attention to this sound? The sound of her heart beating?

"Yes," I hastened to respond. "Of course I hear it, I hear it very well, it is beating evenly and calmly."

"Try to memorise the intervals of the various sounds you hear. You can choose the principal sounds and memorise them."

I selected the chirping of some insect, the cawing of a crow and the gurgling and splash of the water in the stream.

"Now I shall increase the tempo of my heartbeat and you listen to see what happens all around."

Anastasia's heartbeat increased in frequency, and right away the rhythm of sounds I could hear around me joined in with a heightened tonality.

"That's astounding! Simply incredible!" I exclaimed. "What are you saying, Anastasia, are they so sensitive to the rhythm of your heartbeat?"

"Yes. Everything — absolutely everything: a little blade of grass, a big tree, even the bugs — they all react to any change in the rhythm of my heart. The trees accelerate their inner processes, and work harder to produce oxygen."

"Is this how all the plants and animals in people's environment react?" I asked.

"No. In your world they do not understand to whom they should react, and you do not try to make contact with them. Besides, you do not understand the purpose of such contact, and do not give them sufficient information about yourselves.

"Something similar might happen between plants and the people who work on their little garden-plots, if only people would do everything I outlined to you, imbue the seed with information about themselves and begin to communicate more consciously with their plants. Do you want me to show you what Man will feel when he makes such contact?"

"Of course I want you to. But how will you do that?"

"I shall tune the rhythm of my heartbeat to yours, and you will feel it."

She slid her hand inside my shirt. Her warm palm lightly pressed against my chest. Little by little her heart adjusted its tuning and began beating in the same rhythm as mine. And something most amazing happened: I felt an unusually pleasant sensation, as though my mother and my relatives were right there beside me. A sense of softness and good health came over my body, and my heart was filled with joy, freedom and a whole new sense of creation.

The range of surrounding sounds caressed me and communicated the truth — not a truth comprehensible in all its detail, just something I felt intuitively. I had the impression that all the pleasing and joyous feelings I had ever experienced in my life were now merging into a single and wonderful sensation. Perhaps it is this sensation that is called *happiness.*

But as soon as Anastasia began to change the rhythm of her heartbeat, the wonderful sensation started to leave me. I asked:

"More! Please, let me feel it some more, Anastasia!"

"I cannot do that for long. After all, I have my own rhythm."

"Even just a little bit more," I pleaded.

And once again Anastasia brought back the sensation of happiness, just for a short time, and then everything faded, but not without leaving me with a small taste of the pleasant and radiant sensation as a memory of it. We remained silent for a while, and then I felt like hearing Anastasia's voice again, and I asked:

"Was it this good for the first people — Adam and Eve? You just lie around, enjoy life and prosper — everything at hand?... Only it can become boring if there's nothing to do."

Instead of answering my question, Anastasia asked one of her own:

"Tell me, Vladimir, do many people think of Adam, the first Man, as you thought just now?"

"Probably the majority. But what was there for them to do, in Paradise? It was only later that Man started to develop and invent things. Man developed through labour. He became smarter thanks to labour."

"Yes, labour is needful, but the first Man was infinitely smarter than his descendants today, and his labour was more meaningful, it demanded considerable intelligence, awareness and will."

"But what did Adam do in Paradise? Did he tend a garden? That is something that can be done today by any gardener, not to mention plant-breeding specialists! Nothing more is said in the Bible about Adam's activity."

"If the Bible told everything in detail, it would be impossible to read through it in a single human lifetime. One must *understand* the Bible — there is so much information behind each verse. Do you want to know what Adam did? I shall tell you. But first, remember that it is the Bible that tells us that God assigned Adam the task of giving names and specifying the purpose of every creature living on the Earth. And he — Adam — did this. He did what all the scientific institutions in the world taken together have not yet been able to do."

"Anastasia, do you turn to God yourself, do you ask Him for anything for yourself?"

"What more can I ask, when so much has already been given me? It is my task to thank Him and help Him."

CHAPTER TWENTY-TWO

Who will bring up our son?

On the way back to the river, as Anastasia was escorting me to my motorboat, we sat down to rest in the place where she had left her outer clothing, and I asked her:

"Anastasia, how will we bring up our son?"

"Try to understand, Vladimir: you are not yet ready to bring him up. And when his eyes first take in a conscious awareness of the world, you should not be there."

I seized her by the shoulders and gave her a shaking.

"What are you saying? What liberties are you taking here? I can't understand how you could have come to such one-sided conclusions. Anyway, even though the mere fact of your existence is incredible, that doesn't give you the right to decide everything yourself and in violation of all the rules of logic!"

"Calm down, Vladimir, please. I do not know what logic you have in mind, but do try and make sense of it, calmly."

"What am I to make sense of? The child is not only yours, he's mine too, and I want him to have a father, I want him to be well taken care of, and get an education."

"Please understand, he does not need any kind of material benefits, as you see them. He will have everything right from the start. Even in his infancy he will be taking in and making sense of so much information that your kind of education will be simply ludicrous. It is the same as sending a learned mathematician back to Grade One.

"You want to bring the baby some kind of senseless toy, but he has absolutely no need of it whatsoever. You are the one who needs it for your own self-satisfaction: 'Oh look at me, I'm so good and caring!' If you think that you will do some good by offering your son a car or anything else along that line, well, he can get it himself just by wishing for it. Be calm and think about something specific you could tell your son, think about what you could teach him, think about what you have done in life that he might find interesting."

Anastasia continued talking in soft, quiet tones, but her words still made me tremble.

"You see, Vladimir, when he begins to make sense of creation, you will look like an underdeveloped creature next to him. Do you really want that, do you really want your son to see you standing there like a dimwit? The only thing that can bring the two of you together is your level of mental purity, but few attain that level in your world. You must strive to attain it."

I realised that it was absolutely useless to argue with her, and I cried out in despair.

"Does that mean he'll never know anything about me?"

"I shall tell him about you, about your world, when he is able to comprehend it in a meaningful way and make his own decisions. What he will do then, I do not know."

Despair, pain, resentment, fearful conjecture — all these swirled around in my brain. I felt like smashing this beautiful intellectual recluse's face with all my might.

I understood everything. And what I understood left me breathless.

"It's all clear! Now it's all clear to me! You... You had no-body to bang with to give you a child. That business at the beginning — that was all just an act, you sly vixen! You made yourself into a nun! You needed a child. But you *did* go to Moscow. She 'sold her mushrooms and berries'. Ha! You could have got yourself a shag there right on the street. All you had to do was take off that jacket and shawl of yours and you would have had takers right off. Then you wouldn't have needed to spin your web and trap me in it.

"Of course! You needed a man who was dreaming about a son. And now you've got yours! Did you ever think about the child? About your son? One destined in advance to live the life of a recluse. To live the way *you* think he should. Come on now, here she's been sounding off about 'the truth'. You've got an awful lot of gall, you hermit!

"What is it with you — truth as a last resort? Well, did you ever think about me? Me! *I* dreamt about a son! I dreamt about passing along my business to him. I'd teach him to be a businessman. I wanted a son to love. And now how am I supposed to live? To live and know that your precious little son is crawling around unprotected somewhere out in the wilds of the taiga? With no future. With no father. That's what breaks my heart. But that's not something you can understand, you forest bitch!"

"Perhaps," Anastasia quietly responded, "your heart will gain the awareness it needs and everything will be all right? A pain like that will cleanse the soul, accelerate thought and summon you to creation."

But I was still burning with rage and anger. I wasn't in control of myself. I grabbed a stick. I ran away from Anastasia and began beating the stick against a small tree with all my might until the stick broke.

Then I turned to look at Anastasia standing there and... no sooner had I seen her than, incredibly, the anger started to leave. I thought to myself: oh, now I've gone and done it again — I lost control of myself and went wild. Just like the last time, when I swore at her.

Anastasia was standing there against a tree, one arm stretched upward, her head bent forward, as though withstanding the onslaught of a hurricane. With my anger completely gone, I went closer and began looking at her. Now her hands were clasped to her chest, her body slightly trembling. She didn't speak, only her kind, kind eyes were looking at me with the same tenderness as before. We stood there that way for some time, just looking at each other. And I started reflecting along these lines:

There's no doubt about it — she is incapable of lying.

She didn't have to say anything, but...

She knew it would be hard, and yet she spoke. Of course, that is another extreme. How can you possibly live if you must always tell the truth, and say only what you think?! But what can you do if that's the way she is and can't be anything else?

What's done is done. Everything happened the way it happened. Now she will be the mother of my son.

She will *be a mother, if she said so. Of course, she'll be a pretty strange mother. That lifestyle of hers... And her way of thinking... Oh, well, there's nothing to be done with her.*

Still, she's physically very strong. And kind. She really knows Nature well, knows the animals. And she's smart. In her own peculiar way, at least.

In any case she knows a lot about raising children. She kept wanting to talk about children the whole time. She'll nurture the boy. Somebody like her will definitely nurture him. She'll get him through the cold, through snowstorms even. They mean nothing to her. She'll nurture him, yes indeed. And she'll bring him up right.

And somehow I've got to adapt to the situation. I'll come and see them in the summertime, like going to a dacha. No way in the winter — I wouldn't make it. But in the summer I can play with my son. He'll grow up, and I'll tell him about people in big cities...

At any rate, this time I've got to apologise to her...

And I said:

"I'm sorry, Anastasia, I got nervous again."

And right off she said:

"You are not to blame. Only do not be hard on yourself. Do not worry. After all, you were concerned about your son.

You were afraid that things would turn out bad for him, that the mother of your son was just an ordinary bitch. That she could not love with real human love. But you must not worry. You must not get upset. You talked that way because you did not know, you did not know anything about my love, my darling."

CHAPTER TWENTY-THREE

Through a window of time

"Anastasia, if you are so smart and omnipotent, that means you could help me too?"

She looked up at the sky, and then again at me.

"In the whole of the Universe there is no being capable of more powerful development and greater freedom than Man. All other civilisations bow before Man. All sorts of civilisations have the capability of developing and bringing themselves to perfection, but only in one direction, and they are not free. The greatness of Man is beyond even their grasp. God — the Great Mind — created Man and to no one else gave He more than to Man."

I could not make sense — at least right off — of what she was saying. And again I uttered the same question, pleading for help, not fully understanding what kind of help I needed.

She asked me:

"What is it that you have in mind? Do you want me to cure all your physical ailments?

"That is a simple matter for me. I already did this six months ago, only in the principal area of need no benefit came about: the dark and destructive elements common to people of your world have not lessened in you. And your various aches and pains are trying to come back again... 'She's a witch, a mad-woman hermit, I ought to be getting out of here at once!' you are probably thinking, right?"

"Yes," I answered in amazement. "That is exactly what I was thinking — you read my mind?"

"I surmised that that is what you might be thinking. Indeed, it is written all over your face. Tell me, Vladimir, do you not... well... remember, at least a little, having seen me before?"

The question dumbfounded me, and I began carefully examining her facial features. Especially her eyes. I really began to think that I might have seen them somewhere before, but where?

"Anastasia, you said yourself that you spend all your time in the forest. How then could I have seen you?"

She gave me a smile and ran off.

A short while later Anastasia came out from behind the bushes dressed in a long skirt, a brown buttoned cardigan, her hair done up in a shawl. But without the quilted jacket in which she had greeted me on the riverbank. And the shawl was tied just a bit differently. Her clothes were clean, though not stylish, and her shawl covered her forehead and neck... and I remembered her.

CHAPTER TWENTY-FOUR

A strange girl

The summer before, our convoy ship had docked at one of the villages not far from these parts. We needed to buy bulk meat for the restaurant and spend some time in port.

Sixty kilometres farther on there would be a particularly dangerous section of the river, which meant our ship could not travel through there at night (certain sections of the river were not equipped with navigation lights). So as not to waste time, we began announcing over our outdoor loudspeaker system as well as the local radio that we were throwing a party that evening aboard our vessel.

The sleek white ship standing at the dock, glistening with a huge array of lights, and alive with the music pouring forth from it inevitably attracted the young people of the village to such occasions. Indeed, on this particular evening, practically the entire local youth population could be seen making its way to the ship's gangplank.

Upon coming aboard, like any first-time visitors, they immediately set about taking a look around the whole ship to see what they could see. After touring the main, middle and upper decks, they ended up congregating in the restaurant and bar. The female contingent, as a rule, took to dancing, while the male half preferred drinking. The unusual circumstance of being on a ship plus the music and alcohol always engendered a state of excitement, occasionally making big trouble for the crew. Almost always there was not enough time, and the party-goers made a collective appeal to extend the festivities just a bit longer — say, by half an hour, and then more and more into the night.

On this particular occasion I was alone in my cabin. I could hear the music wafting up from the restaurant, as I was trying to make modifications to the convoy's schedule for the remainder of the trip. All at once I felt myself being stared at. I turned around and glimpsed her eyes on the other side of the window glass. That was nothing unusual — visitors often liked looking into the ship's cabins.

I got up and opened the window. She didn't go away. She continued looking at me with some embarrassment. I felt I wanted to do something for this woman standing alone on the deck just outside my cabin. I wondered why she wasn't dancing like the others — perhaps she was somehow unhappy? I offered to show her around the ship, and she silently nodded. I took her all over the ship, showed her the main office — which frequently impressed visitors with its elegant appointments: the rug covering the floor, the soft leather furniture, the computers. Then I invited her into my cabin, which consisted of a study-cum-sleeping-quarters and a carpeted reception room equipped with fine furniture, TV and VCR. I was probably most delighted at the time to impress a poor country girl with the achievements of our civilised world.

I opened in front of her a box of candies, poured two glasses of champagne and, thinking to add the finishing touches to the impression, put on a videotape of Vika Tsyganova[1] singing "Love and death" (*Liubov i smert*). The videotape included a number of other songs performed by my favourite artists. She lightly touched the champagne glass to her lips, looked intently at me, and asked:

"A challenge, eh?"

---

[1]*Viktoria (Vika) Tsyganova (née Zhukova)* — a popular Russian singer born 1963 in Khabarovsk in the Russian Far East. Her singing and stage career began in the mid-1980s. Since then she has produced numerous albums. The song "Love and death" was recorded in 1994.

I expected just about any kind of question except that one. The expedition had *indeed* turned out to be quite a challenge, what with the difficult navigation conditions on the river and the crew (mainly students from the marine academy) smoking pot and pilfering merchandise from the store. We were frequently behind schedule and couldn't get to our planned stops on time where our arrival had been advertised in advance. These burdens and other worries often deprived me of the opportunity not only to admire the landscape along the river but even to get a normal sleep.

I muttered something meaningless to her — something like, "Never mind, we'll get through!", then turned toward the window and polished off my glass of champagne.

We went on talking about this, that or the other, listening to the videotape in the background. We talked right up until the ship docked once more at the end of the party cruise. Then I escorted her to the gangplank. Upon returning to my cabin, I made a mental note: there was something very strange and unusual about this woman, and I was left with an unexpected feeling of lightness and brightness after talking with her. That night I had my first good sleep in many days. At long last I understood why: the woman on the ship had been Anastasia.

"So that was you, Anastasia?!"

"Yes. It was there, in your cabin, that I memorised all the songs which I later sang to you in the forest. They were playing while we were talking. You see how simple it all is?"

"How did you happen to come on board?"

"I was interested in seeing what was going on, how you all lived. After all, Vladimir, I had been spending my whole time just taking care of dachniks.

"That day I had hurried to the village, sold the dried mushrooms which the squirrels had collected, and bought a ticket to your party cruise. Now I know a lot more about the class of people you call entrepreneurs. And I know you pretty well too.

"I feel I owe you a huge apology. I did not know how things would turn out, that I would be so drastically altering your future. Only I can no longer do anything about it, since *they* have seen to the fulfilment of this plan, and *they* are answerable only to God. For a time now you and your family will have great difficulties and challenges to overcome, but then that will all pass."

Still not understanding what Anastasia was specifically talking about, I intuitively felt that something was about to unfold itself to me that would go way beyond the usual parameters of our existence, something directly concerning me.

I asked Anastasia to tell me in more detail what she meant by altering my destiny, and "challenges". Listening to her at the time, I simply could not imagine how accurately her predictions would soon come to be realised in real life. She continued her recounting, once more bringing me back to events of the past year.

"Back then, on the ship," she said, "you showed me everything, even your cabin, treated me to candies, offered me champagne, and then escorted me to the gangplank, but I did not leave the riverbank right away. I stood on the shore near some bushes, and I could see through the lighted windows of the bar how the young people of the village were still dancing and having a good time.

"You showed me everything, but you did not take me to the bar. I guessed why — I was not appropriately dressed, my head was covered in a shawl, my cardigan was not stylish, my skirt was too long. But I could take off the shawl. My cardigan was neat and clean, and I had pressed my skirt carefully with my hands before I came to see you."

It was true: I had *not* taken Anastasia to the bar that evening, precisely on account of her rather strange clothes, beneath which, as it was now clear, this young girl had been hiding her remarkable beauty — something that immediately set her apart from everyone else. And I said to her:

"Anastasia, why would you have wanted to go to the bar? Do you mean you would have gone dancing there in your galoshes? Anyway, how would you know what dances young people do today?"

"I was not wearing galoshes at the time. When I exchanged my mushrooms for money to buy a ticket to your ship, I also bought a pair of shoes from the same woman. Granted, they were old shoes, and were tight on me, but I cleaned them with grass. As for dancing, all I would need is a one-time look, and that would be it. And what a dancer I would be!"

"You were, I suppose, offended at me that night?"

"I was not offended. But if you had taken me to the bar, I do not know whether that would have been a good or a bad move, but events might have turned out differently, and all this might not have happened. But I do not now regret that events happened the way they did."

"So *what* happened? What happened that night that was so terrible?"

"After you escorted me off the ship, you did not return right away to your cabin. First you dropped in to see the captain, and then the two of you headed for the bar. For you that was a normal thing to do. The moment you entered you both made an impression on the public. The captain looked prim and proper in his uniform. You were very elegant and gave a most respectable appearance. You were known to many in this village — the famous Megré. The owner of a convoy of ships unique in these parts. And you fully realised that you were making an impression.

"You sat down at a table with three young country girls. They were all only eighteen years old, just out of school.

"The waiters immediately brought champagne, candies and new wine-glasses to your table — prettier than the ones that were there before. You took one of the girls by the hand, bent over and started whispering something in her ear... compliments, I understand they are called. Then you danced with her several times and the conversation continued. The girl's eyes were radiant, as if she were in another world, a fairy-tale world. You took the girl out on deck, and gave her a tour of the ship, just as you had me. You took her into your cabin and treated her to champagne and candies just like me. But there was something a little different in the way you behaved with this young girl. You were in a cheerful mood. With me you were serious and even morose, but with her you were cheerful. I could see all that very well through the lighted window of your cabin and, possibly, I felt a little as though I wanted to be there in the place of that girl."

"You don't mean to tell me you were *jealous*, Anastasia?"

"I do not know, it was somehow an unfamiliar feeling for me."

I recalled that evening and these young country girls who were trying so hard to look older and more modern.

The next morning Captain Senchenko[2] and I once again had a laugh at their night-time antics on the dock. The night before, in my cabin, I'd realised that this girl was in such a state that she was ready to go to any lengths... but I didn't have any thought about wanting to possess her. I told Anastasia about this, and she replied:

"Still, you had stolen her heart. The two of you went out on deck, it was drizzling, and you threw your jacket over the girl's shoulders. Then you took her back to the bar."

[2] *Alexander Ivanovich Senchenko* — former captain of the *Patrice Lumumba*, later employed with the State River Transport Inspection Agency. Captain Senchenko was qualified to navigate not only the river, but Obsk Bight, where the Ob flows into the Karsk Sea.

"What were you doing, Anastasia, standing the whole time in the bushes in the rain?"

"That was nothing. The drizzle was good and caressing. Only it interfered with my view. And I did not want my skirt and shawl to get wet. They were my mother's. My mother left them to me. But I was very lucky. I found a cellophane bag on the shore. I took off my skirt and shawl, put them in the bag and hid it under my cardigan."

"Anastasia, if you didn't go home and it started to rain, you should have come back to the ship."

"I could not have done that. You had already seen me off, and you had other concerns. Besides, everything was shutting down.

"When the party came to an end and the ship was due to depart, at the girls' request, especially the girl who was with you in your cabin, you delayed the departure. At that point everything was in your power, including their hearts, and you were intoxicated with this power. The young people of the village were grateful to the girls, and the girls too felt imbued with a sense of power, through you. They completely forgot about the young lads who were with them in the bar, guys they had been friends with in school.

"You and the captain escorted them to the gangplank. Then you went back to your cabin. The captain went up to the bridge, and then the signal sounded, and the ship slowly, very slowly began to pull away from the dock. The girl you had danced with stood on the shore beside her girlfriends and the young people who had waited around to see the ship off.

"Her heart was beating so strongly, it was almost trying to leap out of her breast and fly away. Her thoughts and feelings were all mixed up.

"Behind her back could be seen the outlines of the village houses with their darkened windows, while in front of her the sleek white steamship was departing for ever, illuminated with a host of lights, still abundantly pouring forth its music across the water and the night-time riverbank.

"The sleek white ship was where *you* were, after saying so many marvellous things to her she had never heard before, so charming and alluring.

"And all that was slowly distancing itself from her, for ever.

"Then she decided to do something in the sight of everyone. She squeezed her fingers into a fist and began shouting desperately: 'I love you, Vladimir!' And she did it again, and again. Did you hear her shouting?"

"Yes," I replied.

"You could not help hearing her, and members of your crew heard her too. Some of them went out on deck and began laughing at the girl.

"I did not want them to laugh at the girl. Then they stopped laughing, as if they had suddenly come to their senses. But you did not come out on deck, and the ship continued slowly moving away. She thought you could not hear her, and she continued stubbornly crying out: 'I love you, Vladimir!'.

"Then some of her girlfriends joined in, and they all cried out together. I wondered what that feeling was like — *love,* which makes people lose control of themselves, or, perhaps, I wanted to help that girl, and so I shouted with them: 'I love you, Vladimir!'

"It seemed as though I had forgotten at that moment that it was not enough just to simply utter words — there definitely had to be behind them feelings, an awareness and trustworthiness of natural information.

"Now I know how strong that feeling is, and it is hardly subject to reason.

"The country girl later began to go into a slump and take to the bottle, and it was a challenge for me to help her. Now she is married and burdened down with everyday cares. And I have had to add her love to mine."

The story of the girl threw me a little off balance. Anastasia's account managed to resurrect that evening in my memory in full detail, and everything had really happened just as she said. It was very real.

Anastasia's unique declaration of love did not make any impression on me. After seeing her lifestyle and getting to know how she looked at the world, I saw her more and more as some unreal personage, even though here she was, sitting right beside me and all I had to do was reach out my hand and touch her. A consciousness accustomed to judge things by other criteria could not accept her as an existing reality. And while at the beginning of our encounter I *had* been attracted to her, she no longer aroused in me the emotions I once had. I asked:

"So, you think these new feelings appeared in you just by chance?"

"They are desirable, they are important," replied Anastasia. "They are pleasant even, but I wanted you to love me too. I realised that once you got to know me and my world a little more closely, you would not be able to accept me as a normal person — as simply *Man*. Perhaps you would even be afraid of me occasionally...

"And that is exactly what has happened. I myself am to blame. I have made many mistakes. I was anxious, for some reason, all the time. I was in a hurry, and I did not have the time to explain everything to you as I should. Perhaps it all just turned out silly? Eh? Do I need to reform myself?"

And with those words her lips hinted at a sad smile. She touched her breast with her hand, and I at once remembered what had happened that morning when I was in the glade with Anastasia.

CHAPTER TWENTY-FIVE

Bugs

That day I had decided to join in Anastasia's morning routine. Everything went fine at first — I stood under the tree and touched various little shoots. She kept telling me about different herbs, and then I lay down beside her on the grass. We were both completely naked, but even I wasn't cold — that might have been, of course, due to my running through the forest with her. I was in a splendid mood. I felt a sense of lightness, and not just physically, but inside me as well.

It all started when I felt a pinching sensation on my thigh. I raised my head and saw a small army of bugs crawling along my thigh and lower leg — including ants, and some sort of beetle. I lifted my arm to swat them, but to no avail. Anastasia seized my arm in mid-air and held it, saying: "Do not touch them." Then she got up on her knees in front of me, bent over and pinned my other hand to the ground. I lay there as if crucified. I tried to free my arms, but couldn't — I felt that was an impossibility. Then I tried to jerk myself free, with great effort. She kept restraining me, with very little effort, her smile never fading from her face. And still my body felt more and more crawling things, all tickling, biting and pinching, and I came to the conclusion that they were starting to eat me alive.

I was in her hands both literally and figuratively. Taking stock of the situation, I realised that nobody knew where I was, nobody would come here looking for me, and if they should happen to wander by, they would see my picked-over bones (indeed, if they saw any bones at all). And all sorts of things flashed through my head at that moment, and this was no doubt the reason my instinct for self-preservation kicked in, dictating the only feasible course of action in the situation. In desperation I sunk my teeth with all my might into Anastasia's bare breast, at the same time jerking my head from side to side. Upon hearing her scream I immediately loosened my grip on her breast. Anastasia loosened *her* hold, jumped up, one hand holding her breast, the other stretched upward, waving. She tried to smile. I too jumped up and shouted at her, feverishly brushing the crawling things off my body.

"You wanted to feed me to those vermin, you forest witch! Well, I don't give in that easily!"

She continued waving and responding with a forced smile to the elements of Nature around her, which had begun reacting warily to her situation. Anastasia looked at me and slowly — not with her usual spritely gait — walked toward the lake, her head bowed. I kept standing in the same spot for some time, thinking what I should do next — return to the riverbank? But how would I find the way? Follow Anastasia, but what would be the point? Nevertheless, I headed for the lakeshore.

Anastasia was sitting on the shore, rubbing tufts of grass between the palms of her hands and dabbing its juice on that part of her breast where a huge bruise left by my bite was clearly visible. It was probably very painful for her. But what had been her thought in attempting to restrain me? I hovered around her for a little while before asking:

"Does it hurt?"

Without turning her head, she replied:

"It hurts more inside." And she silently continued rubbing in the juice from the tufts of grass.

"Why were you thinking to play tricks on me?"

"I was trying to be helpful. The pores of your skin are all plugged up, they cannot breathe. The little bugs would have cleaned them out. It is not that painful — in fact it is rather pleasant."

"And the snake I saw, wasn't it touching my leg with its stinger?"

"It was not doing you any harm. Even if it had released its venom, it would have been only on the surface, and I would have rubbed it in at once.[1] The skin and muscles on your heel are deteriorating."

"That's on account of a car accident," I said.

For a time neither of us spoke. The whole situation felt rather silly. Not really knowing what to say, I asked her:

"What happened? Why did not that invisible someone help you again, as before, when I lost consciousness?"

"The reason he did not help, was that I was smiling. And when you began biting me, I tried to smile."

I began to feel guilty toward her. Picking up a tuft of grass, I rubbed it between my hands as hard as I could, then knelt down in front of her and began dabbing her bruise with my moistened palms.

---

[1] *rubbed it in* — It should be noted that ointments with snake's venom are used for skin and muscle disorders. Contrary to popular belief, the venom of the vast majority of snakes is only *slightly* toxic for humans. As long as it does not penetrate into the blood-stream all at once, but gradually through the skin and muscular tissue, the concentration of poison in the blood never reaches dangerous levels.

CHAPTER TWENTY-SIX

Dreams — creating the future

Now that I have learnt about Anastasia's feelings, about her desire to show, in spite of all her extraordinary traits, that she is still Man — a normal, natural human being, I realised what mental anguish I had caused her that morning. Once again I apologised to her. Anastasia responded that she wasn't angry, but now, after what she had done, she was afraid for me.

"What could you have possibly done that could be so frightful?" I asked, and once again I heard for the umpteenth time a story nobody should put forward seriously if they expect to be considered as normal as all the other people in our society. Nobody talks that way about themselves.

"When the ship left," Anastasia went on, "and the young people headed back to the village, I stood for a while all by myself on the riverbank, and I felt good. Then I ran off to my forest. The day passed as usual, but in the evening, when the stars had already come out, I lay down on the grass and began dreaming, and then worked out this plan."

"What kind of plan?"

"You see, the things that I know are partially known by various people of the world you live in. Collectively they know practically everything, only they do not fully understand how it works. Then I went and fancied how you will go to a large city and tell many people about me and my explanations. You will do this using the same methods by which you usually spread any kind of information: you will write a book. A great many people will read it and the truth will unfold to them. They will have fewer ailments, they will change their attitude toward children and work out a whole new way of educating them. People will become more loving, and the Earth will begin to emit more radiant energy. Artists will paint my portrait, and each portrait will be their very best masterpiece. I shall try to inspire them. They will make what you call a movie, and it will be the grandest film ever made. You will look at all this and remember me. You will meet wise people who will understand and appreciate what I told you, and they will explain a lot of things to you.

"You will trust their word more than mine, and realise that I am not a witch, but actually Man, a human being. It is just that I have more information inside me than other people. What you write will be of tremendous interest, and you will become rich. You will have money in the banks of nineteen countries, and you will visit holy places and cleanse yourself of all the darkness that is in you. You will remember me and begin to love me, you will have the desire to see me again and to see your son. You will desire to become worthy of your son.

"My dream was so clear, but possibly a bit pleading, too. That is probably why everything happened the way it did. *They* took it as a plan of action and decided to carry people through the dark forces' window of time. That is permitted if the plan is formulated in detail on the Earth, in the heart and mind of an individual Man, an Earth dweller. No doubt *they* took this as a grandiose plan, perhaps they added something themselves, and this is why the forces of darkness have been hard at work of late. They have never been this active before. I realised this from the ringing cedar. Its ray has become a lot more powerful lately. And the ringing has got louder — the cedar is hurrying to give back its light and its energy."

As I listened to Anastasia, I became more and more convinced that she was utterly crazy, that maybe she had long ago escaped from some asylum and was living here in the forest, and here I had gone and slept with her! And now she might have a child. What a tale, indeed! Still, seeing how serious and concerned she was as she talked with me, I tried to calm her down.

"Don't you worry, Anastasia! Your plan is obviously unrealisable, and so there's no need for the forces of darkness and light to fight each other. You don't have a detailed enough knowledge about our everyday life, its laws and conventions. The thing is that an awful lot of books are being published right now, but even the works of well-known authors aren't selling that well. I'm no writer, and so I don't have either the talent or ability or education to write anything."

"That is correct. You did not have these earlier, but now you do," she declared in response.

"Okay," I kept trying to assuage her fears, "even if I tried, nobody would print it, or believe in your existence."

"But I do exist. I exist for those for whom I exist. They will believe and help you just as I shall later help them. And together with those people we..."

I couldn't make sense of what she was saying right off, and once more I made an effort to calm her down:

"I shan't even make an attempt to write anything. There's absolutely no sense in it, don't you get it?"

"Believe me, you shall. *They* have already created a whole network of circumstances that will make you do this."

"What am I, think you — a puppet in somebody's hands?"

"And so much depends on you. But the forces of darkness will try to stop you with all the tricks in their arsenal. They will even try to drive you to suicide by creating an illusion of hopelessness."

"Enough, Anastasia! That's it! I'm sick and tired of listening to your fantasies."

"You think they are just fantasies?"

"Yeah, yeah, fantasies!" And I stopped short. It hit me all of a sudden as I calculated the timing in my head, and I understood. Everything Anastasia told me about her dreams, about our son, she had thought up last year, long before I knew her as well as I do now, long before I slept with her. Now, a year later, it was coming to pass.

"So, that means it's already coming to pass?" I asked her.

"Of course. If it had not been for *them* — and for me too, a little — your second expedition would not have been possible. After all, you were scarcely able to make ends meet after the first one, and you did not even have any claim to the ship."

"You mean to say you influenced the shipping line and the firms that helped me?"

"Yes."

"So you drove me to ruin and inflicted damage on them. What right have you to interfere like that? And here I've left the ship behind and am sitting here with you. Maybe right now everything's going to pieces back there. You've probably got some kind of hypnotic ability. No, worse than that, you're a witch, and that's it. Or a crazy hermit. You don't have anything — not even a house — and here you go philosophising in front of me, you sorcerer!

"I am an entrepreneur! Do you have any idea what that means? I'm an entrepreneur! Even if I am dying, my ships still ply the river, they bring goods to people. That's what *I* do — I bring things to people and I can give you any items you need. But what can *you* give me?"

"I? What can I give you? I can give you a drop of heavenly tenderness and I can give you rest. You will be a genius of bright-eyed cleverness. As your image I am blest."

"Image? Who needs your image? What sense can that express?"

"It will help you write the book for people."

"Oh, please! There you go again doing goodness-knows-what with that mysticism of yours! So, you can't just live like a normal person, are you sure?"

"I have never done anything bad to anyone and I never can. I am a human being! I am Man! If you are so concerned about earthly goods and money, just wait a little — it will all come back to you. I do owe you an apology for dreaming like that — dreaming that you will have a time of troubles, but for some reason I could think of no alternative back then. You do not see the logic, you need to be compelled to see it through the help of circumstances in your world."

"Excuse me!" I couldn't hold out any longer. "What's this about being 'compelled'? You do something like that, and you still want to be treated as a normal human being?!"

"I am Man, a human being, a woman!" Anastasia's agitation was clearly noticeable as she explained: "I only wanted, and I still only want, the good, I want only the light! I want you to be purified. That is why I thought back then about your trip to holy places, about the book. *They* have accepted this, and the forces of darkness are always fighting with them, but never have the dark forces scored a major victory."

"And what about you?" I countered. "With all your intelligence, information and energy, are you just going to stand and watch from the sidelines?"

"In a confrontation on this scale between two great principles, my own efforts count for precious little — help is going to be needed from many others in your world. I shall seek them out and find them, just as I did that time when you were in hospital. Only you need to develop a little more of that conscious awareness. You need to overcome the bad within yourself."

"I'd like to know just what's so bad within myself — what did I do wrong when I was in hospital? And how could you have treated me when you weren't there beside me?"

"Back then you simply did not feel my presence, but I was right there with you. When you were on the ship, I brought you a little branch of the ringing cedar which Mama had broken off before she died. I left it in your cabin when you invited me in. You were ill even then. I could feel it. Do you remember the branch?"

"Yes," I replied. "In fact, that branch hung on the wall of my cabin for some time, many of my crew noticed it, and I brought it back to Novosibirsk. But I didn't pay any attention to it."

"You simply threw it out."

"But I had no idea..."

"No, you had no idea. You threw it out. And Mama's branch did not succeed in overcoming your illness. Then you went into hospital... When you get back, take a close look at the history of your illness. If you check the chart, you will see that in spite of taking the very best medicine available, there was no improvement.

"But then they gave you some cedar nut oil. Now, according to strict prescription regulations, the doctor was not supposed to do that, but she did it, in spite of the fact that there was not a single mention of it in your medical prescription guide and nothing of the sort had ever been done before. Do you remember?"

"Yes."

"You were being treated by a woman who is a sector head in one of the best clinics in your city. But this sector had nothing to do with your particular illness. She left you there, even though just one floor up there was another sector specifically corresponding to your illness — right?"

"Yes!"

"She would prick you with needles, and turn on some music in the half-darkened room."

Anastasia's account was in complete accord with what had actually happened to me.

"Do you remember this woman?"

"Yes. She was in charge of a sector in the former District Council hospital."[1]

And then all at once Anastasia, her eyes fixed intently on me, spoke several disconnected phrases which immediately shocked me and caused a shiver to run through my whole body: "What kind of music do you like?... Fine... Like that? Not too loud?" And she spoke these phrases in exactly the voice and with the intonation used by the sector head who treated me.

"Anastasia!" I exclaimed.

She didn't let me finish.

"Keep listening. Do not be shocked, for God's sake. Do try... try to make sense of everything I am telling you. Get your mind-forces working, at least a little. It is all very easy, you see, for Man."

And she went on.

"This woman doctor — she is very good. She is a real doctor! I got along with her very well. She is kind and forthright. It was I who did not want you to be transferred to the other sector. That sector would have corresponded to your particular illness, but hers did not. She requested her supervisors to leave you with her, assuring them she would take care of you. She felt up to it. She knew your pains were simply the result of 'something else'. And she tried to counteract that 'something else'. She is a doctor!

"And how did you behave? You kept on smoking and drinking to your heart's content, eating salty and spicy foods, and that in spite of your serious ulcer. You did not deny yourself anything in the way of pleasure. Somehow your sub-conscious got a message, even though you were not aware of it,

---

[1]*District Council hospital* — this was a first-class hospital reserved (in Soviet times) for high-ranking Communist Party officials.

that there was nothing terribly wrong with you, that nothing would happen to you.

"I did not accomplish anything good — rather, the opposite. The darkness in your consciousness did not lessen, nor did your will or sense of awareness improve. When you regained your health, you sent one of your employees to thank the woman who saved your life. You yourself did not call her, not even once. She was waiting for you to call, she had such a feeling of love for you."

"She? Or you, Anastasia?"

"*We*, if that is clearer to you."

I got up and for some reason took a few steps away from Anastasia, who was sitting on a fallen tree. The mixed-up state of my feelings and thoughts caused even greater uncertainty as to how I should think about her.

"Now look, once again you are not understanding how I do things, you are becoming confused, but it is a simple thing to grasp — I do things with the help of my imagination and my ability to analyse possible situations. And now you have started thinking ill of me again."

She fell silent, her head resting on her knees. And I stood there too, without saying a word, thinking: *What's she doing there, talking away and saying all sorts of incredible things at the same time? She keeps on talking, and yet she's concerned that her sayings are not being understood. It's clear she has no idea that any normal person would not accept them, and so would not accept her as a normal person.*

Still, I went over to Anastasia and brushed her cascading braids of hair from her face. Tears were rolling down her cheeks from her large bluish-grey eyes. She smiled and said something quite uncharacteristic:

"'She's just another one of those soppy females, eh?' Right now you are overwhelmed by the very fact of my existence and do not believe your eyes. You do not fully believe, and you cannot even make sense of what I am telling you. You find both my existence and my abilities amazing. You have completely ceased accepting me as a normal human being, as Man. But believe me, I am a human being and not a witch.

"You consider my way of life amazing, but why does not a certain something else seem just as amazing, even paradoxical, to you? Why do people admit the Earth to be a celestial body, the greatest creation of the Supreme Mind with each system component as His greatest achievement, and then go tear this system apart and devote so much effort to its destruction?

"You see a manufactured space ship or aeroplane as something natural, in spite of the fact that all its components are made of broken or re-melted parts of the original supreme system.

"Imagine a being who breaks off a piece of an aeroplane in flight and uses its parts to make himself a hammer or a scraper, and then praises himself for having succeeded in making a primitive tool. He does not understand that one cannot keep breaking pieces off a flying aeroplane indefinitely.

"How can you not grasp that our Earth must not be tortured like that?...

"The computer is considered to be an achievement of the human mind, but few realise that the computer may simply be compared to a prosthesis of the brain.

"You can imagine what would happen to a person with normal, healthy legs if they walked on crutches all the time. Naturally, their leg muscles would atrophy.

"No machine will ever be superior to the human brain, provided the brain is kept in constant training."

Anastasia rubbed at a tear rolling down her cheek and stubbornly persisted in elucidating the incredible revelations stemming from her extraordinary logic.

At the time I had no idea how everything she said would arouse millions of people, set the minds of scholars astir and, even as mere hypotheses, prove to be without parallel anywhere in the world.

According to Anastasia, the Sun is something like a mirror. It reflects emanations from the Earth which are invisible to the eye. These emanations come from people in a state of love, joy or some other radiant feeling. Reflecting off the Sun, they return to Earth in the form of sunlight and give life to everything on the planet.[2]

She brought up a whole array of supporting arguments which were not that simple to grasp.

"If the Earth and other planets were simply consumers of the Sun's grace of light," she said, "it would be extinguished, or burn unevenly, and its glow would be off-kilter. In the Universe there is and can be no lopsided process. Everything is interrelated."

[2]Interestingly, the idea that Sun has no radiance of its own is in fact quite widespread in both science and religion. For example, a prominent Russian engineer and scientist living in France, Dr Georges Lakhovsky (1869–1942), a bioenergetics pioneer, author of *The secret of life: Cosmic rays and radiations of living beings* and one of the most respected European scientists of his time, has suggested that "The Sun is a cold black body". Viktor Schauberger (see footnote 1 in Chapter 16: "Flying saucers? Nothing extraordinary!") argues along the same lines, as discussed in Callum Coats's book *Living energies*. Dr Philip Callahan (1923–), a prominent entomologist and radio engineer, author of numerous scientific articles and books, speaks about *tachons*, particles travelling faster than the speed of light, and attempts to detect them in solar rays *and* around people in a state of love (e.g., saints or meditating yogis). George Ivanovich Gurdjieff (1872?–1949) was a spiritual thinker whose thought had a profound influence on such prominent intellectuals of the twentieth century as naturalist Aldo Leopold (1887–1948), originator of land ethics and author of *A Sand County almanac*, and economist E.F. Schumacher (1911–1977), author of *Small is beautiful: Economics as if people mattered*. Gurdjieff maintained that Sun "neither shines nor warms" and devoted an entire chapter in his *Beelzebub's tales to his grandson* to a discussion of this seemingly paradoxical proposition.

She cited, too, the words of the Bible: "And the life was the light of men".[3]

Anastasia also stated that one Man's feelings can be transmitted to another by reflecting off the celestial bodies, and she demonstrated this by the following example:

"Nobody on Earth can deny that you can feel when somebody loves you. This feeling is especially noticeable when you are with a person who loves you. You call it intuition. In fact, invisible light-waves emanate from the one who loves. But the love can be felt, if it is strong enough, even when the individual is absent. By drawing upon this feeling and understanding its nature, one can do wonders. This is what you call miracles, mysticism or incredible abilities. Tell me, Vladimir, do you not feel a bit better with me now? Somehow lighter, warmer, more fulfilled?"

"Yes," I replied. "For some reason I *have* started to feel warmer."

"Now watch what happens when I concentrate on you even more strongly."

Anastasia lowered her eyelids ever so slightly, slowly stepped back a few paces and stopped. A pleasant feeling of warmth started running through my body. It gradually intensified, but didn't burst into flame, and didn't make me hot. Anastasia turned and began to slowly walk away, hiding behind the thick trunk of a tall tree. The sensation of pleasant warmth did not lessen, and to it was added another — as though something were helping my heart pump blood through my veins, and with every heartbeat came the impression that the blood-streams were instantly reaching to every little vein in my body. The soles of my feet broke out into a heavy sweat and became very moist.

[3]John 1: 4 (*Authorised King James Version*).

"You see? Now is it all clear to you?" Anastasia said as she triumphantly re-appeared from behind the tree, confident that she had proved something to me. "You see, you felt all that when I went behind the tree-trunk, and your sensations even increased when you could not see me. Tell me about them."

I told her, and then asked in turn:

"What does the tree-trunk show?"

"What do you think? The waves of information and light went directly from me to you. When I hid myself, the tree-trunk was supposed to significantly distort them, since it has its own information and its own glow, but this did not happen. The waves of feelings began falling directly upon you, reflecting off the celestial bodies, and even intensified. Then I caused what you call a 'miracle' — your feet began to perspire. You failed to mention that fact."

"I didn't think it was important. How do my feet perspiring constitute a miracle?"

"I chased all sorts of diseases out your body through your feet. You should feel a lot better now. It is even noticeable on the outside — you are not slouching as much."

Indeed, I *was* feeling better physically.

"So, when you concentrate like that, you dream up something and whatever you want comes to pass?"

"That describes it, more or less."

"And does what you dream about always come to pass — even when you're asking for something besides bodily healing?"

"Always. As long as it is not an abstract dream. As long as it is detailed down to the minutest aspects and does not contradict the laws of spiritual being. I do not always manage, however, to come up with a dream like that. Thought has to proceed extremely quickly and there must be a corresponding vibration of feelings, and then it will definitely come true.

It is a very natural process. It happens in the lives of many people. Ask around among your acquaintances. Perhaps you will find some among them who have dreamt this way, and their dream has come true either fully or partially."

"Detailed... thinking... proceeding extremely quickly... Tell me, when you were dreaming about the poets and artists and the book, was that all in detail too? Did your thought proceed quickly then?"

"Extraordinarily quickly. And everything was so specific, down to the finest detail."

"So now, you think, it's going to come true?"

"Yes, it will."

"There wasn't anything else you dreamt about at the time? You've told me everything about your dreams?"

"Not everything."

"Then tell me everything."

"Do you... do you really want to listen to me, Vladimir? Really?"

"Yes."

Anastasia's face brightened, as though illuminated by a flash of light.

It was with inspiration and excitement that she continued her incredible monologue.

CHAPTER TWENTY-SEVEN

Across the dark forces' window of time

"During that night of my dreams I thought of how to transport people across this window of time of the dark forces. My plan and conscious awareness were precise and real, and *they* accepted them.

"In the book you are going to write there will be unobtrusive combinations, formulations made up of letters, and they will arouse in the majority of people good and radiant feelings. These feelings are capable of overcoming ailments of body and soul, and will facilitate the birth of a new awareness inherent in people of the future. Believe me, Vladimir, this is not mysticism — it is in accord with the laws of the Universe.

"It is all very simple: you will write this book, guided only by feelings and your heart. You will not be able to do otherwise, since you have not mastered the technique of writing, but through your feelings you can do *anything*. These feelings are already within you. Both mine and yours. They are not something you are aware of just yet. But they will be understood by many. When they are embodied in signs and patterns, they will be stronger than Zoroaster's fire.[1] Do not hide anything that has happened to you, even your most intimate

---

[1] *Zoroaster* (ca. 628–551 B.C.) — a Persian mystic, also known as *Zarathustra,* who compared the nature of God to an eternal, uncontainable flame. Zoroastrianism is practised today principally in India (where adherents are known as *Parsees*) and in isolated areas of Iran.

experiences. Free yourself from any sense of shame and do not be afraid of appearing ridiculous. Humble your pride.

"I have opened my whole being to you — my body and my soul. Through you I want to open myself to everyone. Now I am permitted to do this. I know what a terrible mass of dark forces will descend upon me, they will try to counteract my dream, but I am not afraid of them. I am stronger and I will succeed in seeing my plan come true, and I will succeed in giving birth and raising my son. Our son, Vladimir.

"My dream will break down many of the devices of the forces of darkness, which for millennia have been acting on people destructively, and it will cause many to work for good.

"I know that you find yourself unable to believe me at the moment — you are prevented from doing this by the conventions and many dogmas planted in your brain by the circumstances of existence in the world in which you live. The possibility of transport through time seems incredible to you. But your concepts of time and distance are all relative. These dimensions cannot be measured by metres or seconds, but by the degree of one's conscious awareness and will.

"The purity of the thoughts, feelings and perceptions held by the majority is what determines the place of humanity in time and the Universe.

"You believe in horoscopes, you believe in your complete dependence on the position of the planets. This belief has been attained through the aid of the devices of the dark forces. This belief is slowing down the movement of the channel of light, allowing its dark counterpart to advance and increase in size. This belief is leading you away from a conscious awareness of the truth, the essence of your earthly being. Analyse this question very carefully. Think about how God created Man in His image and likeness.[2] Man has been granted the

[2]*His image and likeness* — see Gen. 1: 26, 27.

greatest of freedoms — the freedom to choose between the darkness and the light. Man has been given a soul. The whole visible world is subject to Man, and Man is free even when it comes to his relationship to God — to love Him or not to love Him. Nobody and nothing can control Man apart from his own will. God wants Man's love in return for His love, but God wants the love of a free Man, perfect in His likeness.

"God has created everything we can see, including the planets. They serve to guarantee the order and harmony of all life — not only plants and animals, they also help human flesh, but there is no way they have power over Man's heart and mind. It is not they who control Man, but Man controls *their* movements through his sub-conscious.

"If a single individual wanted a second Sun to flare up in the sky, it would not appear. Things are arranged this way so that planetary catastrophes do not happen. But if everybody together wanted a second Sun, it would appear.

"In making up a horoscope, it is necessary first of all to take into account the basic dimensions — the level of Man's temporal awareness, his strength of will and his spirit, the aspirations of his soul and the degree to which it participates in the life of the here and now.

"Favourable and unfavourable astrological signs, magnetic storms, high and low pressure — these are all subject to will and conscious awareness.

"Have you never seen a happy and joyful person on a cloudy or stormy day — or, on the other hand, a sad and depressed person on a sunny day with a most favourable astrological prediction?

"You think that I am simply indulging in a crazy person's fantasy when I say that the patterns and formulations of letters I shall put in the book will heal people and enlighten them. You do not believe me because you do not understand. And yet in fact it is so simple.

"You see, right now I am talking to you in your language, using your speech idioms, and I even try sometimes to speak with your voice inflections. It will be easy for you to memorise what I say, because this is *your* language, belonging exclusively to you, although understandable to many people. It contains no incomprehensible words or obscure idioms. It is simple and therefore understandable to the majority. But there are certain words, or word orders, which I have changed, just a little — but only a little. Right now you are in an excited state and therefore, whenever you recall this state, you will recall everything I have told you. And you will write down what I have said.

"And that is how my combinations of letters will fall into place in your book.

"These combinations are very important. They can do wonders, just like prayer. After all, many of you already know that prayers are specific combinations and specific patterns of letters. These combinations and patterns are strung together, with God's help, by people who have had an illuminating experience.

"The forces of darkness have always tried to deprive Man of the opportunity of drawing upon the grace emanating from these combinations. To this end they have even changed the language, introduced new words and removed old ones, and distorted the meaning of words.

"At one time, for example, there were forty-seven letters in your language. Now there remain thirty-three alone. The forces of darkness have imported other combinations and fashions of their own, stirring up base and dark elements, attempting to lead Man astray by fleshly lusts and passions. But I have restored the original purity of combinations using only the letters and symbols in use today, and they will now be effective. I tried so hard to find them... and I did! I have brought together all the best from different times. I collected a good many, and have hidden them in the lines that you will write.

"As you can see, they are simply a translation of the combinations of signs from the depth of eternity and infinity of the Universe — exact in sense, meaning and purpose.

"Write about everything you have seen, hold back nothing — neither the bad nor the good, nor even the intimate or absurd — and then they will be preserved.

"You yourself will be convinced of this, please believe me, Vladimir. You will become convinced once it is written down. In many who read what has been written, feelings and emotions will be found which they are not yet able to fully understand or are not fully aware of. They will confirm this for you — you will see and hear it confirmed. And radiant feelings will appear in them, and then many will themselves understand, through the help of these feelings, a great deal more than what is written by your hand. Try writing at least a little. When you are convinced that people feel these combinations, when a dozen, or a hundred, or a thousand people confirm it for you, you will then believe and write down everything. Only believe. Believe in yourself. Believe in me.

"Later I can tell you things even more significant, and people will understand and feel them too. I am talking about the raising of children. You were interested to know about flying saucers and mechanical objects, rockets and planets. But I so wanted to tell you more about the raising of children, and I shall do so. I shall explain it when I instil in you a greater sense of conscious awareness. However, all this needs to be read when there is no interference from sounds of manufactured, artificial devices around. Such sounds are harmful and lead Man away from the truth. Let only the sounds of the God-created natural world be heard. They carry within themselves truthful information and grace, and increase one's conscious awareness. Then the healing effect will be significantly more powerful.

"Once again, of course, you have your doubts when you think of me, and do not believe in the healing power of the word. But there is no mysticism here — no mere fantasy or contradiction of the laws of spiritual being.

"When these radiant feelings appear in Man, they cannot help but exert a beneficial influence on literally every organ of his body. It is these radiant feelings that are the most powerful and effective remedy against any kind of bodily complaint. God has healed through the help of such feelings, as have prophets and saints. Read the Old Testament and see for yourself. Certain people in your world, too, are healing through the help of these feelings. Many of your doctors know about this. Ask them if you do not believe me. After all, it is easier for you to believe them. The stronger and brighter the feeling, the greater effect it has on the person it is directed to.

"I have always been able to heal with my ray. Great-Grandfather taught me and explained everything when I was still a child. I have done this many times with my dachniks.

"Now my ray is many times more powerful than Grandfather's and Great-Grandfather's. That is because, they say, there has arisen in me another feeling, the one called love.

"This feeling is so great, so pleasant, and a little fiery too. I want to share it with everyone, and with you. As for me, I want good for everyone and everything, just as God wanted."

Anastasia spoke her monologue with extraordinary inspiration and confidence, as though aiming it across space and time. And then she fell silent. I looked at Anastasia, amazed by her uncharacteristic fervour and confidence, and then asked:

"Anastasia, is that it? Are there no further nuances in your plans or dreams?"

"The rest, Vladimir, is just trifles, nothing of great significance. I merely included them — little things as simple as *ABC* — as I was formulating the plan. There was just one sticking point, concerning you, but I managed to resolve it."

"Well, I need a bit more detail here. What kind of sticking-point was it, that concerned me?"

"You see, I made you into the richest person on the Earth. And I also made you the most famous. This will happen by and by. But when the details of my dream unfolded... As yet it had not taken off, so to speak, it had not yet been taken up by the forces of light. The forces of darkness — they are always trying to inject their own harmful input, like all sorts of side effects, exerting a destructive influence on the person at the centre of the dream, and on other people too.

"My thoughts were dashing along ever so quickly, but the forces of darkness were still keeping pace. They had left many of their other earthly affairs in their attempts to concentrate their devices on my dream. But then I came up with something. I outwitted them. And I caused all their devices to turn about and work for the good. The forces of darkness lost their bearings for less than a split second, but that was enough for my dream to be snatched up by the forces of light and transported into radiant infinity, well beyond their sight and reach."

"And just what did you come up with, Anastasia?"

"Unexpectedly for them, I extended, just by a little, the dark forces' window of time — the time you will need to meet the various challenges. In doing so I deprived myself of the possibility of using my ray to help you. They were confounded, failing to see any logic on my part. But during this moment I very quickly shone my light on people who will be in touch with you in the future."

"And what does all this mean?"

"People will help you, will help realise my dream. They will do this with little rays of their own, which will be almost uncontrollable. But there will be a lot of them, and together you will make the dream come true in physical reality. You will be carried *across* the dark forces' window of time. And you will carry others with you.

"And becoming rich and famous will not make you greedy or arrogant. Because you will understand that money is not the point — it will never buy you the warmth or the genuine compassion of the human soul.

"You will understand this when you make your way across that window of time, when you see and get to know these people. And they too will understand. As for the deep knee-bends... This kind of relationship with the banks is something I also thought up because you are altogether negligent in taking care of your body. But this way, at least, you will be getting some exercise whenever you withdraw money from your account. Some of the bank officials will do it, besides. And never mind if it looks a little funny. It means you will find yourself free from the sin of pride.

"So it has turned out that all these challenges and trials which the forces of darkness have concocted in their window of time will serve to strengthen you and those around you. All this will increase your sense of conscious awareness. And it will ultimately save you from the dark temptations they are so proud of. Their own actions will save you. This is why they lost their bearings for a split second! Now they will never be able to catch up to my dream!"

"Anastasia! My dear, precious dreamer! My fantasy-maker!"

"Oh... How good of you to say that! Thank you! Thank you! It was so good of you to say 'My dear'!"

"You're welcome. But, you see, I also called you a fantasy-maker. A dreamer. You're not offended?"

"Not at all. You do not know yet, how accurately my dreams always come true, when they turn out so clearly and in such detail. This one will come true without fail. It is my favourite dream, the clearest of them all. And the book you write will come into being, and people will start having extraordinary feelings, and these feelings will call people—"

"Wait, Anastasia! You're getting carried away again. Calm down."

Only a short time had gone by since my interruption of Anastasia's fervent stream of speech, which seemed indeed but a fantasy.

I couldn't quite grasp the significance behind this monologue of hers. Everything she said sounded *too* fantastic. Only a year later Mikhail Fyrnin,[3] editor of the magazine *Chudesa i prikliuchenia* (Wonders and Adventures), after reading my manuscript containing this monologue, excitedly handed me the latest issue of his magazine — the issue of May 1996.

The contents of the magazine overwhelmed me with excitement. Two major scholars, both academicians, — Anatoly Akimov[4] and Vlail Kaznacheev[5] — talked in their articles

---

[3]*Mikhail A. Fyrnin* — an editor with the publishing house *Molodaya gvardia (Young Guard)* for more than 25 years, where he worked in particular on a series entitled "Lives of remarkable people". One of his more recent major projects was the compilation of *Sobranie myslei Dostoevskogo (Collection of Dostoevsky's thoughts)*, published in Estonia in 2003.

[4]*Anatoly Evgenevich Akimov* — Director of the International Institute of Theoretical and Applied Physics of the Russian Academy of Natural Sciences.

about the existence of a Supreme Mind, the close inter-relationship of Man and the Universe, as well as about certain rays, invisible to normal sight, emanating from Man. Scientists have now been able to identify them with special equipment, and the magazine included two photographs of these rays emanating from people.

But science has only begun to talk about what Anastasia has not only known from childhood, but has been applying in her daily life, in her endeavours to help others.

How was I to know a year earlier that this girl standing before me in an old skirt (the only one she possessed) and uncomfortable-looking galoshes, nervously picking at the buttons on her cardigan — this girl named *Anastasia* — actually possessed a vast store of knowledge as well as the ability to influence human destinies. Or that the pulse-beats of her soul are in fact capable of counteracting the dark and destructive forces threatening mankind. Or that the well-known Russian healer Vladimir Mironov[6] would tell a gathering of his assistants that "We are all ants compared to her", adding that the world has not yet known a power greater than hers and regretting that even after spending such a long time with her I had still not understood her.

Many people were to feel the energy of a tremendous power emanating from the book.

---

[5]*Vlail Petrovich Kaznacheev* (1924–) — a prominent member of the Russian Academy of Medical Sciences from Novosibirsk, specialising in the inter-relationship between Man and Nature, including bio-systems and information processes. A decorated World War II veteran, Dr Kaznacheev has received numerous awards for his research and publications.

[6]*Vladimir Andreevich Mironov* — a Doctor of Alternative Medicine, who runs his own natural therapy clinic in south-central Moscow, and has published several books and numerous articles on the subject.

Following the first small-scale printing of this book, for which I have to give credit to Anastasia herself as one author, would come a sprinkling of verses in abundance, washing away dirt like a spring rain.

Now, dear reader, this is the very book which you are holding in your hands and which you are reading at this moment. Whatever feelings it is arousing in your heart is for you alone to judge. What do you feel? What is it calling upon you to do?

Staying there alone in her glade in the taiga, Anastasia will use her ray of goodness to eliminate any barriers standing in the way of her dream. And she will gather and inspire more and more people to make her dream come true.

And so, at my challenging moments three Moscow students[7] will come to my side and stand by me. They will not receive any significant compensation for their efforts and will even end up helping me financially. Earning their living wherever they can, they — especially Lyosha Novichkov — will spend nights keyboarding the *Anastasia* text into their computers.

They will not cease their keyboarding work, even after their difficult examination session begins.

And Moscow Printshop Number Eleven will put out a 2,000-copy print run. They'll do this on their own, by-passing a publishing house. But even before this, the journalist Evgenia Kvitko of the agricultural paper *Krestyanskie vedomosti* will be the first to tell about Anastasia in the press. Later Katya Golovina from *Moskovskaya pravda*, and then *Lesnaya*

---

[7]*three Moscow students* — the reference is to Alexey (Lyosha) Novichkov, Artem Semenov and Anton Nikolaikin, who will eventually support Vladimir in a number of ways in carrying out the provisions of Anastasia's plan (see Book 2 in the series, especially the end of Chapter 17: "The beginning of *perestroika*").

gazeta, Mir novostei and Radio Rossiya. The magazine *Chudesa i prikliuchenia* (Wonders and Adventures), which publishes articles by the brightest lights of Russian academia, will throw tradition to the wind and devote several issues to Anastasia, explaining:

"In their boldest dreams our academics come nowhere near the insights of Anastasia, the wise woman of the Siberian taiga. Purity of thought makes Man omnipotent and omniscient. Man is the apex of creation."

Anastasia will be published only by the major press outlets in Moscow. Anastasia herself seems to have made that choice in preference to the tabloids, in a careful effort to preserve the purity of her dream.

But none of this became clear to me until a year after my visit with her. Not understanding her at the time, and not fully believing, I had my own take on the experience, and tried to shift the conversation to a topic I was more familiar with — namely, entrepreneurs.

CHAPTER TWENTY-EIGHT

Strong people

The highest evaluation of your personality
comes from those around you.

Anastasia talked a lot about the people we call entrepreneurs, about their influence on public spirituality, and then took a twig and drew a circle on the ground. Inside it she drew many little circles, with a dot in the middle of each one. Off to the side there were more circles. It was like a map of the planets within the earthly world, and she kept adding many details, and said:

"The large circle is the Earth — a planet inhabited by people. The little circles are small groups of people, linked together into groups. The dots are the people in charge of these groups. The way these heads relate to the people in their group, what they make them do, what kind of psychological climate they create through their influence will determine whether the people around them feel good or bad. If the majority feel good, a bright ray emanates from each of them and from the group as a whole. If bad, then the ray is dark."

And Anastasia shaded in some of the circles, making them dark.

"Naturally, their inner state is influenced by many other factors as well, but in the space of time during which they are in this group, the principal thing is their interrelationship with the person in charge. For the Universe it is very important that a bright radiance should emanate from the Earth. The radiance of the light of love and good. This is mentioned in the Bible, as well: 'God is love'.[1]

"I feel sorry, very sorry, for the people you call entrepreneurs. They are the most miserable of all. I would so much like to help them, but it is difficult for me to do that all by myself."

"You're mistaken, Anastasia. The most miserable people in our society are the pensioners, people who can't find work, can't afford a roof over their heads, or even food or clothing. An entrepreneur is someone who has all these things in greater abundance than other people. He has access to pleasures which others can't even dream about."

"What specifically, for example?"

"Well, even if you take the average entrepreneur, he will have a modern car and apartment. He will have no problems whatsoever with food and clothing."

"And what about joy? What does he find satisfaction in? Come and see for yourself."

Once again Anastasia led me to the grass and, like the first time, when she showed me the woman dachnik, she began to show me other scenes.

"You see? There he is, sitting in a car you, in fact, would call pretty snazzy. You see — he is sitting alone in the back seat, and the car is air-conditioned — it has its own micro-climate, so to speak. His chauffeur is driving it very smoothly. But look and see how worried and pensive the entrepreneur sitting in the back seat is — he is thinking, working out plans, he is afraid of something. See — he has picked up what you call a telephone. He is upset... Yes, he has just received some news... Now he must quickly evaluate the situation and make a decision. He is all tensed up... Thinking. Now he is ready, the decision has been made. Now look, look — he appears to be sitting peacefully, but his face betrays doubt and concern. And there is no joy."

---

[1]I John 4: 8 & 16 (*Authorised King James Version*).

"That's *work*, Anastasia."

"That is a way of life, and there is no respite in it from the moment he wakes in the morning until the moment he goes to bed at night, or even in his sleep. And he sees neither the leaves unfolding on the trees nor the streams of spring.

"All around him are perennially envious rivals, desiring to take over his possessions. His attempts to fence himself off from these by what you call bodyguards and a house — more of a citadel, actually — do not bring any complete sense of peace, since fear and worry have crept in and will forever remain with him.

"This goes on until his dying day, and just before the end of his life, he feels a sense of regret that he is obliged to leave it all behind."

"An entrepreneur has his joys," I observed. "They come when he obtains a desired result, or fulfils a plan he's thought up."

"Not true, Vladimir. He never gets to enjoy his acquisitions, since along comes another plan immediately to take its place — a more complicated plan, and the whole process begins again from scratch, only with greater challenges."

This forest princess painted me a rather sad and gloomy picture of our outwardly well-off social class, and this was not a picture I felt like accepting. I attempted a counter-argument:

"You forget, Anastasia, their ability to reach a set goal and obtain the good things in life, excited glances from women, respect by people around them."

To which she replied:

"Sheer illusion. There is nothing of the sort. Where have you ever seen a respectful or an excited glance directed at a passenger in a snazzy car or at the owner of the fanciest house in town? Not a single person will confirm what you have just said. These are but glances of envy, indifference and irritation.

And even women cannot love these people, because their feeling is mixed in with their desire to possess not only the man but his property too. The men, in turn, cannot really love a woman, for there is no way they can free up enough room for such an important feeling."

It was useless to look for further arguments, since what she said could be confirmed or refuted only by the people she was talking about. As an entrepreneur myself, I never really thought about what Anastasia was describing, never analysed how many minutes of joy I actually experienced, and most certainly could not do this for anyone else. For some reason it is simply not accepted in entrepreneurs' circles to whine or complain — everyone tries to show himself as successful and content with life.

This is no doubt why most people hold the stereotype image of the entrepreneur as someone who has received more than his share of good things in life. Anastasia was perceiving not the externally expressed feelings, but those which are more delicate and hidden in the inner recesses of one's heart. She was measuring a person's state of well-being by the amount of light she could detect in them. As to the scenes and situations she was able to see, I felt I was picturing them more from listening to her. I mentioned this to Anastasia, and she responded:

"I shall help you now. It is simple. Close your eyes, lie down on the grass, arms out to the sides, and relax. Picture in your mind the whole Earth, try to see its colour and the pale bluish glow emanating from it. Then narrow the focus of your imagination's ray so that it does not take in the whole Earth. Rather, make it narrower and narrower until you see concrete details. Look for people where the bluish light is stronger than in other places. Keep on narrowing your ray and you will eventually focus on one person, or a small group. Now try again, with my help."

She took me by the hand, ran her fingers along mine, resting her fingertips in my palm. The fingers of her other hand, which was lying on the grass, were pointed upward. I went through in my mind all the steps she outlined, and began to get a fuzzy image of three people sitting at a table engaged in a lively conversation. I couldn't understand what they were saying, as I wasn't picking up any voices at all.

"No," said Anastasia, "those are not entrepreneurs. Wait a moment, we shall find some."

She searched and searched with her ray, peering into offices both large and small, private clubs, party celebrations and bordellos... The bluish glow was either very weak or not there at all.

"Look — it is night-time here already, and this entrepreneur is sitting alone in a smoky office. Something is not right... But look at that one, how contented he looks, in a swimming pool, surrounded by pretty girls. He is tipsy, but there is no glow. He is simply trying to run away from something, his feeling of self-satisfaction is artificial...

"This one is at home. There is his wife, and his little one is asking him something... The telephone is ringing... You see there, he has become serious again, and pushed his family to the background..."

All sorts of situations became illuminated one after another, some of them outwardly good and some not so good... until we happened upon a most frightening scene. All at once appeared a room, probably in some apartment, quite nice-looking, but...

On a round table lay a naked man, his hands and feet tied to the table legs, his head hanging over, his mouth covered with brown sticky tape. At the table were sitting two burly-looking youths — one of them with a close-shaven head, the other with smooth, slick hair. A little distance away, under a floor lamp, there was a young woman in an arm-chair. Her mouth was also taped over, and she was tied to the chair with her linen sash bound tight around her waist. Both her legs were tied to the chair legs. She was wearing nothing but a torn undergarment. Next to her was sitting a thin, wiry man who was taking a drink of something, possibly cognac. On a small table in front of him lay a chocolate bar. The youths sitting at the round table weren't drinking. I could see them pouring some kind of liquid over the chest of the man lying on the table — vodka, or pure alcohol, and set it alight. A break-in, I surmised.

Anastasia shifted her ray away from this scene. But I cried out: "Go back! Do something!"

She went back to the scene and replied:

"I cannot. It has already happened. This cannot be stopped now. It should have been stopped earlier, but now it is too late."

I watched spellbound and suddenly got a clear glimpse of the woman's eyes, filled with sheer horror and not even pleading for mercy.

"Do something!" I cried to Anastasia. "If you have any heart at all, do at least something!"

"But it is not within my power. Everything has been, so to speak, programmed in advance, but not by me. I cannot interfere directly. They have the upper hand right now."

"But where's that goodness of yours — your powers?"

Anastasia didn't say a word. The horrifying scene began to blur a little. Then the older man who had been drinking the cognac suddenly disappeared.

All at once I felt a weakness throughout my body.

I could also feel the arm Anastasia was touching start to grow numb.

I could hear her bland and weakened voice say, with evident difficulty in getting out the words:

"Take your hand away, Vladi—." She couldn't even finish saying my name.

I stood up, and drew my hand away.

My arm just hung there as if paralysed (as happens sometimes when you get a tingling sensation in your arms or legs)
and went completely white. Then I wiggled my fingers a little
and the numbness began to go away.

I looked at Anastasia in shock. Her eyes were closed. The
blush had drained from her cheeks and it seemed as though
there was not a drop of blood left under the skin on her hands
and face.

She did not even seem to be breathing as she lay there. The
grass for about three metres all around her had also become
white and bent over. I realised something terrible had happened and cried out:

"Anastasia! What's happened to you, Anastasia?"

But there was not even the slightest response to my cry.
Then I grabbed her by the shoulders and shook her body,
which was no longer supple, but had somehow gone limp.
There was no response — her completely white, bloodless
lips remained silent.

"Can you hear me, Anastasia?!"

She opened her eyelids ever so slightly and looked at me
through her dimmed eyes, which had lost all their characteristic
expression. I grabbed a flask of water, lifted up Anastasia's head
and tried to give her something to drink, but she was unable to
swallow. I looked at her, feverishly wondering what to do.

At long last she managed to move her lips just a tiny bit and
to whisper:

"Carry me over there... to the tree."

I lifted her limp body and carried it out of the circle of
whitened grass, and laid it down by the nearest cedar tree.
After some time she started to come round, and I asked:

"What happened to you, Anastasia?"

"I tried to fulfil your request," she quietly said, and a minute
later added: "I think I succeeded."

"But you look so bad — you almost died!"

"I violated the natural laws. I interfered in something I should not have. That required all my strength and energy. I am surprised that they held out at all."

"Why did you take such a risk, if you knew it was so dangerous?"

"I had no choice. After all, you wanted me to do something. I was afraid that if I did not fulfil your request, you would lose all respect for me. You would think that all I can do is talk, that I am all words... And that I could not do anything in real life."

Her eyes looked at me enquiringly and pleadingly. Her soft voice trembled a little as she spoke.

"But I cannot explain to you how to do it, how this natural system works. I feel it, but I cannot explain to you in a way you could understand, and your scholars, probably, will not be able to explain it either."

She bowed her head, fell silent for a while, as though mustering her strength. Then she looked at me once more with pleading eyes and said:

"Now you are going to be even more persuaded that I am abnormal, or a witch."

All at once I felt the tremendous urge to do something good for her, but what? I wanted to tell her that I did consider her a normal human being, a beautiful and intelligent woman, but in all honesty I didn't feel about her the way I usually felt about women, and she with that intuition of hers would not believe me.

And then I suddenly recalled her story about how her great-grandfather customarily greeted her as a child. About how this old grey-haired fellow would stand on one knee before the little Anastasia and kiss her hand. I got down on one knee before Anastasia, grasped hold of her still pale and slightly cold hand, kissed it and said:

"If you are indeed abnormal, then you are the best, the kindest, the cleverest and the most beautiful of all abnormal people ever!"

At long last a smile once more alighted upon Anastasia's lips, and her eyes looked at me in gratitude. A rosy blush was coming back to her cheeks.

"Anastasia, that was quite a depressing scene. Did you choose it deliberately?"

"I was looking for something good, just as an example, but I could not find anything. They are all held in the grip of their worries and cares. They are constantly facing their problems all alone. They have practically no spiritual communication."

"So what can be done? What can you suggest, apart from pitying them? And I should tell you: these are strong people, these entrepreneurs."

"Very strong," she agreed, "and most interesting. It is as though they are living two lives in one. One life is known only to them — not even their family are aware of it — while the other is the outward life, which people around them see. They can only be helped through increasing their sincere, spiritual communication with each other. They need to strive, with complete sincerity, for purity of thought."

"Anastasia, in all probability I shall try to do what you have asked. And I shall try to both write a book and establish an organisation of entrepreneurs with pure thoughts, but only in a way that I can understand."

"It will be difficult for you. I shall not be able to offer you sufficient help, I have little strength left. It will take a long time for my strength to recover. For a time I shall not be able to see at a distance with my ray. I am even having difficulty seeing you right now with my ordinary eyesight."

"Don't tell me you're going blind, Anastasia!"

"I think it will all get better. Only it is a pity that for some time I shall not be able to help you."

"You don't need to help me, Anastasia. Just try to keep yourself for your son and help other people."

I needed to leave, to catch up to my ship. After waiting until she had started to regain her almost normal appearance, I got into the motorboat. Anastasia took hold of the bow with her hand and pushed the boat away from the shore. The boat was swept up and began floating downstream with the current.

Anastasia stood in the water almost up to her knees. The hem of her long skirt got wet and flapped about in the waves.

I gave the starting-cord a tug. The motor roared into life, breaking the silence I had grown accustomed to over the past three days. The boat gave a jerk forward, picked up more and more speed, and soon began to distance itself from the diminutive figure of the taiga recluse standing all alone in the shallow water near the riverbank.

All at once Anastasia rushed out of the water and started running along the bank after the boat.

Her long hair, trailing behind her from the headwind, looked like a comet's tail. She tried to run very fast, probably using up all her remaining strength in an effort to do the impossible — catch up to a speeding motorboat. But even *she* wasn't up to that. The distance between us gradually increased. I started feeling sorry for her fruitless efforts. Wanting to shorten the difficult moments of parting, I pushed down on the gas lever with all my might. Then the thought flashed through my head that Anastasia might think that I had taken fright once more and was running away.

The motor, now roaring in bursts, lifted the boat's bow out of the water, making it speed forward faster and faster, and increasing the distance between us even more.

As for her... Oh Lord! What was she doing?

Anastasia ripped off the wet skirt that was slowing her down and cast aside her torn clothes. She increased her tempo, and the incredible happened: the distance between her and the boat gradually began to *decrease*.

On the path ahead of her loomed a steep slope, leading to an almost vertical drop-off. Continuing to press the gas lever to the limit, I thought that the incline would stop her in her tracks and bring this difficult episode to a quick end.

But Anastasia continued her headlong rush, occasionally stretching out her arms in front of her, as though using them to sense the space ahead.

Could it be that her eyesight had become so poor that she couldn't see the slope?

Without slowing down in the least, Anastasia ran straight up the slope. Reaching the top, she fell on her knees, threw up her arms toward the sky, turned slightly in my direction, and began shouting something. I could hear her voice over the wild roar of the motor and the noise of the waves. I heard as though in a whisper:

"There are sha-a-allows ahe-e-ad, sha-a-allows, su-u-unken lo-o-ogs!"

I quickly jerked my head forward, not fully able to grasp what was happening, and gave such a hard pull on the rudder that the lower side of the sharply tilted boat almost submerged to the point of taking on water.

A huge sunken log, one end grounded in a sandbar, the other barely visible on the surface, lightly scraped against the side of the speeding boat. If it had been a direct hit, it would easily have torn a gaping hole in the thin aluminium bottom.

Once out in mid-channel, I turned to glance at the cliff and whispered in the direction of the lonely figure standing on her knees, which was slowly being transformed into a vanishing dot:

"Thank you, Anastasia!"

CHAPTER TWENTY-NINE

Who are you, Anastasia?

The ship was waiting for me at Surgut.[1] The captain and crew were awaiting my instructions. But there was no way I could concentrate my thought on working out the subsequent itinerary, and ordered the ship's crew to continue standing in port at Surgut, hold parties for the local population to come and have a good time, and keep up the promotion and sales exhibits.

My thoughts were occupied with my experiences with Anastasia. At a local shop I purchased a great deal of popular-science literature, books on extraordinary phenomena and people's unusual abilities, as well as the history of Siberia. I squirrelled myself away in my cabin, trying to find in all these books some sort of plausible explanation.

In addition, I wondered whether Anastasia's shouting of "I love you, Vladimir!" in her attempts to help the village girl could have really engendered in her a feeling of love for me.

How is it that mere words, which we often utter without putting a sufficient amount of suitable feeling into them, could have affected Anastasia — in spite of the differences in our ages and views on life and lifestyles?

The popular-science literature gave me no clues. Then I picked up the Bible. And there it was — my answer. At the

[1]*Surgut* — a city of 270,000, founded in the 16th century on the banks of the River Ob, which shares its proximity to the 60th parallel of latitude with St Petersburg, Helsinki, Oslo, Churchill (Manitoba) and Whitehorse (Yukon). Surgut is a large centre of oil and gas industry.

very outset of the Gospel according to John I read: "In the beginning was the *Word,* and the *Word* was with God, and the *Word* was God."[2]

For the umpteenth time it struck me how laconic and precise were the definitions of this amazing book.

Immediately a lot of things became clearer in my mind. Anastasia, incapable as she was of trickery or deceit, could not just simply utter meaningless words. I remembered her saying:

"It seemed as though I had forgotten at that moment that it was not enough just to simply utter those words — there definitely had to be behind them feelings, an awareness and trustworthiness of natural information."[3]

O God!!! How disappointingly her hopes had turned out! Why had she addressed these words to me — here I was no longer in my prime, someone with a family, enslaved to a great many of this world's temptations, dark and destructive, as she herself said? With her degree of inner purity she deserves someone else entirely. But who could fall in love with her, given such an extraordinary lifestyle, mentality and intellect?

At first glance she comes across as an ordinary girl, albeit extremely beautiful and attractive. But once you get to know her it is as though she is transformed into some kind of creature living way beyond the bounds of the rational.

It may very well be that this impression of mine is due to my imperfect knowledge of things, my insufficient understanding of what constitutes our being. Others might have an entirely different perception of her.

I recalled that even at our parting I did not feel any particular desire to kiss or embrace her. I don't know whether she would have wanted me to or not. Anyway, what exactly

---

[2]John 1: 1 *(Authorised King James Version).*
[3]See Chapter 24: "A strange girl" above.

did she want? I recalled her telling me of her dreams. What a strange philosophical bent her love had: organise a fellowship of entrepreneurs to help them? Write a book passing along her advice to people? Carry people across the dark forces' window of time?

And she believes it all! She is convinced that that's how it will all turn out. Oh, I was a good one — I promised I would try and organise a fellowship of entrepreneurs and write a book. Now she'll probably be having even more fantastic dreams about that. She might have thought up something simpler, more realistic.

An inexplicable sense of pity for Anastasia arose in my heart. I could imagine her sitting there in her forest waiting and dreaming that everything would work out that way in broad daylight. Fine, if she were simply content to wait and dream. But, who knows, she may go beyond that and start taking steps on her own, focusing that ray of goodness of hers, expending the colossal energy of her heart and believing in the impossible. And even though she showed me what she could do with her ray and attempted to explain to me how it works, somehow my consciousness still couldn't accept it as something real. Judge for yourselves, dear readers — in her own words, she aims her ray at a person, illuminates this person, this Man, with an invisible light, and imparts to him her feelings and aspirations toward goodness and light.

"No, no, do not just think that I am interfering with a person's mental make-up, that I am violating his heart and mind," I remember her telling me. "Man is free — people are free — to accept or reject me. Only to the degree that they themselves find it to their liking, something close to their heart, will they be able to accept these feelings as their own. Then they will become lighter and brighter in their appearance too, and your diseases will leave them, either partially or completely. My grandfather and great-grandfather can do this, and I have always been able to — Great-Grandfather taught me, when he played with me in my childhood. But now my ray has become many times stronger than Grandfather's and Great-Grandfather's, because in me has been born that extraordinary feeling called love. It is so bright and clear, and even a little fiery. There is such a lot of it, and I want to share it."[4]

"With whom, Anastasia?" I had asked.

"With you, with others, with anyone who can accept it. I want everyone to experience good. When you begin to do what I have dreamt of, I shall bring many of these people to see you, and together you..."

Remembering all this, picturing her in my mind, I suddenly realised that I couldn't help but carry out — at least *try* to carry out her wishes. If I didn't, I would be tormented with doubt for the rest of my life, along with the feeling that I had betrayed Anastasia and her dream. Perhaps her dream wasn't all that realistic, but it was something she passionately desired.

I made my decision, and the ship headed full steam for Novosibirsk.

The unloading and disassembly of the exhibit equipment I left to my firm's executive director. After somehow managing to settle matters with my wife, I set out for Moscow.

I set out for Moscow to make — or at least try to make — Anastasia's dream come true.

To be continued...

----

[4]See Chapter 27: "Across the dark forces' window of time" above.

CHAPTER THIRTY

Author's message to readers

Dear readers, thank you. Thank you all who have responded to Anastasia with kindness and understanding. Indeed, I could not imagine that she would actually be capable of arousing so many feelings and emotions. I would so like to answer all your letters individually, but for the time being at least, this is physically impossible. The last lines of this book were penned in the Caucasus, where I have been working with local archaeologists and enthusiasts in investigating the dolmens[1] Anastasia told me about. And we found them. Saw them with our own eyes. Took pictures. These are ancient stone constructions, ten thousand years old. They have functional significance even for people living today.

They are located in the south, in the mountains of the Caucasus, not far from the cities of Novorossiysk, Gelendzhik and Tuapse.[2] They are the precursors of the pyramids of

---

[1] *dolmen* — a megalithic tomb (also known as a *portal tomb*) built of heavy upright stones (each weighing between 5,000 and 13,000 kg) with an even larger flat one on top and a small sealed opening at the front. While this specific type of tomb construction is unique to the north-western Caucasus, the term *dolmen* is also applied to megalithic configurations in Britain, Ireland, the Mediterranean and Northern Europe.

[2] *Novorossiysk* — port on the Black Sea in the Krasnodar region, with a population of just over 200,000, founded after the Russo-Turkish War of 1828–29; *Gelendzhik* — a resort town on the Black Sea about 45 km south-east of Novorossiysk, dating from the 1840s; *Tuapse* — a small port on the Black Sea just a few kilometres south-east of Gelendzhik, mentioned as early as the Byzantine chronicles of the 6th century B.C. (in the Greek variant: *Topsida*), although evidence of human life here is said to date back thousands of years.

Egypt. But the local residents didn't pay any attention to the dolmens, not appreciating their purpose. Even though the dolmens were classified as historic monuments, they were ransacked by the local population. Their huge stones were carted off, and even used to build a church in the settlement of Beregovoe,[3] which to me is nothing short of sheer blasphemy. Perhaps it was for the same reason that forty priests were cruelly tortured to death in the Kuban region[4] during the revolutionary period of Russian history — one priest for each dolmen stone. People carried these stones off, not fully appreciating their significance.

Now that Anastasia has spoken about them, I think all this will change. It is amazing, but a fact: much of what she said has already been confirmed.

And even the fluctuations she talked about — the background radiation of the Earth fluctuating near the dolmens — have been detected and reported on by local health officials. Out of all the things Anastasia told or showed to me, I have decided to publish only what has been directly or indirectly corroborated by scientific experiments, material objects or historical facts.

Though I am starting to think that we'd better simply listen some more with our hearts too. It would be quicker that way. The other method of confirmation takes up an awful lot of time. As with the dolmens, for example.

It took me pretty much half a year to collect historical data and trek through the Caucasus mountains to see the dolmens with my own eyes, and take pictures of them. I was, finally, convinced. But at the end of the day it turns out that if I'd

[3]*Beregovoe* — a small outpost (*stanitsa*) located in a valley 5 km inland from the coast, 30 km to the south-east of Gelendzhik.

[4]*Kuban region* — the area of the Krasnodar region that forms the basin of the Kuban River in the north-western Caucasus.

simply believed right off, I could have used this half-year to greater advantage. It turns out that a great deal depends on one's ability to believe.

I did get a chance to visit Anastasia a second time. I got a chance to see the son she bore, and how she relates to him. A most unusual relationship. In addition, I had the opportunity of finding out from the people who ferried me to the spot on the riverbank about the various attempts on the part of both individuals and groups to penetrate Anastasia's domain and find her dwelling-place for themselves. Many, no doubt, wish to see and talk with her out of well-meaning motives. But the people who ferried me also told me about a group of scoundrels who set up camp on the riverbank, sent out a helicopter to take pictures of the area, and tried to capture her. She was obliged to emerge from the taiga to talk with them and then send them packing, despite their attempts to restrain her physically. I shall tell all about that in the second book.[5]

I only ask people not to touch her, to leave her alone. Now, after the experience with these rotters, local hunters have taken it upon themselves to shoot strangers on sight. That's bad, of course. But I say, let them shoot. It turns out the local hunters knew about her existence long before I came along. Only they never told anyone. And they never encroached upon her territory themselves. The locals talked with her only when she came out to them. I started having pangs of conscience for having told about her without hiding the location, especially in the first edition of the book, and for not changing the names of people I mentioned, or even the name of the ship.

Anastasia calmed my fears a little when she said:

[5] This actually ended up being described in the initial chapters of Book 3, rather than in Book 2.

"Never mind. After all, I was the one who wanted to reveal myself to everybody."

But I'm wiser now. I shouldn't have mentioned specific names. And in future I shall try to be more circumspect.

But still I want to emphasise: *please don't disturb her.* She herself will tell everything she feels is necessary to reveal. We must not do to her what we have already done to one Siberian family — the Lykovs, described by Vasily Peskov in his *Komsomolskaya Pravda* article "Dead-end in the taiga". As far as I know, the only member of this family remaining is Agafia, who is dying of cancer, left helpless, taken out of the taiga.[6] A real tragedy, how things have turned out. The Lykov family lived in the taiga for many years, but died out after contact with our 'enlightened' civilisation. Which way of life, then, is the real "dead-end"?

I can understand why so many people want to contact Anastasia. But it is impossible for her to meet and talk with everyone. And, after all, Anastasia does have a young child to care for.

There is an 'Anastasia' club or community organisation operating in Gelendzhik, headed by Valentina Larionova,[7] an ethnographer of thirty years' experience. She has organised a group of local ethnographers, along with people from a variety of professions, who are sensitive to the spiritual legacy of

[6] *Agafia Lykova* — For the story of the Lykovs, see footnote 3 in Chapter 2: "Encounter". After this book was first published in 1996, Agafia's health improved and she returned to her original home, where she was subsequently visited by the original *Komsomolskaya Pravda* correspondent, Vasily Peskov.

[7] *Valentina Terentevna Larionova* — an ethnographer (and at one time a member of the Gelendzhik city council) who not only has taken special interest in the dolmens since the first publication of this book in Russian, but is one of the many who can bear personal testimony to the healing value of Anastasia's advice as set forth herein. More will be said about Ms Larionova in Book 2 (see, especially, Chapter 33: "Your sacred sites, O Russia!").

their region and its ecological problems. This was one of the first clubs to be organised by readers of the *Anastasia* book.[8]

The members of the Gelendzhik club have made what is to my mind a remarkable discovery. On the basis of information provided by Anastasia, they have restored to Russia — and, quite possibly, to the world — the forgotten shrines of our ancestors, and are now receiving people wishing to visit them and conducting tours to the places mentioned by Anastasia.

About Gelendzhik, for example, Anastasia had this to say: "This city could be richer than Jerusalem or Rome, but because of its rulers' neglect of our pristine origins, this city is dying."

I believe this and other cities and settlements will be restored not by 'the rulers of this world', but by the hearts of ordinary people aroused by Anastasia.

And there's more. Many healers, wizards and preachers are now speaking out regarding Anastasia. "We are like ants compared to her," said the chairman of the Russian Healers' Foundation Vladimir Mironov.[9]

I have seen a video recording of a speech given in front of a large audience by the leader of a religious denomination, in which he referred to Anastasia as "the ideal of womanhood to which we should aspire". He added: "Her ability to draw inferences and conclusions and level of intellect far surpasses that of humanity today." This video is now being copied and distributed.

Much the same type of reaction is coming from people with extraordinary abilities living in India.

Still another religious leader said that while Anastasia is currently studying our life, she has not yet managed,

---

[8] *Anastasia* clubs have spread to many towns and cities in Russia and abroad, and since then have grown into a powerful social movement.

[9] *Vladimir Andreevich Mironov* — see footnote 6 in Chapter 27: "Across the dark forces' window of time".

unfortunately, to meet up with a real man. Later I was told that there is one chap very much like Anastasia living in Australia, and that the two should meet.

I, of course, do not have any pretensions to being a "real man", far from it, even in my thinking. But perhaps it is still premature to think in terms of arranging a marriage? And it isn't right to idealise her to such an extent.

It is this idealisation of Anastasia that has prevented a timely recognition of what she has done. Just think calmly and rationally about what has happened. A child has been born. And I have held him in my arms, I have heard his little heart beating. There is a child. He is growing up. But he has no official birth certificate. He will grow up and want to go somewhere — maybe abroad, for instance — maybe he'll want to see the world. Who will issue him a passport to travel abroad? What country is he a citizen of? What shall we tell him then? "Oh well, you know, somehow we haven't thought about any documents for you. You just stay here in the taiga."

I checked with a legal firm on the question of a birth certificate. The lawyer said Anastasia would have had to give birth in a hospital — then, even if she didn't have a medical record, they could have at least issued her a memo regarding the birth, which she could have used to obtain a proper birth certificate.

"The other alternative," said the lawyer, "would be for her to abandon her child to an orphanage. They would issue him documents there. Orphanages can do that. And then have him adopted." But somehow this alternative was not at all appealing. And I doubt that Anastasia would ever agree. So what to do? When I talked with her about a birth certificate, she responded:

"Of course, it would be fine if he had one, just like everyone else. I suppose I let that slip by without really thinking about it. But do not be concerned, everything will still work out."

Note how she said: "I suppose I let that slip by without really thinking about it." I wonder how many other things she has let 'slip by' — things which could be taken care of at a future stage. That means we can't fully count on everything working out exactly the way she said. I think we need to examine it all very carefully and at some point make adjustments to adapt it to *our* reality.

On another point, I hear talk about what a poor entrepreneur I am — not being able to print enough copies to keep pace with the demand!

Indeed. I really can't at the moment. I have refused to sell exclusive rights to the book to any one publisher. I certainly don't want anyone to have exclusive control over the manuscript and put out whatever print-runs they fancy.

The publishers I talked with gave me this: "...The style needs to be edited and made more literary. In its present form it is only Anastasia's explanations and monologues that make the book worth anything at all."

My language is seen as "stilted". They suggest I think up a catchier title — something like "Dead-end in the taiga", "The healer-girl", or even "The girl from outer space". But I do not consider Anastasia to be from outer space, nor do I consider her to be at a dead-end in the taiga. She herself, after all, simply wants to be Man, a normal human being. Of course I can always exercise my author's privilege even in confrontation with publishing houses, but a lot of time would be wasted on that.

I have been using the proceeds of the initial print-runs to pay for subsequent runs in the print-shop,[10] by-passing the publishing houses altogether. So things will even out in the long run. If someone is interested in assisting along this line

---

[10] A reference to Moscow Printshop Number Eleven (see the end of Chapter 27: "Across the dark forces' window of time").

to our mutual advantage, I'd be happy to listen, but without the condition of exclusive rights.

I should also say a few words about a certain situation involving my relationship with my family. The Moscow group now looking after distribution of the book has received a number of letters and telephone calls about this. There have been complaints that calls and letters to my home address indicated in the book have not been met with any intelligible response.

I left Novosibirsk, as I mentioned, directly upon my return from the expedition. Subsequent events will be described in my next book.

Now I have learnt that my firm is falling apart. And there has been nobody there to reply to enquiries. I'll see to it and bring it back to life once I finish my writing. As for my wife, I have only spoken to her on the telephone. It was a deeply personal conversation. However, I beg my correspondents' forgiveness for not responding right off and for my delay in sending out copies of the books.

At present my daughter Polina is there. I have met with her. She will fix everything up, and in future there should be no repetition of the trouble. I have had long talks with my daughter and she understands everything. A little later I plan to get a mobile telephone and then I shall be able to spend more time chatting with you personally.

I shall definitely respond to all the letters coming in and maybe even publish some of them. They are worth publishing. There are letters about Russia, about love, about bright aspirations. They show the same energy Elena Ivanovna Roerich[11] talks about in her book *Living ethics*. Thank you for these letters. But one letter in particular, a letter from a thirteen-year-old girl from Kolomna[12] named Nastia[13] deserves to

[11]*Elena Ivanovna Roerich* — see footnote 18 in Chapter 1: "The ringing cedar".

be answered right here and now, along with other girls who have written and will be writing. Here is her letter:

Dear Vladimir Megré,

My name is Nastia Shapkina, from the city of Kolomna. I am 13 years old, and I am in Grade 7 at school. I read your book "The Ringing Cedar. Anastasia". I really, really liked it. Not just 'liked' — that's not the best word here (it sounds too dry) — after reading the book I got a warm and happy feeling in my heart. They told me a lot about it in hospital — I've got a serious illness, and I have to go to hospital every two months, and I really want to get well. And your book was like a ray of light amidst all this darkness and vulgarity. I really want to meet with you, and especially with Anastasia. Could you help me?

Right now you're probably thinking: "How brash and impolite she is!", but that's not true. You see, that's the way we all are — until we see with our own eyes, we don't believe anyone. I don't even know whether to believe or not (Mama doesn't believe, and no one around here believes), it is so fantastic. And yet, why not? — to be honest, I believed, I really did, but all my friends keep saying "Fairy tales, fairy tales!" I'm confused. Please help me. I think you are a very brave man. You have written the truth — maybe you haven't yet told the whole story, but you've told a good part of it, that's for certain.

What happened between you and Anastasia — the way you offended her, and then it turned out she wasn't to blame — all sorts of things — yet still, I think, you shouldn't offend a person that way, even if, let's say, she's abnormal or a fake (but that's strictly my personal opinion — you may not agree with it).

---

[12]*Kolomna* — a city 100 km south-east of Moscow, where the Moskva River flows into the Oka.

[13]*Nastia* — a diminutive form of the name *Anastasia* (a common girl's name in modern Russian).

Vladimir (sorry, I don't know your patronymic[14]), did Anastasia have a child or not, and if she did, is it a boy or a girl, and what did your wife think of that?

And my last question: you wrote that Anastasia's grandfather and great-grandfather rubbed the piece of cedar with their fingers, but you never said that Anastasia did this too. Did she really not do it, or did you just happen to leave it out?

Please answer me (I know you get whole bagfuls of letters, but please, just a few lines).

Good-bye!!!

Anastasia

Dear Nastia,

You will most certainly be a healthy, spiritually strong and pretty girl. I shall ask Anastasia the next time I visit her to help you. True, Anastasia has a unique approach to healing. She looks upon illness as a conversation between God and Man. An illness can be a warning or a deliverance from something even more terrible, and she showed me examples of this — I'll be telling about them later in a new book. I shall try and persuade her. Though she's pretty stubborn about sticking to her views. She says it's only Man himself, through his spirit and conscious awareness, who can cure anything without negative side-effects, while outside interference is often harmful.

[14]*patronymic* — see footnote 9 in Chapter 1: "The ringing cedar". A child writing to an adult would normally use the combination of first name *plus* patronymic in addressing the adult. The author's patronymic is *Nikolaevich*.

Nastia, judging by your reaction to the book, you seem to be already healthier spiritually than a lot of people, and that's the main thing. I'm beginning to realise that that's really the case. As far as whether people around you believe or don't believe in Anastasia's existence, I'll answer you by quoting what someone said at one of my get-togethers with readers. When that question was put to me for the umpteenth time, he got up and declared in a loud voice: "Look, people! You're holding in your hands an impulse of inspiration, a thought bursting forth, a call to action, an idea! It's right there in your hands. What more do you want? A sample of her blood, urine and feces for analysis? Is there no way you can do without that? After all, the greatest and most important proof is already sitting right there in your hands!"

You see, Nastia, I've come to the realisation that Anastasia is an uncomfortable concept for many, and they'd rather she didn't exist at all. After all, she's breaking down a whole lot of technocratic dogmas, conventions and priorities. Against the background of purity emanating from her we suddenly start to become aware of our own filth, and that's not always what we want. Especially when we like to think of ourselves as so good and smart and conscientious, no matter what we do.

Anastasia said: "I exist for those for whom I exist."[15]

I didn't think there was anything special hidden in this statement. Anyone who wants to believe can believe. If they don't want to believe, they don't have to. However, I was mistaken. Some people read and nothing happens with them. Others... They find a great feeling of love, kindness and inspiration welling up in their heart. And, like a shower of spring rain, the world feels this grand poetry of love, a poetry of the heart which is capable of perceiving the light, magnifying it and sharing it with others. These are the people who feel her and know that she does exist.

---

[15] *I exist for those for whom I exist* — see Chapter 26: "Dreams — creating the future" above.

As for my wife, Nastia, she reacted the way most women probably would. We've only spoken on the telephone. But my daughter Polina is ready to help me. She understands everything, and brings me letters. She was the one who brought me yours.

You say it was wrong on my part to offend Anastasia that way. Of course it's wrong. I would never do anything like that again. The same people can be different at different times.

Our son was born. He's such a strong little lad. Smiles all the time. And Anastasia is happy and enjoying her life.

My best to you, and to your Mama.

I wish you joy and happiness in your life. You deserve it.

You're a strong girl. And you can make your friends happier too, more consciously aware of things.

A word about religious believers — their enquiries and questions.

I have spoken about Anastasia with members of the clergy from our Orthodox Church, as well as with representatives of various denominations. Some of them are quite favourably disposed to her. Others say, with some apprehension, that she's most likely a heathen — she could break down people's faith in religious doctrine, or resurrect idolatry or something nobody knows about yet — and it's wrong for her not to be baptised.

Her attitude to religion will be discussed in greater detail in the second book, and it is really quite extraordinary. I'll just mention a few points here.

"You see," she told me, "it is good that they are already talking about the soul, about kindness and the light. Who is the most worthy? I am unable to say."

"But what about the sects?" I countered. "The sects that have been banned. Now everyone says that they took the wrong path. Their actions were wrong."

"Do you think so? Then think of this: a group of soldiers is out on patrol. One of them in the lead has broken off or gone to one side and gets blown up by a mine. Yes, you can say: 'He took the wrong path, his actions were wrong.' But you can also say that these same actions saved other people's lives."

"In any case, Anastasia, which religion do you think is closest to you, the one most comprehensible?"

"Vladimir, let us say you had never seen your parents or talked with them. You would probably be happy to hear anyone talk about them. Even if they each talked about them a little differently. Where the truth lies, you can judge for yourself after reflecting on everything inside you. After all, you are their offspring, you are your parents' child. As for me, though, I do not need any intermediaries."

Well, okay. That's enough about doubts. There are some rather pleasant phenomena that Anastasia has somehow managed to bring about in our reality.

I was especially sceptical that she would actually be able to infuse something into the text of the book. These are her own 'combinations'[16] and rhythms, as she said, coming from the depths of eternity. But after the first edition came out,

---

[16]'*combinations*' — see Chapter 15: "Attentiveness to Man" and Chapter 27: "Across the dark forces' window of time" above.

in a run of only four thousand copies, something incredible happened. Many people were so moved by feelings and emotions that poetic verses began flooding in all by themselves. There are a whole lot of them now. These are just ordinary people, not professional poets, who have been writing. There are enough poems to date to put out a whole separate volume of them.[17]

In the Moscow group devoted to studying Anastasia phenomenon, they say that nowhere in the world, in the past or present, has there ever been a person or image capable of provoking such a huge poetic outpouring in so short a time.

Another surprising thing is that while in the first book there is almost nothing said about *faith*, or *Russia*, the majority of the readers' poems speak directly about faith and Russia, and bright aspirations. And it seems to me they do this most inspiringly. And this had a calming effect on my thought about Anastasia's influence. After all, the Bible tells us how to distinguish the bad from the good, the false prophet from the bearer of truth — it says "By their fruits ye shall know them."[18]

And if Anastasia's aspirations and her combinations bring forth such radiant poetic feelings, those are undoubtedly good fruits.

And I even thought: *If this goes on much longer she's going to turn half the population of Russia into poets, enamoured of their Motherland, the Earth, and all Nature around them.*

I sorted the poems into several categories: anonymous poems, signed poems, poems by soldiers and poems by government officials. And do you know what this kind of sorting shows?

---

[17]In the meantime, a 544-page volume of readers' poetry, art and letters has been published in Russian, under the title: *V luche Anastasii zvuchit dusha Rossii. Narodnaya kniga* (The soul of Russia sings in Anastasia's ray. A people's book).

[18]Matth. 7: 20 (*Authorised King James Version*).

It shows that there is absolutely no point in dividing society up the way we sometimes do, and blaming our troubles on certain categories of people — like entrepreneurs, the military, government officials. Their hearts all beat in exactly the same way, and across all these categories there are people sincerely striving for the light, for the good.

As for our troubles... They're something we probably all produce by ourselves.

In this edition of the book I have decided to publish one poem from each category.

1. ANASTASIA'S RAY

Into our busy, bustling life
Of lonely souls in crowds immersed,
From the vast Universe of Space
A Ray broke through to the Earth.

It glistened brighter than the light
Of the Sun or of gold of purest hue:
"My people! Greetings! Here I am
As your brother, speaking to you.

"I have been sent to you by love!
Sent to you by the ages' call.
Come to me and take of mine —
I give myself to all.

"Wait, there, my friend, where are you going?
Why is there sadness on your face?
You've been forsaken... Yes, I know...
I know all time and space.

"Dear people! What are you thinking, people?
The world is beautiful, no end.
I can do everything, dear people,
Because I am your friend!"

But the crowd only surged against the Ray,
Rushing along on their fashion-shod feet,
And kept on shoving it away
Into a puddle in the street.

The Ray dipped into the dirty slush...
It felt no offence, and shed no tear.
But all at once the slush burst forth
In a water-spring crystal-clear.

And then a little boy came running —
And fearing no punishment therefrom,
He leapt feet first into the puddle,
And drew on the Ray's sweet balm.

His Mama got angry with despair
And wildly waved her arms in dread,
But Pushkin's[19] statue on the square
Suddenly came to life and said:

"Now wait! You must not spank the boy!
He did not act just out of fun!

---

[19] *Alexander Sergeevich Pushkin* (1799–1837) — Russia's best-loved poet, considered to be 'the father of Russian literature', to whom many a Russian poet since then acknowledges a debt of gratitude. His influence on the Russian literary language is comparable to Shakespeare's on English. He is immortalised in portraits and statues in hundreds of Russian towns and cities.

Pay heed to him — your hearts will be
Illumined by your son!

"Come near and feel his moistened hands,
Come close and touch your blessed son,
And you will find there in his palms
All that the poets have sung —

"All they've created through the ages —
Reflected there within the heart."
"Mama! Mamochka! My Mama!"
The little boy hugged his mum.

"Mama, can you hear the singing,
Hear the song of happy birds?
You know, dear Mama, yes, you know it.
I shall write you a verse.

"And now you will be happy, Mama.
For that is what I want for you.
You see, I hear it, yes I hear it...
I think I can do it, too."

Into our busy, bustling life
Of lonely souls in crowds immersed,
From the vast Universe of Space
A Ray broke through to the Earth.

Author unknown

2. ANASTASIA (ANAS)

(on the image and heroine of V. Megré's book Anastasia*)*

In Russia Megré wrote this brand new idea
In book publications and newspaper lines,
The Ringing Cedar or *Ana-sta-si-ya,*[20]
Which drew attention to himself at the same time.

It's not the first time that this name I've heard spoken,
And yet it is still not that common a name:
Yes, *Ana-sta-si-ya* — so music-evoking,
Or *Stas-ya,* or *Stacie* — they all mean the same.
The Stacies I know live in cities of shadows,
Their character simple, of good honest worth
But here in the taiga, in a cedar-ringed meadow,
I glimpse a fair Goddess — the fairest on Earth.
Anas — a Siberian of Nature's creation —
In harmony with her environment lives.
Her conscious awareness, her love, inspiration,
To animals, plants, all around her she gives.

Her feelings and thoughts are in tune with the living,
The mind of the Cosmos is simple and clear.
In all of our wide world, believe me, there's nothing
Escaping her knowledge of stars or light-years.

Clairvoyant, Anas cures disease at all stages,
The great ringing cedar enhances her reach.

---

[20] *Ana-sta-SI-ya* — see footnote 1 in Chapter 9: "Who lights a new star?". A diminutive form would be *STAS-ya* (*Stacie* in English). In this poem she is also called *Anas* (stress on second syllable).

She draws upon cultures of all lands and ages
For logic and meaning and richness of speech.

An analyst practising Nature's ecology,
Her meaning of life is in tune with the world.
Intuitive grasper of highest astrology,
There's nothing impossible for this precious girl.

N. Mikhailov, Moscow

3. THE KIND WIZARD-GIRL

Gelendzhik's
Dolmens.
The years... wind back...
Time has opened a window, just a crack,
For the stretches of infinity
To be understood, evaluated,
Felt through and through, recognised as fact.
Stepping over my threshold-limit
Through the light of good in the blue expanses way up high,
I come to you, Anastasia,
Born again
In the twinkling of an eye!
You are a flower of Consciousness and Will,
Your might from cedar trees and forest leaves,
And from such charming, mystical, magical thoughts
That I'm ready to be one who simply believes.

Every beast and insect, raven and jay,
Every serpent, blade of grass and hay,
You wizard-girl, kind maven of the way...
So many aroused by what you have to say...
Your thoughts, ideas, even stronger now today,
Shed light on all the Earth with their bright Ray!

O.T. Vialshina, Gelendzhik

4. ANASTASIA'S LOVE

To the woman of my beloved

I shall pray for you, for you are loved,
The woman of my own beloved,
As his heart's desire, you will be blest,
You will be blest, as I wished for you the best.

Keep him safe when he is strong, or weak, or brave,
Keep him safe when he may irrationally behave,
Keep him, keep my beloved safe and sweet,
My days, it seems, have flashed by in a beat,
Their crazy dance has burnt me with its heat,
My years have started passing all too fleet,
My son has started walking on his feet.

"Your Papa is the very best, my son,
The very best!

It is I who did not manage to open up to *him,*
In life, my son, that can happen on a whim,
Another woman takes his fancy and steps in."

You are both caressed by the gentle breeze of spring
Which tells me in the whisper of the leaves
How he feels the warmth,
How he feels the joy
Both from your hands
And from your lips.
I shall not dare distract him
From the warmth and tenderness of your eyes.

But should that not be enough,
I shall send you
A ray of sunlight
To relieve you of your grief.

The years will fly past
Just like a stormy night.
Life will seem to you like an empty room.
I, as a fading star, falling to Earth from above,
Shall chase from your soul the night-time gloom.
And I shall be able to pray, please do believe,
So that you, by the light-ray illumed,
Need feel no withering love,
I shall be able to pray, for you are loved,
The woman of my own beloved.

Author unknown

5. TO ANASTASIA

To a woman I dedicate this verse.
I write as an air force flyer.
A poet I could never be.
But my heart flared true.
My breast with fire did burst.
Anastasia!
Do not think me brash.
I can't stop loving you.
Your image, a touching pulse for good,
Pulsed louder than any engine ever could.
My engine failed... Visibility nil...
An explosion, in the twinkling of an eye...
But then your Ray of Light,
Your image, flashed and blessed,
On fragile wings it kept me in flight.
A single moment it took.
Only one. I wished — as I looked until
My landing gear touched safely down —
That I were a blade of grass upon the ground,
By your fingers tenderly caressed.

Author unknown

6. THE CEDAR FOREST RINGS AND CHIMES
To Vladimir Megré

Ah, the fragrance of Siberian cedars!
The smell of resin very strong
The taiga vast, almost half a globe sweeping,
Stretching to one grand endless song.
The cedars keep peace since times of old,
Maintaining the energy of the Earth.
To brighten the pulse-beat of the soul
They ring for all mankind these words:

"Here dwells among us Anastasia
In spiritual purity's forest art.
She watches over Mother Russia
Through people's holiness of heart.

"She sends out thoughts, and calls to action,
To the highway leading to heavenly light —
The essence of Veles, Krishna, Rama,
Shiva, Buddha, Allah, Christ.

"These holy thoughts, the Star-bright Logos —
Old Russian purity their theme —
Are flying like snowstorms, calling the ages
To penetrate to the heart of the dream.

"With me are forces of light, unchanging,
I exist for all who walk and plod.
I give to all a bright awakening
Who do not turn their back on God.

"Bow before Holy Russia's leading,
Bow to her Gods, our creators above —

In the never-ceasing ring of the cedars —
Which deify the light as love.

"So, Russians, turn! and with your soul
Pay heed to all that heaven gives:
On the rivers of Lena, Yana and Ob
God's Temple of all the Russias lives.

"Step out on the upward road to the light!
The Cosmic Self-Programming path discern!
We look to your goals, as you answer aright,
So Russia may to her Gods return.

"Preserver of the Cosmic energy of Nature,
The ringing cedar waits for the one
Who loves his Russia as God the Saviour,
Whose heart its course for others has run.

"Then live in peace and love for Nature,
Brook no dishonesty, live aright,
Draw wisdom's radiance from the people's favour,
And show to others the pathway to light!

"Such people are called by Anastasia
To accept my energy's gentle load,
So that the bright forces' attentive idea
May help those climbing up the road."

The cedars call everyone to hope for the prize
On the path to divinity, to beauty's gleam:
"Awaken, my people! Open your eyes!
Reach out to others, to the heart of the dream!"

The cosmic expanse opens wide its doors
To awakened pilgrims on their climb.
To those united on their upward course
The whole cedar forest rings and chimes.

Ya. N. Koltunov, President of the Cosmos Society
of the Russian Space Exploration Committee, Moscow

7. TWO GODDESSES

Do not come here to see my shame
Or think with mute reproach to bless:
Nor hand nor secret stare can claim
To lift the cross from my poor chest.

No earth-bound cry will scare away
The soul of heavenly confusion.
It will not blight the holy ray
Of mind and feeling's interfusion.
The world is full of sun and storm,
Of finger-snaps and love's fire too,
Here ashes, flame, blood, tears are born
Where mind is false, but feelings true!

Wild honey becomes bitter, surely —
No sweetness from the wormwood's bloom
Pretenders will not grasp the worldly,
The afterlife the wise will doom.

All stories, letters, poems, flowers,
Will waken to the heavenly blue!
I see two Goddesses, two powers:
These are my Poetry and You!

Verse should not be debased as phantom,
It will not see a final breath!
You are immortal, we are random
In poems, just like birth and death.

G. Pautov, physicist
Krasnodar

CHAPTER THIRTY-ONE

Author's message to entrepreneurs

The author's attempt to organise a fellowship of Russian entrepreneurs in accord with certain spiritual principles has revealed an evident desire for such a coming together on the part of many entrepreneurs. Notices were sent out all over Moscow. A wider distribution throughout Russia would have entailed a substantial expenditure. The lack of funding and, consequently, the ultimate failure of the project, led to nowhere. Anastasia's plans began to seem unrealisable.

During my second visit with her, however, she told me there were no dead-end situations, only that I should not have altered the sequence she had prescribed. The book should have come first, which would have spread the right information and prevented the organisational principles from being tied to monetary concerns.

This second visit also settled one other question. An organisational task force had been set up in Moscow to spearhead the formation of the fellowship, but we could not come to a decision on either the selection criteria for new members or how the selection committee should be constituted.

Anastasia stated the following:

"One's heartfelt impulsion and one's aspiration to strive for such a fellowship are the principal criteria for eligibility. Nobody has the right to refuse access to anyone manifesting such qualities. One's past record is irrelevant. For the one who was most worthy yesterday may well turn out to be the least worthy today, and vice-versa. Subsequently, when you get together to determine the eligibility criteria according to the impulses of your hearts, you will also be able to work out the specific terms on which applicants are accepted into the fellowship."

The blame for altering the sequence prescribed by Anastasia falls, of course, on me. To all those Moscow entrepreneurs who wanted to join the fellowship I hereby offer my sincere apologies — first, for postponing the initial conference to a later date and, secondly, for the consequent drain on your time and finances.

The task force was indeed made up of high-profile entrepreneurs. Many of you had limited time to devote to the project. But you found the time, or stole it from something else, you worked on drafting documents and the principles for the future society. The secretariat too, made up of Muscovites, was similarly fuelled by enthusiasm. In addition, Moscow students put together a magnificent computer version of the future society's catalogue. It made it all the more painful for me to look back, once I realised my mistake, and see the hopelessness of the situation. The only way out was to muster the strength needed to correct the mistake and write the book. Without a word of explanation to anyone (explanations seemed impossible at that point!) I went off by myself and began to write.

It is only now that the book exists and is spreading more and more right across Russia and starting to fulfil the function specified for it by Anastasia that I can talk about the future. I am more confident now about the possibility of seeing such a society actually come into being.

The reaction to the book indicates that it will attract a sufficient number of entrepreneurs from the various regions of the country. The conference will take place. There will be a fellowship!

In acting on my own, I may well have offended some of those who worked alongside me in Moscow.

I should particularly like to single out three Moscow students[1] who gave their all to assisting and participating in the secretariat of the future society. They were the ones who keyboarded the text of the first book on their computers, and kept on keyboarding even after their exam session started. I wasn't in a position to compensate them for their work. They knew this, they understood the situation, but still went on keyboarding. Others too would have probably reacted with understanding, had they known the whole picture. If that applies to any of you, I apologise for my lack of trust in you and for my temporary disappearance.

Of course there is a great deal more I need to learn and understand, including the degree to which Anastasia herself has been involved in all this. I'd like to know just how this reclusive young woman from the Siberian taiga managed not only to draw up plans like these but also to have them implemented in real life. It's not that she is predicting the future. She is literally *creating* the future, she struggles to bring it about and feels the struggle in her heart. In fact, it is something on the order of a master business plan which she has formulated in her head, keeping track of all its details down to the nuances of the psychological factors involved. She is working her hardest to bring it about, and calling on us to participate in its realisation.

But we are not simply 'blind mice', but normal, professionally experienced adults, and we must understand that a single individual, especially one still relatively inexperienced in the business world, cannot foresee everything ahead of time.

Anastasia affirms:

"Just the organisation alone, the spiritual — yes, *spiritual* — contact among such people as entrepreneurs, is a salutary

[1] *three Moscow students* — see footnote 7 in Chapter 27: "Across the dark forces' window of time".

reaction of cosmic proportions. There is no need to dictate what will happen next. What will happen next will point out its own path and set its priorities in the occurrences of daily life."

What kind of reaction is this? What path is she alluding to?

Even though her aspiration to the light can be felt intuitively, nevertheless, we must make sense of everything ourselves and work out the details.

I wish you all happiness and success!

Dreams coming true
Editor's Afterword

In the summer of 1996 a tired-looking man was standing on a street corner in downtown Moscow, with a self-published 96-page volume in his hands, trying to sell it to passers-by. The book's title was *The Ringing Cedar. Anastasia*, and the man called himself Vladimir Megré.

A woman stopped by, looked at the inconspicuous cover, talked to the author and bought a copy. Next day she was back — smiling, her eyes shining — to pick up an entire pack, to give to everybody she knew.

As it was, the first print-run of 2,000 copies of *Anastasia* sold out in a matter of weeks. What happened next was as miraculous as the story Vladimir Megré had written down: new print-runs first of 2,000, then of 10,000, sold out within weeks. Not long afterward, *millions* more were printed and sold. By 1999 Vladimir Megré was one of Russia's most popular authors, and the seven books published to date have sold over 10 million copies in their original Russian alone, not counting their translated editions in more than a dozen languages.

The books in the *Ringing Cedars Series* started producing incredible changes in people's hearts and minds, the effect of which is now being felt throughout Russia and beyond. What happened here? How can it be that, with no advertisement other than word-of-mouth, this book by an unknown author became a national, then an international best seller, distributed initially by readers alone before it was accepted by even a single bookstore? How can it be that one copy from this first

2,000-copy print-run actually found its way to the stacks of the U.S. Library of Congress?[1]

Why have people of all ages — from schoolchildren to pensioners — and in all walks of life — from teachers to public officials and from scientists to clergymen — felt such inspiration from the book to the point of writing poetry and creating works of art?

Why did a former member of the Russian parliament, an economist by the name of Dr Viktor Medikov, write an entire book, *Putin, Megré and Russia's future,*[2] stating that the Ringing Cedars was becoming Russia's new national idea?

Why did the Supreme Mufti[3] of Russia, Talgat Tajuddin, publicly declare in a televised interview: "I *love* these books. I read them and get a lot out of them for myself"? Why have leaders of other confessions made equally laudatory remarks?

Why did my mother once bring home a copy of *Anastasia* from her yoga class on the recommendation of her instructor, and gingerly request that I read it?

Why, when, applying to enter the doctoral programme in Forestry at six top-rated American universities, I submitted a research proposal based on the ideas set forth by Anastasia, I was accepted by all of them? Four of the schools, in fact, offered me full financial support with a scholarship. And here I am now at the University of Missouri at Columbia, writing

---

[1] *Zveniashchii kedr: Anastasiia*, printed by Moscow Printshop Number Eleven in 1996, bears the Library of Congress Control Number 98171763. A copy from the first 1997 printing of Book 2, *Zveniashchie kedry Rossii* (The Ringing Cedars of Russia), has also been included in the Library of Congress collection (LCCN 98216313).

[2] *Putin, Megré i budushchaia Rossiia*, published in 2003, is also found at the Library of Congress, with Control Number 2003710013.

[3] *Mufti* — a Muslim scholar who interprets *Shari'a* law.

my Ph.D. dissertation on the significance of ideas from the Ringing Cedars for the future of forestry and agriculture in Russia and the world as a whole.

But here comes the most striking part: how can it be that all these developments — from the wild popularity of the Ringing Cedars Series to the outpouring of reader's poetry and art — had been described in the very first book *before* coming to pass?

As it is, true to what Anastasia said in the very first volume, millions of people have been moved by her words, many thousands have planted trees, written poetry and songs, or created works of art — all inspired by the book. Readers' clubs have proliferated throughout Russia and abroad. Numerous readers' conferences throughout Russia and Europe have brought together thousands of people, asking questions they had never even thought of before. In just the scant few years since the book's initial publication, Russia has witnessed the birth of a powerful eco-village movement, inspiring thousands of people to leave their jobs in large cities and, despite formidable obstacles, move to one of the many eco-settlements now sprouting all over the country. Russian emigrants to Germany, America and Canada have been flocking back to their homeland to establish new self-sufficient homesteads on their ancestors' lands. In the eco-village where my family now owns a plot of land, our neighbours include economists, singers, entrepreneurs, engineers, writers, mechanics, managers and executives, artists, peasants; young families, single mothers, pensioners and even schoolchildren — coming from all over Russia and other countries once part of the Soviet Union: from Moscow to Irkutsk and from Ivanovo to Kazakhstan and Tajikistan.

Whence comes all this inspiration?

The answer is simple: *Anastasia* resonates so strongly in tune with people's hearts that one cannot fail to inwardly recognise the truth emanating from it. How many times have I heard personal examples of this instant recognition: people who have been searching for years or decades for meaningful answers to questions on the purpose of life, on Man's place in Nature, have finally found them in this book!

But should it be surprising that the image of a way of life founded on the ideals of love, beauty and non-violence, as presented by Anastasia, would resonate so strongly with our inner self? After all, does not every one of us want to live in a free society of kind and happy people, in a world without wars, crime or oppression? In a world where not a single tear need run down a child's cheek, and where families live in love and prosperity? Do we not want to live without monstrous industries destroying and polluting both Nature and Man? Do we not want to enjoy creative labour for the benefit of both our families and our communities, instead of suffering through boring jobs merely to enrich faceless corporations? Do we not want a society based on mutual help and co-operation, rather than competition?

But, you may say, this was just Anastasia's *dream*. Or just Vladimir Megré's dream. And "a dream is simply a dream".[4] But cannot each of us dream of a desirable future and then act to bring this future about? Is it not what John Lennon was singing about in his *Imagine*:

> *You may say I'm a dreamer,*
> *But I'm not the only one.*
> *I hope someday you'll join us*
> *And the world will live as one.*

Is it not what one of the greatest economists of the twentieth century, E.F. Schumacher, was referring to in his seminal work *Small is beautiful?*[5]

Now, it might be said that this is a romantic, a utopian, vision. True enough. What we have today, in modern industrial society, is not romantic and certainly not utopian, as we have it right here. But it is in very deep trouble and holds no promise of survival. We jolly well have to have the courage to *dream* if we want to survive and give our children a chance of survival... [The crises of the industrial society] will become worse and end in disaster, until or unless we develop a new life-style which is compatible with the real needs of human nature, with the health of living nature around us, and with the resource endowment of the world.

Fortunately, the disaster may still be averted, as more and more people in Russia and throughout the world, drawing their inspiration from the Ringing Cedars, acquire "the courage to dream" and create an image of radiant reality for themselves and their children, and then get down to work in this direction.

The spiritual and practical revelations presented in this book are unparalleled in so many areas that their discussion could fill entire volumes. Let me but mention Anastasia's "beloved dachniks" — a discovery of exceptional significance.

As it happens, the most obvious and significant things often go the most easily unnoticed. This is particularly true about Russia's *dacha* movement. Judge for yourself — Anastasia and Vladimir Megré were the first to speak about the importance of *dachniks*. Now it turns out that according to widely available official statistics, published every year in

---

[4]See Chapter 7: "Anastasia's ray".

[5]E.F. Schumacher, *Small is beautiful: Economics as if people mattered* (New York, Harper & Row, 1973), p. 162 (in the 1989 edition).

Russia's primary statistical source *Rossiya v tsifrakh*, over 35 million families — and this amounts to 70% of the country's population — grow their own food on their plots and collectively provide far more vegetables, fruit, and even meat and milk than the whole country's commercial agriculture taken together.[6] Why had nobody paid attention to these numbers earlier? Why didn't they ever surface in the discussion on the present and future of Russian — and, indeed, the world's — agriculture? Why did nobody take seriously President Boris Yeltsin's confession that he was spending his weekends tending a vegetable garden, growing potatoes and radishes?

Should you choose to research for yourself the questions discussed by Anastasia, you will soon discover the truth of her assertion that *her* knowledge is already shared — at least partially — by a number of people in our world, and that "collectively they know practically everything, only they do not fully understand how it works".[7]

Take communication with plants, for example. It sounds incredible at first, but it only requires a reading of Peter Tompkins and Christopher Bird's well-researched *The secret life of plants*[8] to gain an entirely new perspective and conclude: She must be right!

But could it be possible that all diseases are curable through such interaction with plants, as Anastasia argues? It would take a complex and lengthy scientific study to test this hypothesis. Fortunately, this is not necessary, as — in addition to a growing number of personal testimonials from thousands of people — there is factual evidence at hand that can dispel

[6]The spiritual, social and economic significance of dacha movement is discussed in great detail in Book 5 of the series, *Who are we?* Dr Medikov referred to this book as "expressing Russia's new national idea".

[7]See Chapter 26: "Dreams — creating the future".

[8]New York: Harper & Row, 1973.

any doubts. Over centuries and millennia the Hunzakut, a people living in a valley in northern Pakistan, have been practising an agriculture very similar to the one described by Anastasia. Eating food *exclusively* from their family garden plots and thus establishing a closed loop of matter- and information-exchange between people and their plants, they are recognised as the most healthy and long-living people on Earth. The Hunzakut commonly live to more than 100 years, and men becoming fathers at age 90 is not a rarity.[9] Can it be that this information exchange between an individual person and a plant Anastasia talks about is the missing link to understanding human nutrition? Even in the absence of scientific studies, why not try it? The science will catch up.

Furthermore, why should we be sceptical about Anastasia's ability to live without concern for acquiring food or clothing — effortlessly relying on Nature for a complete life-support system? Is not the exact same ideal of life taught to humanity in the Bible: "He who watches the wind will not sow and he who looks at the clouds will not reap"[10] or "Take no thought for your life, what ye shall eat, or what ye shall drink".[11] Also, in our own not-so-distant past, Nobel Laureate Albert Schweitzer testified on the basis of his experiences in Africa: "In return for very little work nature supplies the native with nearly everything that he requires for his support".[12]

Looking around, should one doubt that truly happy children can *only* be raised in Nature? Jean Liedloff, who spent two and a half years in a society living in close relationship

[9]See, for example, *Secrets of the soil* by Peter Tompkins and Christopher Bird (Yonkers, N.Y.: Rare Bird Press, 1998), or numerous other books written about the Hunzakut people.

[10]Ecclesiastes 11: 4 (*New American Standard Bible*).

[11]Matthew 6: 24 (*Authorised King James Version*).

[12]A. Schweitzer, *On the edge of the primeval forest: Experiences and observations of a doctor in Equatorial Africa* (London: A.C. Black, 1934), p. 112.

with Nature — and consequently knowing no such things as crying children, crime or depression — speaks about this in her book *The continuum concept*[13] with very much the same conclusions as Anastasia.

Again, this list could continue. In fact, researchers could — and probably will — write volumes of commentary on almost every statement contained in *Anastasia*.

Yes, doubts naturally do creep in. It still sounds all too improbable to our traditional way of thinking. And even if the heart feels a genuine light emanating from the book, the mind often refuses to accept it as real. This is an all too familiar dilemma, fully experienced even by Vladimir Megré himself. However, as the series progresses and you come to embrace the ever more significant revelations set forth in the subsequent volumes, and immerse yourself in their ever more poetic language, the idea that it could all be "simply thought up" should gradually melt away.

You hold in your hands a flower which will unfold its petals to reveal a most remarkable masterpiece, unique in all of Russia's literature and, possibly, the world's as well. Indeed, its significance goes far beyond *literature*. This book possesses a tremendous, unprecedented potential to change life on our whole planet for the better.

Do you know of any other book that in a matter of just a few years has succeeded in not only stirring the hearts and minds of millions of people, but also arousing these same people to extraordinary acts of creation in their everyday lives, developing new modes of expression in all the arts, taking or embracing non-violent initiatives to preserve and enhance life on this planet as we know it? Every day more and more people are joining in. Now that the Ringing Cedars is globally available

---

[13]London: Duckworth, 1975; rev. ed. 1977. From 1985 published by Addison-Wesley.

in English, the realisation of Anastasia's dream is certain to take on planetary proportions. I have no doubt about it.

In the winter of 2003, at my office in downtown Moscow — just one block away from the street corner outside the Taganskaya metro station where Vladimir Megré had been selling the first copies of his book only six years earlier[14] — Igor Vladimirov, head of the Anastasia Readers' Club in St Petersburg, mused one day, looking at the snowflakes dancing outside the window:

"Wouldn't it be wonderful to have *Anastasia* published in English?"

"It would," I agreed.

"You are a professional project manager, and you speak English fluently. Isn't that true?"

"Yes, more or less."

"Then *why are you sitting here?!*"

We laughed. A subsequent chain of circumstances and events led me to certain people — including Vladimir Megré himself — who became instrumental in carrying out the English translation project.

The story of the unusual coincidences and struggles behind this edition could easily form the stuff of a suspense thriller (which I shall probably write one day). In the meantime I take comfort in the fact that you are now holding a masterfully translated volume in your hands. This alone is a good indication that dreams really do come true.

Columbia, Missouri, USA
January 2005   Leonid Sharashkin

---

[14] At the time I was employed as Programme Manager at the Moscow headquarters of WWF Russia — a branch of the World Wide Fund for Nature (also known in America and Canada as the World Wildlife Fund) — just a five-minute walk from the Taganskaya station. Megré's initial attempts to sell and promote his book are painstakingly described in Book 2.

THE RINGING CEDARS SERIES AT A GLANCE

Anastasia (ISBN 978-0-9801812-0-3), Book 1 of the Ringing Cedars Series, tells the story of entrepreneur Vladimir Megré's trade trip to the Siberian taiga in 1995, where he witnessed incredible spiritual phenomena connected with sacred 'ringing cedar' trees. He spent three days with a woman named Anastasia who shared with him her unique outlook on subjects as diverse as gardening, child-rearing, healing, Nature, sexuality, religion and more. This wilderness experience transformed Vladimir so deeply that he abandoned his commercial plans and, penniless, went to Moscow to fulfil Anastasia's request and write a book about the spiritual insights she so generously shared with him. True to her promise this life-changing book, once written, has become an international bestseller and has touched hearts of millions of people world-wide.

The Ringing Cedars of Russia (ISBN 978-0-9801812-1-0), Book 2 of the Series, in addition to providing a fascinating behind-the-scenes look at the story of how *Anastasia* came to be published, offers a deeper exploration of the universal concepts so dramatically revealed in Book 1. It takes the reader on an adventure through the vast expanses of space, time and spirit — from the Paradise-like glade in the Siberian taiga to the rough urban depths of Russia's capital city, from the ancient mysteries of our forebears to a vision of humanity's radiant future.

The Space of Love (ISBN 978-0-9801812-2-7), Book 3 of the Series, describes the author's second visit to Anastasia. Rich with new revelations on natural child-rearing and alternative education, on the spiritual significance of breast-feeding and the meaning of ancient megaliths, it shows how each person's thoughts can influence the destiny of the entire Earth and describes practical ways of putting Anastasia's vision of happiness into practice. Megré shares his new outlook on education and children's real creative potential after a visit to a school where pupils build their own campus and cover the ten-year Russian school programme in just two years. Complete with an account of an armed intrusion into Anastasia's habitat, the book highlights the limitless power of Love and non-violence.

Co-creation (ISBN 978-0-9801812-3-4), Book 4 and centrepiece of the Series, paints a dramatic living image of the creation of the Universe and humanity's place in this creation, making this primordial mystery relevant to our everyday living today. Deeply metaphysical yet at the same time down-to-Earth practical, this poetic heart-felt volume helps us uncover answers to the most significant questions about the essence and meaning of the Universe and the nature and purpose of our existence. It also shows how and why the knowledge of these answers, innate in every human being, has become obscured and forgotten, and points the way toward reclaiming this wisdom and — in partnership with Nature — manifesting the energy of Love through our lives.

Who Are We? (ISBN 978-0-9801812-4-1), Book 5 of the Series, describes the author's search for real-life 'proofs' of Anastasia's vision presented in the previous volumes. Finding these proofs and taking stock of ongoing global environmental destruction, Vladimir Megré describes further practical steps for putting Anastasia's vision into practice. Full of beautiful realistic images of a new way of living in co-operation with the Earth and each other, this book also highlights the role of children in making us aware of the precariousness of the present situation and in leading the global transition toward a happy, violence-free society.

The Book of Kin (ISBN 978-0-9801812-5-8), Book 6 of the Series, describes another visit by the author to Anastasia's glade in the Siberian taiga and his conversations with his growing son, which cause him to take a new look at education, science, history, family and Nature. Through parables and revelatory dialogues and stories Anastasia then leads Vladimir Megré and the reader on a shocking re-discovery of the pages of humanity's history that have been distorted or kept secret for thousands of years. This knowledge sheds light on the causes of war, oppression and violence in the modern world and guides us in preserving the wisdom of our ancestors and passing it over to future generations.

The Energy of Life (ISBN 978-0-9801812-6-5), Book 7 of the Series, re-asserts the power of human thought and the influence of our thinking on our lives and the destiny of the entire planet and the Universe. It also brings forth a practical understanding of ways to consciously control and build up the power of our creative thought. The book sheds still further light on the forgotten pages of humanity's history, on religion, on the roots of inter-racial and inter-religious conflict, on ideal nutrition, and shows how a new way of thinking and a lifestyle in true harmony with Nature can lead to happiness and solve the personal and societal problems of crime, corruption, misery, conflict, war and violence.

The New Civilisation (ISBN 978-0-9801812-7-2), Book 8, Part 1 of the Series, describes yet another visit by Vladimir Megré to Anastasia and their son, and offers new insights into practical co-operation with Nature, showing in ever greater detail how Anastasia's lifestyle applies to our lives. Describing how the visions presented in previous volumes have already taken beautiful form in real life and produced massive changes in Russia and beyond, the author discerns the birth of a new civilisation. The book also paints a vivid image of America's radiant future, in which the conflict between the powerful and the helpless, the rich and the poor, the city and the country, can be transcended and thereby lead to transformations in both the individual and society.

Rites of Love (ISBN 978-0-9801812-8-9), Book 8, Part 2, contrasts today's mainstream attitudes to sex, family, childbirth and education with our forebears' lifestyle, which reflected their deep spiritual understanding of the significance of conception, pregnancy, homebirth and upbringing of the young in an atmosphere of love. In powerful poetic prose Megré describes their ancient way of life, grounded in love and non-violence, and shows the practicability of this same approach today. Through the life-story of one family, he portrays the radiant world of the ancient Russian Vedic civilisation, the drama of its destruction and its re-birth millennia later — in our present time.

Vladimir Megré
The Ringing Cedars Series

Translated from the Russian by John Woodsworth
Edited by Dr Leonid Sharashkin

RINGING
CEDARS
PRESS

Published by Ringing Cedars Press
www.ringingcedars.com

PENGUIN BOOKS

BRAINCHILDREN

Daniel C. Dennett is Distinguished Professor of Arts and
Sciences and Director of the Center for Cognitive Studies at
Tufts University in Massachusetts. He is the author of *Content
and Consciousness* (1969); *Brainstorms* (1978); *Elbow Room* (1984);
The Intentional Stance (1987); *Consciousness Explained* (1992;
Penguin, 1993); the highly acclaimed *Darwin's Dangerous Idea*
(1995; Penguin, 1996); *Kinds of Minds* (1996); and *Brainchildren*
(Penguin, 1998).